W9-BMV-536

DEC 2 / 2005

CONTENTS

Graphic Classics:
H.G. WELLS

THE INVISIBLE MAN ©2002 RICK GEARY

Cover illustration by Seth Frail
Back cover illustration by Nick Miller
Additional illustrations by Kent Steine, Chris Moore,
Rick Geary and Jim Nelson

Graphic Classics: H.G. Wells is published by Eureka Productions. Second edition (2005), ISBN 978-0-9746648-3-9. Price US $11.95. Available from Eureka Productions, 8778 Oak Grove Road, Mount Horeb, WI 53572. Tom Pomplun, designer and publisher, tom@graphicclassics.com. Eileen Fitzgerald, editorial assistant. This compilation and all original works ©2005 Eureka Productions. All rights revert to creators after publication. Graphic Classics is a trademark of Eureka Productions. The Graphic Classics website is at http://www.graphicclassics.com. Printed in Canada.

CARVER PUBLIC LIBRARY

H.G. Wells' THE INVISIBLE MAN

adapted by
Rod Lott
illustrated by
Simon Gane

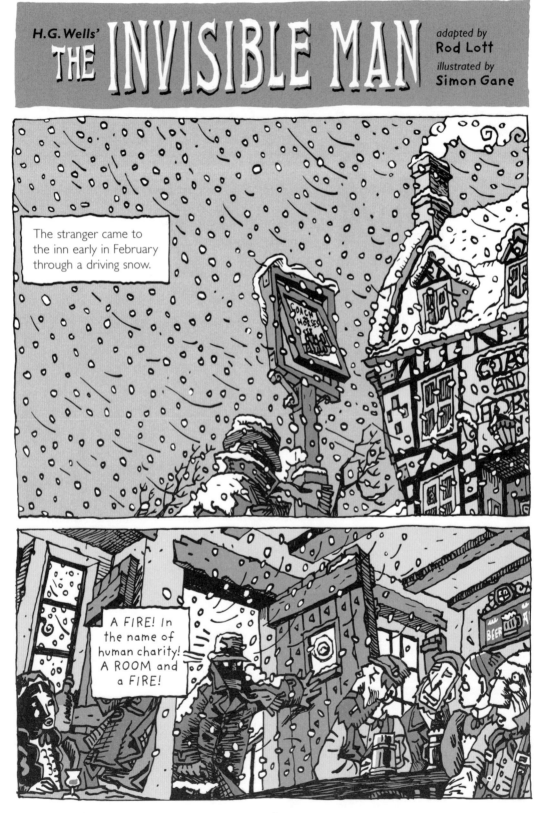

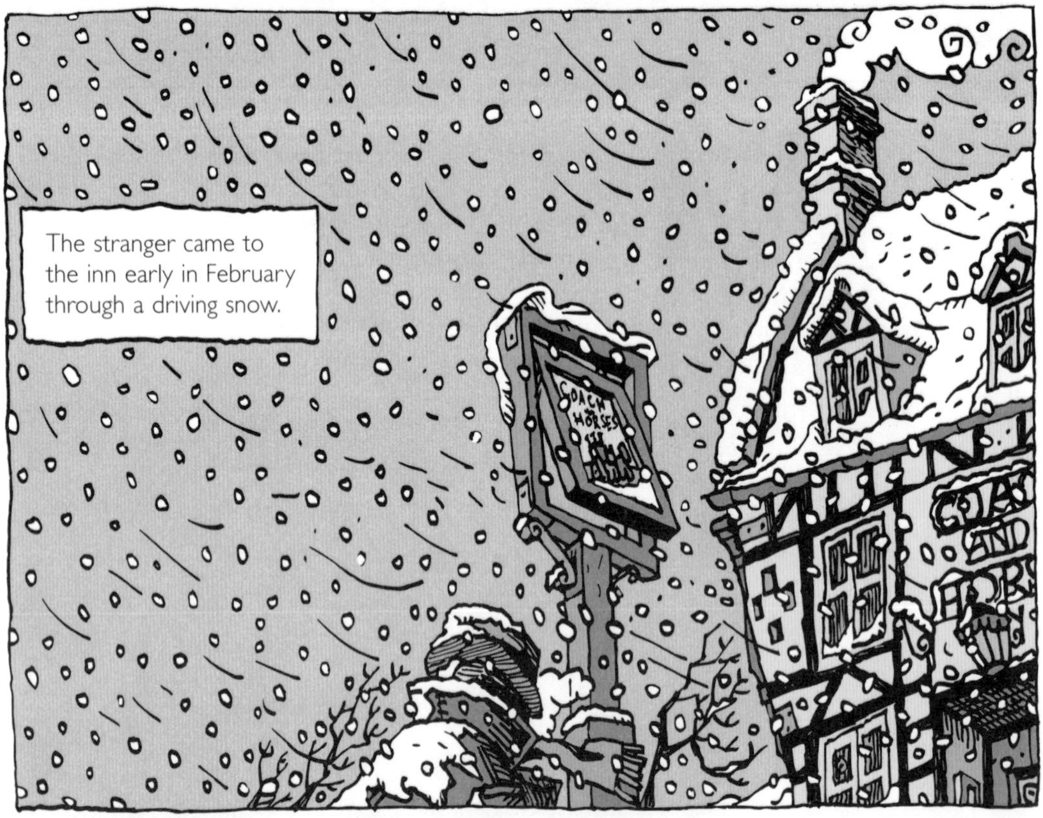
The stranger came to the inn early in February through a driving snow.

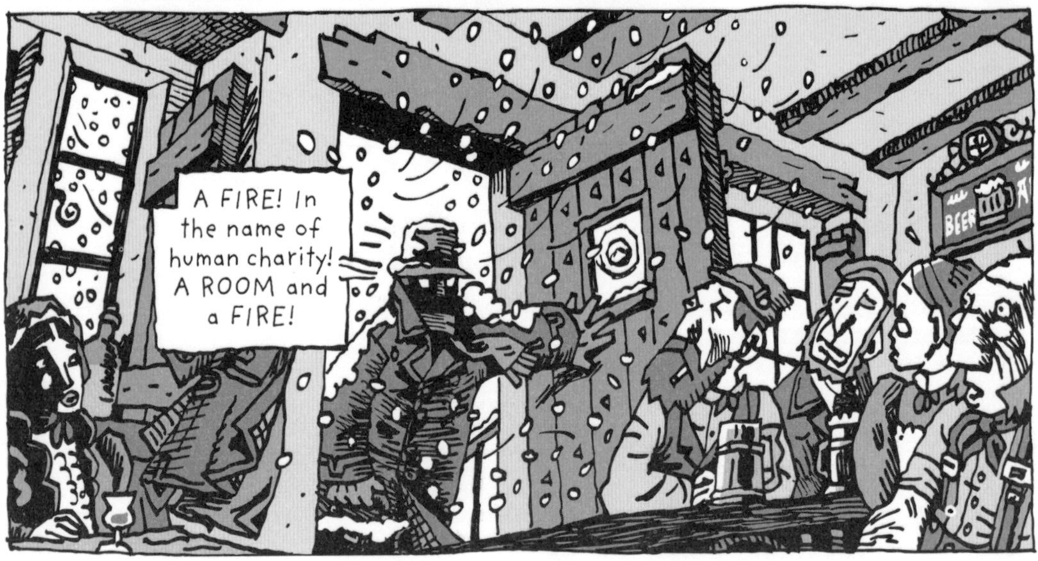
A FIRE! In the name of human charity! A ROOM and a FIRE!
BEER

He stamped and shook the snow from himself and followed Mrs. Hall into the parlour. For a guest to stop in the wintertime was an unheard-of piece of luck, and Mrs. Hall was resolved to show herself worthy of her good fortune.

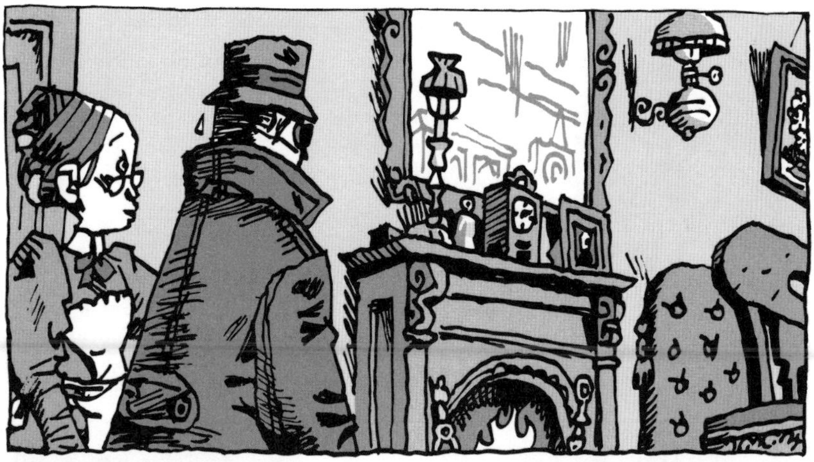

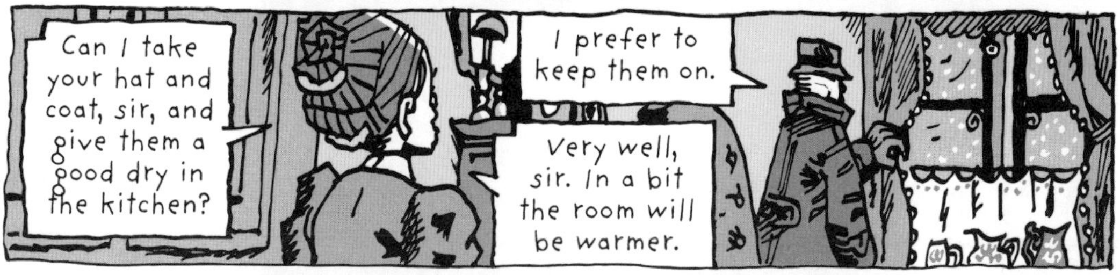
Can I take your hat and coat, sir, and give them a good dry in the kitchen?
I prefer to keep them on.
Very well, sir. In a bit the room will be warmer.

When she returned with the breakfast, she noticed the overcoat and hat had been put over a chair in front of the fire.

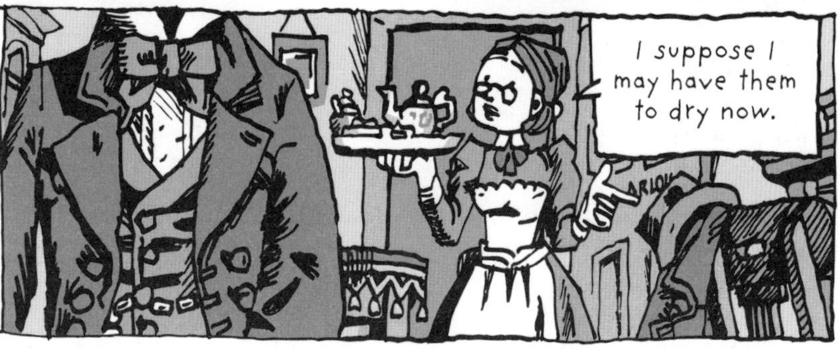
I suppose I may have them to dry now.

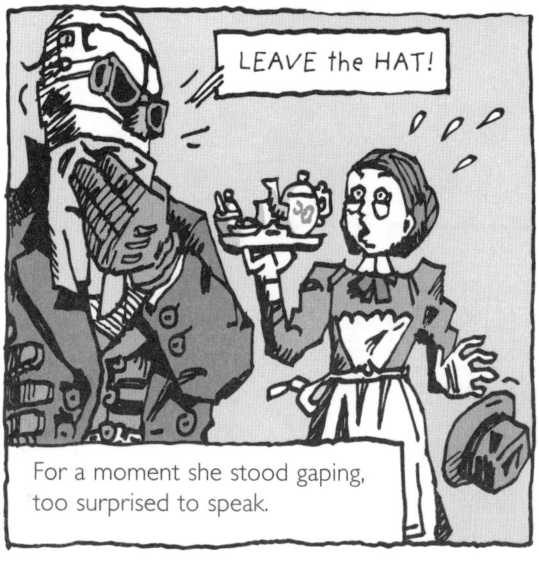
LEAVE the HAT!

For a moment she stood gaping, too surprised to speak.

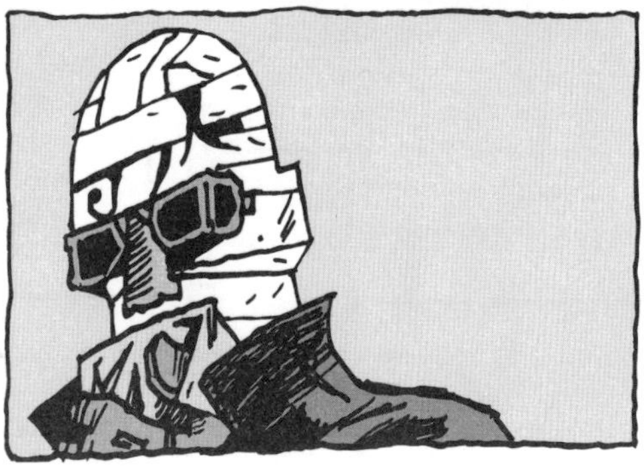

He held a cloth over the lower part of his face, so that his mouth was completely hidden. But it was the bandages which startled Mrs. Hall. Not a scrap of his face was exposed except his pink, peaked nose.

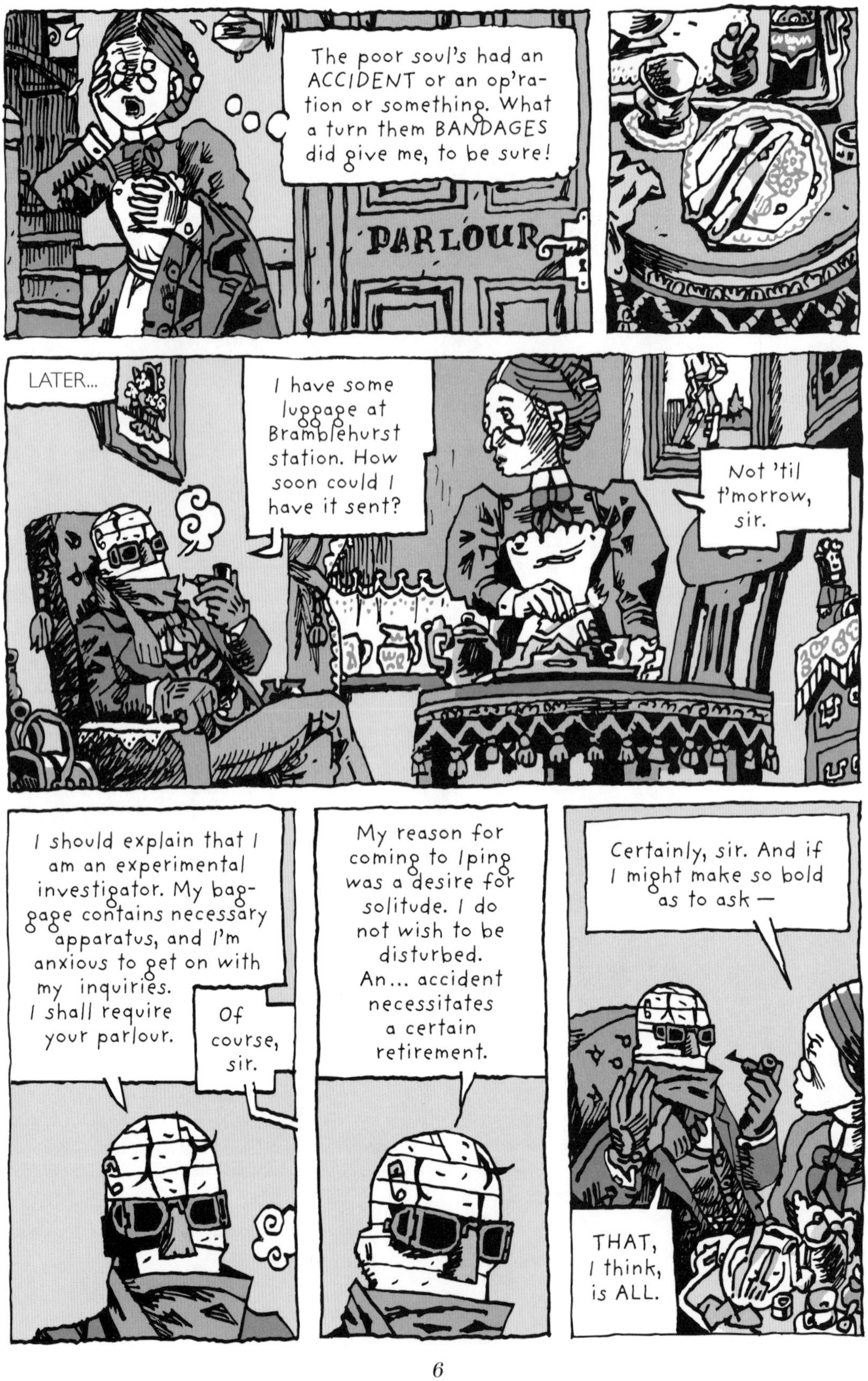
The poor soul's had an ACCIDENT or an op'ration or something. What a turn them BANDAGES did give me, to be sure!
PARLOUR
LATER...
I have some luggage at Bramblehurst station. How soon could I have it sent?
Not 'til t'morrow, sir.
I should explain that I am an experimental investigator. My baggage contains necessary apparatus, and I'm anxious to get on with my inquiries. I shall require your parlour.
Of course, sir.
My reason for coming to Iping was a desire for solitude. I do not wish to be disturbed. An... accident necessitates a certain retirement.
Certainly, sir. And if I might make so bold as to ask —
THAT, I think, is ALL.

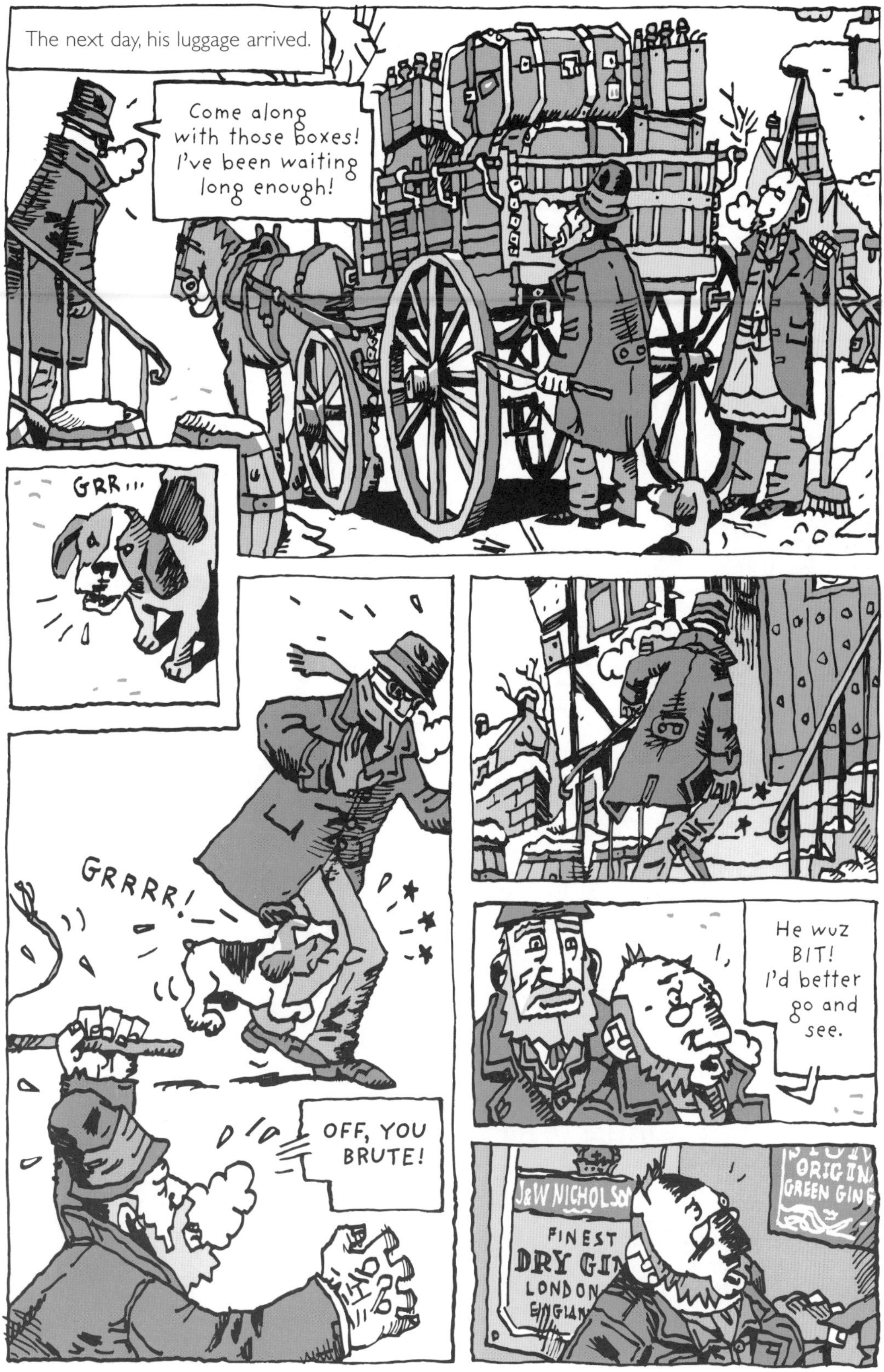
The next day, his luggage arrived.
Come along with those boxes! I've been waiting long enough!
GRR...
GRRRR!
OFF, YOU BRUTE!
He wuz BIT! I'd better go and see.
J&W NICHOLSON
FINEST DRY GIN LONDON ENGLAND
ORIGINAL GREEN GINGER

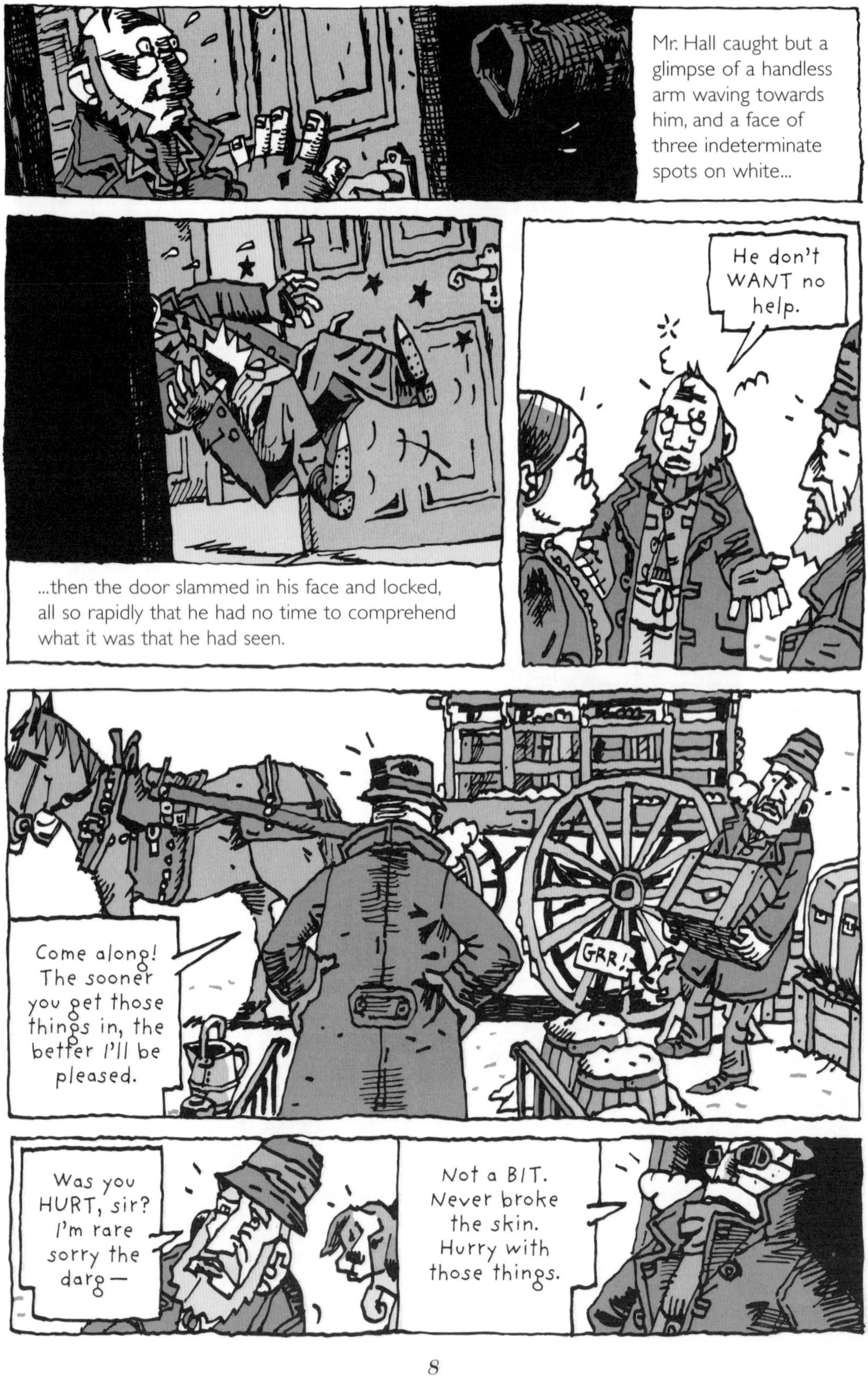
Mr. Hall caught but a glimpse of a handless arm waving towards him, and a face of three indeterminate spots on white...
...then the door slammed in his face and locked, all so rapidly that he had no time to comprehend what it was that he had seen.
He don't WANT no help.
Come along! The sooner you get those things in, the better I'll be pleased.
GRR!
Was you HURT, sir? I'm rare sorry the darg—
Not a BIT. Never broke the skin. Hurry with those things.

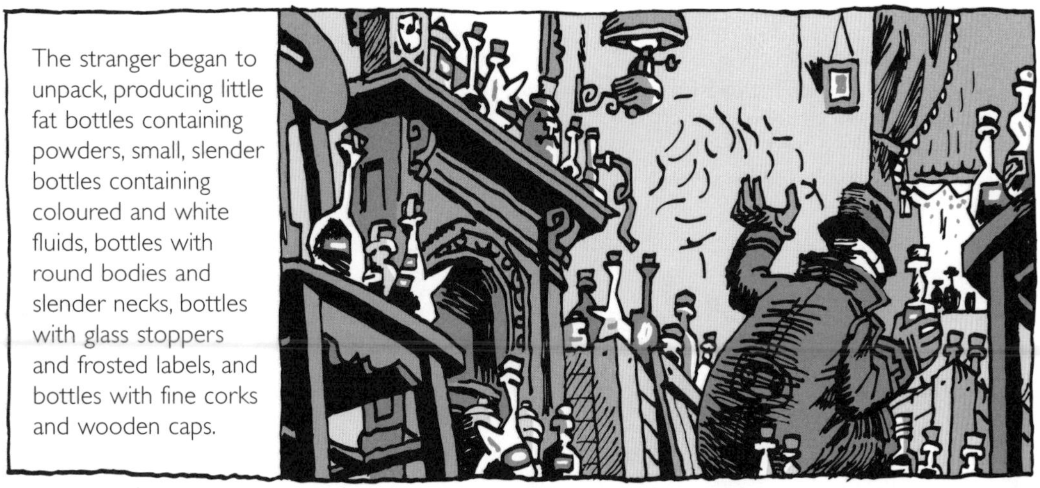
The stranger began to unpack, producing little fat bottles containing powders, small, slender bottles containing coloured and white fluids, bottles with round bodies and slender necks, bottles with glass stoppers and frosted labels, and bottles with fine corks and wooden caps.

The stranger immediately set to work. When Mrs. Hall took his dinner to him, he was so absorbed, he did not hear her until she had swept away the bulk of the straw and put the tray on the table…

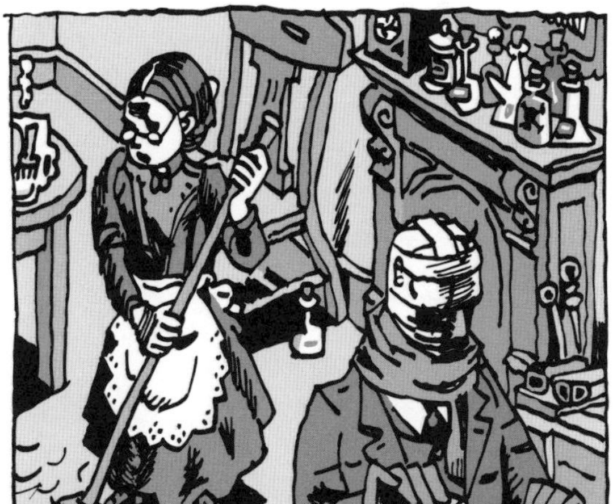

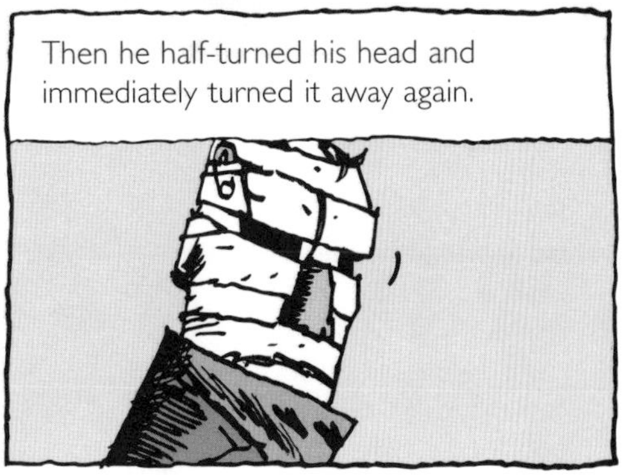
Then he half-turned his head and immediately turned it away again.

But she saw he had removed his glasses, and it seemed to her that his eye sockets were extraordinarily hollow.

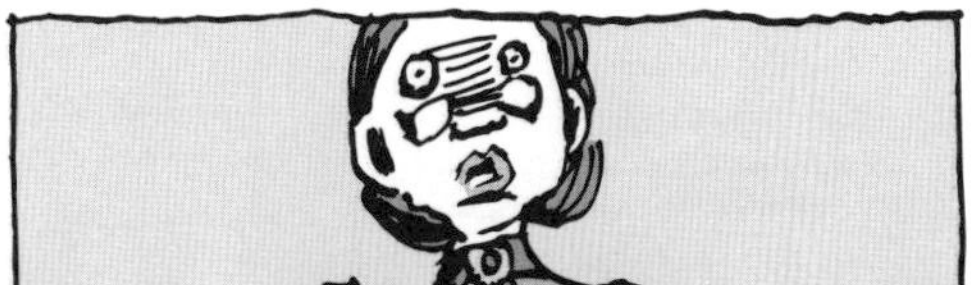

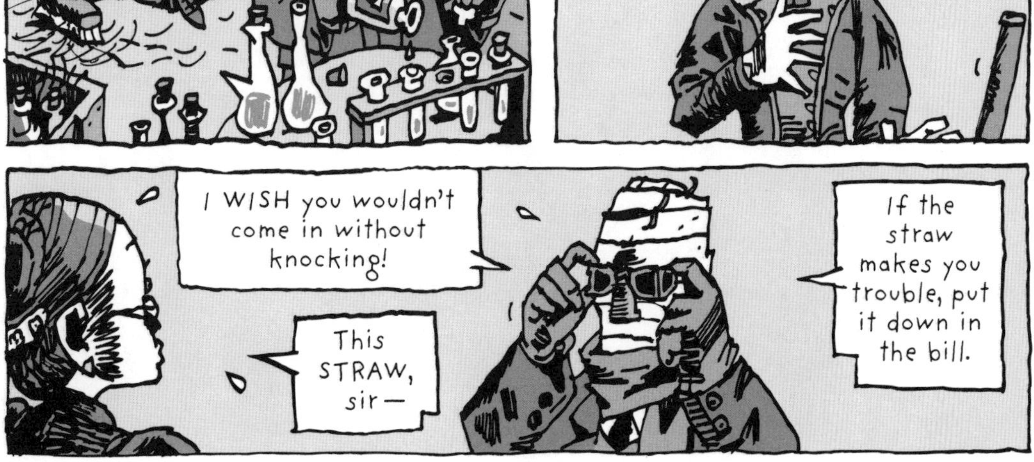
I WISH you wouldn't come in without knocking!
This STRAW, sir—
If the straw makes you trouble, put it down in the bill.

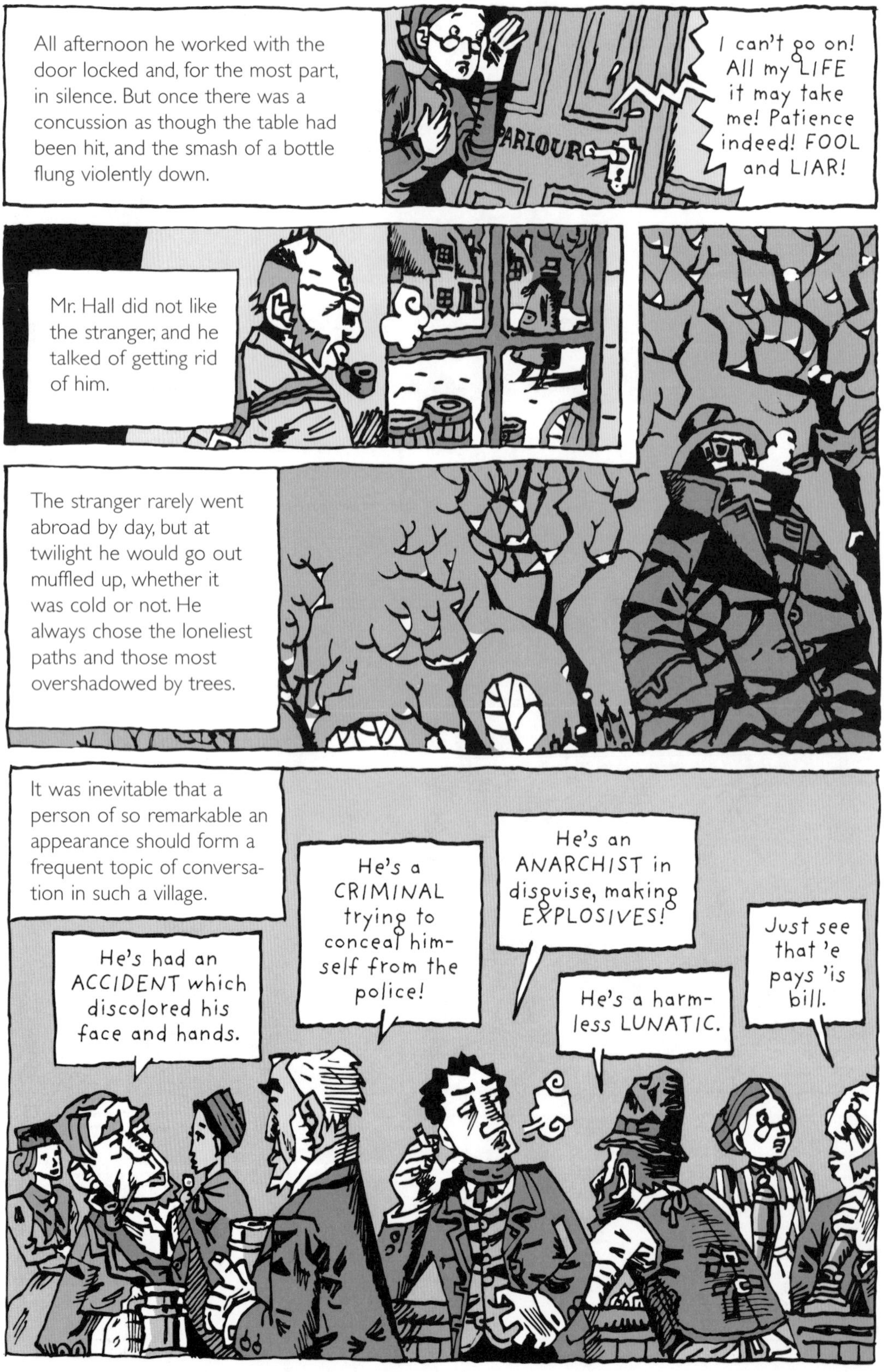
All afternoon he worked with the door locked and, for the most part, in silence. But once there was a concussion as though the table had been hit, and the smash of a bottle flung violently down.
PARLOUR
I can't go on! All my LIFE it may take me! Patience indeed! FOOL and LIAR!
Mr. Hall did not like the stranger, and he talked of getting rid of him.
The stranger rarely went abroad by day, but at twilight he would go out muffled up, whether it was cold or not. He always chose the loneliest paths and those most overshadowed by trees.
It was inevitable that a person of so remarkable an appearance should form a frequent topic of conversation in such a village.
He's had an ACCIDENT which discolored his face and hands.
He's a CRIMINAL trying to conceal himself from the police!
He's an ANARCHIST in disguise, making EXPLOSIVES!
He's a harmless LUNATIC.
Just see that 'e pays 'is bill.

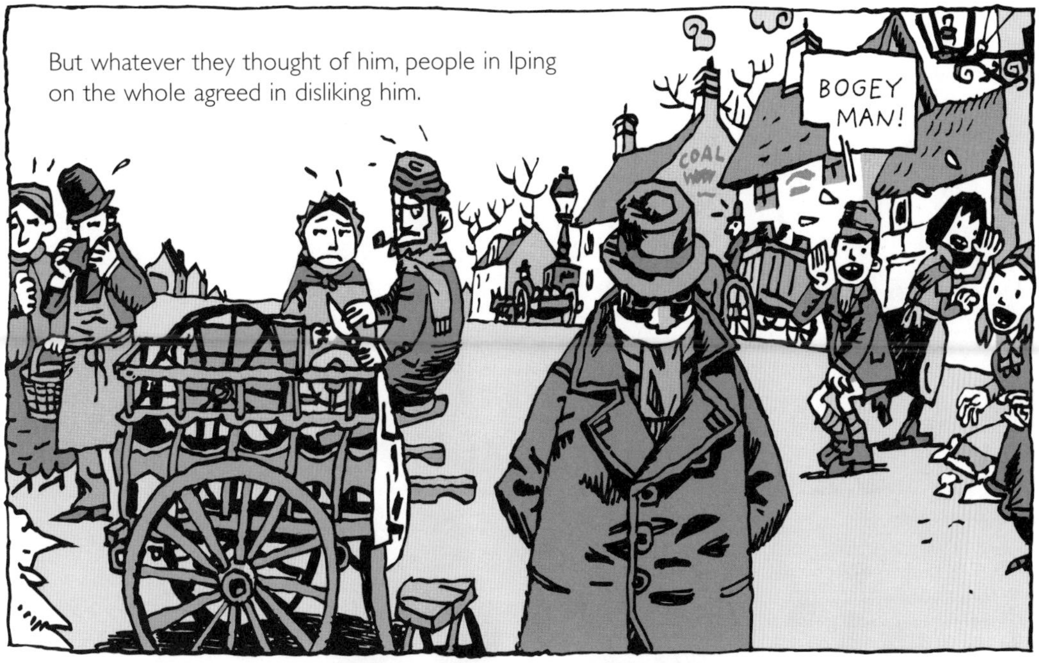
But whatever they thought of him, people in Iping on the whole agreed in disliking him.
BOGEY MAN!
COAL

Cuss, the village's general practitioner, was devoured by curiosity. The bandages excited his professional interest, and the report of the thousand and one bottles further aroused his jealous regard.

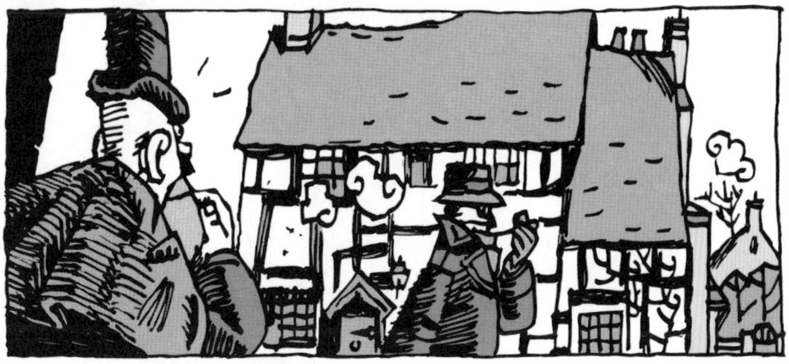

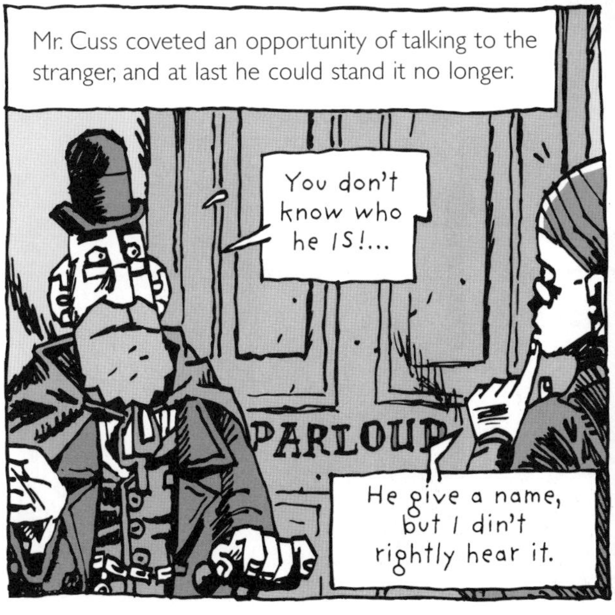
Mr. Cuss coveted an opportunity of talking to the stranger, and at last he could stand it no longer.
You don't know who he IS!...
PARLOUR
He give a name, but I din't rightly hear it.

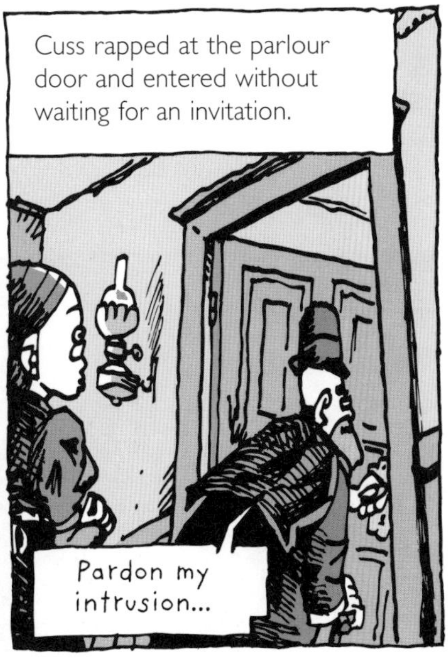
Cuss rapped at the parlour door and entered without waiting for an invitation.
Pardon my intrusion...

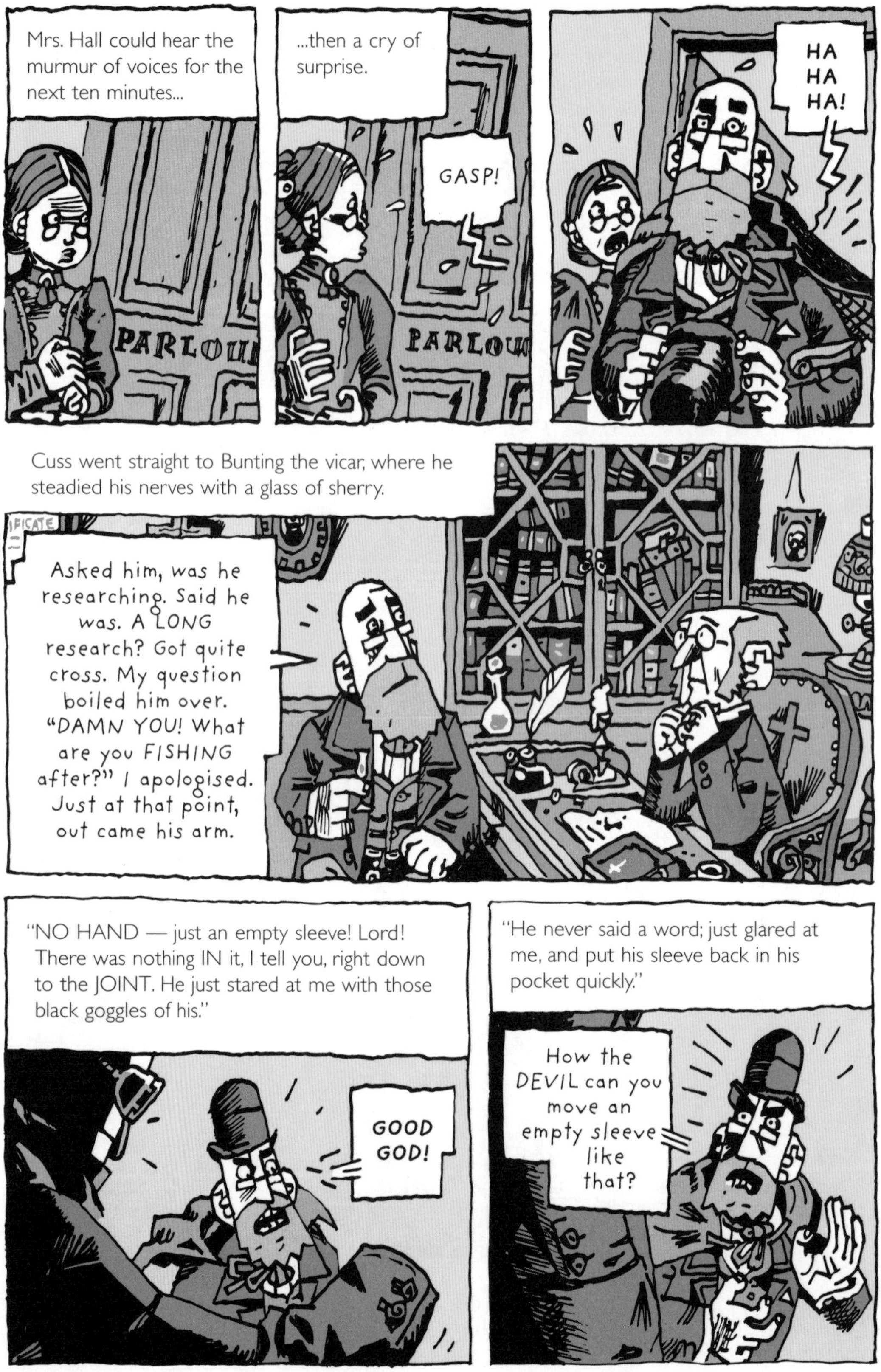
Mrs. Hall could hear the murmur of voices for the next ten minutes...
PARLOU
...then a cry of surprise.
GASP!
PARLOU
HA HA HA!
Cuss went straight to Bunting the vicar, where he steadied his nerves with a glass of sherry.
Asked him, was he researching. Said he was. A LONG research? Got quite cross. My question boiled him over. "DAMN YOU! What are you FISHING after?" I apologised. Just at that point, out came his arm.
"NO HAND — just an empty sleeve! Lord! There was nothing IN it, I tell you, right down to the JOINT. He just stared at me with those black goggles of his."
GOOD GOD!
"He never said a word; just glared at me, and put his sleeve back in his pocket quickly."
How the DEVIL can you move an empty sleeve like that?

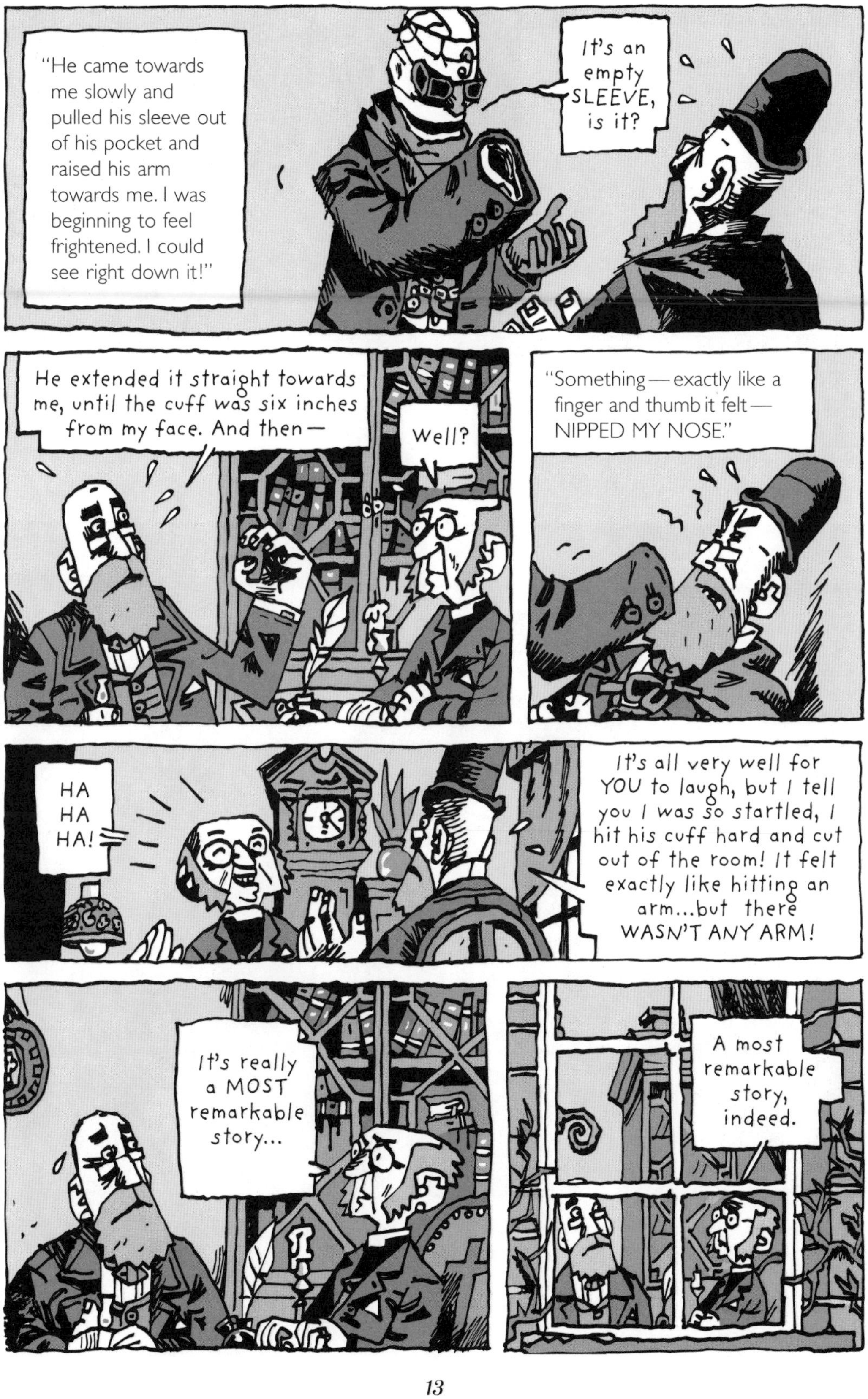
"He came towards me slowly and pulled his sleeve out of his pocket and raised his arm towards me. I was beginning to feel frightened. I could see right down it!"
It's an empty SLEEVE, is it?
He extended it straight towards me, until the cuff was six inches from my face. And then—
Well?
"Something—exactly like a finger and thumb it felt—NIPPED MY NOSE."
HA HA HA!
It's all very well for YOU to laugh, but I tell you I was so startled, I hit his cuff hard and cut out of the room! It felt exactly like hitting an arm...but there WASN'T ANY ARM!
It's really a MOST remarkable story...
A most remarkable story, indeed.

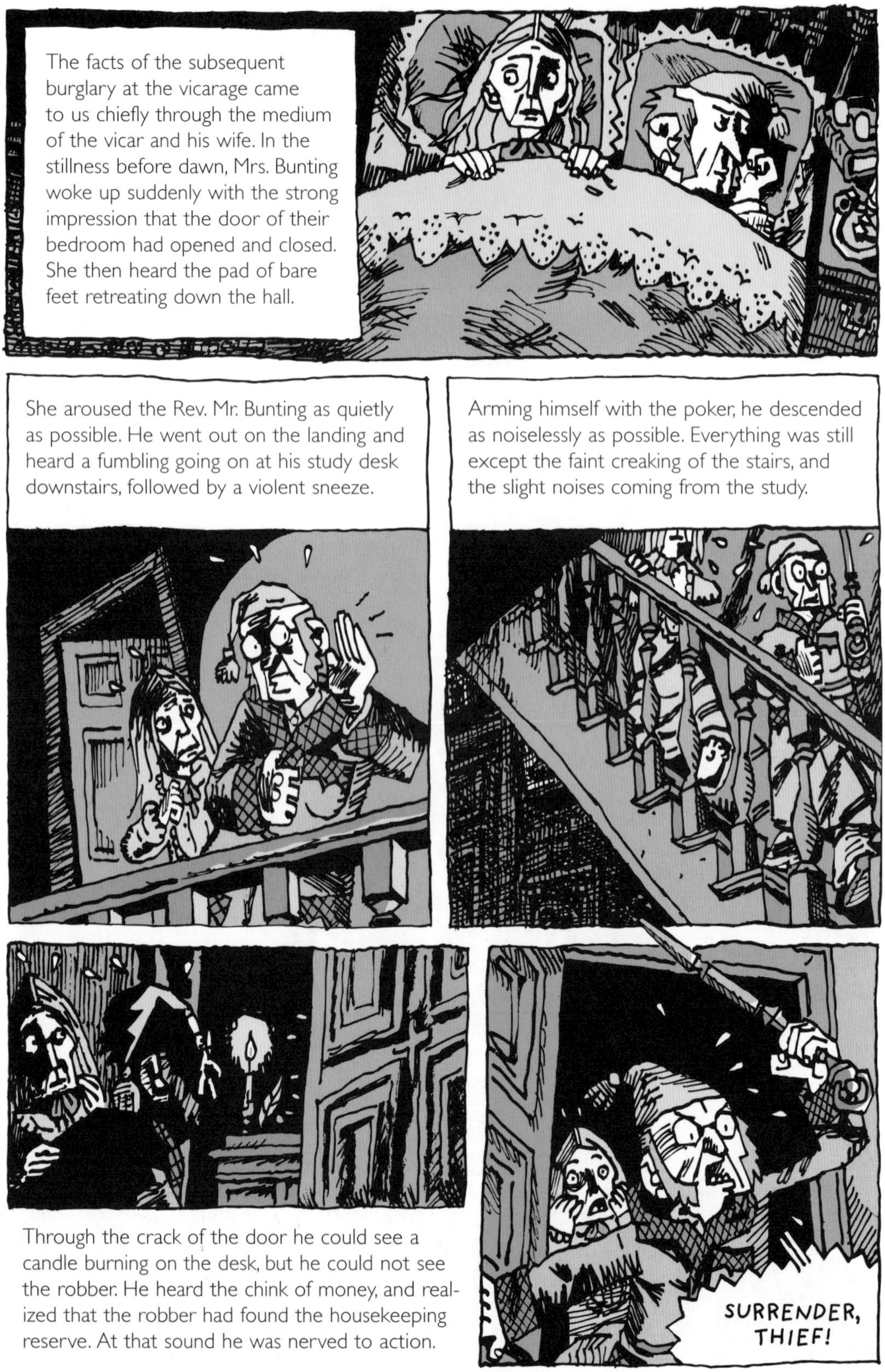
The facts of the subsequent burglary at the vicarage came to us chiefly through the medium of the vicar and his wife. In the stillness before dawn, Mrs. Bunting woke up suddenly with the strong impression that the door of their bedroom had opened and closed. She then heard the pad of bare feet retreating down the hall.
She aroused the Rev. Mr. Bunting as quietly as possible. He went out on the landing and heard a fumbling going on at his study desk downstairs, followed by a violent sneeze.
Arming himself with the poker, he descended as noiselessly as possible. Everything was still except the faint creaking of the stairs, and the slight noises coming from the study.
Through the crack of the door he could see a candle burning on the desk, but he could not see the robber. He heard the chink of money, and realized that the robber had found the housekeeping reserve. At that sound he was nerved to action.
SURRENDER, THIEF!

Mr. Bunting rushed into the room, closely followed by his wife. But the room was perfectly empty. There was not a soul to be found in the house, search as they would.

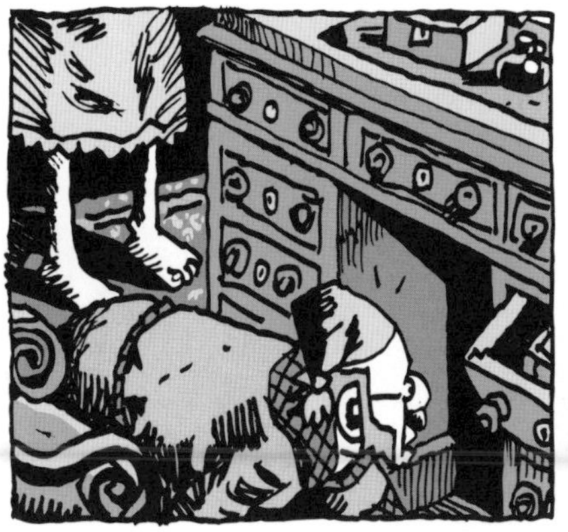

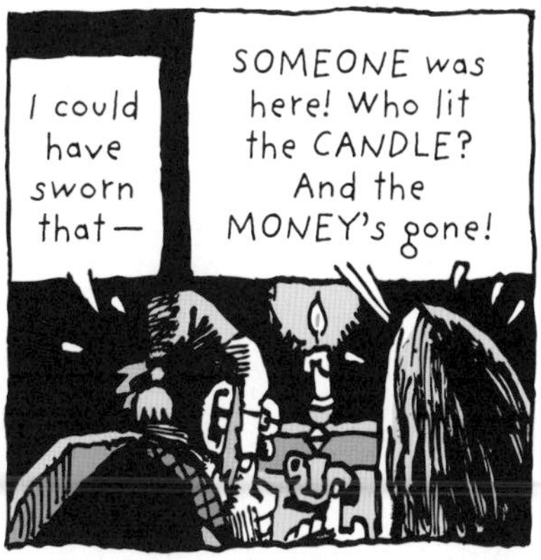
I could have sworn that—
SOMEONE was here! Who lit the CANDLE? And the MONEY's gone!

Now it happened that in the early hours of that day, Mr. Hall had been surprised to find the stranger's door ajar. He entered with Mrs. Hall.

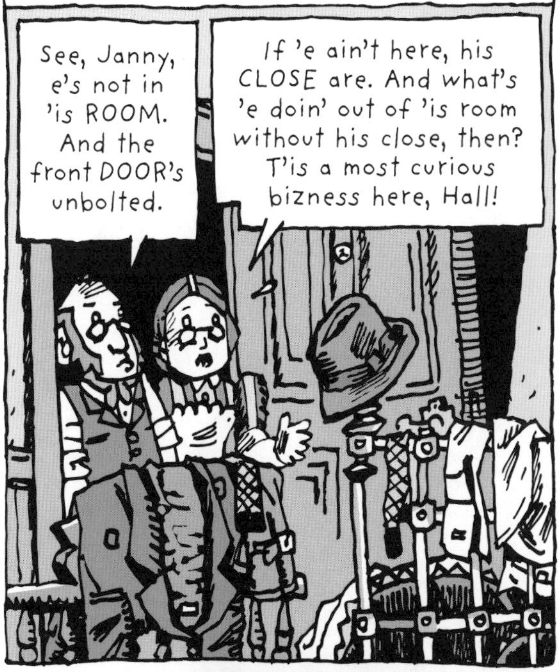
See, Janny, e's not in 'is ROOM. And the front DOOR's unbolted.
If 'e ain't here, his CLOSE are. And what's 'e doin' out of 'is room without his close, then? T'is a most curious bizness here, Hall!

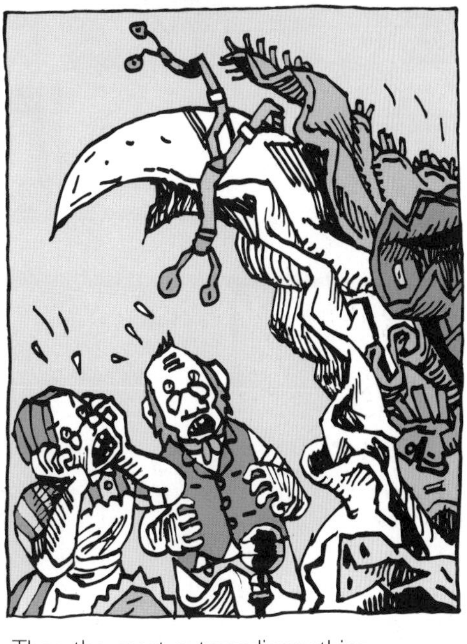

Then the most extraordinary thing happened — the bedclothes suddenly gathered themselves and jumped into the air! The sponge leapt from the washstand and the stranger's hat hopped off the bedpost and dashed straight at Mrs. Hall's face!

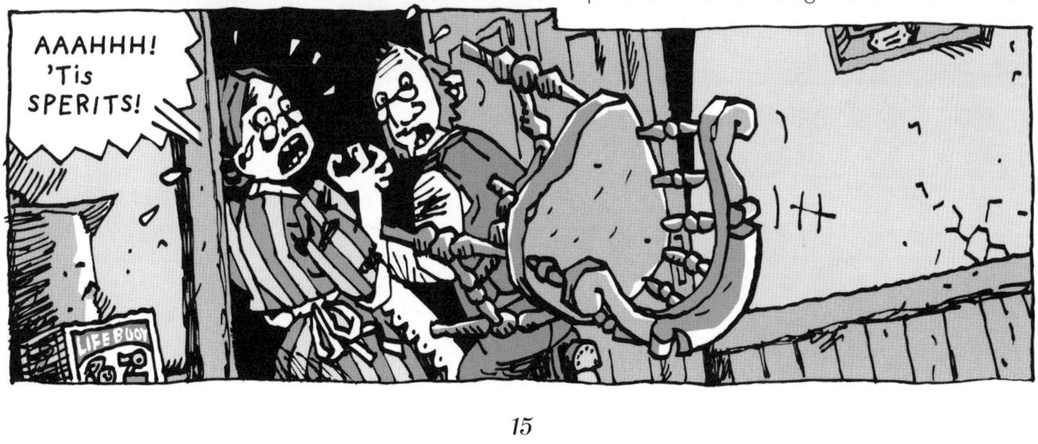
AAAHHH! 'Tis SPERITS!
LIFEBUOY

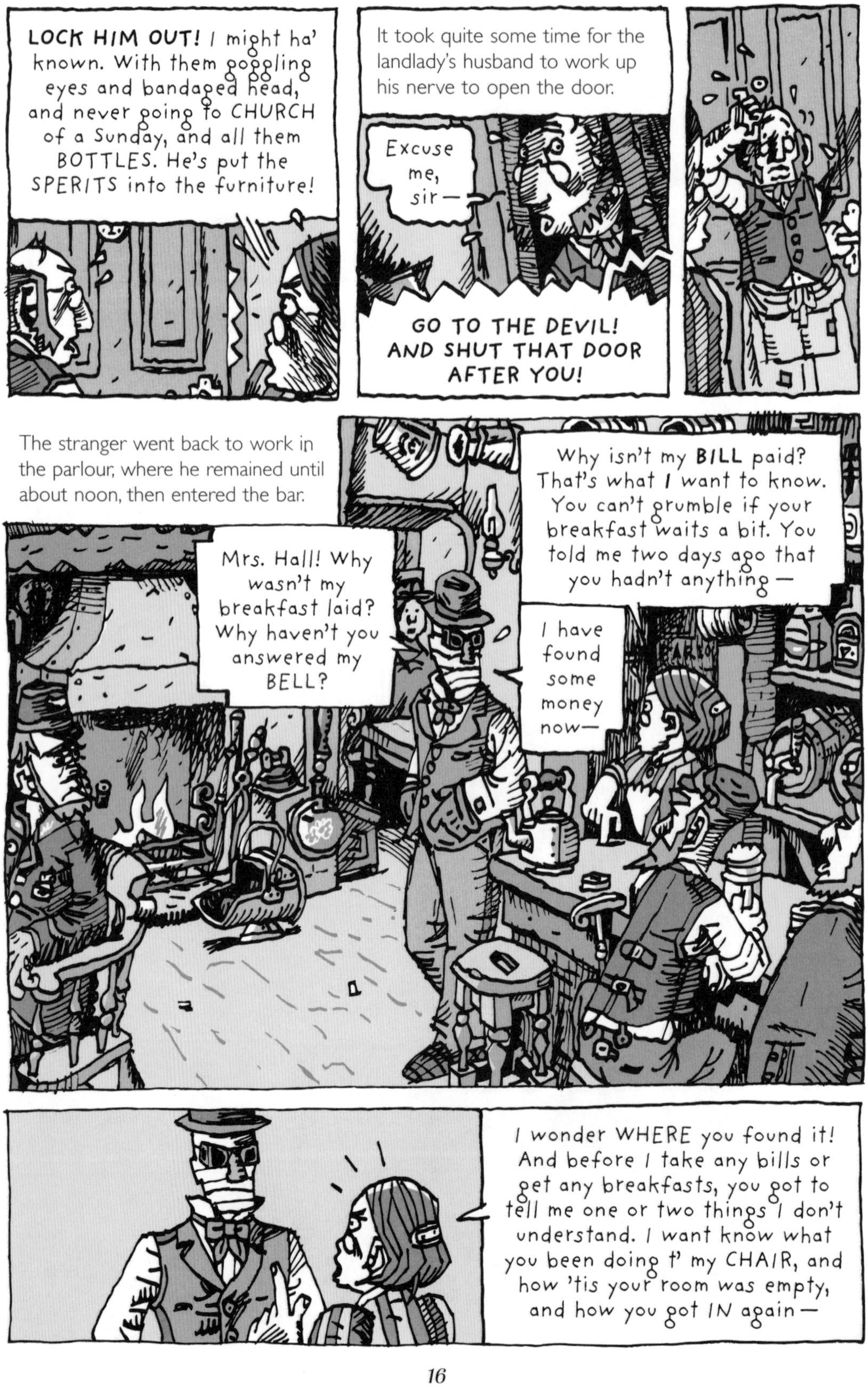
LOCK HIM OUT! I might ha' known. With them goggling eyes and bandaged head, and never going to CHURCH of a Sunday, and all them BOTTLES. He's put the SPERITS into the furniture!
It took quite some time for the landlady's husband to work up his nerve to open the door.
Excuse me, sir—
GO TO THE DEVIL! AND SHUT THAT DOOR AFTER YOU!
The stranger went back to work in the parlour, where he remained until about noon, then entered the bar.
Mrs. Hall! Why wasn't my breakfast laid? Why haven't you answered my BELL?
Why isn't my BILL paid? That's what I want to know. You can't grumble if your breakfast waits a bit. You told me two days ago that you hadn't anything—
I have found some money now—
I wonder WHERE you found it! And before I take any bills or get any breakfasts, you got to tell me one or two things I don't understand. I want know what you been doing t' my CHAIR, and how 'tis your room was empty, and how you got IN again—

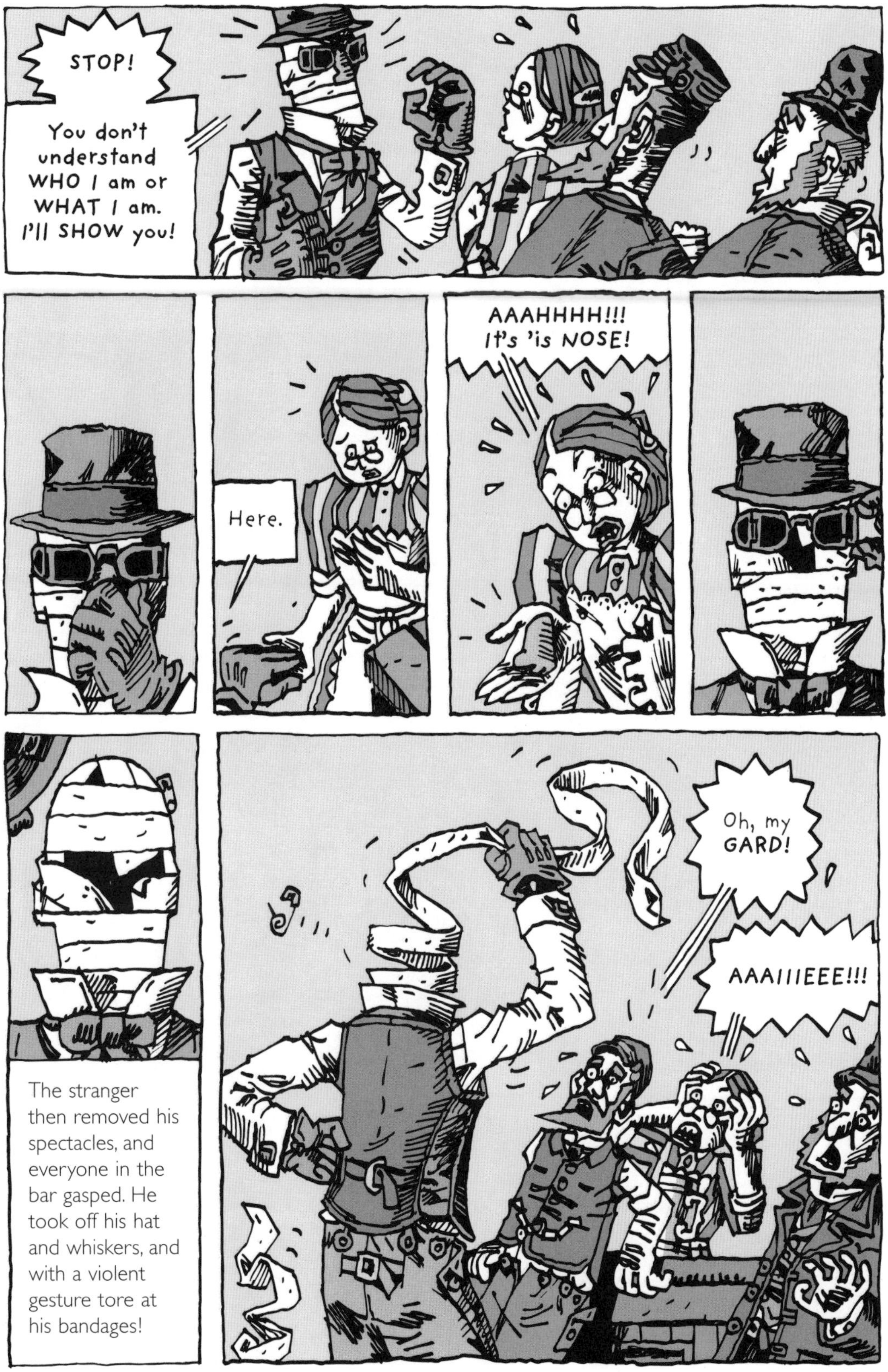
STOP!
You don't understand WHO I am or WHAT I am. I'll SHOW you!
Here.
AAAHHHH!!! It's 'is NOSE!
The stranger then removed his spectacles, and everyone in the bar gasped. He took off his hat and whiskers, and with a violent gesture tore at his bandages!
Oh, my GARD!
AAAIIIEEE!!!

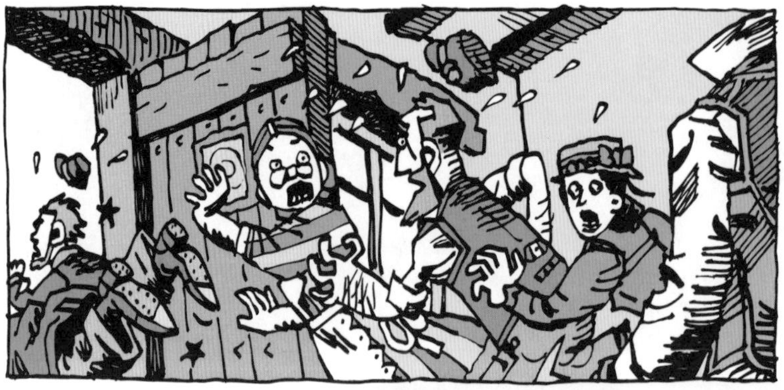

It was worse than anything. They were prepared for scars, disfigurements, tangible horrors, but… nothing! Mrs. Hall shrieked and made for the door, as everyone tumbled on everyone else down the steps…

For the man who stood there in the bar, shouting incoherently and gesticulating toward the panicking villagers, was a solid figure up to the collar of him, and then — nothingness, no visible thing at all!

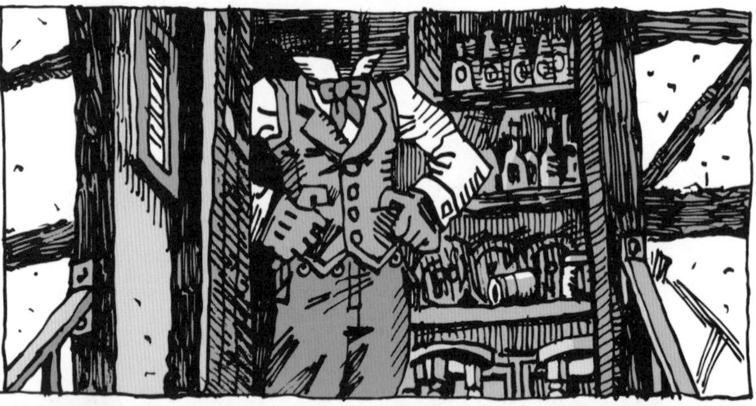

People down the village heard the shouts and shrieks, and a crowd soon gathered in the street. Presently, a little procession marched resolutely towards the house — Mr. Hall, then Mr. Bobby Jaffers, the village constable, followed by three brawny, but rather wary volunteers. They found the barroom empty, and the parlour door closed.

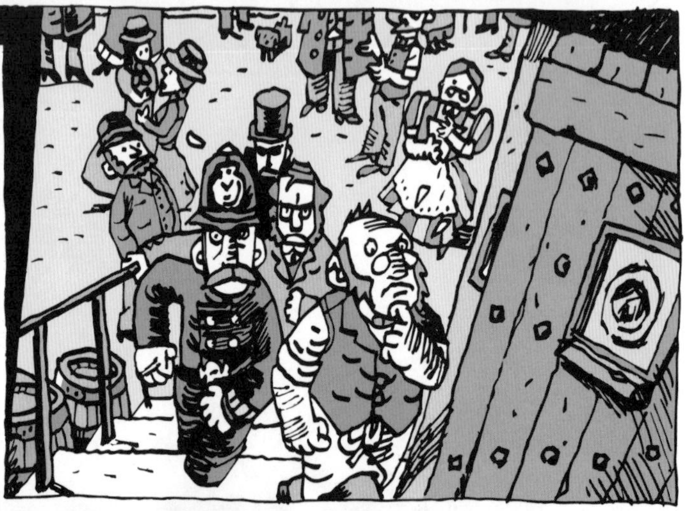

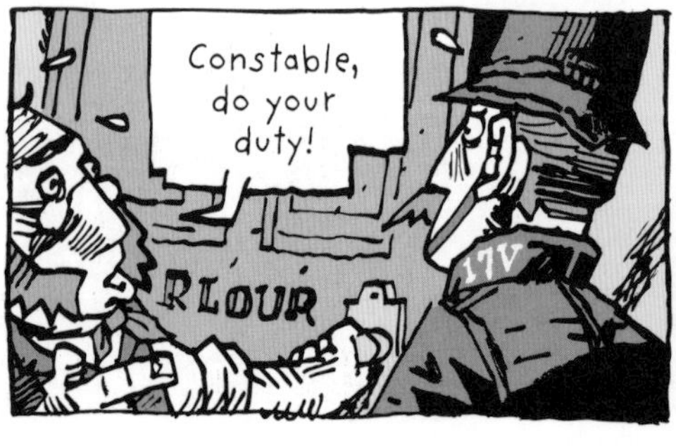
Constable, do your duty!
RLOUR

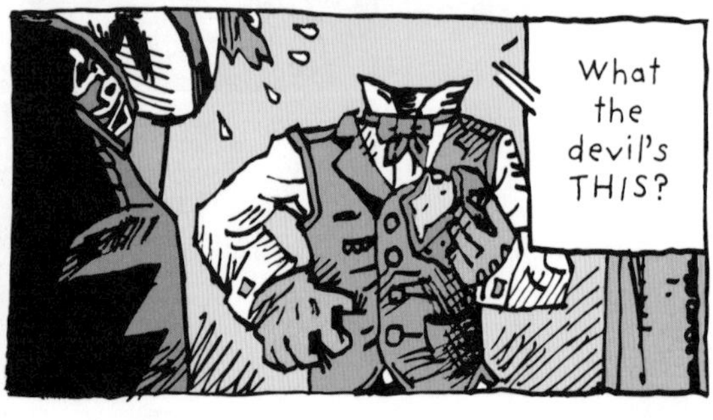
What the devil's THIS?

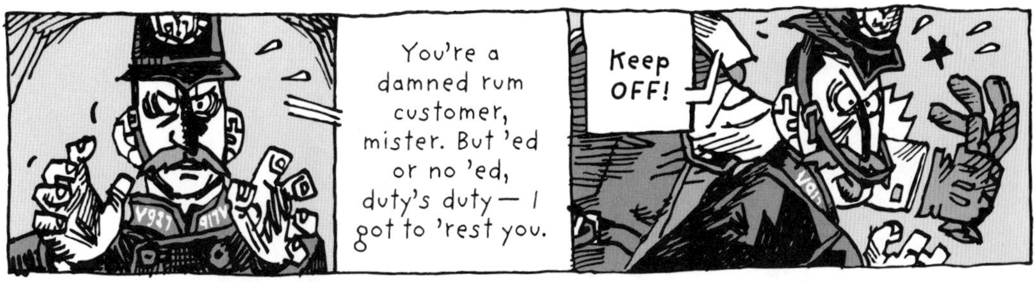
You're a damned rum customer, mister. But 'ed or no 'ed, duty's duty — I got to 'rest you.
Keep OFF!

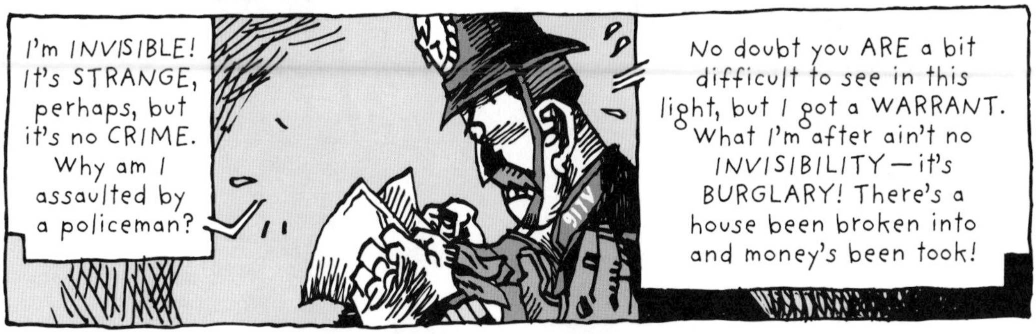
I'm INVISIBLE! It's STRANGE, perhaps, but it's no CRIME. Why am I assaulted by a policeman?
No doubt you ARE a bit difficult to see in this light, but I got a WARRANT. What I'm after ain't no INVISIBILITY — it's BURGLARY! There's a house been broken into and money's been took!

The stranger made an appearance of surrender. But then he quickly flung off his coat, and before anyone realized what was being done, his slippers, socks, and trousers had been kicked off. There was a rush at the fluttering white shirt which was now all that remained visible.

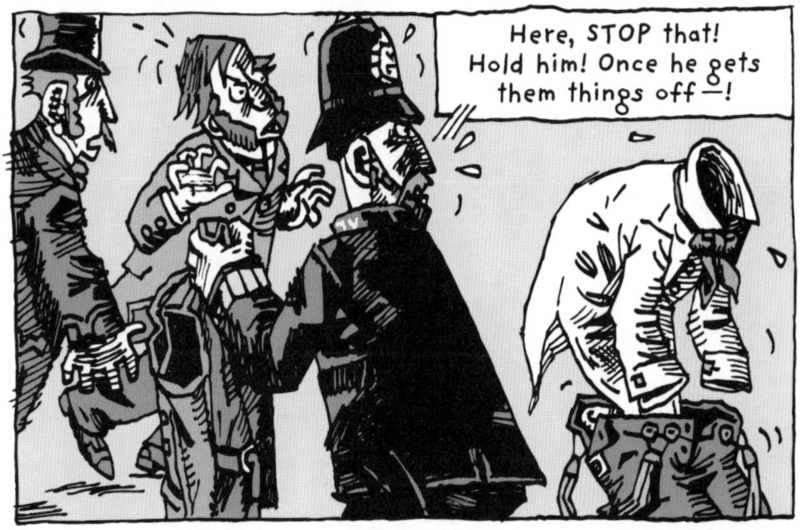
Here, STOP that! Hold him! Once he gets them things off —!

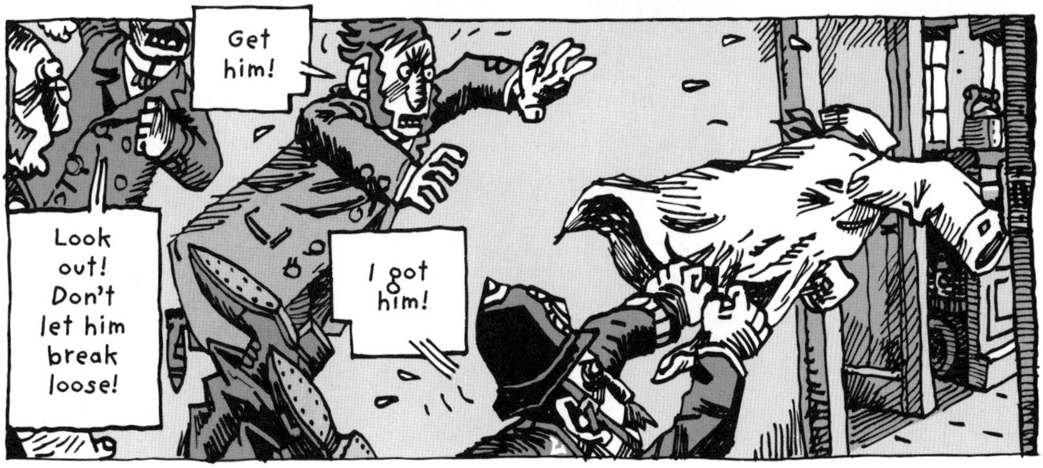
Get him!
Look out! Don't let him break loose!
I got him!

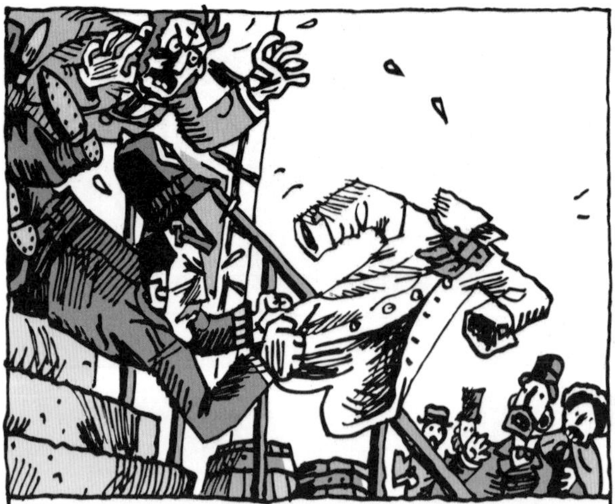

Men staggered right and left as the extraordinary conflict swayed swiftly towards the house door, and went spinning down the steps of the inn. Constable Jaffers clung tenaciously to the fleeing shirt.

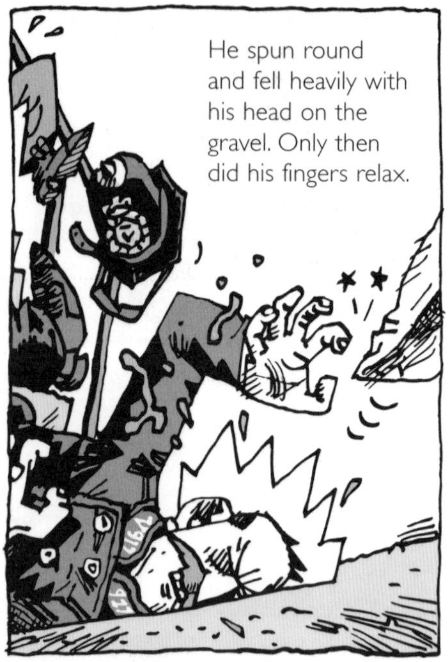
He spun round and fell heavily with his head on the gravel. Only then did his fingers relax.

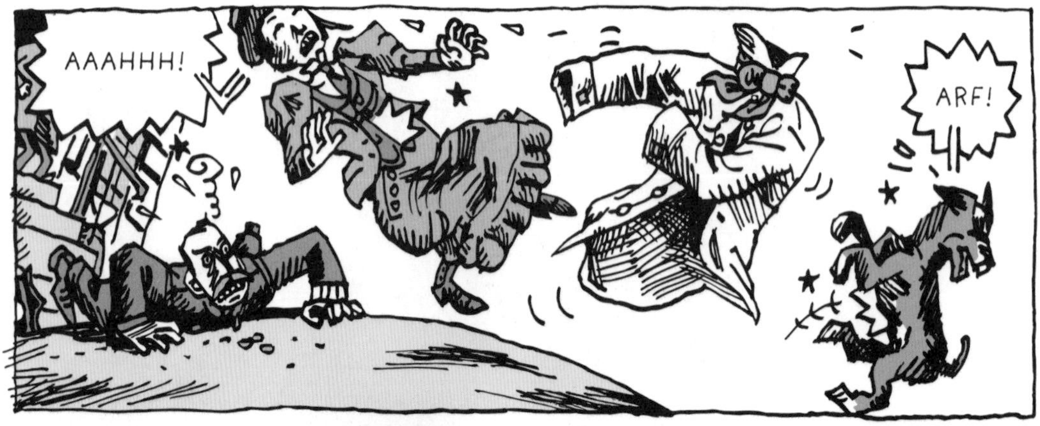
AAAHHH!
ARF!

Thus the transit of the Invisible Man was accomplished. Meanwhile, by the roadside about a mile and a half out of Iping sat Mr. Thomas Marvel. In a leisurely manner—he did everything in a leisurely manner—Mr. Marvel was contemplating trying on a pair of boots. He was not at all startled by a voice behind him.

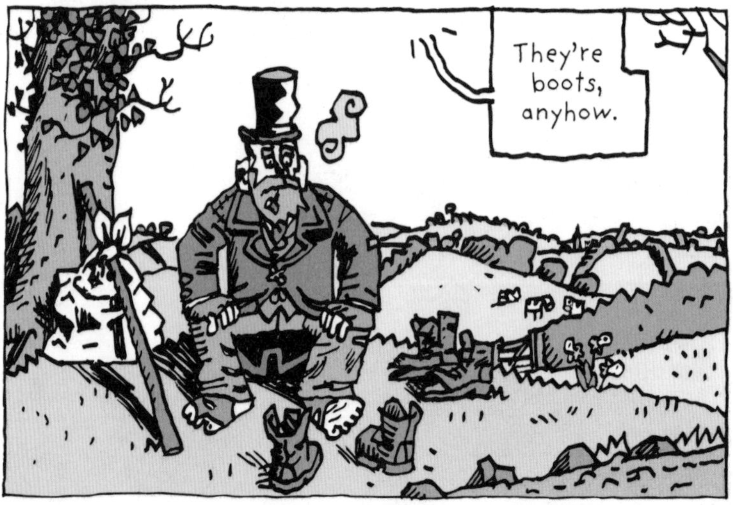
They're boots, anyhow.

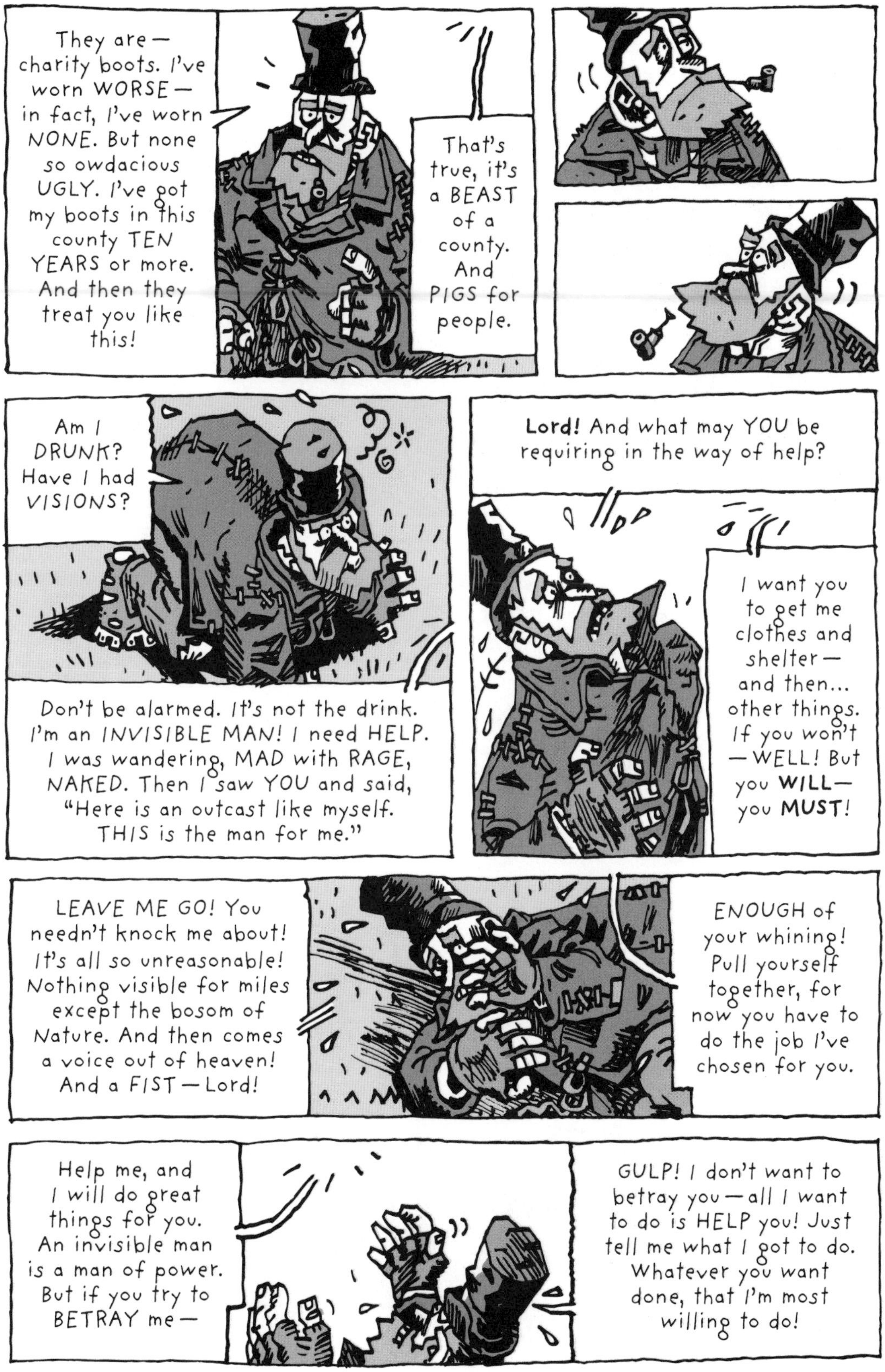
They are—charity boots. I've worn WORSE—in fact, I've worn NONE. But none so owdacious UGLY. I've got my boots in this county TEN YEARS or more. And then they treat you like this!
That's true, it's a BEAST of a county. And PIGS for people.
Am I DRUNK? Have I had VISIONS?
Don't be alarmed. It's not the drink. I'm an INVISIBLE MAN! I need HELP. I was wandering, MAD with RAGE, NAKED. Then I saw YOU and said, "Here is an outcast like myself. THIS is the man for me."
Lord! And what may YOU be requiring in the way of help?
I want you to get me clothes and shelter—and then... other things. If you won't—WELL! But you **WILL**—you **MUST**!
LEAVE ME GO! You needn't knock me about! It's all so unreasonable! Nothing visible for miles except the bosom of Nature. And then comes a voice out of heaven! And a FIST—Lord!
ENOUGH of your whining! Pull yourself together, for now you have to do the job I've chosen for you.
Help me, and I will do great things for you. An invisible man is a man of power. But if you try to BETRAY me—
GULP! I don't want to betray you—all I want to do is HELP you! Just tell me what I got to do. Whatever you want done, that I'm most willing to do!

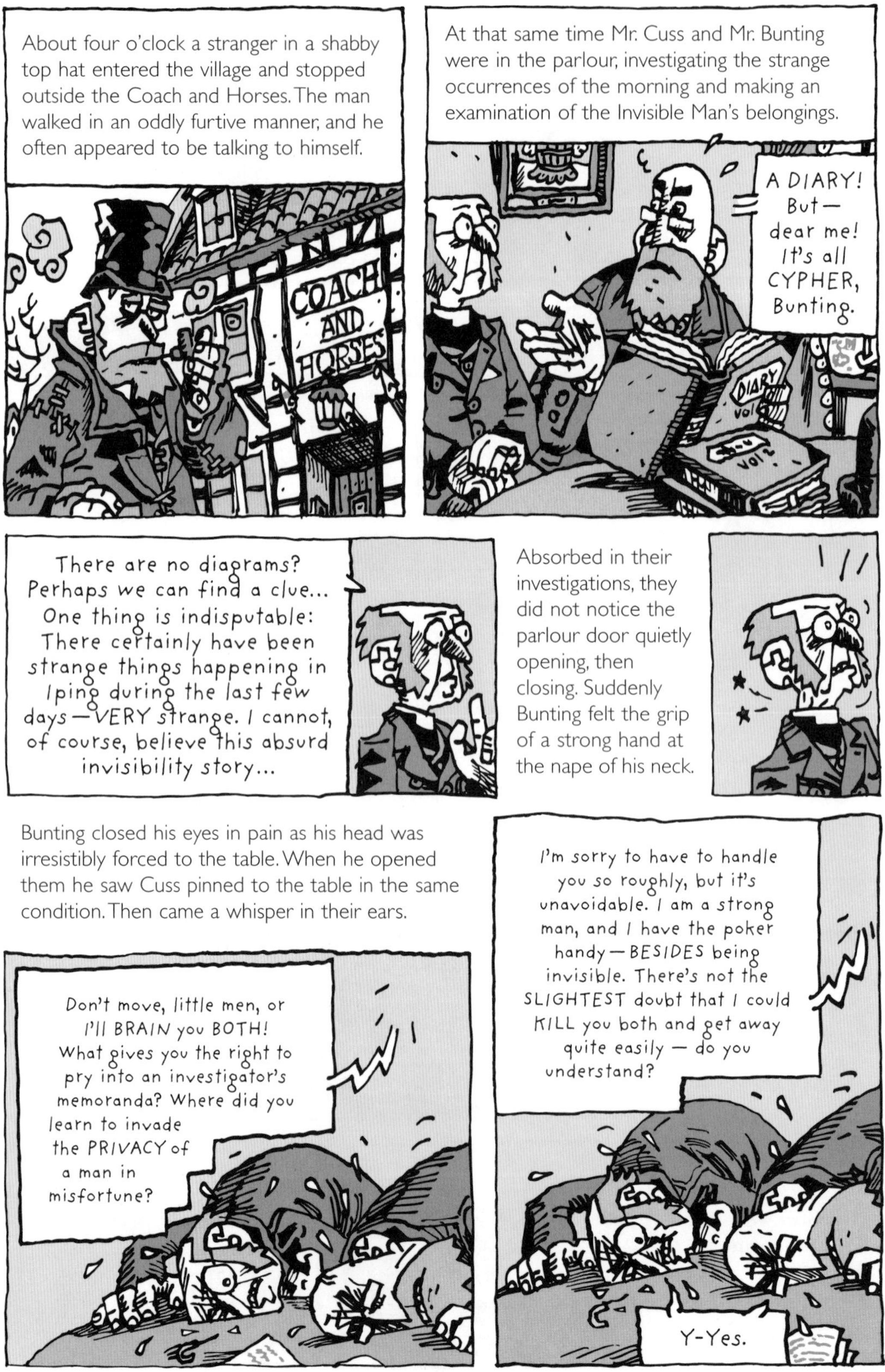
About four o'clock a stranger in a shabby top hat entered the village and stopped outside the Coach and Horses. The man walked in an oddly furtive manner, and he often appeared to be talking to himself.
COACH AND HORSES
At that same time Mr. Cuss and Mr. Bunting were in the parlour, investigating the strange occurrences of the morning and making an examination of the Invisible Man's belongings.
A DIARY! But— dear me! It's all CYPHER, Bunting.
DIARY VOL
There are no diagrams? Perhaps we can find a clue... One thing is indisputable: There certainly have been strange things happening in Iping during the last few days—VERY strange. I cannot, of course, believe this absurd invisibility story...
Absorbed in their investigations, they did not notice the parlour door quietly opening, then closing. Suddenly Bunting felt the grip of a strong hand at the nape of his neck.
Bunting closed his eyes in pain as his head was irresistibly forced to the table. When he opened them he saw Cuss pinned to the table in the same condition. Then came a whisper in their ears.
Don't move, little men, or I'll BRAIN you BOTH! What gives you the right to pry into an investigator's memoranda? Where did you learn to invade the PRIVACY of a man in misfortune?
I'm sorry to have to handle you so roughly, but it's unavoidable. I am a strong man, and I have the poker handy—BESIDES being invisible. There's not the SLIGHTEST doubt that I could KILL you both and get away quite easily — do you understand?
Y-Yes.

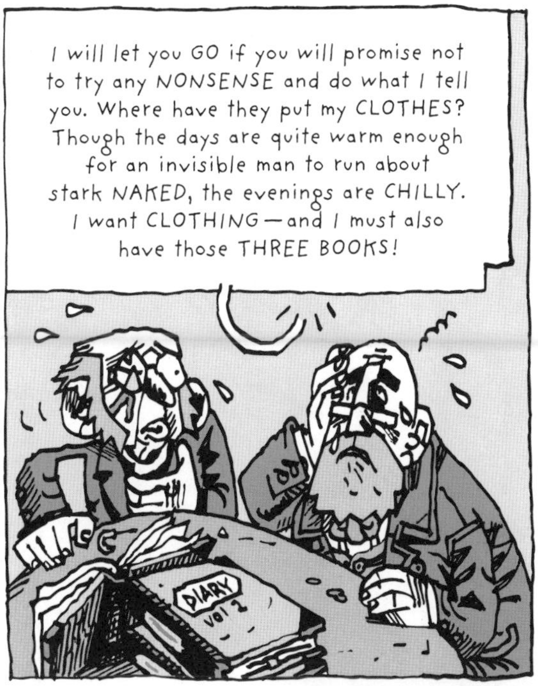
I will let you GO if you will promise not to try any NONSENSE and do what I tell you. Where have they put my CLOTHES? Though the days are quite warm enough for an invisible man to run about stark NAKED, the evenings are CHILLY. I want CLOTHING—and I must also have those THREE BOOKS!
DIARY vol 2

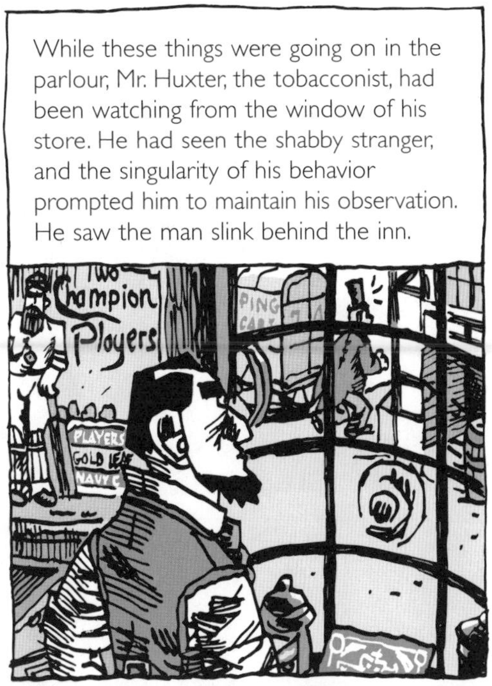
While these things were going on in the parlour, Mr. Huxter, the tobacconist, had been watching from the window of his store. He had seen the shabby stranger, and the singularity of his behavior prompted him to maintain his observation. He saw the man slink behind the inn.
Champion Players

The vagabond soon reappeared, with a big bundle in one hand, and three books tied together in the other. Conceiving he was witness to some petty larceny, Mr. Huxter stepped out of his shop and gave chase.

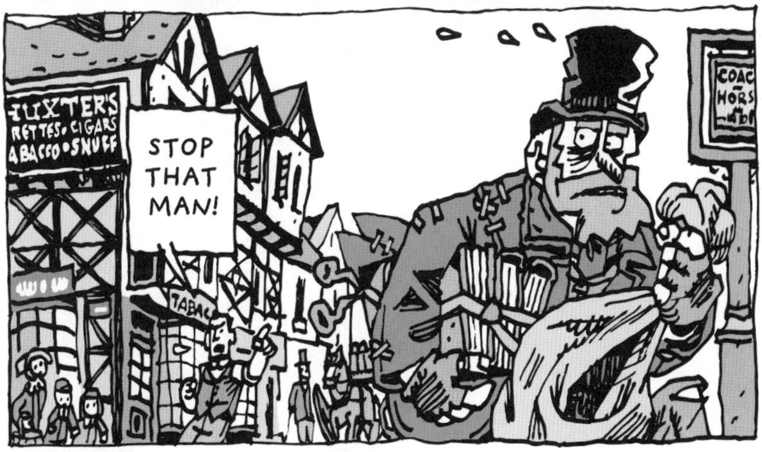
STOP THAT MAN!

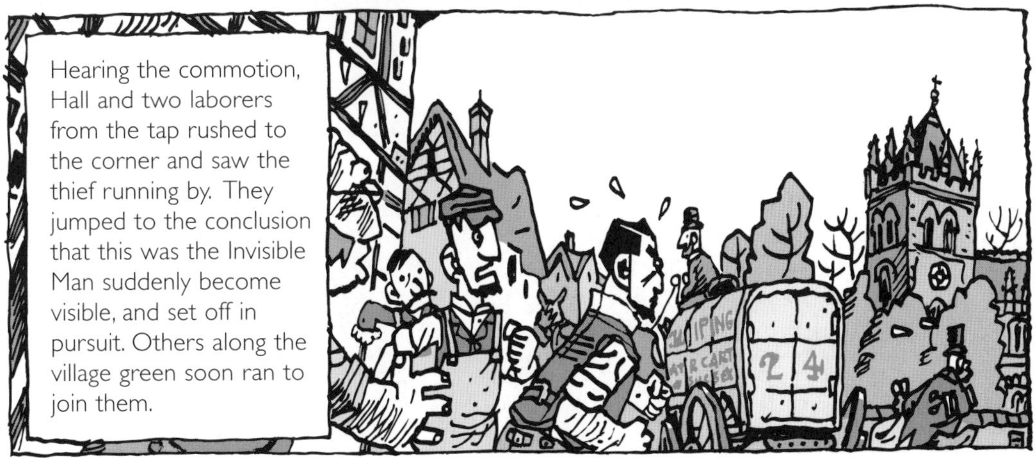
Hearing the commotion, Hall and two laborers from the tap rushed to the corner and saw the thief running by. They jumped to the conclusion that this was the Invisible Man suddenly become visible, and set off in pursuit. Others along the village green soon ran to join them.
24

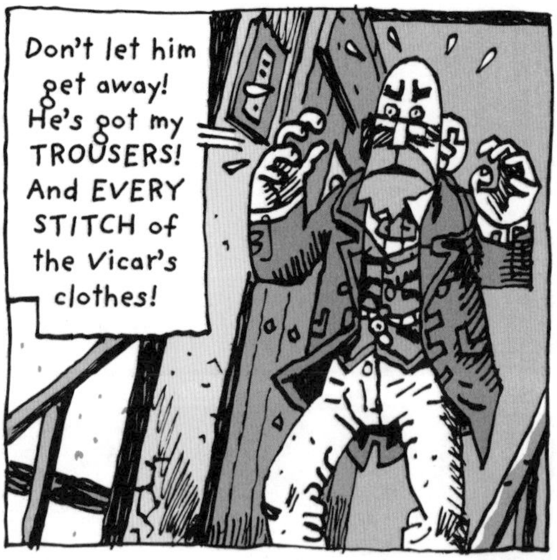
Don't let him get away! He's got my TROUSERS! And EVERY STITCH of the Vicar's clothes!

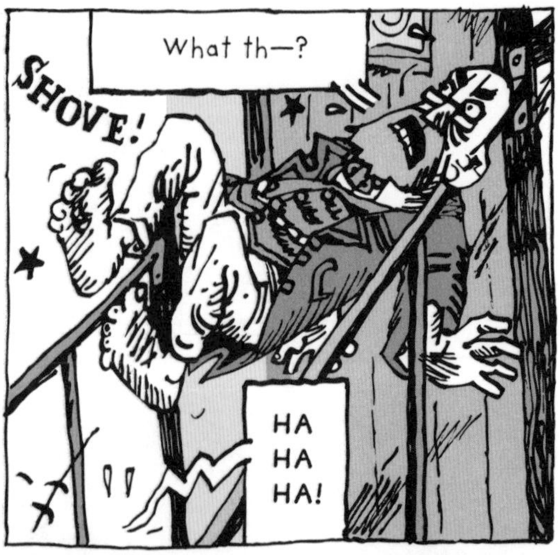
What th—?
SHOVE!
HA HA HA!

The Invisible Man amused himself for a little while by breaking all the windows in the Coach and Horses. Then he thrust a street lamp through the parlour window of Mrs. Gribble.

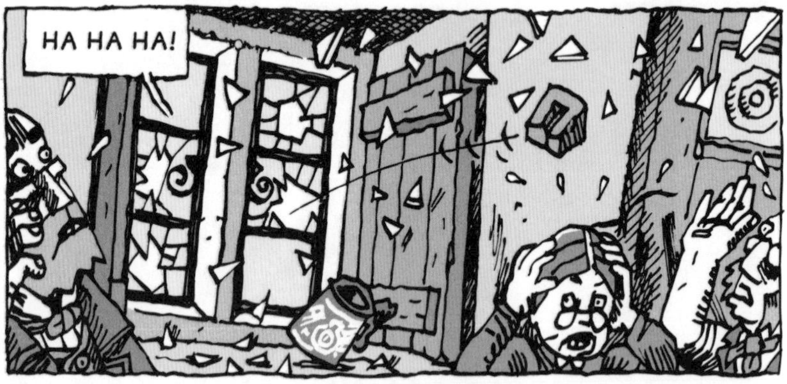
HA HA HA!

This was the culmination of an extraordinary day in the town: all that day, from the tills of local shops, money had been making off in handfuls, floating quietly along, then dodging quickly from approaching eyes. And then the telegraph wire to Aberdeen had mysteriously been cut.

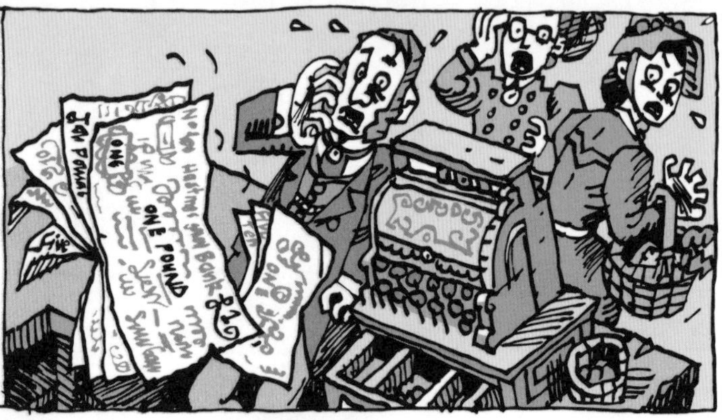

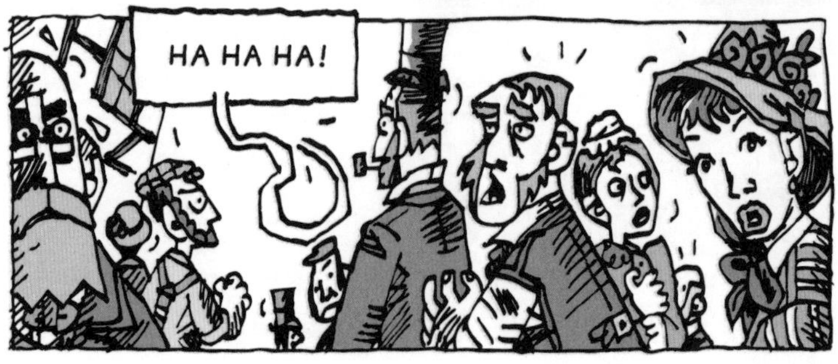
HA HA HA!

The Invisible Man's temper, never very good, seems to have gone completely, and he began smiting and breaking for the mere satisfaction of hurting. Finally it stopped, and the Invisible Man was neither heard, seen, nor felt again in Iping.

The next day, at The Jolly Cricketers in nearby Port Burdock, footsteps approached, running heavily. The door was opened violently, and Marvel, weeping and dishevelled, rushed in, shrieking with terror.

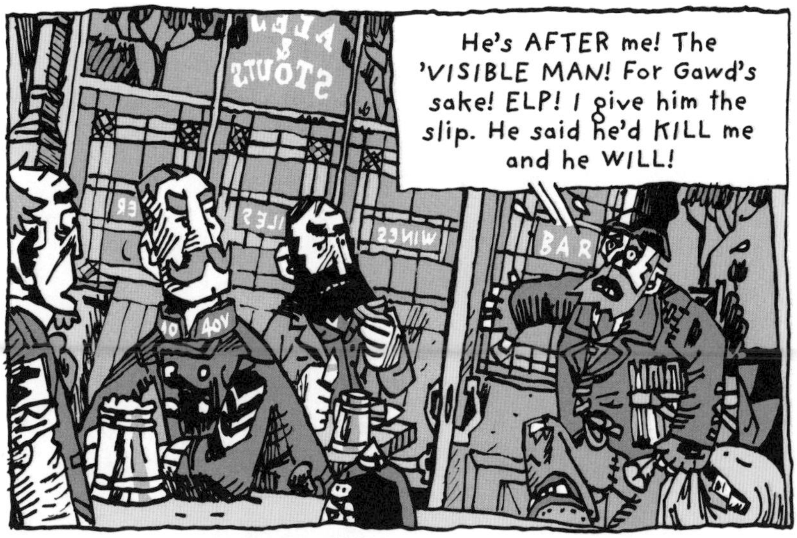
He's AFTER me! The 'VISIBLE MAN! For Gawd's sake! ELP! I give him the slip. He said he'd KILL me and he WILL!
BAR

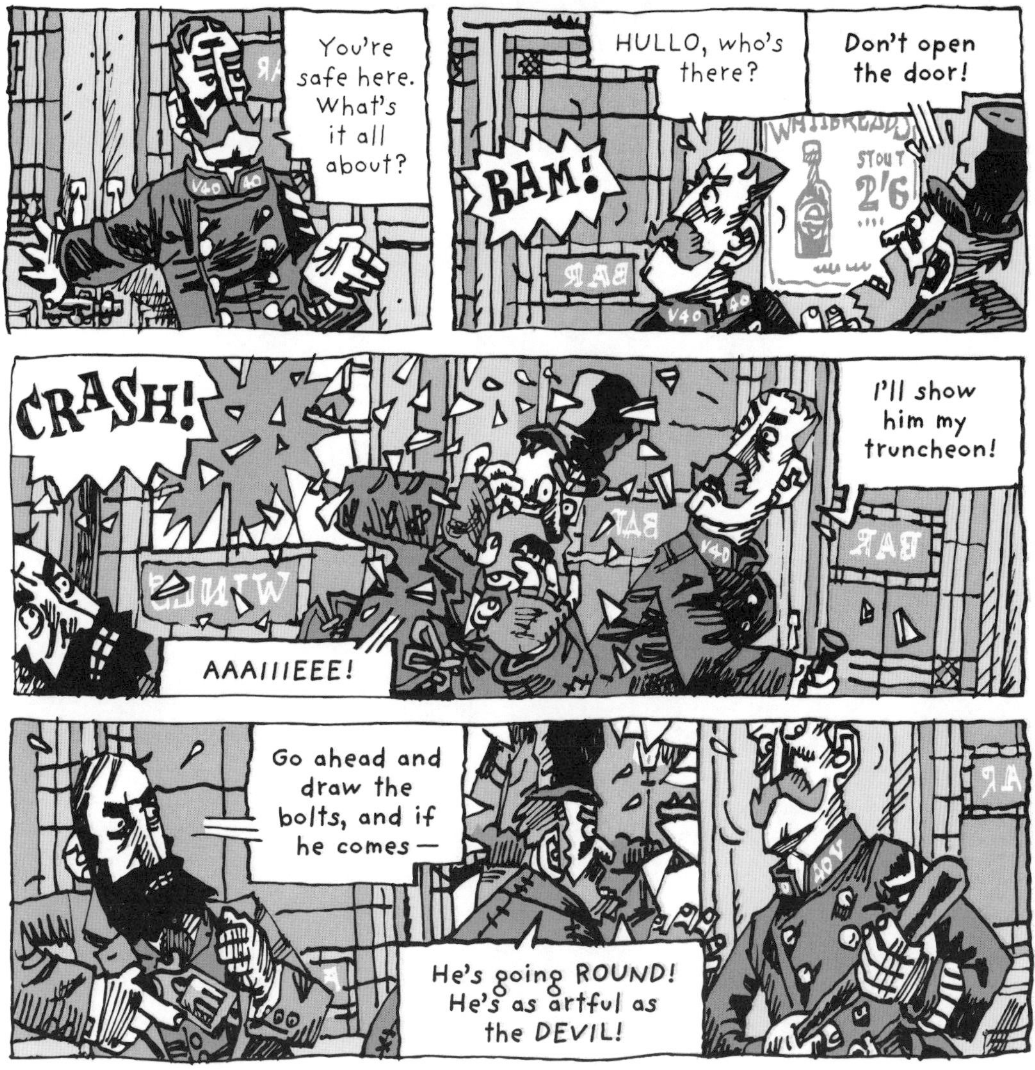
You're safe here. What's it all about?
HULLO, who's there?
Don't open the door!
BAM!
STOUT 2'6
BAR
CRASH!
I'll show him my truncheon!
AAAIIIEEE!
Go ahead and draw the bolts, and if he comes —
He's going ROUND! He's as artful as the DEVIL!

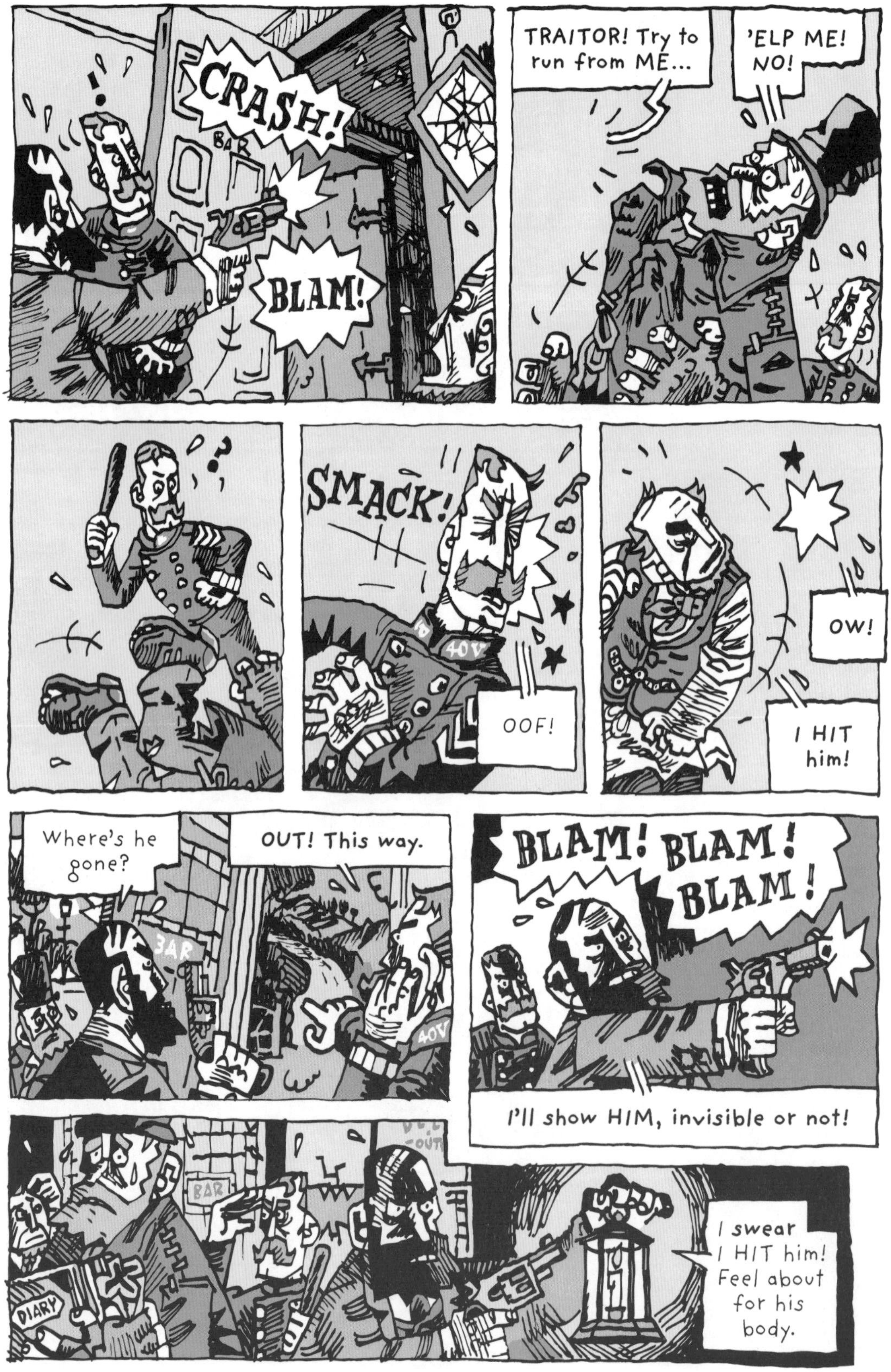
CRASH!
BAR
BLAM!
TRAITOR! Try to run from ME...
'ELP ME! NO!
SMACK!
40V
OOF!
OW!
I HIT him!
Where's he gone?
OUT! This way.
BAR
40V
BLAM! BLAM! BLAM!
I'll show HIM, invisible or not!
BAR
DIARY
I swear I HIT him! Feel about for his body.

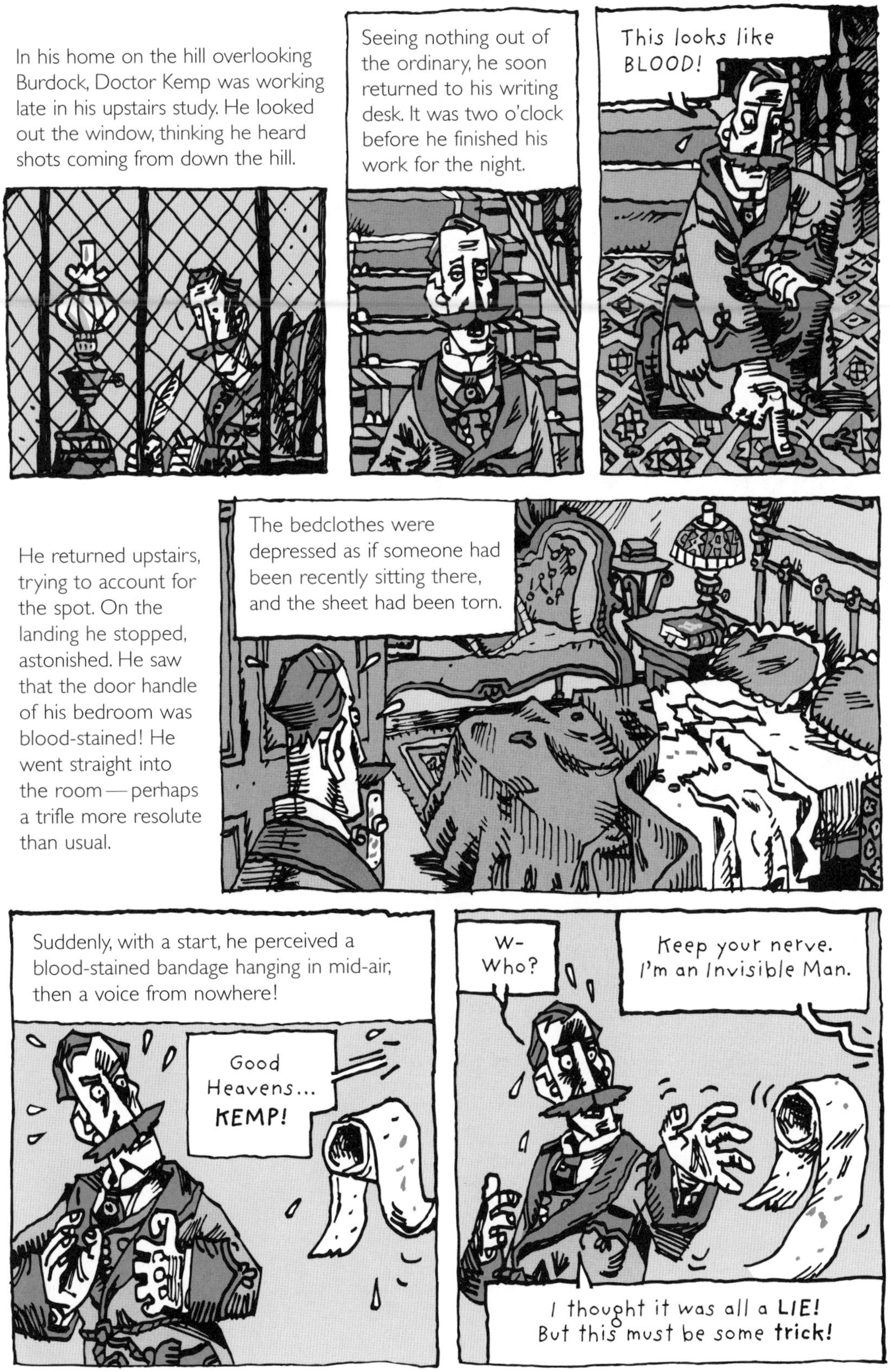
In his home on the hill overlooking Burdock, Doctor Kemp was working late in his upstairs study. He looked out the window, thinking he heard shots coming from down the hill.
Seeing nothing out of the ordinary, he soon returned to his writing desk. It was two o'clock before he finished his work for the night.
This looks like BLOOD!
He returned upstairs, trying to account for the spot. On the landing he stopped, astonished. He saw that the door handle of his bedroom was blood-stained! He went straight into the room — perhaps a trifle more resolute than usual.
The bedclothes were depressed as if someone had been recently sitting there, and the sheet had been torn.
Suddenly, with a start, he perceived a blood-stained bandage hanging in mid-air, then a voice from nowhere!
Good Heavens... KEMP!
W- Who?
Keep your nerve. I'm an Invisible Man.
I thought it was all a LIE! But this must be some trick!

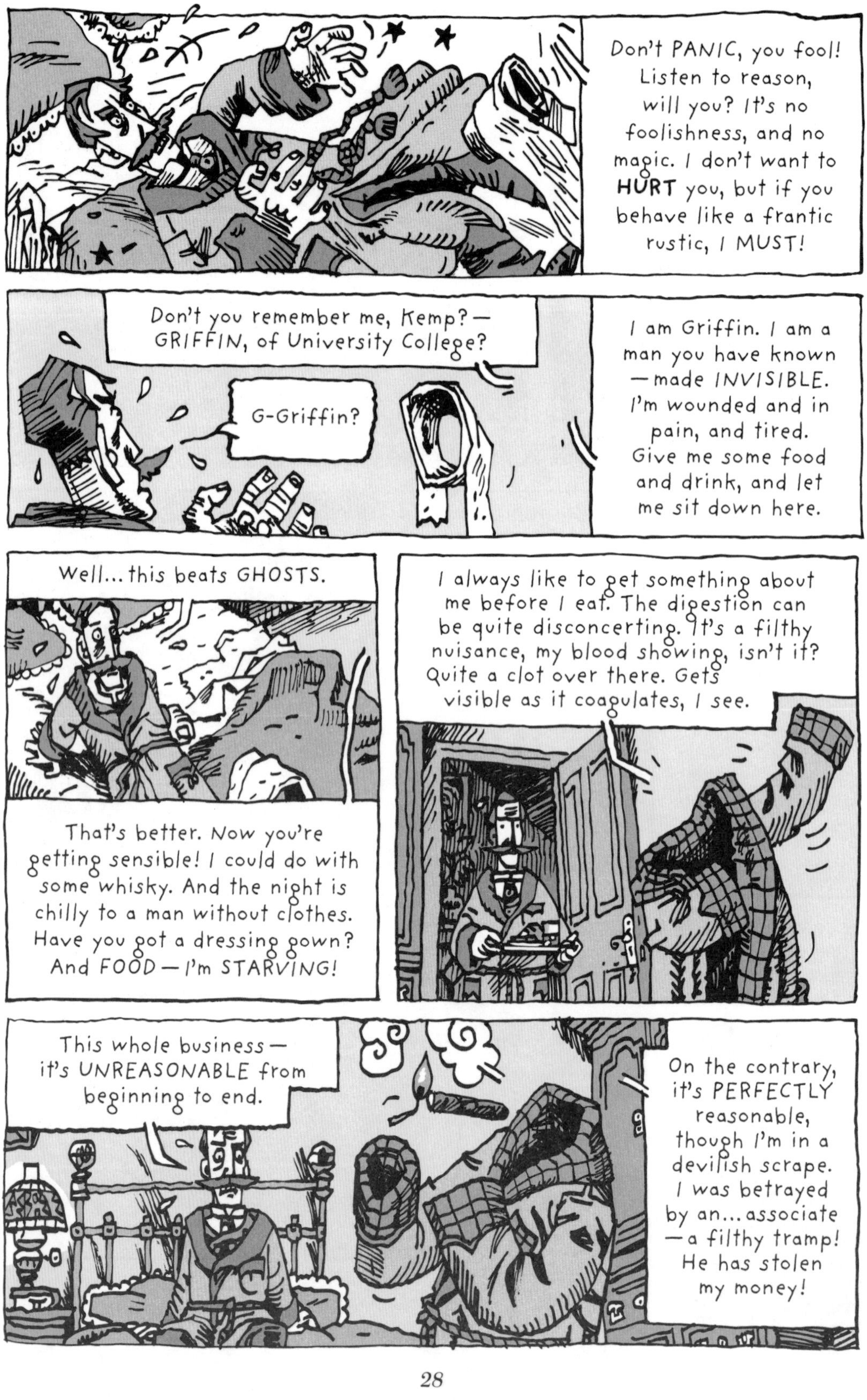
Don't PANIC, you fool! Listen to reason, will you? It's no foolishness, and no magic. I don't want to HURT you, but if you behave like a frantic rustic, I MUST!
Don't you remember me, Kemp?—GRIFFIN, of University College?
G-Griffin?
I am Griffin. I am a man you have known—made INVISIBLE. I'm wounded and in pain, and tired. Give me some food and drink, and let me sit down here.
Well... this beats GHOSTS.
That's better. Now you're getting sensible! I could do with some whisky. And the night is chilly to a man without clothes. Have you got a dressing gown? And FOOD—I'm STARVING!
I always like to get something about me before I eat. The digestion can be quite disconcerting. It's a filthy nuisance, my blood showing, isn't it? Quite a clot over there. Gets visible as it coagulates, I see.
This whole business—it's UNREASONABLE from beginning to end.
On the contrary, it's PERFECTLY reasonable, though I'm in a devilish scrape. I was betrayed by an... associate—a filthy tramp! He has stolen my money!

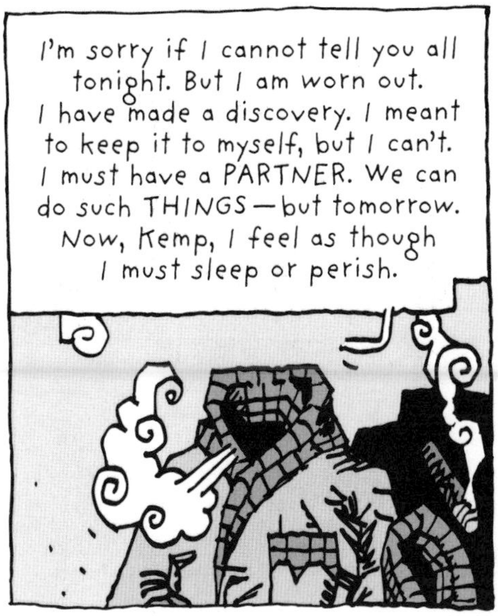
I'm sorry if I cannot tell you all tonight. But I am worn out. I have made a discovery. I meant to keep it to myself, but I can't. I must have a PARTNER. We can do such THINGS—but tomorrow. Now, Kemp, I feel as though I must sleep or perish.

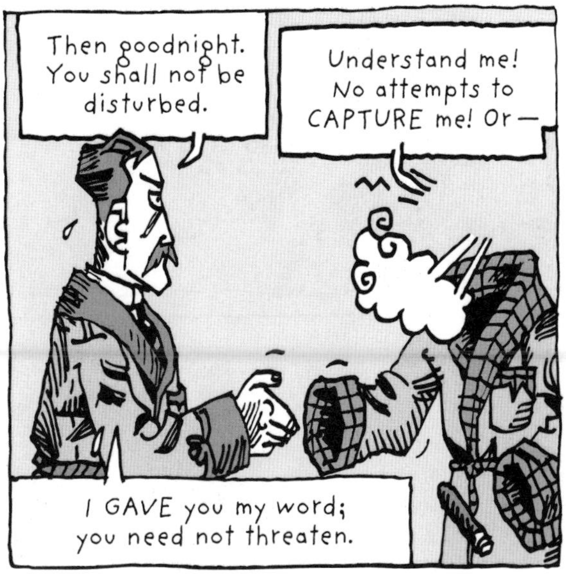
Then goodnight. You shall not be disturbed.
Understand me! No attempts to CAPTURE me! Or—
I GAVE you my word; you need not threaten.

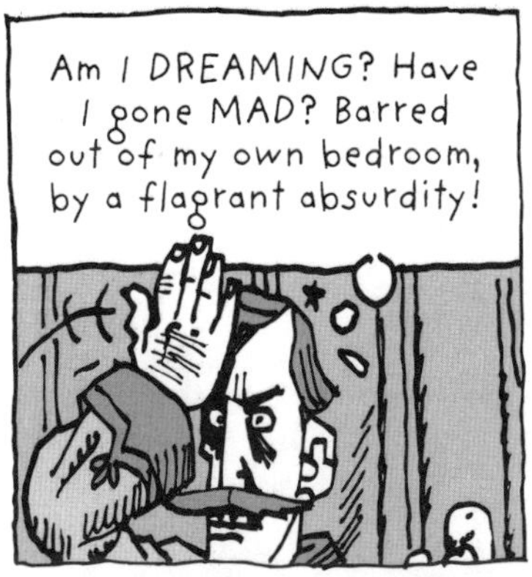
Am I DREAMING? Have I gone MAD? Barred out of my own bedroom, by a flagrant absurdity!

Dr. Kemp went into his little consulting room and caught up the morning's *St. James' Gazette*.

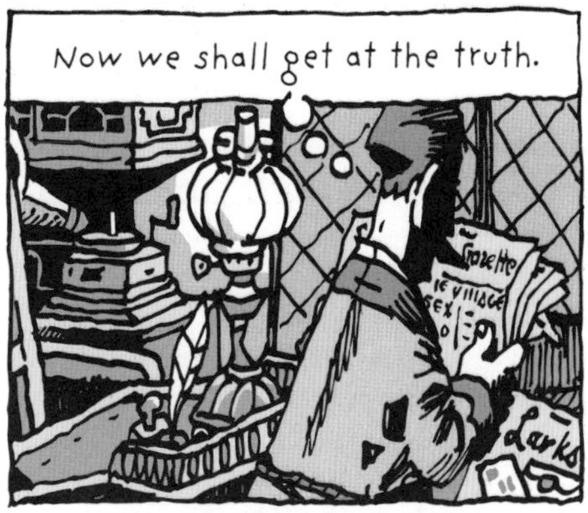
Now we shall get at the truth.

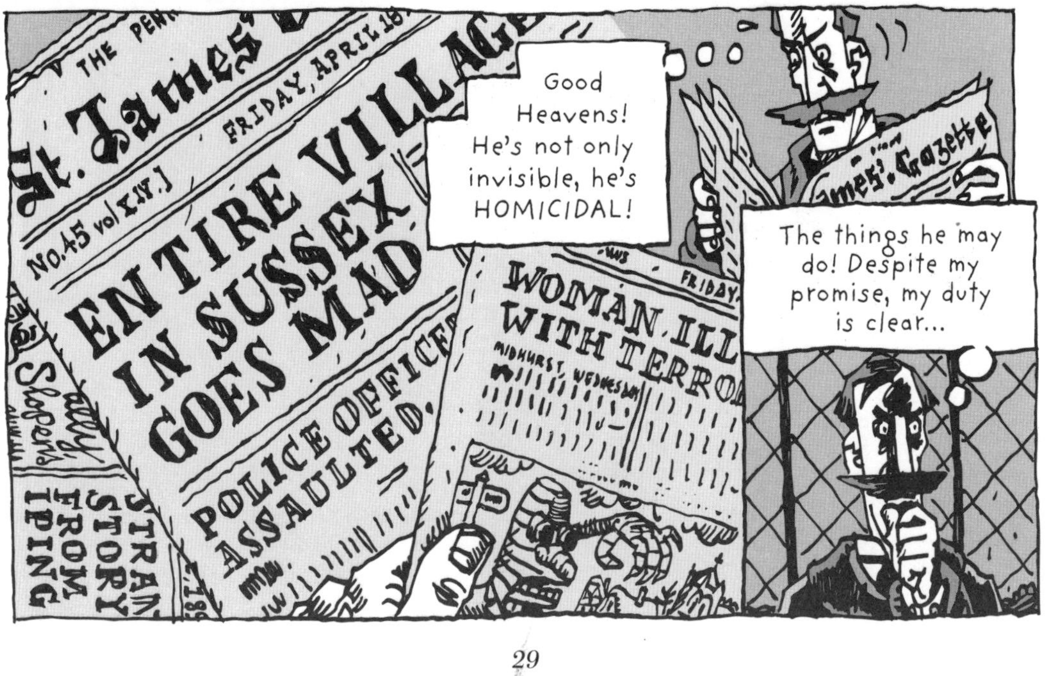
St. James'
FRIDAY, APRIL 18
ENTIRE VILLAGE IN SUSSEX GOES MAD
POLICE OFFICER ASSAULTED.
WOMAN ILL WITH TERRO
STRAN STORY FROM IPING
Good Heavens! He's not only invisible, he's HOMICIDAL!
The things he may do! Despite my promise, my duty is clear...

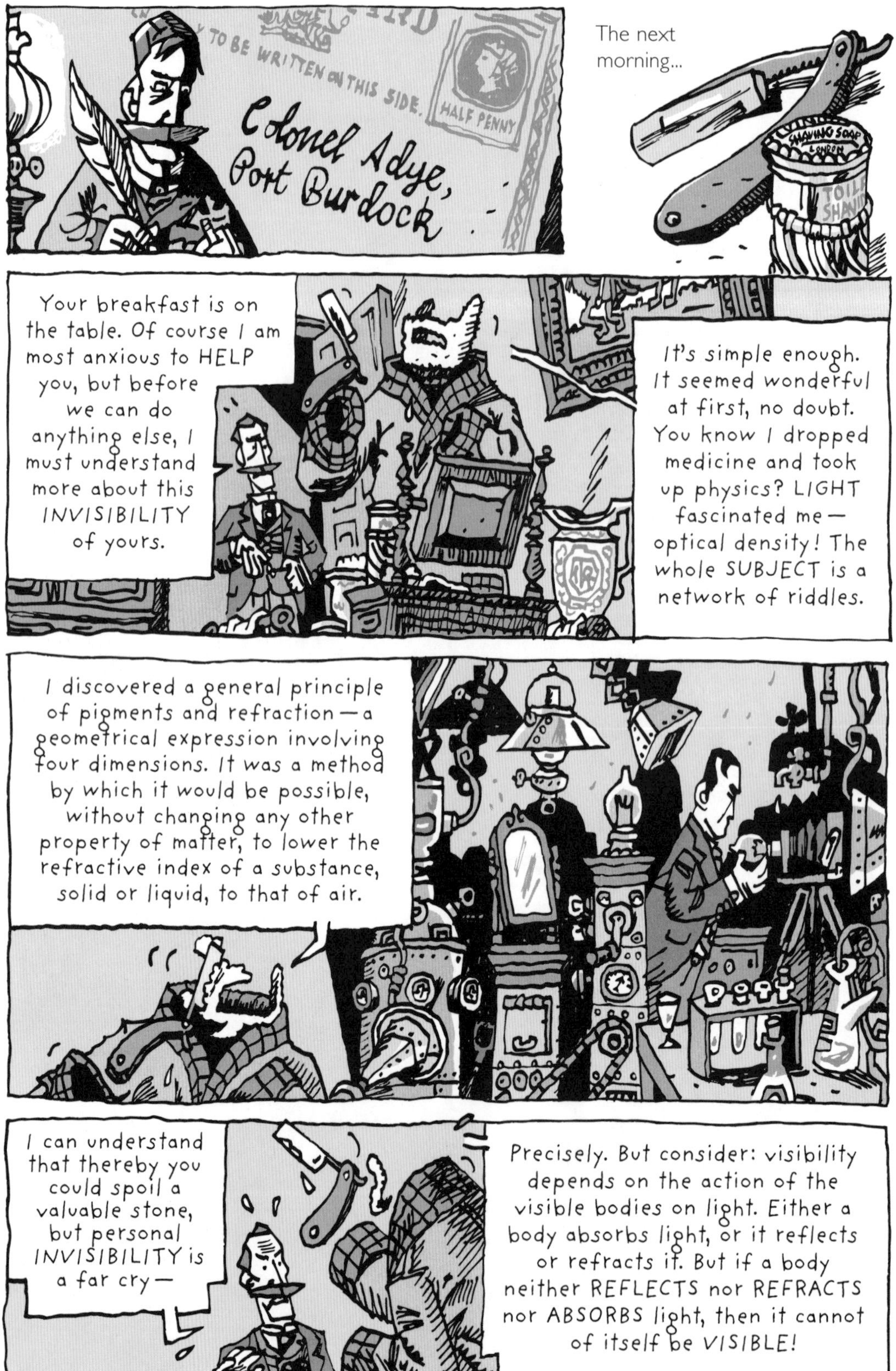
TO BE WRITTEN ON THIS SIDE.
HALF PENNY
Colonel Adye, Port Burdock
The next morning...
SHAVING SOAP
LONDON
Your breakfast is on the table. Of course I am most anxious to HELP you, but before we can do anything else, I must understand more about this INVISIBILITY of yours.
It's simple enough. It seemed wonderful at first, no doubt. You know I dropped medicine and took up physics? LIGHT fascinated me— optical density! The whole SUBJECT is a network of riddles.
I discovered a general principle of pigments and refraction—a geometrical expression involving four dimensions. It was a method by which it would be possible, without changing any other property of matter, to lower the refractive index of a substance, solid or liquid, to that of air.
I can understand that thereby you could spoil a valuable stone, but personal INVISIBILITY is a far cry—
Precisely. But consider: visibility depends on the action of the visible bodies on light. Either a body absorbs light, or it reflects or refracts it. But if a body neither REFLECTS nor REFRACTS nor ABSORBS light, then it cannot of itself be VISIBLE!

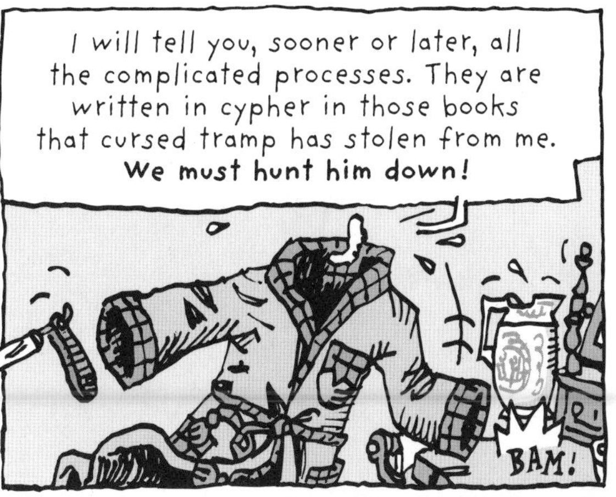
I will tell you, sooner or later, all the complicated processes. They are written in cypher in those books that cursed tramp has stolen from me. **We must hunt him down!**
BAM!

"We must get those books back again! But the essential phase was to place the object whose refractive index was to be lowered between two radiating centers of an ethereal vibration. My first experiment was with a bit of wool fabric."

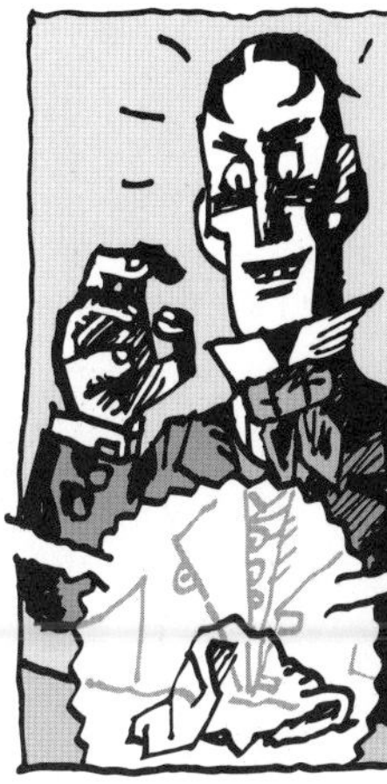

"It was the strangest thing to see it fade like a wreath of smoke and vanish. Then I found a lean white cat outside. I processed her. After all the rest had faded, there remained two little ghosts of her eyes."

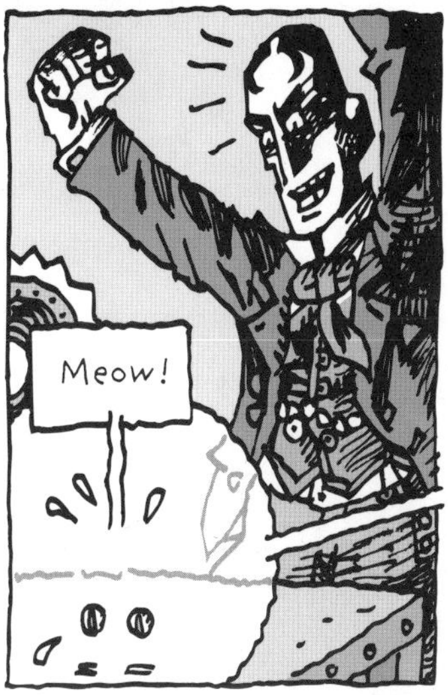
Meow!

"Then someone came knocking. It was the old woman from downstairs, who suspected me of vivisecting."

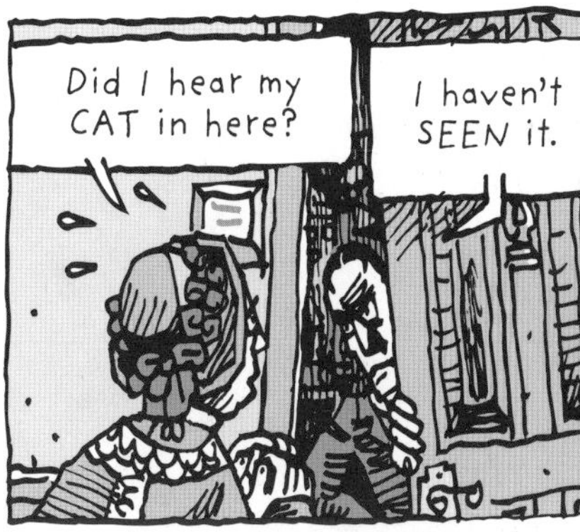
Did I hear my CAT in here?
I haven't SEEN it.

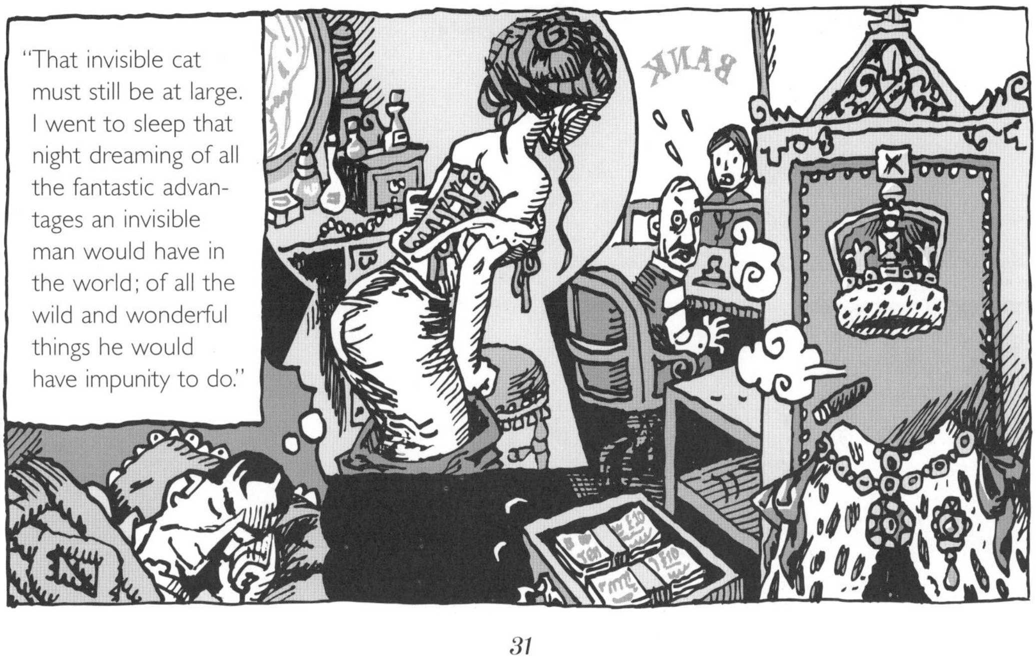

"That invisible cat must still be at large. I went to sleep that night dreaming of all the fantastic advantages an invisible man would have in the world; of all the wild and wonderful things he would have impunity to do."

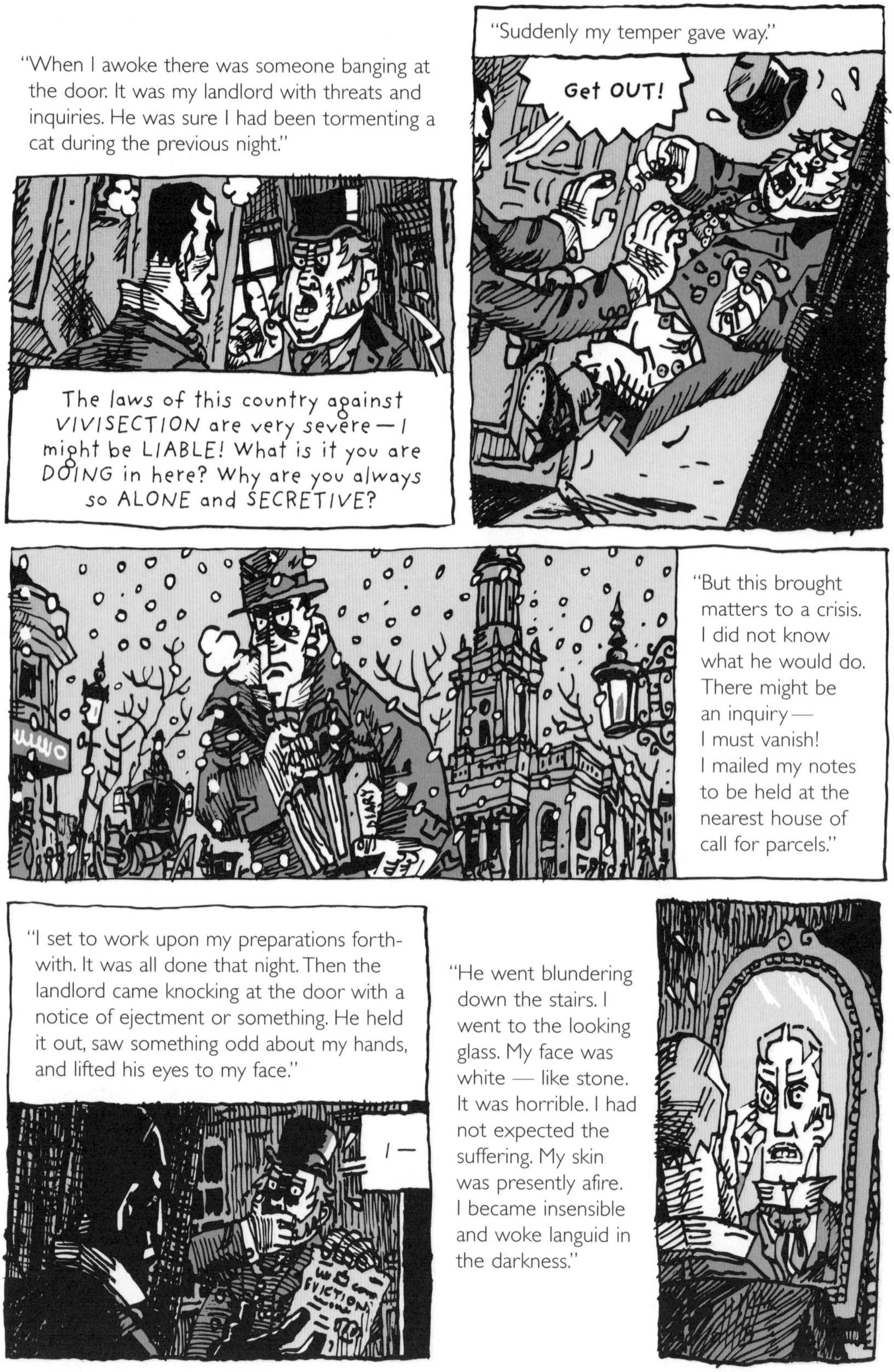
"When I awoke there was someone banging at the door. It was my landlord with threats and inquiries. He was sure I had been tormenting a cat during the previous night."
The laws of this country against VIVISECTION are very severe — I might be LIABLE! What is it you are DOING in here? Why are you always so ALONE and SECRETIVE?
"Suddenly my temper gave way."
Get OUT!
"But this brought matters to a crisis. I did not know what he would do. There might be an inquiry — I must vanish! I mailed my notes to be held at the nearest house of call for parcels."
DIARY
"I set to work upon my preparations forth-with. It was all done that night. Then the landlord came knocking at the door with a notice of ejectment or something. He held it out, saw something odd about my hands, and lifted his eyes to my face."
I —
"He went blundering down the stairs. I went to the looking glass. My face was white — like stone. It was horrible. I had not expected the suffering. My skin was presently afire. I became insensible and woke languid in the darkness."

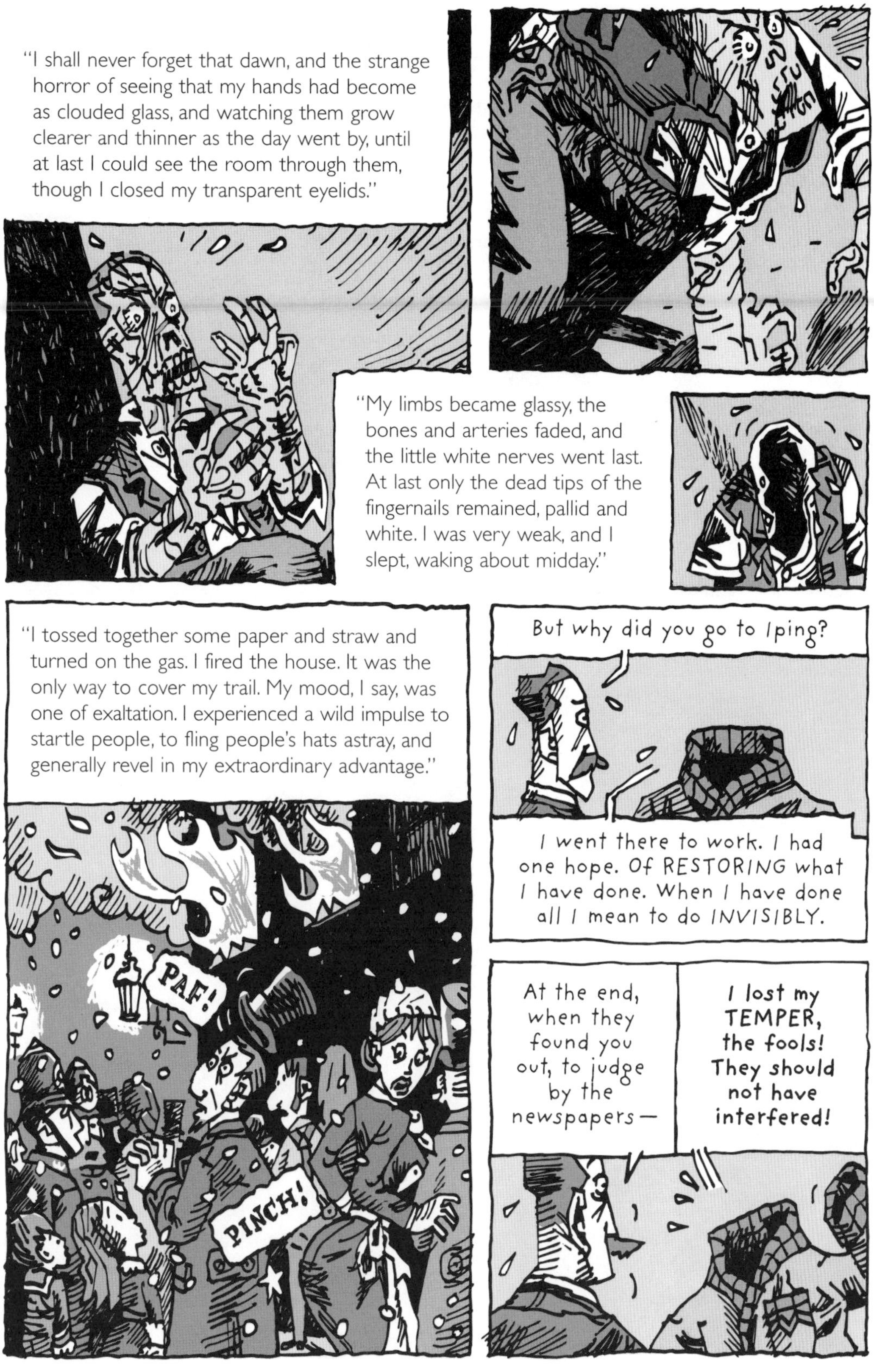
"I shall never forget that dawn, and the strange horror of seeing that my hands had become as clouded glass, and watching them grow clearer and thinner as the day went by, until at last I could see the room through them, though I closed my transparent eyelids."
"My limbs became glassy, the bones and arteries faded, and the little white nerves went last. At last only the dead tips of the fingernails remained, pallid and white. I was very weak, and I slept, waking about midday."
"I tossed together some paper and straw and turned on the gas. I fired the house. It was the only way to cover my trail. My mood, I say, was one of exaltation. I experienced a wild impulse to startle people, to fling people's hats astray, and generally revel in my extraordinary advantage."
PAF!
PINCH!
But why did you go to Iping?
I went there to work. I had one hope. Of RESTORING what I have done. When I have done all I mean to do INVISIBLY.
At the end, when they found you out, to judge by the newspapers —
I lost my TEMPER, the fools! They should not have interfered!

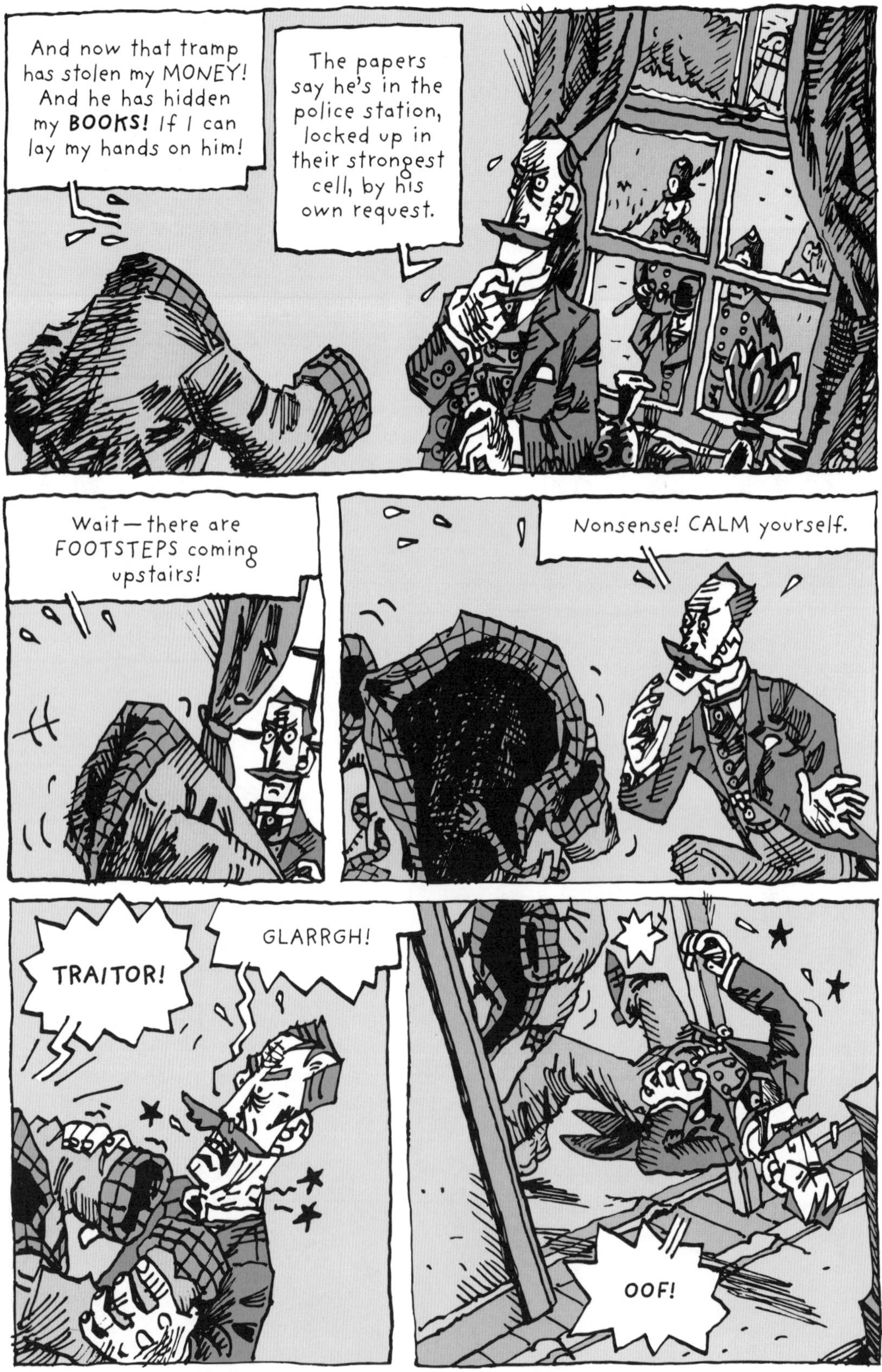
And now that tramp has stolen my MONEY! And he has hidden my **BOOKS!** If I can lay my hands on him!
The papers say he's in the police station, locked up in their strongest cell, by his own request.
Wait—there are FOOTSTEPS coming upstairs!
Nonsense! CALM yourself.
TRAITOR!
GLARRGH!
OOF!

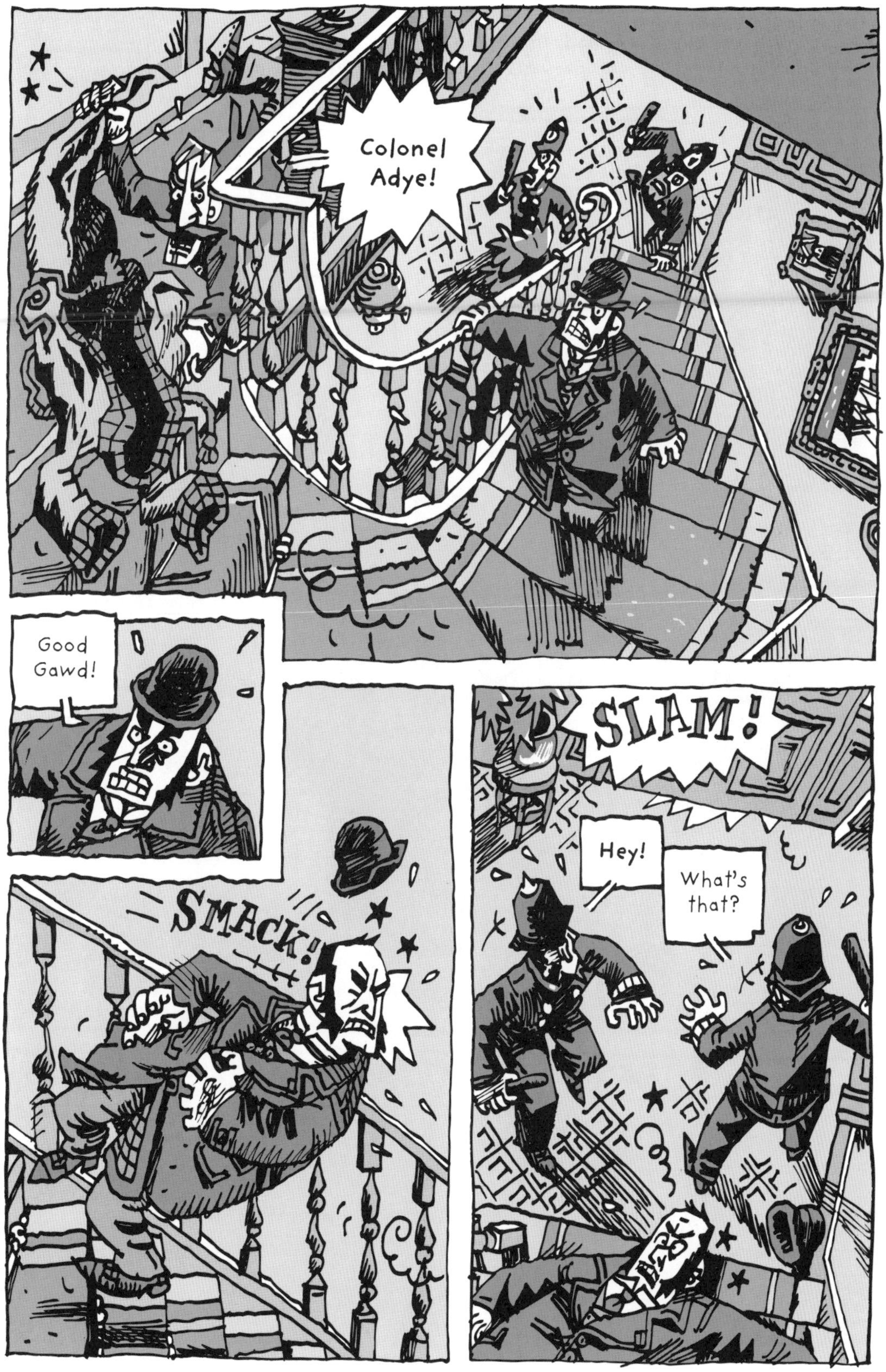
Colonel Adye!
Good Gawd!
SMACK!
SLAM!
Hey!
What's that?

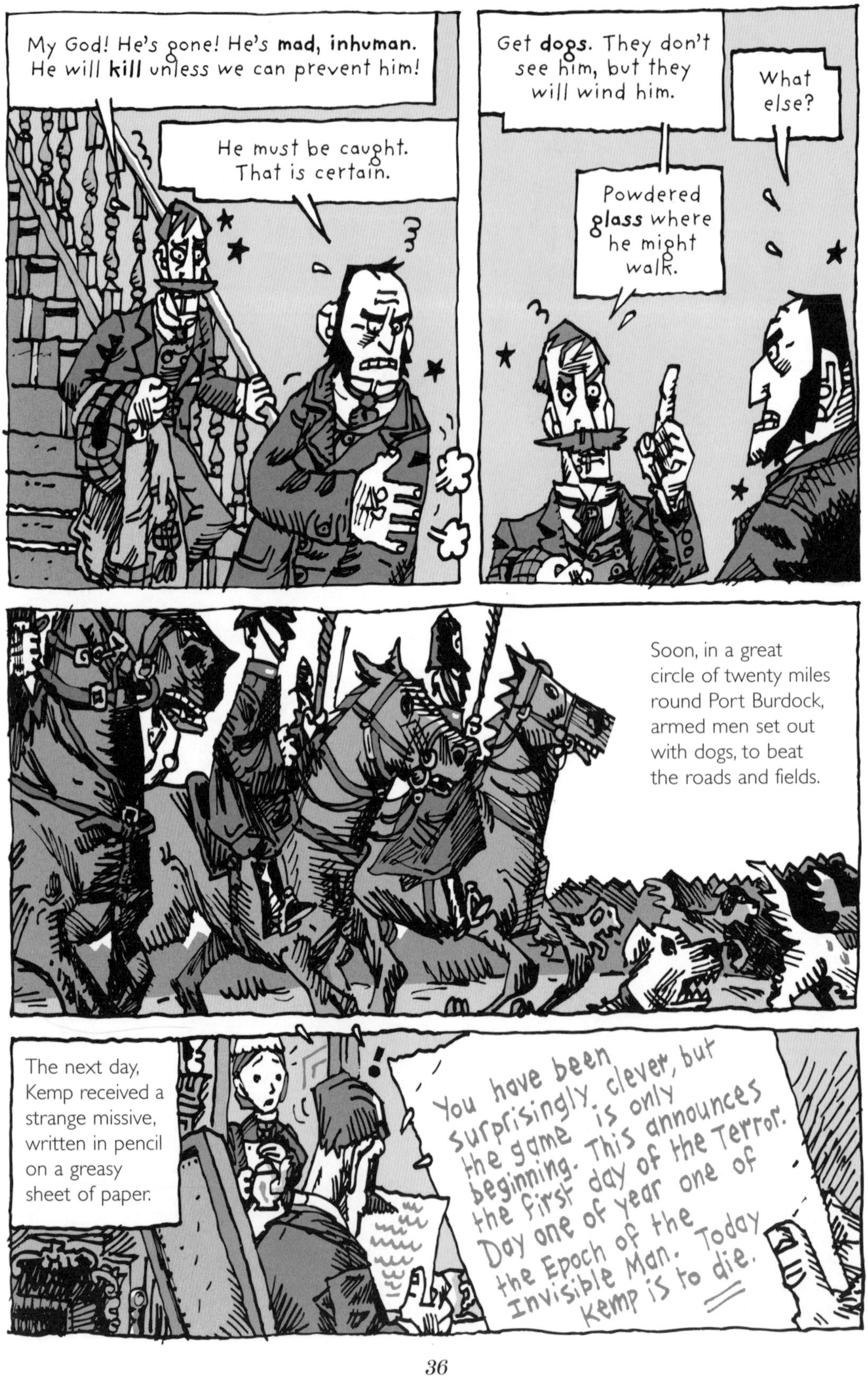
My God! He's gone! He's **mad, inhuman.** He will **kill** unless we can prevent him!
He must be caught. That is certain.
Get **dogs**. They don't see him, but they will wind him.
What else?
Powdered **glass** where he might walk.
Soon, in a great circle of twenty miles round Port Burdock, armed men set out with dogs, to beat the roads and fields.
The next day, Kemp received a strange missive, written in pencil on a greasy sheet of paper.
You have been surprisingly clever, but the game is only beginning. This announces the first day of the Terror. Day one of year one of the Epoch of the Invisible Man. Today Kemp is to die.

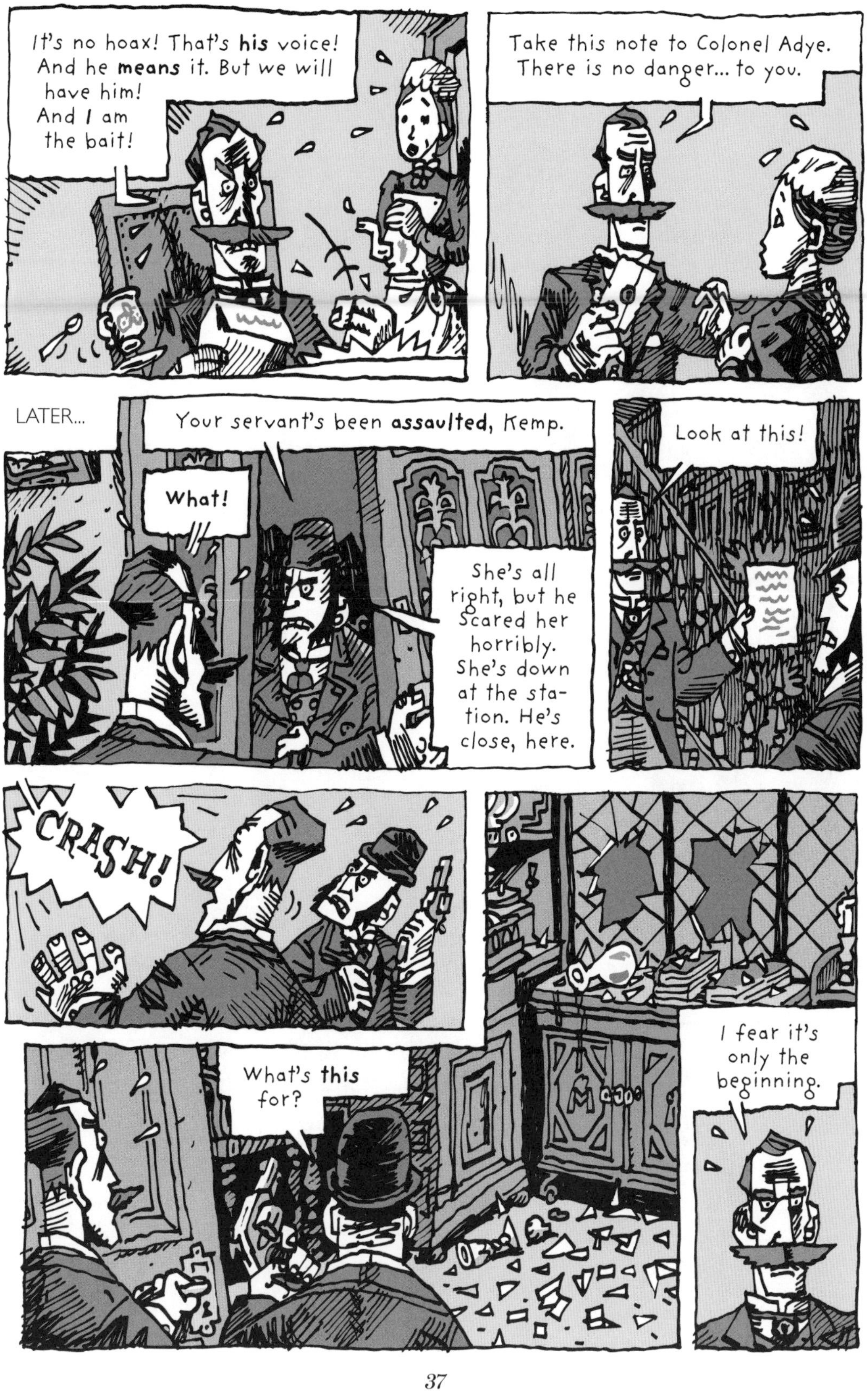
It's no hoax! That's **his** voice! And he **means** it. But we will have him!
And **I** am the bait!
Take this note to Colonel Adye. There is no danger... to you.
LATER...
Your servant's been **assaulted**, Kemp.
What!
She's all right, but he scared her horribly. She's down at the station. He's close, here.
Look at this!
CRASH!
What's **this** for?
I fear it's only the beginning.

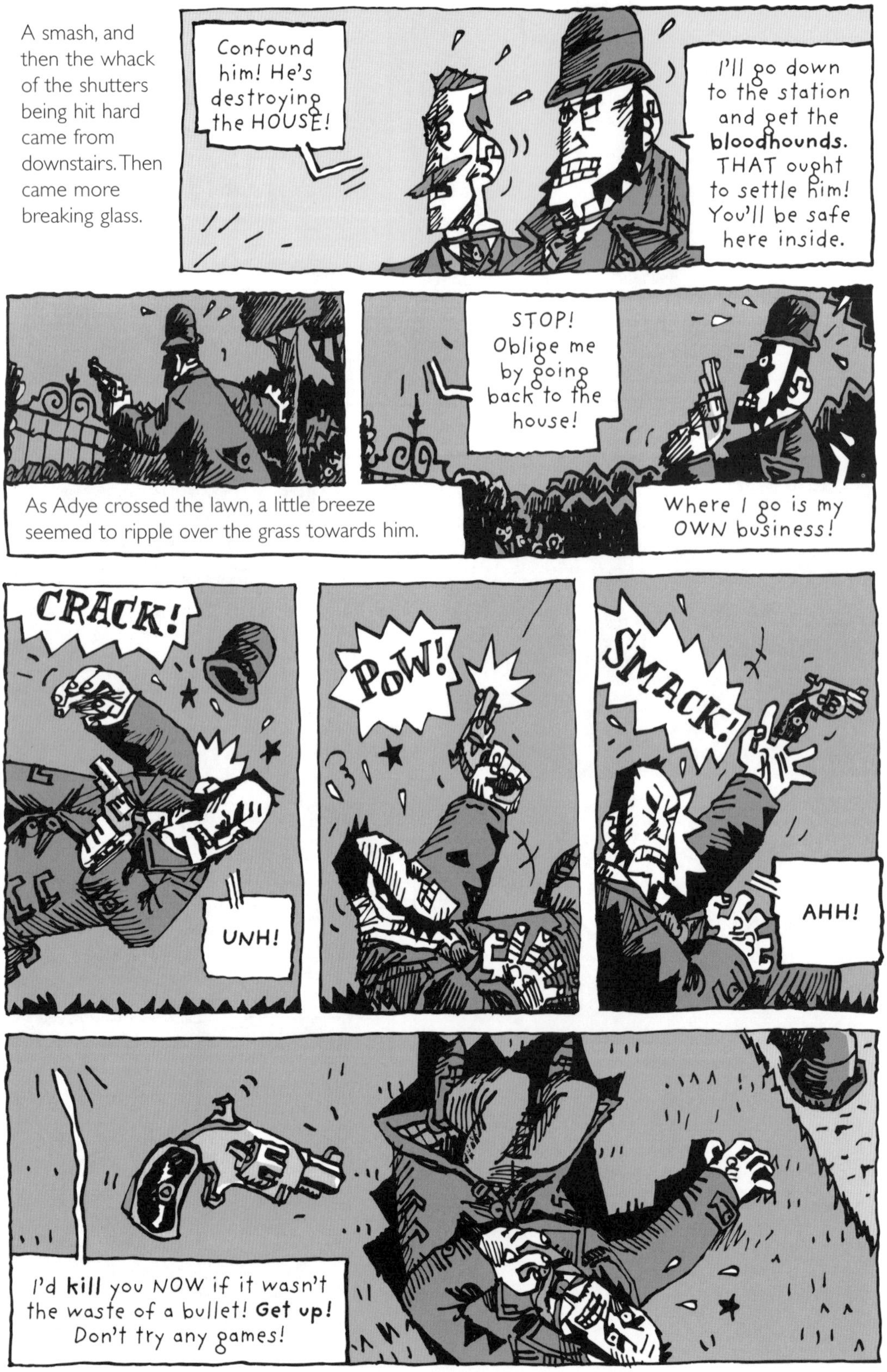
A smash, and then the whack of the shutters being hit hard came from downstairs. Then came more breaking glass.
Confound him! He's destroying the HOUSE!
I'll go down to the station and get the **bloodhounds.** THAT ought to settle him! You'll be safe here inside.
As Adye crossed the lawn, a little breeze seemed to ripple over the grass towards him.
STOP! Oblige me by going back to the house!
Where I go is my OWN business!
CRACK!
UNH!
POW!
SMACK!
AHH!
I'd **kill** you NOW if it wasn't the waste of a bullet! **Get up!** Don't try any games!

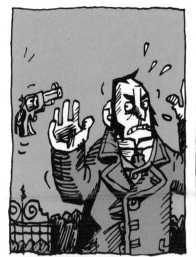

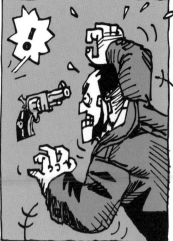

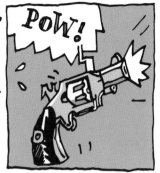

!
POW!
Adye stepped towards the house, then suddenly turned and clutched at the revolver. There was a puff of smoke and he fell forward.
Kemp watched in horror as Adye raised himself on one arm, fell back, and lay still. He then heard a crash coming from the kitchen and cautiously went to investigate.
CRRRACK!
LORD!
HA HA HA!
BAM! BAM! BAM!
The Invisible Man! He's KILLED Adye!
What's that smashing?
He's breaking into the KITCHEN!

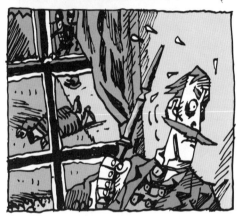

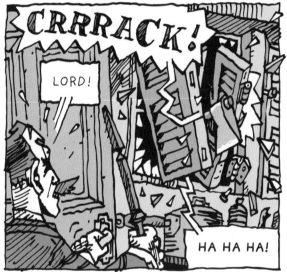

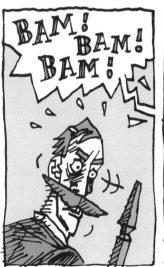

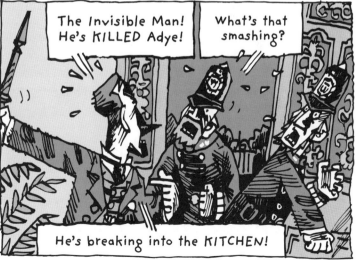

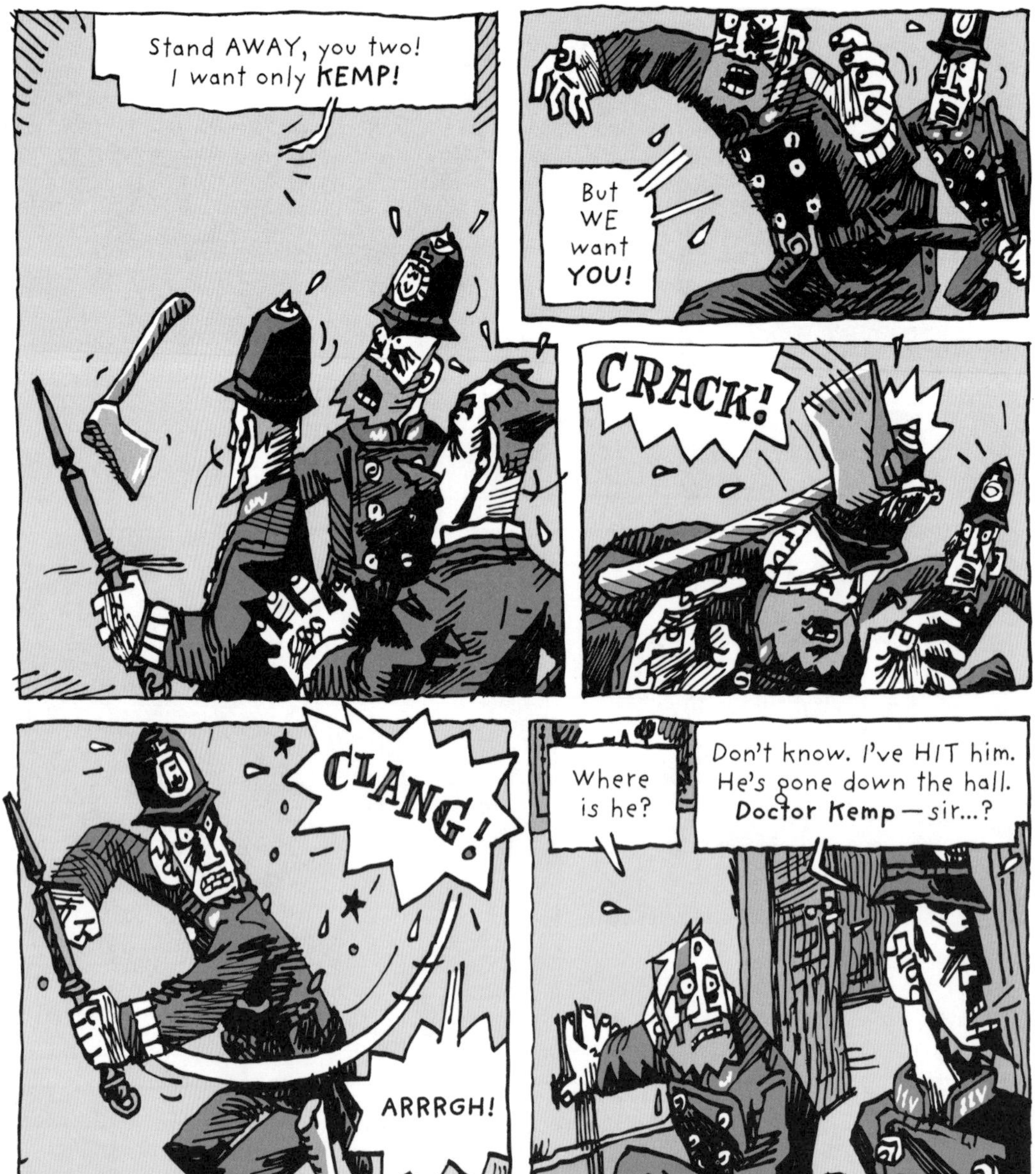
Stand AWAY, you two! I want only KEMP!
But WE want YOU!
CRACK!
CLANG!
ARRRGH!
Where is he?
Don't know. I've HIT him. He's gone down the hall. Doctor Kemp—sir...?

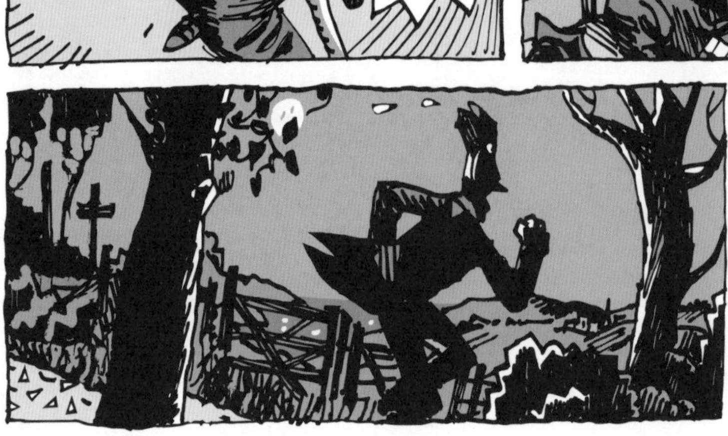

Kemp was rushing down the hill. Wherever a patch of rough ground intervened, or wherever he saw the broken glass the police had spread, he crossed it and left the bare invisible feet that followed to take what line they would.

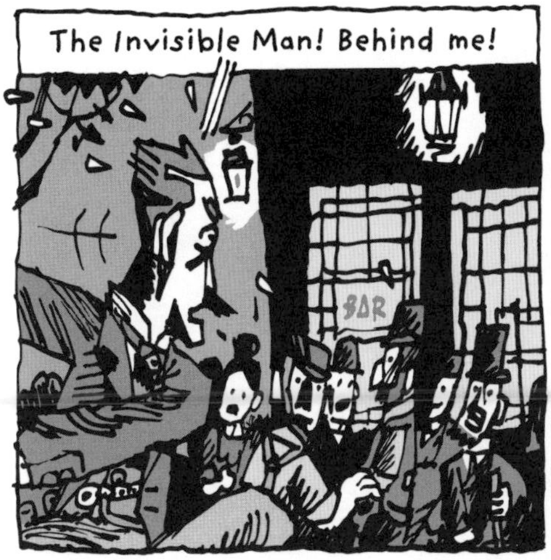
The Invisible Man! Behind me!
BAR

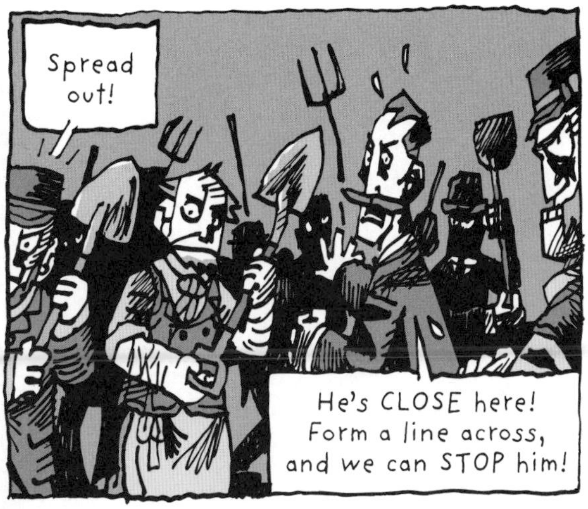
Spread out!
He's CLOSE here! Form a line across, and we can STOP him!

Kemp was suddenly hit hard, and eager hands found his throat, as he vainly grasped the wrists of his assailant.

Then a spade came whirling through the air above him and struck something with a dull thud. The grip on his throat relaxed.

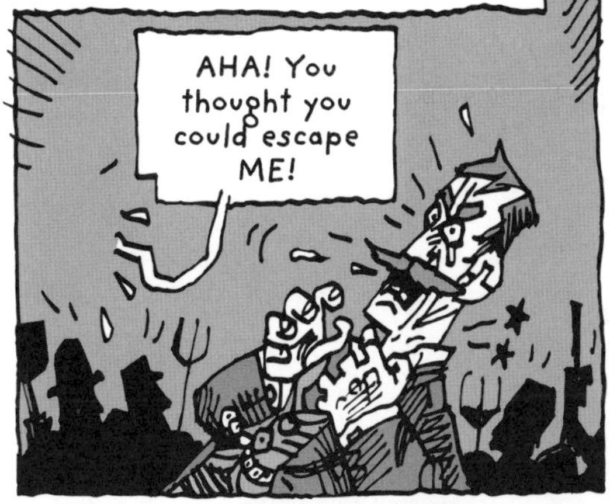
AHA! You thought you could escape ME!

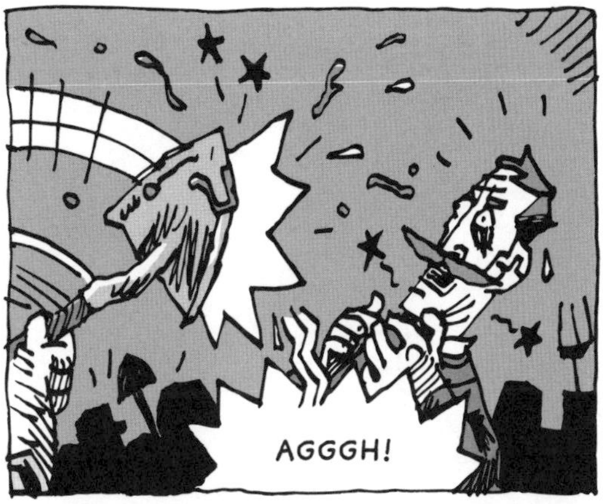
AGGGH!

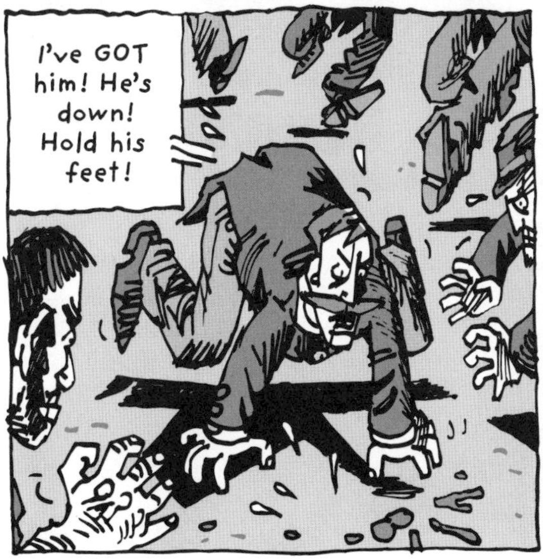
I've GOT him! He's down! Hold his feet!

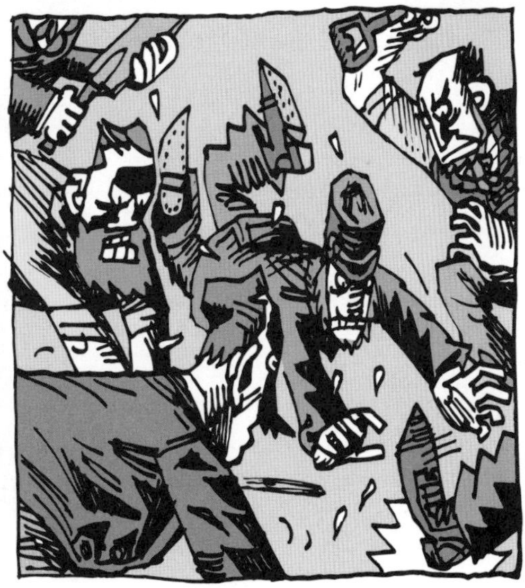

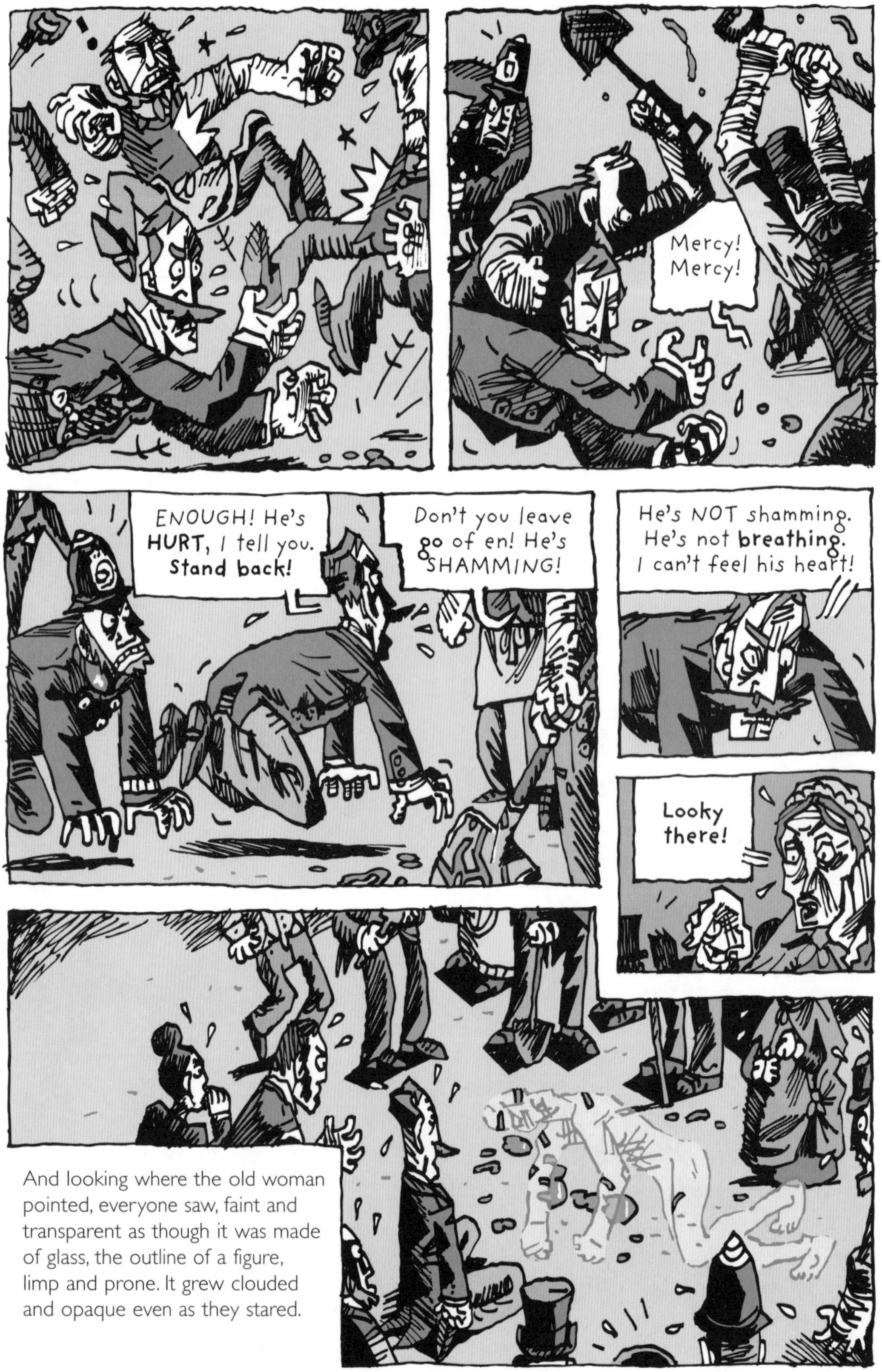
Mercy! Mercy!
ENOUGH! He's **HURT**, I tell you. **Stand back!**
Don't you leave go of en! He's SHAMMING!
He's NOT shamming. He's not **breathing**. I can't feel his heart!
Looky there!
And looking where the old woman pointed, everyone saw, faint and transparent as though it was made of glass, the outline of a figure, limp and prone. It grew clouded and opaque even as they stared.

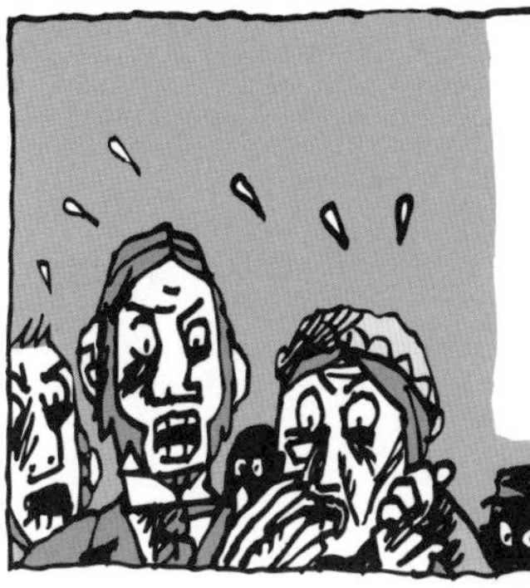

Beginning at his hands and feet and creeping along his limbs to the center of his body, that strange change continued. It was like the slow spreading of a poison. First came the little white nerves, then the flesh and skin. Presently they could see his crushed chest and the dim outline of his drawn and battered features.

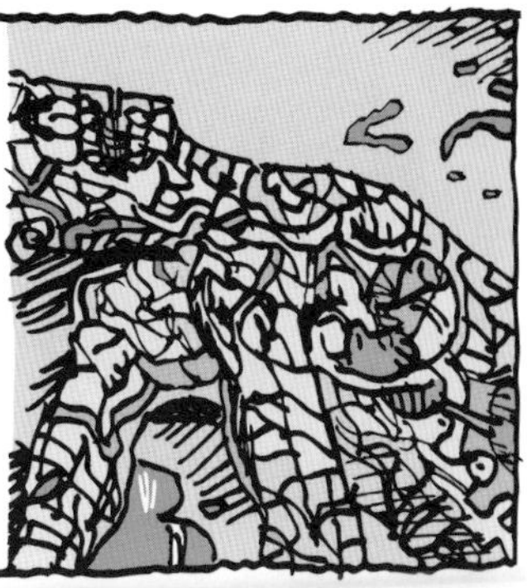

When at last the crowd made way for Kemp to stand erect, there lay, naked and pitiful on the ground, the bruised and broken body of a young man. His hands were clenched, his eyes were wide open, and his expression was one of anger and dismay.

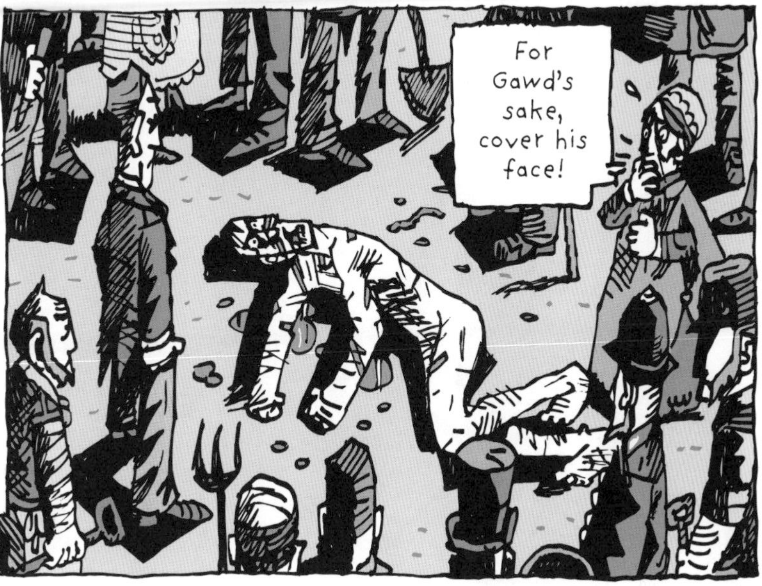
For Gawd's sake, cover his face!

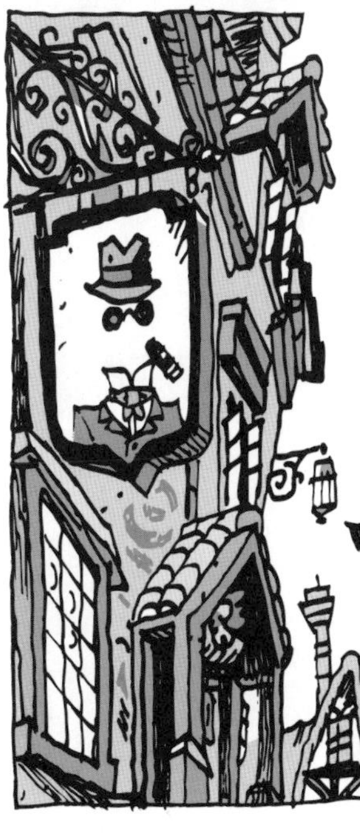

So ends the story of the strange and evil experiment of the Invisible Man. And if you would learn more you must go to a little inn near Port Stowe and talk to the landlord. Drink generously, and the landlord will tell you of how the lawyers tried to do him out of the treasure found upon him.

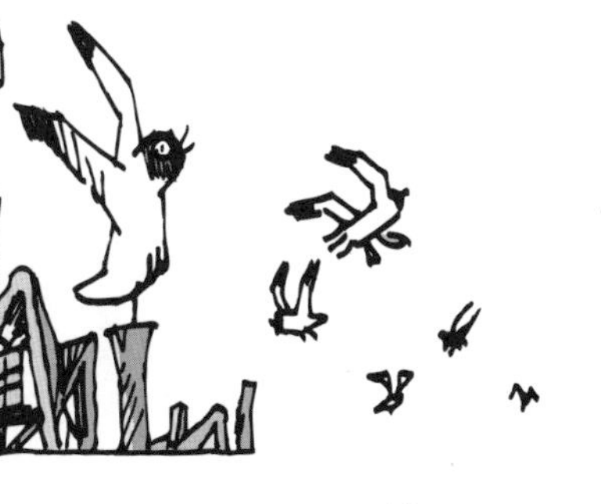

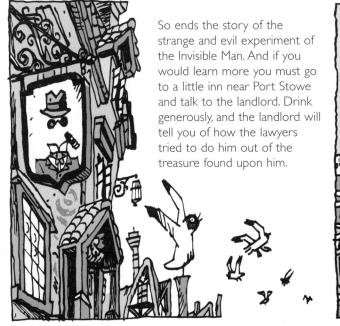

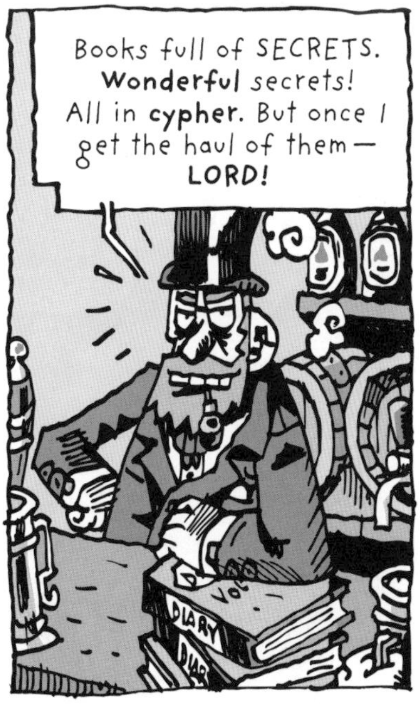
Books full of SECRETS. **Wonderful** secrets! All in **cypher**. But once I get the haul of them — **LORD!**
DIARY

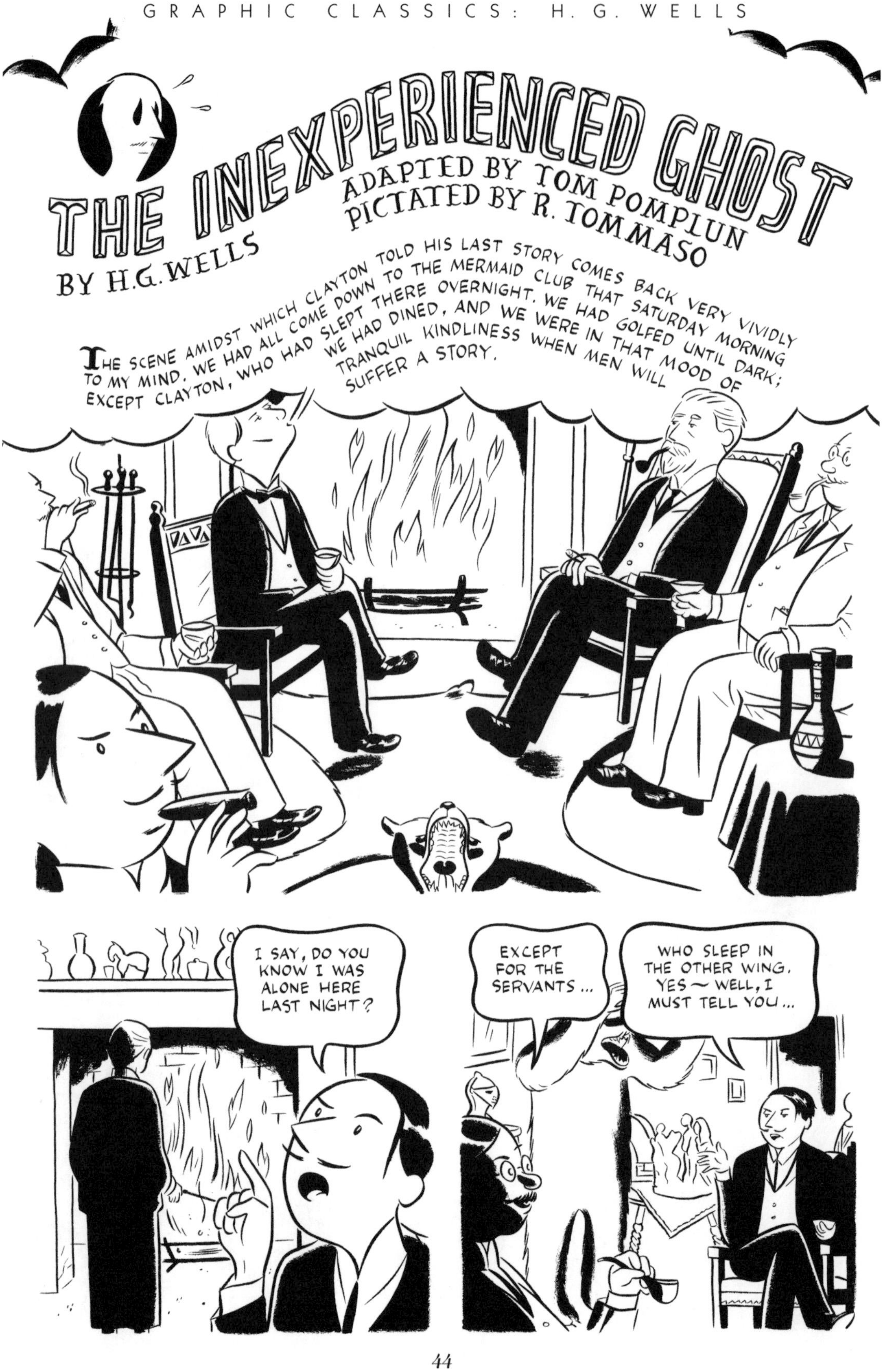
THE INEXPERIENCED GHOST
BY H.G. WELLS
ADAPTED BY TOM POMPLUN
PICTATED BY R. TOMMASO
THE SCENE AMIDST WHICH CLAYTON TOLD HIS LAST STORY COMES BACK VERY VIVIDLY TO MY MIND. WE HAD ALL COME DOWN TO THE MERMAID CLUB THAT SATURDAY MORNING EXCEPT CLAYTON, WHO HAD SLEPT THERE OVERNIGHT. WE HAD GOLFED UNTIL DARK; WE HAD DINED, AND WE WERE IN THAT MOOD OF TRANQUIL KINDLINESS WHEN MEN WILL SUFFER A STORY.
I SAY, DO YOU KNOW I WAS ALONE HERE LAST NIGHT?
EXCEPT FOR THE SERVANTS ...
WHO SLEEP IN THE OTHER WING. YES ~ WELL, I MUST TELL YOU ...

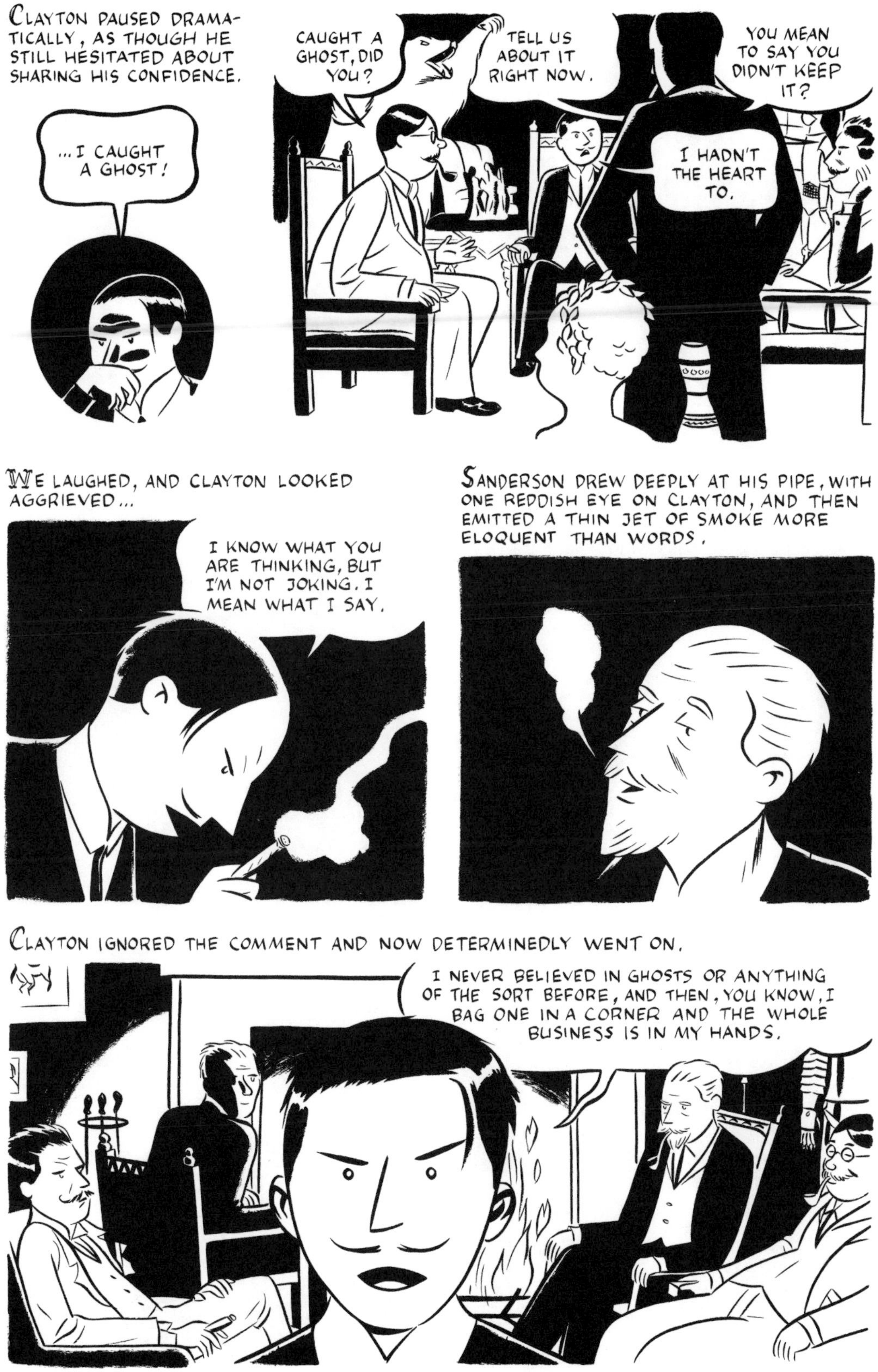
CLAYTON PAUSED DRAMATICALLY, AS THOUGH HE STILL HESITATED ABOUT SHARING HIS CONFIDENCE.
...I CAUGHT A GHOST!
CAUGHT A GHOST, DID YOU?
TELL US ABOUT IT RIGHT NOW.
YOU MEAN TO SAY YOU DIDN'T KEEP IT?
I HADN'T THE HEART TO.
WE LAUGHED, AND CLAYTON LOOKED AGGRIEVED...
I KNOW WHAT YOU ARE THINKING, BUT I'M NOT JOKING. I MEAN WHAT I SAY.
SANDERSON DREW DEEPLY AT HIS PIPE, WITH ONE REDDISH EYE ON CLAYTON, AND THEN EMITTED A THIN JET OF SMOKE MORE ELOQUENT THAN WORDS.
CLAYTON IGNORED THE COMMENT AND NOW DETERMINEDLY WENT ON.
I NEVER BELIEVED IN GHOSTS OR ANYTHING OF THE SORT BEFORE, AND THEN, YOU KNOW, I BAG ONE IN A CORNER AND THE WHOLE BUSINESS IS IN MY HANDS.

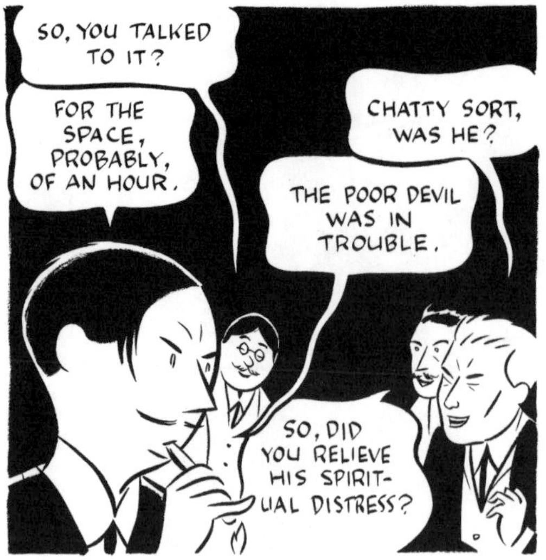
SO, YOU TALKED TO IT?
FOR THE SPACE, PROBABLY, OF AN HOUR.
CHATTY SORT, WAS HE?
THE POOR DEVIL WAS IN TROUBLE.
SO, DID YOU RELIEVE HIS SPIRITUAL DISTRESS?

CLAYTON IGNORED OUR ATTEMPTS AT HUMOR AND WENT ON, A BIT PENSIVELY.

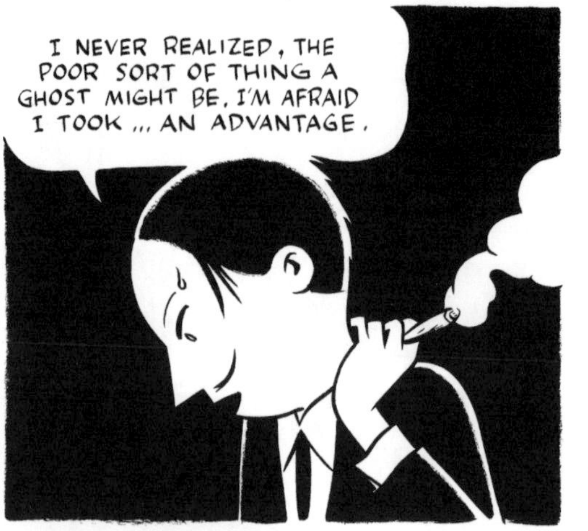
I NEVER REALIZED, THE POOR SORT OF THING A GHOST MIGHT BE. I'M AFRAID I TOOK ... AN ADVANTAGE.

WE WERE NOW ENGROSSED, AND NONE OF US IN A HURRY, SO WE SETTLED BACK FOR A LONG TALE.

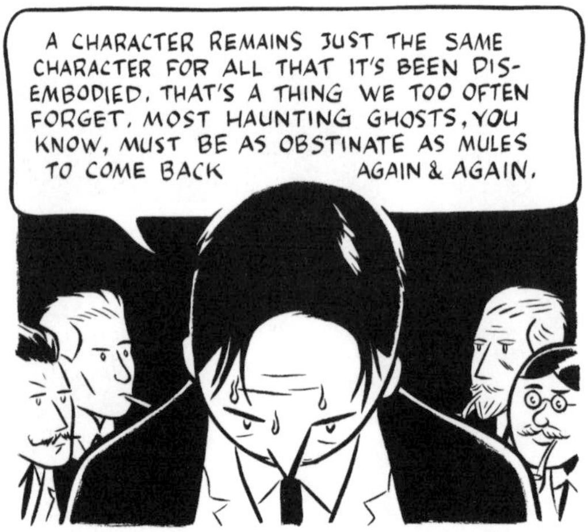
A CHARACTER REMAINS JUST THE SAME CHARACTER FOR ALL THAT IT'S BEEN DISEMBODIED. THAT'S A THING WE TOO OFTEN FORGET. MOST HAUNTING GHOSTS, YOU KNOW, MUST BE AS OBSTINATE AS MULES TO COME BACK AGAIN & AGAIN.

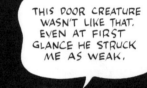

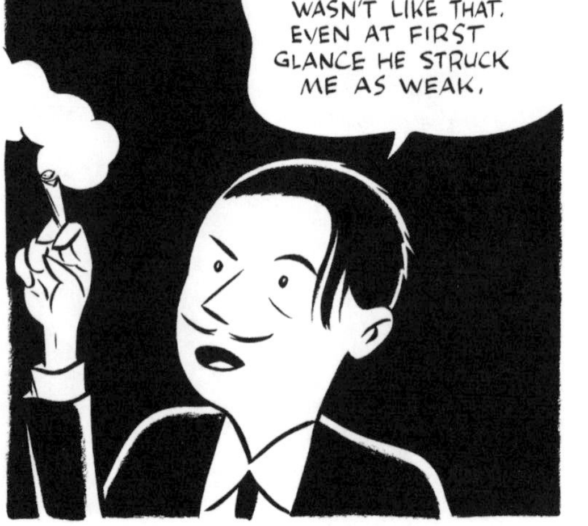
THIS POOR CREATURE WASN'T LIKE THAT. EVEN AT FIRST GLANCE HE STRUCK ME AS WEAK.

"I CAME UPON HIM IN THE HALLWAY. HIS BACK WAS TOWARDS ME, BUT RIGHT OFF I KNEW HIM FOR A GHOST. I COULD SEE THE WINDOW AT THE HALL'S END CLEAN THROUGH HIS CHEST."

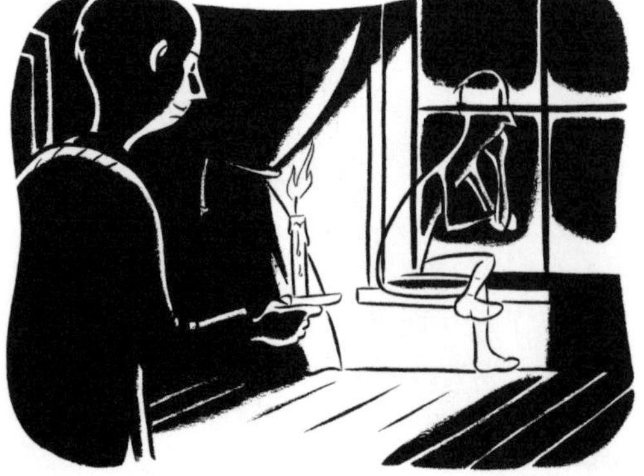

"HE TURNED WHEN HE REALIZED I WAS THERE AND I SAW THE FACE OF AN IMMATURE YOUNG MAN; A WEAK NOSE, A SCRUBBY LITTLE MOUSTACHE, A FEEBLE CHIN AND RATHER BAD EARS. HE SEEMED AS THOUGH HE DIDN'T KNOW IN THE SLIGHTEST WHATEVER HE MEANT TO DO."

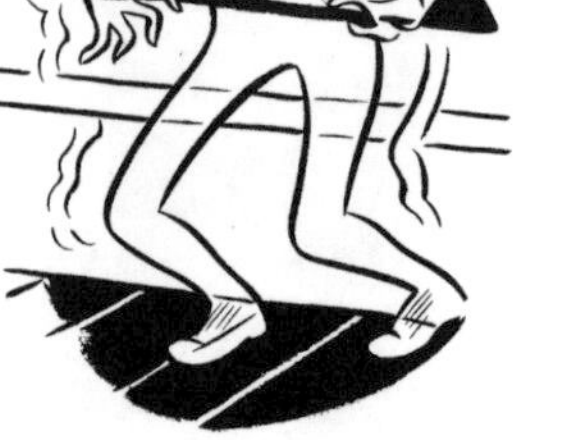

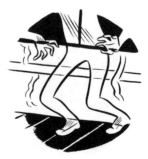

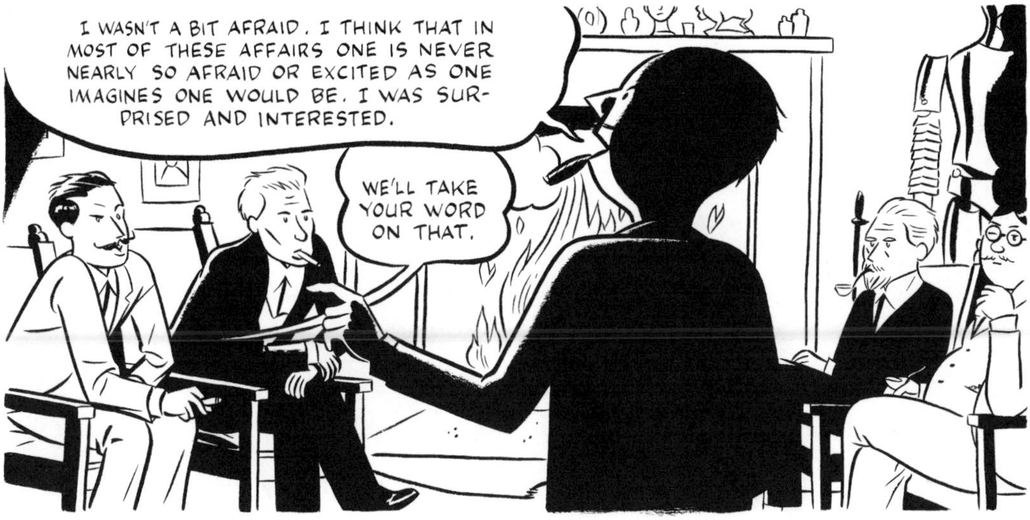
I WASN'T A BIT AFRAID. I THINK THAT IN MOST OF THESE AFFAIRS ONE IS NEVER NEARLY SO AFRAID OR EXCITED AS ONE IMAGINES ONE WOULD BE. I WAS SURPRISED AND INTERESTED.
WE'LL TAKE YOUR WORD ON THAT.

"FOR AN INSTANT WE STOOD AND REGARDED ONE ANOTHER. THEN HE SEEMED TO REMEMBER HIS HIGH CALLING. HE RAISED HIS ARMS IN APPROVED GHOST FASHION AND CAME TOWARDS ME."

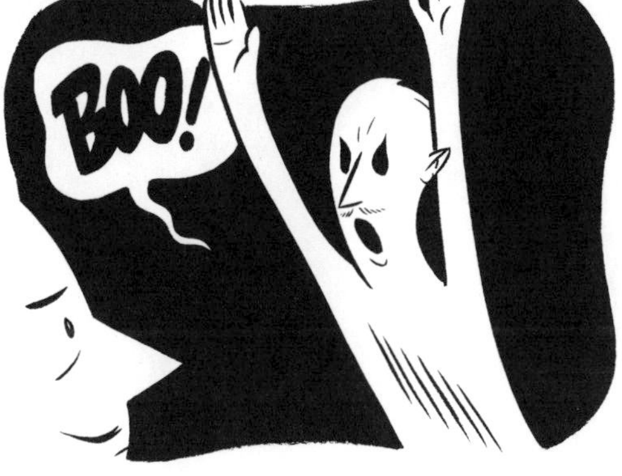
BOO!

"NO, IT WAS NOT A BIT FRIGHTENING. I HAD DINED. I'D HAD A BOTTLE OF CHAMPAGNE, AND PERHAPS TWO OR THREE ~ MAYBE FOUR OR FIVE ~ WHISKIES, SO I WAS NO MORE TERRIFIED THAN IF I'D BEEN ASSAILED BY A FROG."

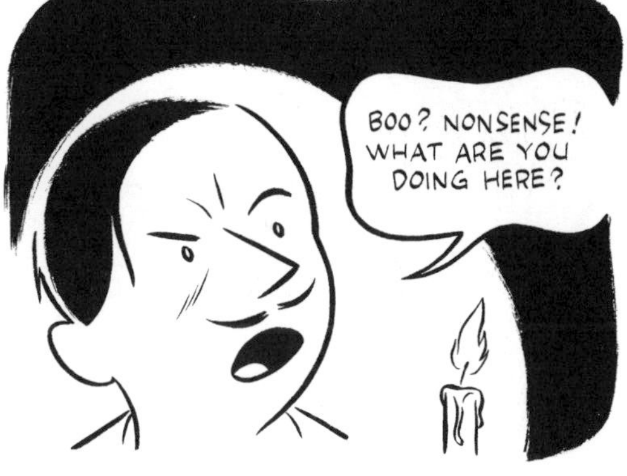
BOO? NONSENSE! WHAT ARE YOU DOING HERE?

"I COULD SEE HIM WINCE. THEN HE GATHERED HIMSELF AND TRIED AGAIN."

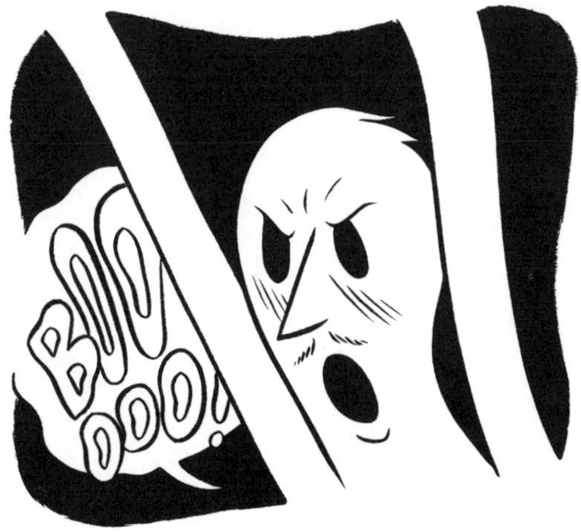
BOOOOO!

"I HELD UP MY CANDLE AND LOOKED HIM RIGHT IN HIS GHOSTLY EYE."

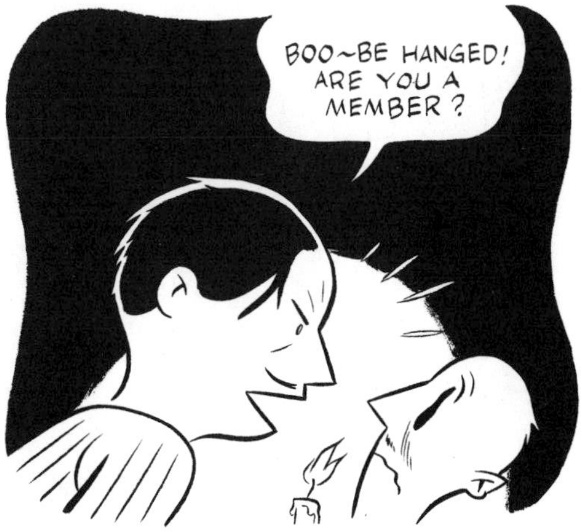
BOO~BE HANGED! ARE YOU A MEMBER?

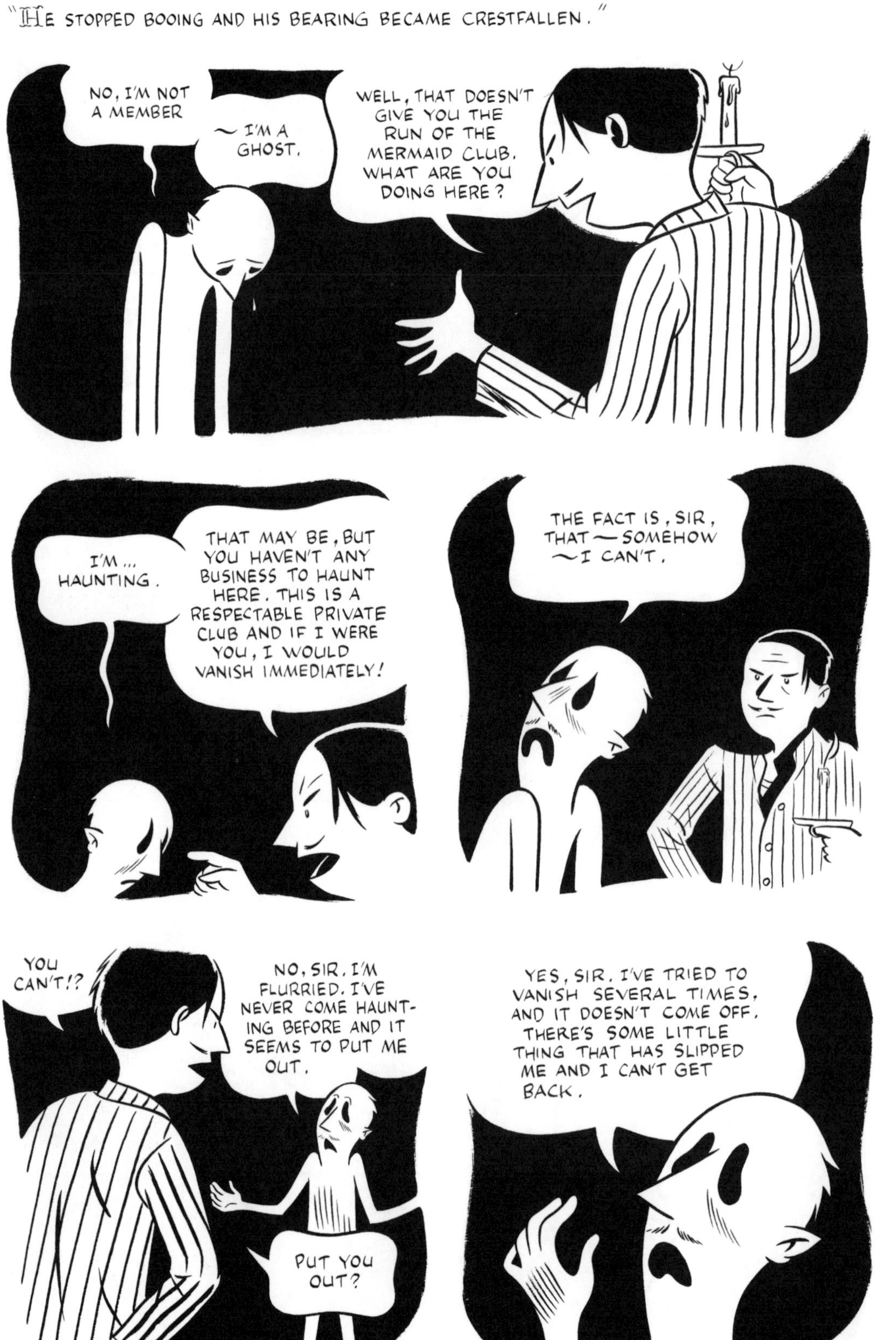
"HE STOPPED BOOING AND HIS BEARING BECAME CRESTFALLEN."
NO, I'M NOT A MEMBER
~ I'M A GHOST.
WELL, THAT DOESN'T GIVE YOU THE RUN OF THE MERMAID CLUB. WHAT ARE YOU DOING HERE?
I'M ... HAUNTING.
THAT MAY BE, BUT YOU HAVEN'T ANY BUSINESS TO HAUNT HERE. THIS IS A RESPECTABLE PRIVATE CLUB AND IF I WERE YOU, I WOULD VANISH IMMEDIATELY!
THE FACT IS, SIR, THAT — SOMEHOW ~ I CAN'T.
YOU CAN'T!?
NO, SIR. I'M FLURRIED. I'VE NEVER COME HAUNTING BEFORE AND IT SEEMS TO PUT ME OUT.
PUT YOU OUT?
YES, SIR. I'VE TRIED TO VANISH SEVERAL TIMES, AND IT DOESN'T COME OFF. THERE'S SOME LITTLE THING THAT HAS SLIPPED ME AND I CAN'T GET BACK.

"THAT, YOU KNOW, RATHER BOWLED ME OVER AND I TRIED TO TAKE HIM BY THE ARM. BUT, OF COURSE, YOU MIGHT AS WELL HAVE TRIED TO TAKE HOLD OF A PUFF OF SMOKE! SO I LED THE WAY DOWN THE HALL TO MY ROOM."

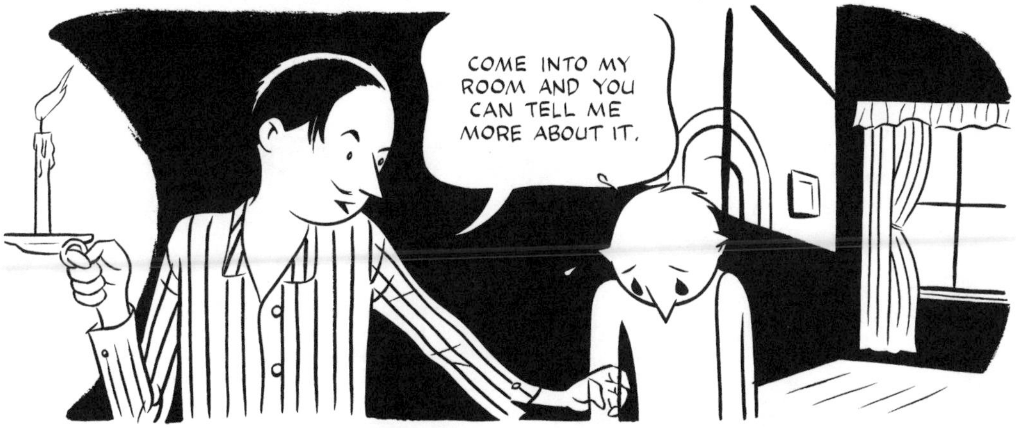
COME INTO MY ROOM AND YOU CAN TELL ME MORE ABOUT IT.

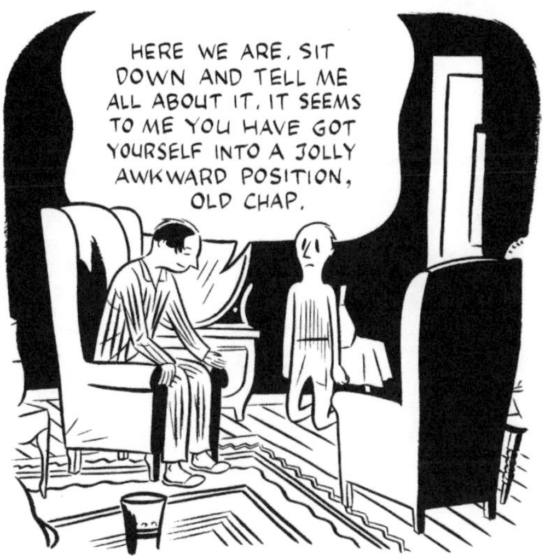
HERE WE ARE. SIT DOWN AND TELL ME ALL ABOUT IT. IT SEEMS TO ME YOU HAVE GOT YOURSELF INTO A JOLLY AWKWARD POSITION, OLD CHAP.

"WELL, HE SAID HE WOULDN'T SIT DOWN; HE'D PREFER TO FLIT UP AND DOWN THE ROOM IF IT WAS ALL THE SAME TO ME. AND SO HE DID, WHILE WE HAD A LONG TALK."

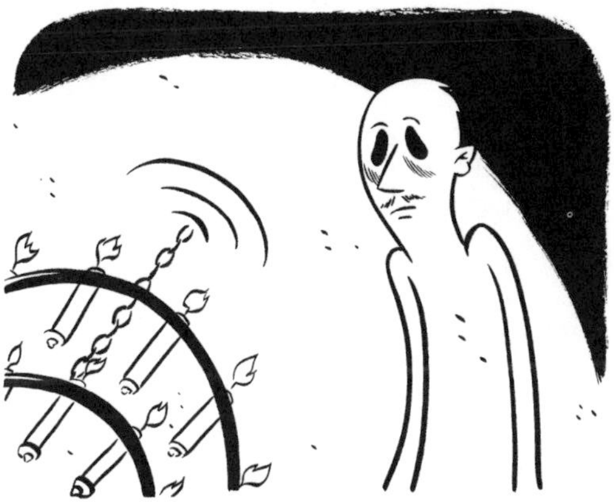

"HE TOLD ME HOW HE HAD BEEN KILLED—HE WENT DOWN INTO THE BASEMENT WITH A CANDLE TO LOOK FOR A LEAKAGE OF GAS—AND DESCRIBED HIMSELF AS A SENIOR ENGLISH MASTER IN A LONDON PRIVATE SCHOOL WHEN THAT RELEASE OCCURRED."

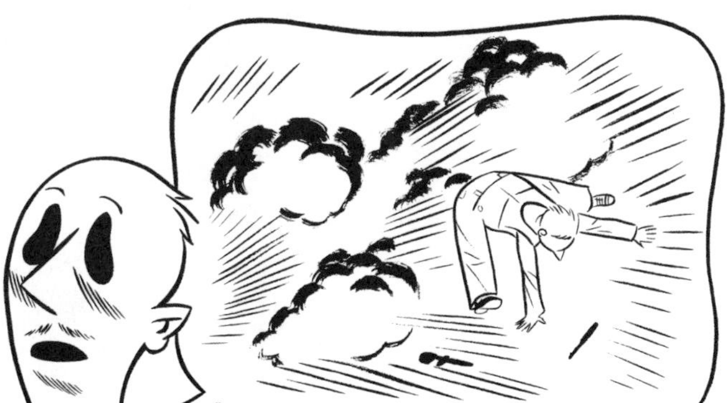

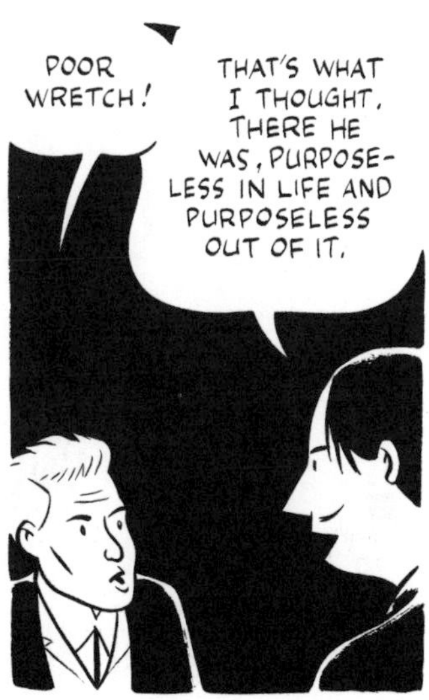
POOR WRETCH!
THAT'S WHAT I THOUGHT. THERE HE WAS, PURPOSE-LESS IN LIFE AND PURPOSELESS OUT OF IT.

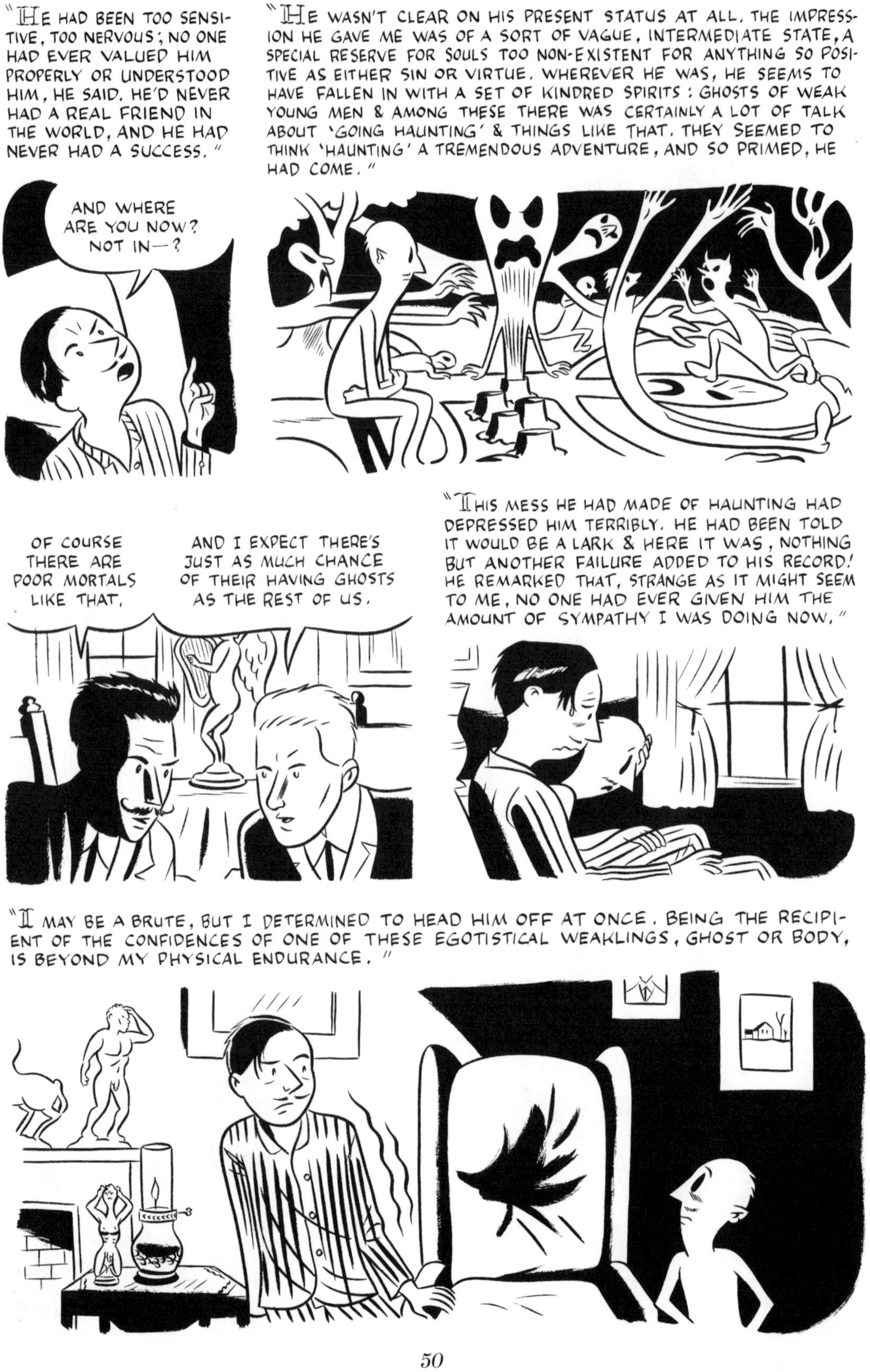
"HE HAD BEEN TOO SENSITIVE, TOO NERVOUS; NO ONE HAD EVER VALUED HIM PROPERLY OR UNDERSTOOD HIM, HE SAID. HE'D NEVER HAD A REAL FRIEND IN THE WORLD, AND HE HAD NEVER HAD A SUCCESS."
"HE WASN'T CLEAR ON HIS PRESENT STATUS AT ALL. THE IMPRESSION HE GAVE ME WAS OF A SORT OF VAGUE, INTERMEDIATE STATE, A SPECIAL RESERVE FOR SOULS TOO NON-EXISTENT FOR ANYTHING SO POSITIVE AS EITHER SIN OR VIRTUE. WHEREVER HE WAS, HE SEEMS TO HAVE FALLEN IN WITH A SET OF KINDRED SPIRITS: GHOSTS OF WEAK YOUNG MEN & AMONG THESE THERE WAS CERTAINLY A LOT OF TALK ABOUT 'GOING HAUNTING' & THINGS LIKE THAT. THEY SEEMED TO THINK 'HAUNTING' A TREMENDOUS ADVENTURE, AND SO PRIMED, HE HAD COME."
AND WHERE ARE YOU NOW? NOT IN—?
OF COURSE THERE ARE POOR MORTALS LIKE THAT.
AND I EXPECT THERE'S JUST AS MUCH CHANCE OF THEIR HAVING GHOSTS AS THE REST OF US.
"THIS MESS HE HAD MADE OF HAUNTING HAD DEPRESSED HIM TERRIBLY. HE HAD BEEN TOLD IT WOULD BE A LARK & HERE IT WAS, NOTHING BUT ANOTHER FAILURE ADDED TO HIS RECORD! HE REMARKED THAT, STRANGE AS IT MIGHT SEEM TO ME, NO ONE HAD EVER GIVEN HIM THE AMOUNT OF SYMPATHY I WAS DOING NOW."
"I MAY BE A BRUTE, BUT I DETERMINED TO HEAD HIM OFF AT ONCE. BEING THE RECIPIENT OF THE CONFIDENCES OF ONE OF THESE EGOTISTICAL WEAKLINGS, GHOST OR BODY, IS BEYOND MY PHYSICAL ENDURANCE."

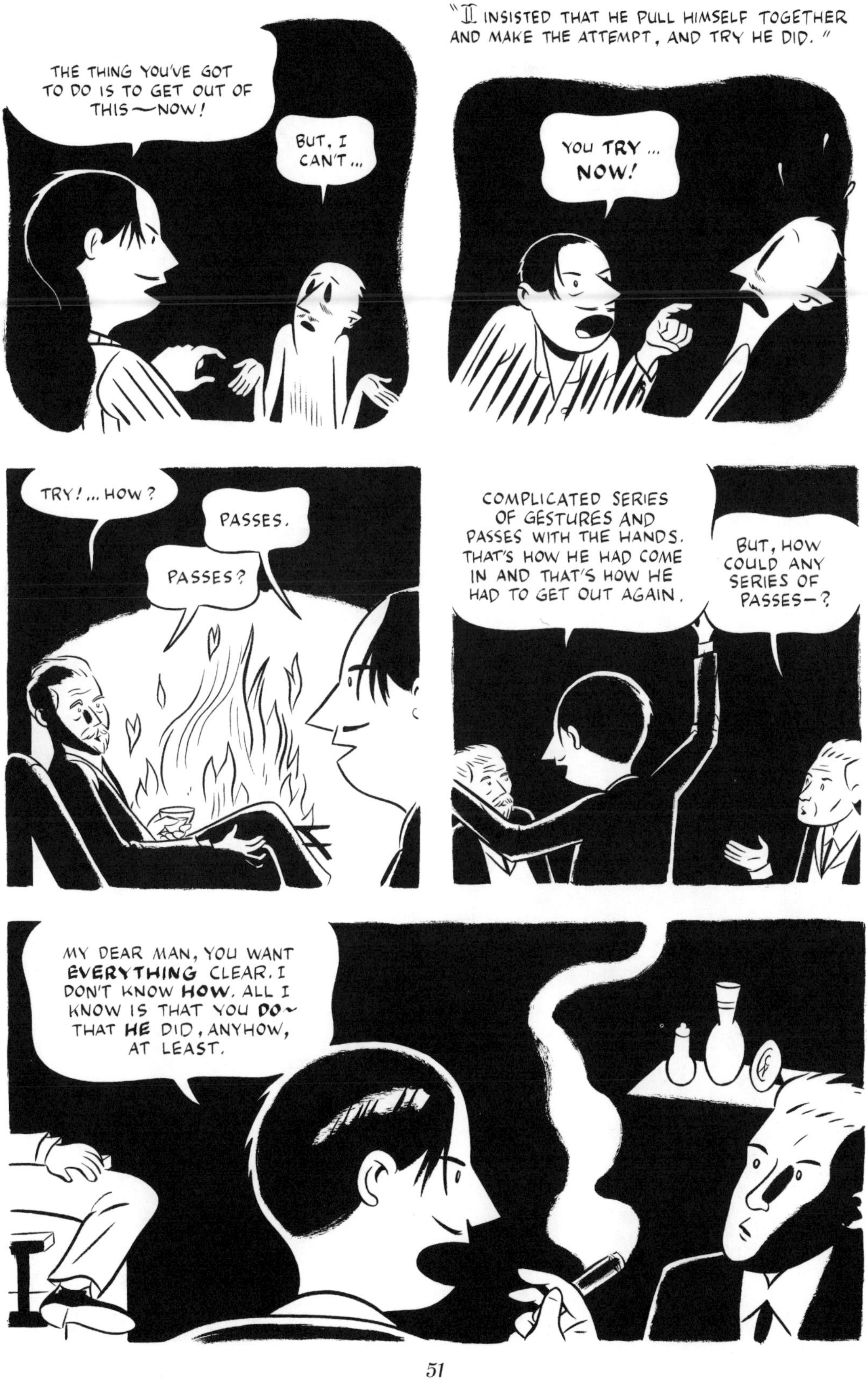
THE THING YOU'VE GOT TO DO IS TO GET OUT OF THIS—NOW!
BUT, I CAN'T...
"I INSISTED THAT HE PULL HIMSELF TOGETHER AND MAKE THE ATTEMPT, AND TRY HE DID."
YOU TRY ... NOW!
TRY! ... HOW?
PASSES.
PASSES?
COMPLICATED SERIES OF GESTURES AND PASSES WITH THE HANDS. THAT'S HOW HE HAD COME IN AND THAT'S HOW HE HAD TO GET OUT AGAIN.
BUT, HOW COULD ANY SERIES OF PASSES—?
MY DEAR MAN, YOU WANT EVERYTHING CLEAR. I DON'T KNOW HOW. ALL I KNOW IS THAT YOU DO— THAT HE DID, ANYHOW, AT LEAST.

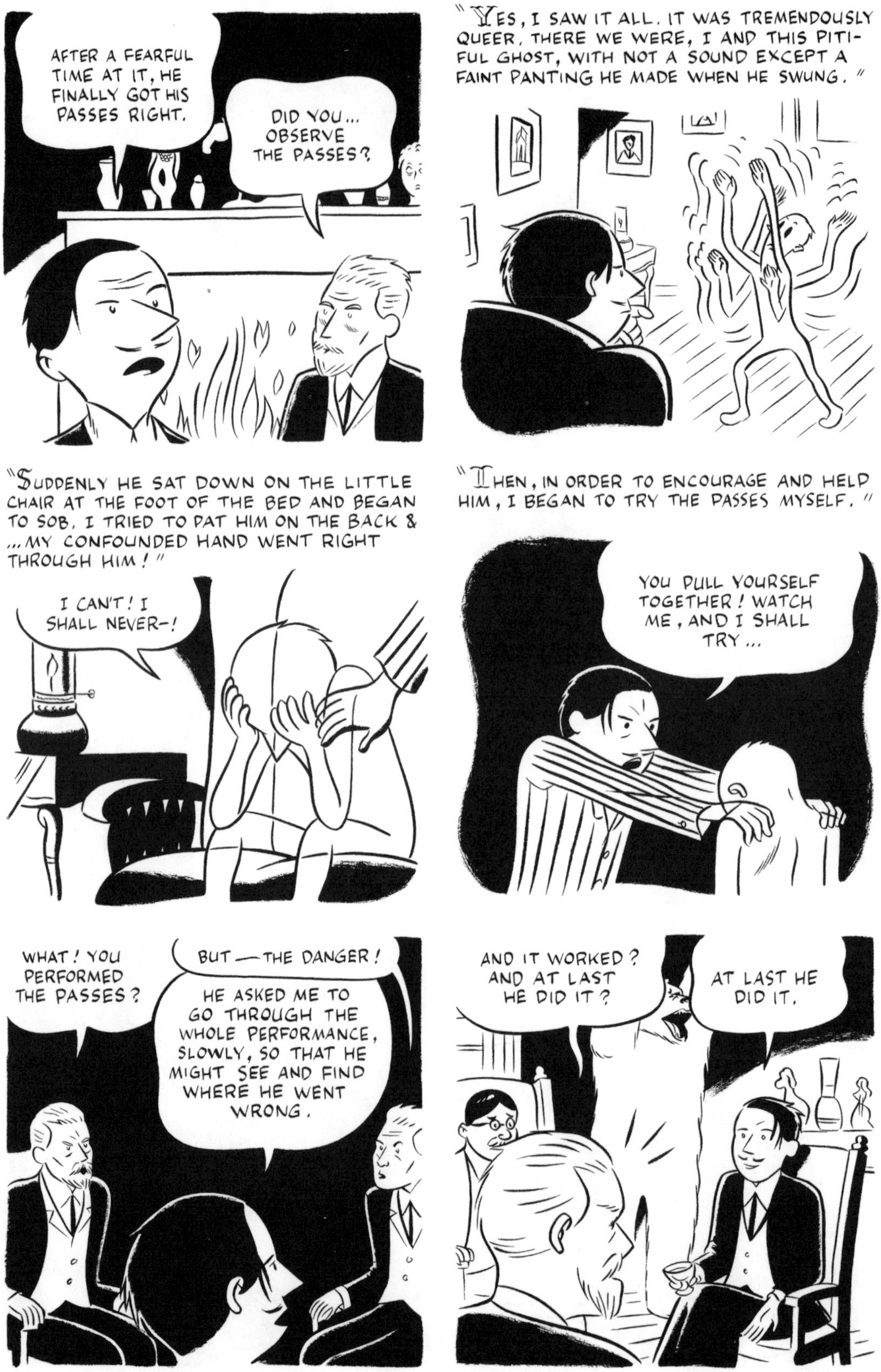
AFTER A FEARFUL TIME AT IT, HE FINALLY GOT HIS PASSES RIGHT.
DID YOU... OBSERVE THE PASSES?
"YES, I SAW IT ALL. IT WAS TREMENDOUSLY QUEER. THERE WE WERE, I AND THIS PITIFUL GHOST, WITH NOT A SOUND EXCEPT A FAINT PANTING HE MADE WHEN HE SWUNG."
"SUDDENLY HE SAT DOWN ON THE LITTLE CHAIR AT THE FOOT OF THE BED AND BEGAN TO SOB. I TRIED TO PAT HIM ON THE BACK & ...MY CONFOUNDED HAND WENT RIGHT THROUGH HIM!"
I CAN'T! I SHALL NEVER-!
"THEN, IN ORDER TO ENCOURAGE AND HELP HIM, I BEGAN TO TRY THE PASSES MYSELF."
YOU PULL YOURSELF TOGETHER! WATCH ME, AND I SHALL TRY...
WHAT! YOU PERFORMED THE PASSES?
BUT — THE DANGER!
HE ASKED ME TO GO THROUGH THE WHOLE PERFORMANCE, SLOWLY, SO THAT HE MIGHT SEE AND FIND WHERE HE WENT WRONG.
AND IT WORKED? AND AT LAST HE DID IT?
AT LAST HE DID IT.

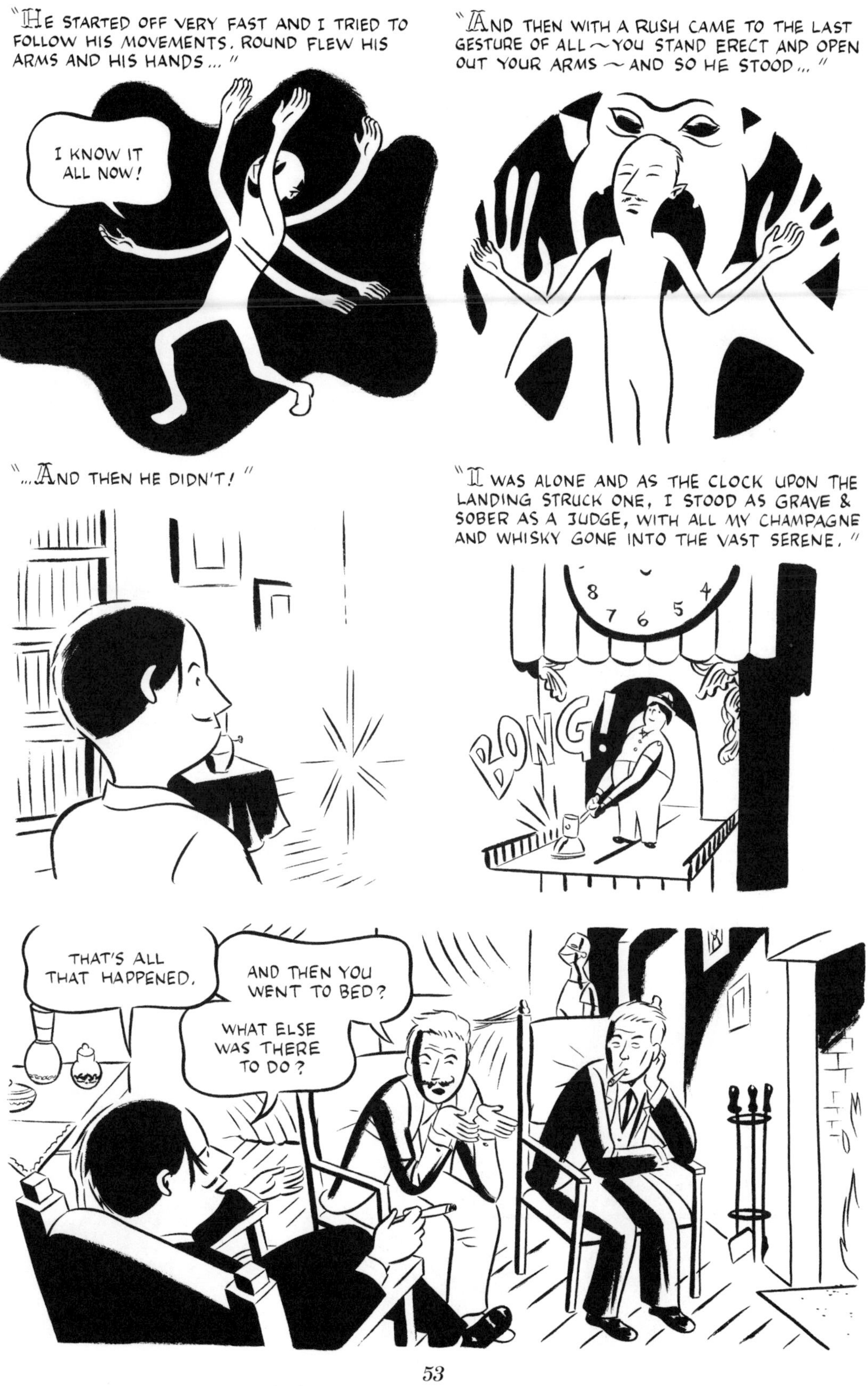
"HE STARTED OFF VERY FAST AND I TRIED TO FOLLOW HIS MOVEMENTS. ROUND FLEW HIS ARMS AND HIS HANDS..."
I KNOW IT ALL NOW!
"AND THEN WITH A RUSH CAME TO THE LAST GESTURE OF ALL ~ YOU STAND ERECT AND OPEN OUT YOUR ARMS ~ AND SO HE STOOD..."
"...AND THEN HE DIDN'T!"
"I WAS ALONE AND AS THE CLOCK UPON THE LANDING STRUCK ONE, I STOOD AS GRAVE & SOBER AS A JUDGE, WITH ALL MY CHAMPAGNE AND WHISKY GONE INTO THE VAST SERENE."
BONG!
THAT'S ALL THAT HAPPENED.
AND THEN YOU WENT TO BED?
WHAT ELSE WAS THERE TO DO?

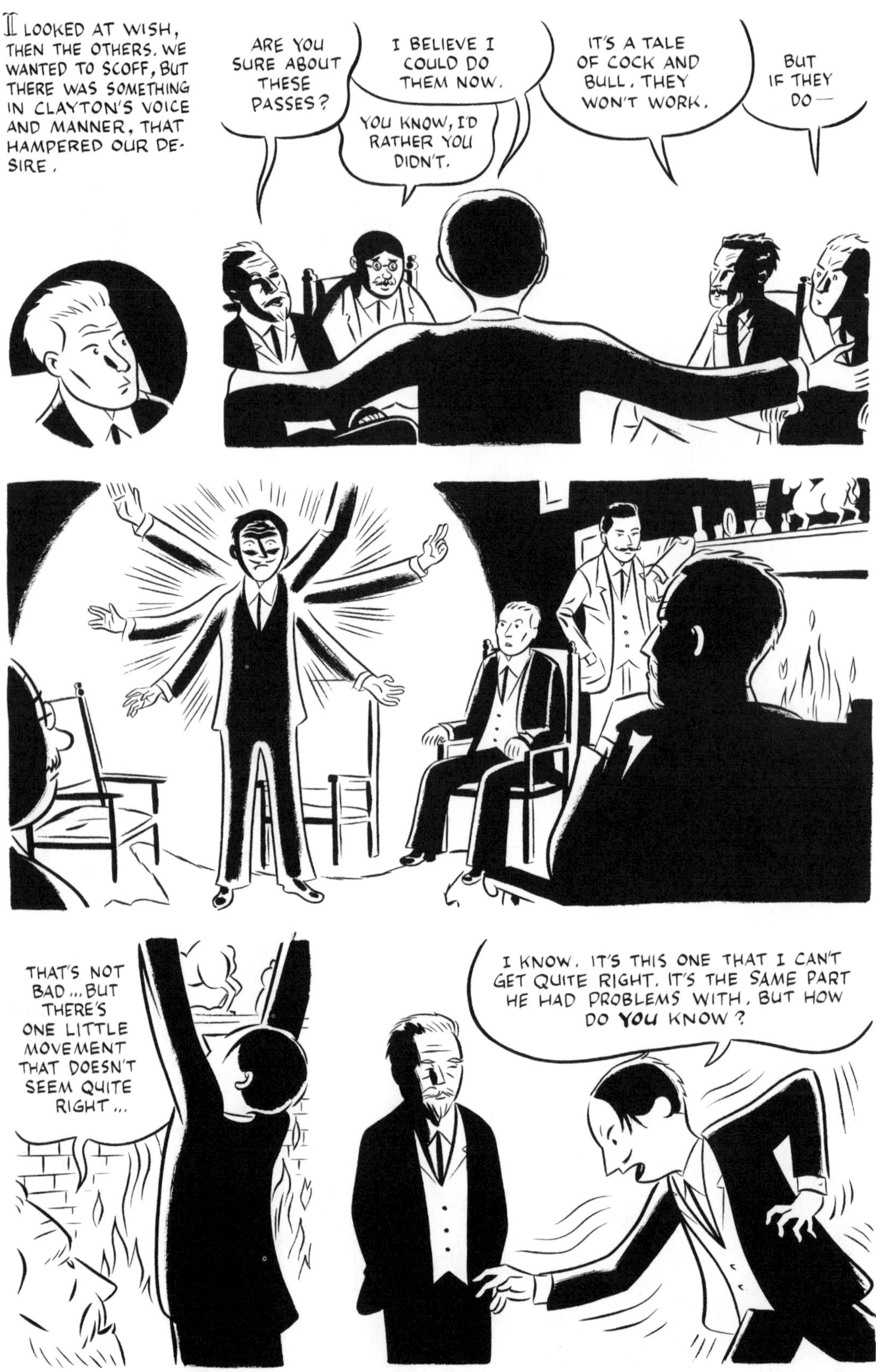
I LOOKED AT WISH, THEN THE OTHERS. WE WANTED TO SCOFF, BUT THERE WAS SOMETHING IN CLAYTON'S VOICE AND MANNER, THAT HAMPERED OUR DESIRE.
ARE YOU SURE ABOUT THESE PASSES?
I BELIEVE I COULD DO THEM NOW.
YOU KNOW, I'D RATHER YOU DIDN'T.
IT'S A TALE OF COCK AND BULL. THEY WON'T WORK.
BUT IF THEY DO—
THAT'S NOT BAD... BUT THERE'S ONE LITTLE MOVEMENT THAT DOESN'T SEEM QUITE RIGHT...
I KNOW. IT'S THIS ONE THAT I CAN'T GET QUITE RIGHT. IT'S THE SAME PART HE HAD PROBLEMS WITH. BUT HOW DO **YOU** KNOW?

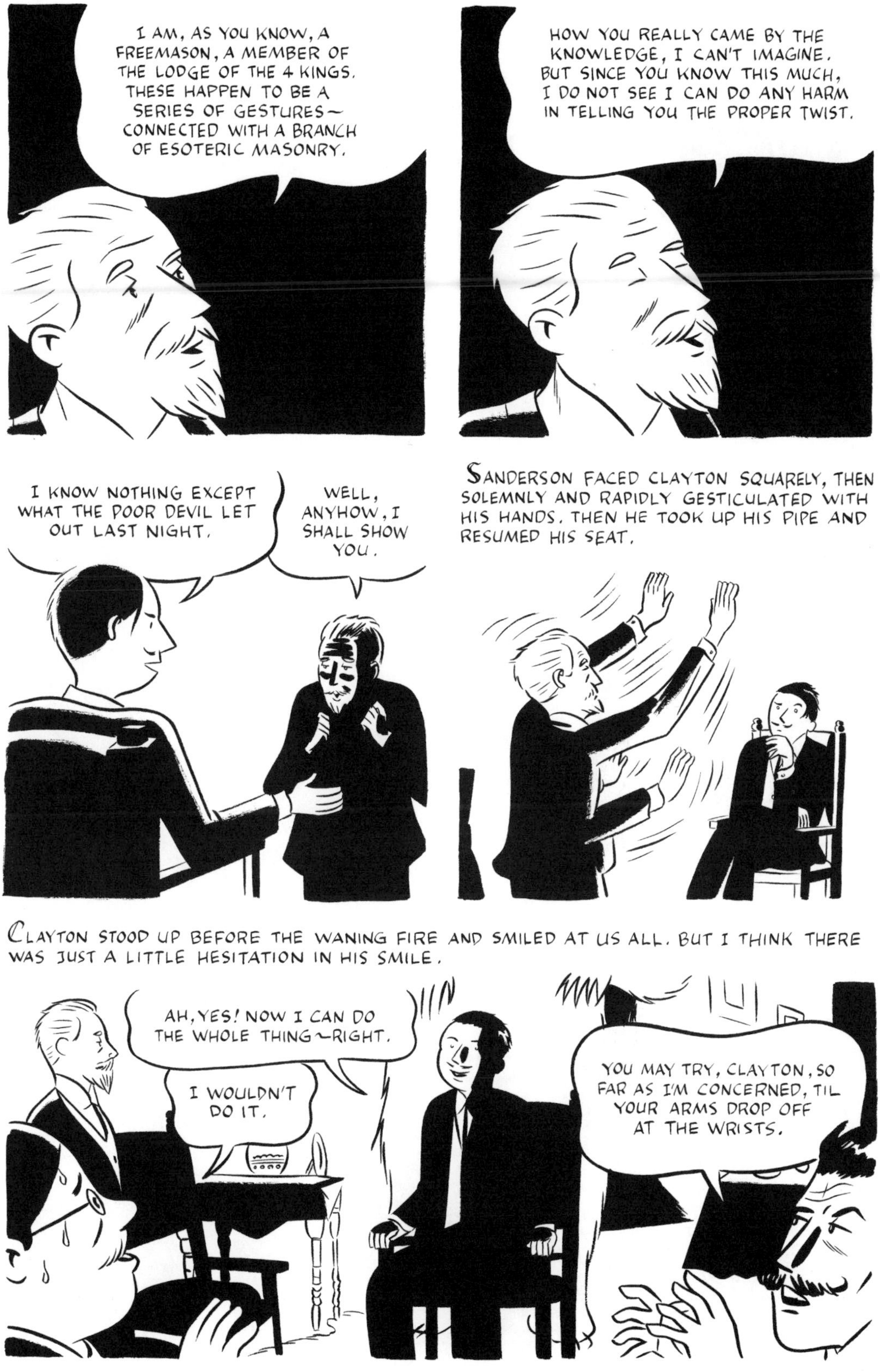
I AM, AS YOU KNOW, A FREEMASON, A MEMBER OF THE LODGE OF THE 4 KINGS. THESE HAPPEN TO BE A SERIES OF GESTURES~ CONNECTED WITH A BRANCH OF ESOTERIC MASONRY.
HOW YOU REALLY CAME BY THE KNOWLEDGE, I CAN'T IMAGINE. BUT SINCE YOU KNOW THIS MUCH, I DO NOT SEE I CAN DO ANY HARM IN TELLING YOU THE PROPER TWIST.
I KNOW NOTHING EXCEPT WHAT THE POOR DEVIL LET OUT LAST NIGHT.
WELL, ANYHOW, I SHALL SHOW YOU.
SANDERSON FACED CLAYTON SQUARELY, THEN SOLEMNLY AND RAPIDLY GESTICULATED WITH HIS HANDS. THEN HE TOOK UP HIS PIPE AND RESUMED HIS SEAT.
CLAYTON STOOD UP BEFORE THE WANING FIRE AND SMILED AT US ALL. BUT I THINK THERE WAS JUST A LITTLE HESITATION IN HIS SMILE.
AH, YES! NOW I CAN DO THE WHOLE THING~RIGHT.
I WOULDN'T DO IT.
YOU MAY TRY, CLAYTON, SO FAR AS I'M CONCERNED, TIL YOUR ARMS DROP OFF AT THE WRISTS.

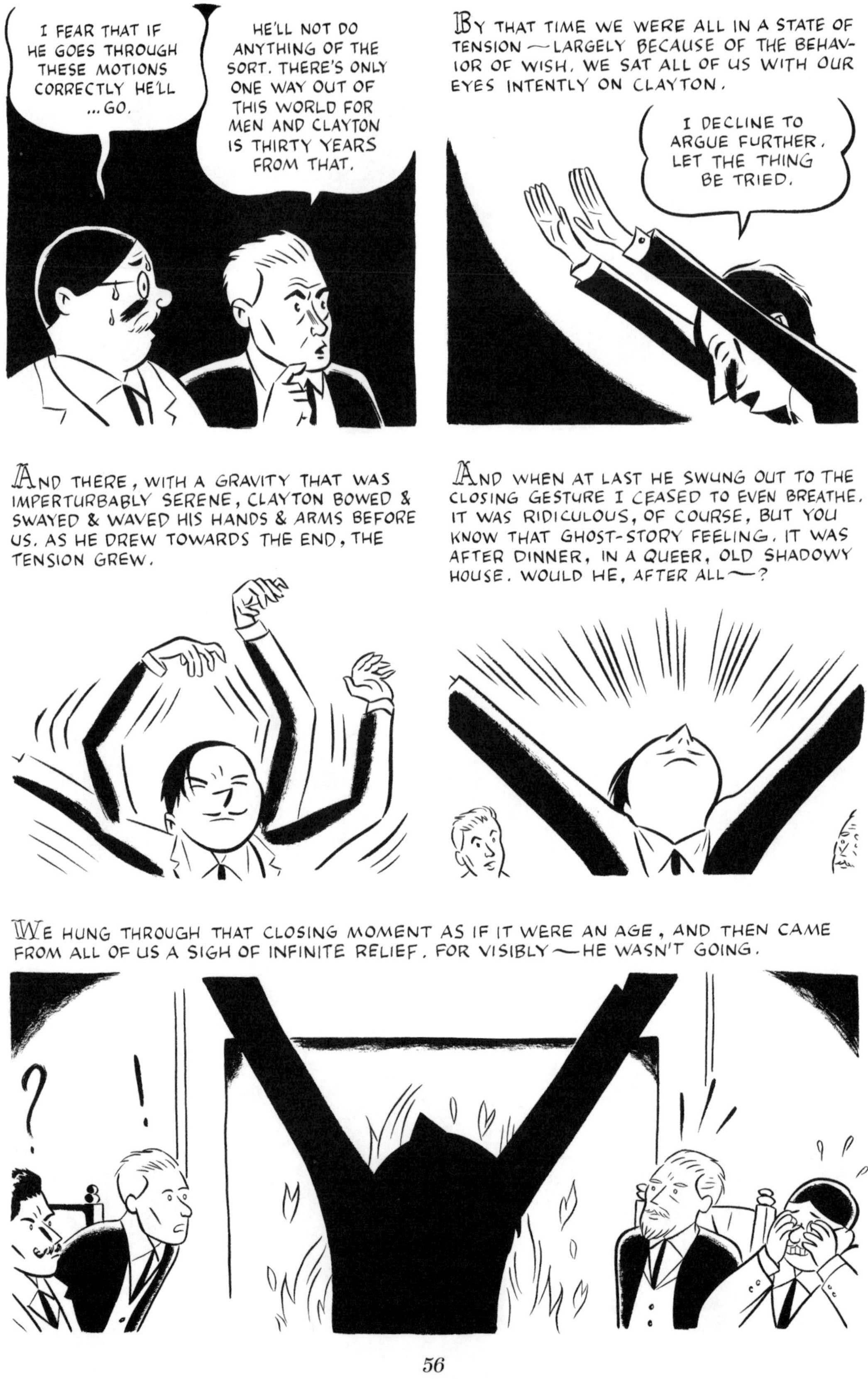
I FEAR THAT IF HE GOES THROUGH THESE MOTIONS CORRECTLY HE'LL ...GO.
HE'LL NOT DO ANYTHING OF THE SORT. THERE'S ONLY ONE WAY OUT OF THIS WORLD FOR MEN AND CLAYTON IS THIRTY YEARS FROM THAT.
BY THAT TIME WE WERE ALL IN A STATE OF TENSION — LARGELY BECAUSE OF THE BEHAVIOR OF WISH. WE SAT ALL OF US WITH OUR EYES INTENTLY ON CLAYTON.
I DECLINE TO ARGUE FURTHER. LET THE THING BE TRIED.
AND THERE, WITH A GRAVITY THAT WAS IMPERTURBABLY SERENE, CLAYTON BOWED & SWAYED & WAVED HIS HANDS & ARMS BEFORE US. AS HE DREW TOWARDS THE END, THE TENSION GREW.
AND WHEN AT LAST HE SWUNG OUT TO THE CLOSING GESTURE I CEASED TO EVEN BREATHE. IT WAS RIDICULOUS, OF COURSE, BUT YOU KNOW THAT GHOST-STORY FEELING. IT WAS AFTER DINNER, IN A QUEER, OLD SHADOWY HOUSE. WOULD HE, AFTER ALL—?
WE HUNG THROUGH THAT CLOSING MOMENT AS IF IT WERE AN AGE, AND THEN CAME FROM ALL OF US A SIGH OF INFINITE RELIEF. FOR VISIBLY—HE WASN'T GOING.
?
!

IT WAS ALL NONSENSE. HE HAD TOLD AN IDLE STORY AND CARRIED IT ALMOST TO CONVICTION, THAT WAS ALL! ... AND THEN, IN THAT MOMENT, THE FACE OF CLAYTON ~ CHANGED.

IT CHANGED AS A LIT HOUSE CHANGES WHEN ITS LIGHTS ARE SUDDENLY EXTINGUISHED. HIS SMILE REMAINED FROZEN ON HIS LIPS, AS HE STOOD THERE, VERY GENTLY SWAYING.

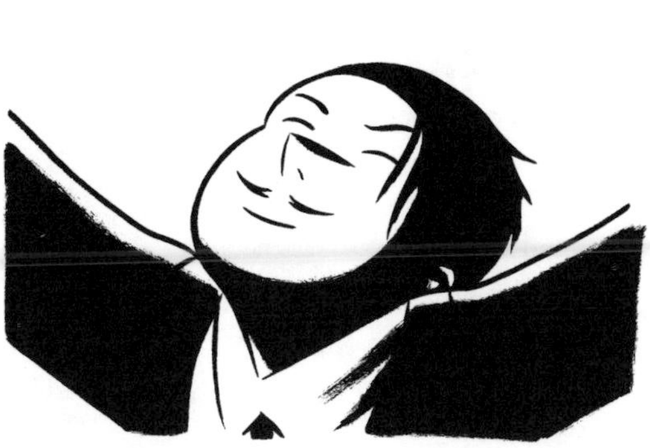

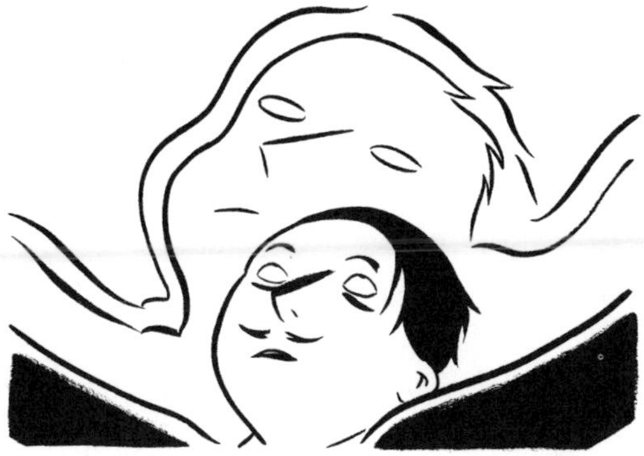

THEN CHAIRS WERE SCRAPING, THINGS WERE FALLING, AND WE WERE ALL MOVING AS HIS KNEES SEEMED TO GIVE. HE FELL FORWARD & EVANS ROSE & CAUGHT HIM IN HIS ARMS.

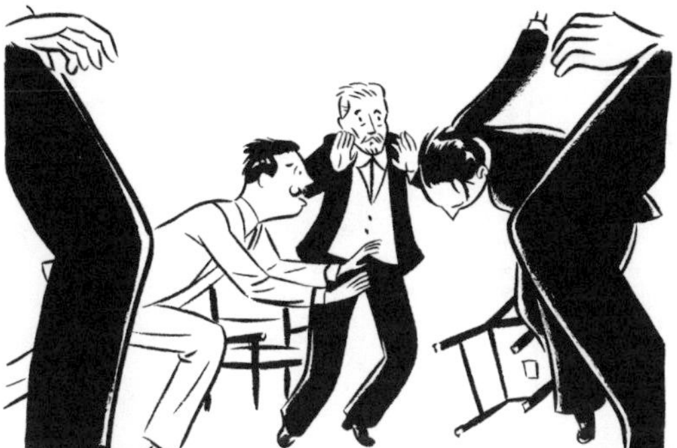

IT STUNNED US ALL. CLAYTON HAD, INDEED, PASSED INTO THE WORLD THAT LIES SO NEAR TO & SO FAR FROM OUR OWN & HE HAD GONE THITHER BY THE ONLY ROAD THAT MORTAL MAN MAY TAKE.

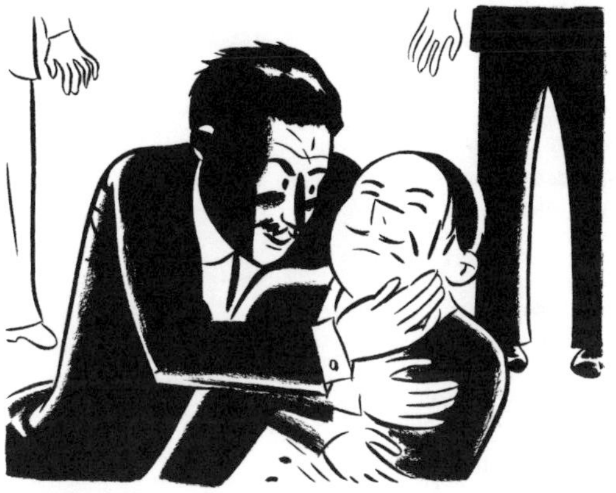

BUT WHETHER HE DID INDEED PASS THERE BY THAT POOR GHOST'S INCANTATION, OR WHETHER HE WAS STRICKEN SUDDENLY BY APOPLEXY IN THE MIDST OF AN IDLE TALE—AS THE CORONER'S JURY WOULD HAVE US BELIEVE—IS NO MATTER FOR MY JUDGING; IT IS JUST ONE OF THOSE INEXPLICABLE RIDDLES THAT MUST REMAIN UNSOLVED UNTIL THE FINAL SOLUTION OF ALL THINGS SHALL COME.

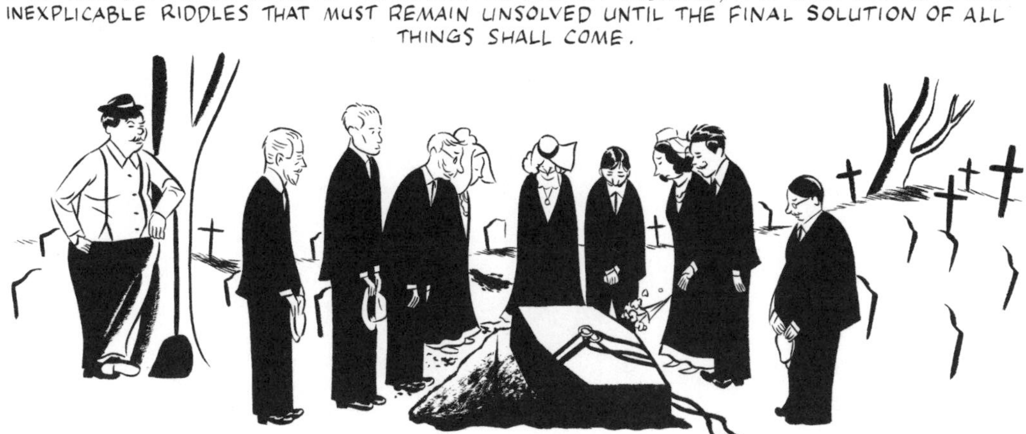

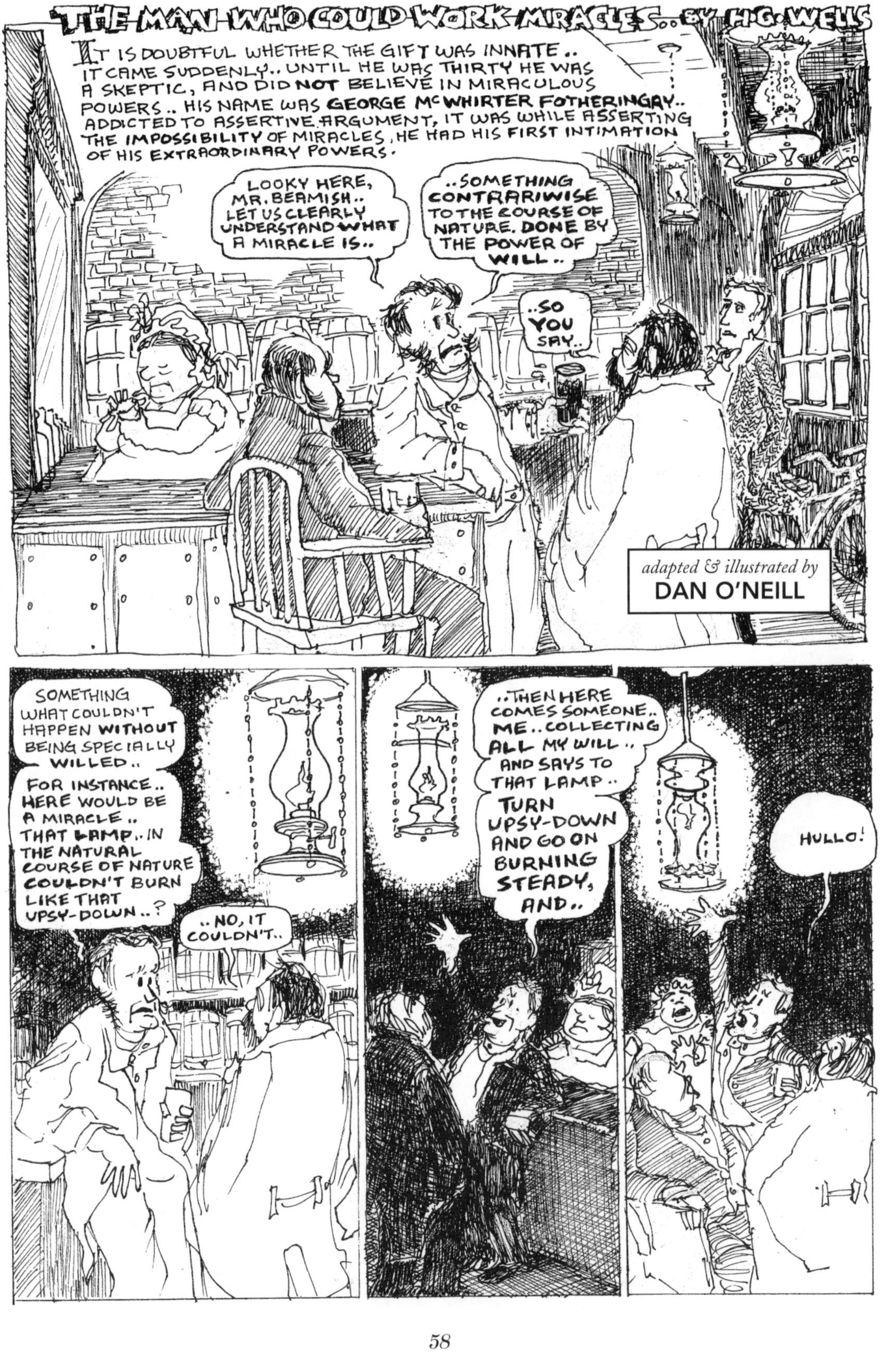
THE MAN WHO COULD WORK MIRACLES.. BY H.G. WELLS
IT IS DOUBTFUL WHETHER THE GIFT WAS INNATE .. IT CAME SUDDENLY.. UNTIL HE WAS THIRTY HE WAS A SKEPTIC, AND DID NOT BELIEVE IN MIRACULOUS POWERS.. HIS NAME WAS GEORGE McWHIRTER FOTHERINGAY.. ADDICTED TO ASSERTIVE ARGUMENT, IT WAS WHILE ASSERTING THE IMPOSSIBILITY OF MIRACLES, HE HAD HIS FIRST INTIMATION OF HIS EXTRAORDINARY POWERS.
LOOKY HERE, MR. BEAMISH.. LET US CLEARLY UNDERSTAND WHAT A MIRACLE IS..
..SOMETHING CONTRARIWISE TO THE COURSE OF NATURE. DONE BY THE POWER OF WILL..
..SO YOU SAY..
adapted & illustrated by
DAN O'NEILL
SOMETHING WHAT COULDN'T HAPPEN WITHOUT BEING SPECIALLY WILLED..
FOR INSTANCE.. HERE WOULD BE A MIRACLE.. THAT LAMP.. IN THE NATURAL COURSE OF NATURE COULDN'T BURN LIKE THAT UPSY-DOWN..?
..NO, IT COULDN'T..
..THEN HERE COMES SOMEONE.. ME.. COLLECTING ALL MY WILL.. AND SAYS TO THAT LAMP..
TURN UPSY-DOWN AND GO ON BURNING STEADY, AND..
HULLO!

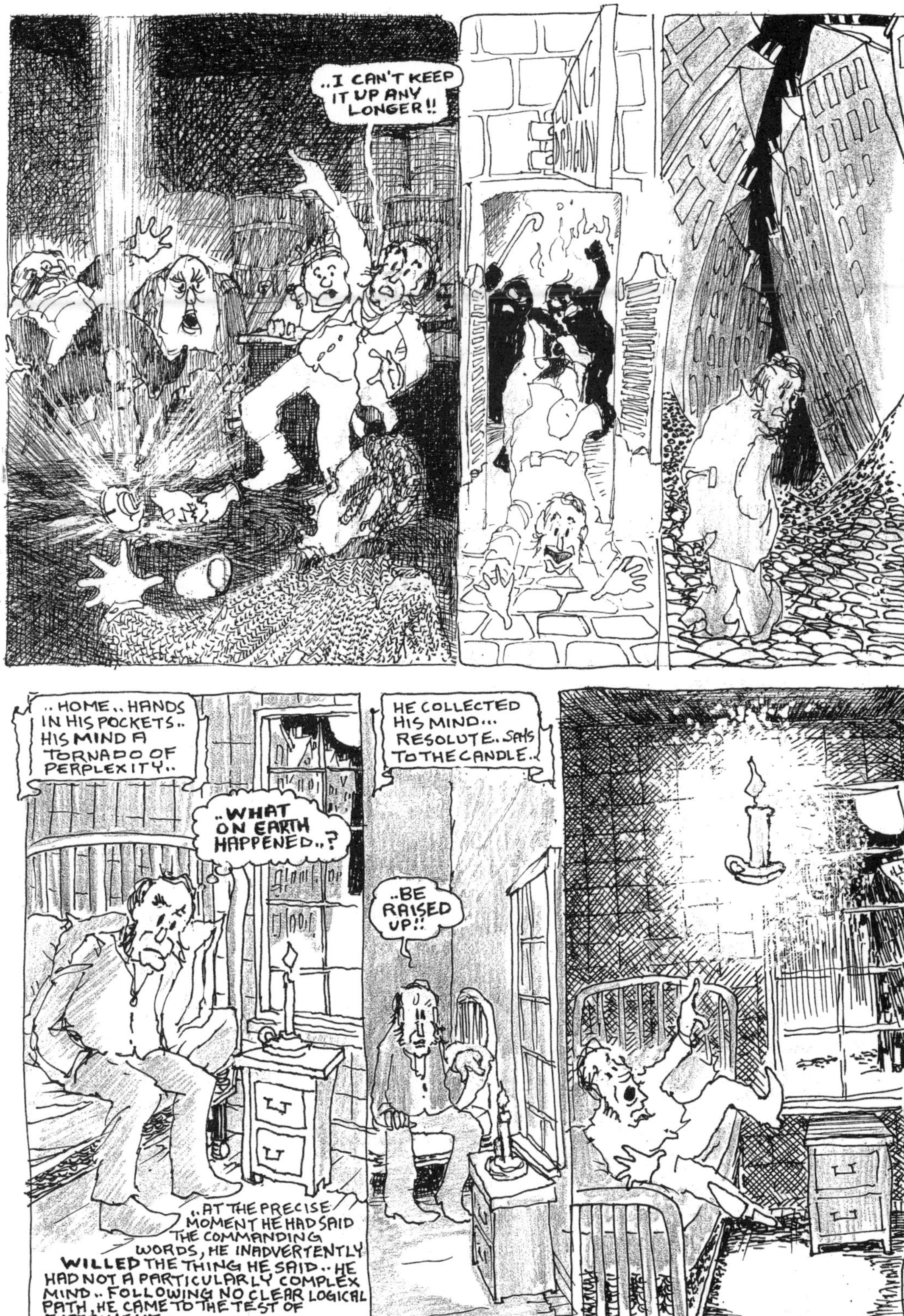
..I CAN'T KEEP IT UP ANY LONGER!!
..HOME.. HANDS IN HIS POCKETS.. HIS MIND A TORNADO OF PERPLEXITY..
..WHAT ON EARTH HAPPENED..?
..AT THE PRECISE MOMENT HE HAD SAID THE COMMANDING WORDS, HE INADVERTENTLY WILLED THE THING HE SAID.. HE HAD NOT A PARTICULARLY COMPLEX MIND.. FOLLOWING NO CLEAR LOGICAL PATH, HE CAME TO THE TEST OF EXPERIMENT..
HE COLLECTED HIS MIND... RESOLUTE.. SAYS TO THE CANDLE..
..BE RAISED UP!!

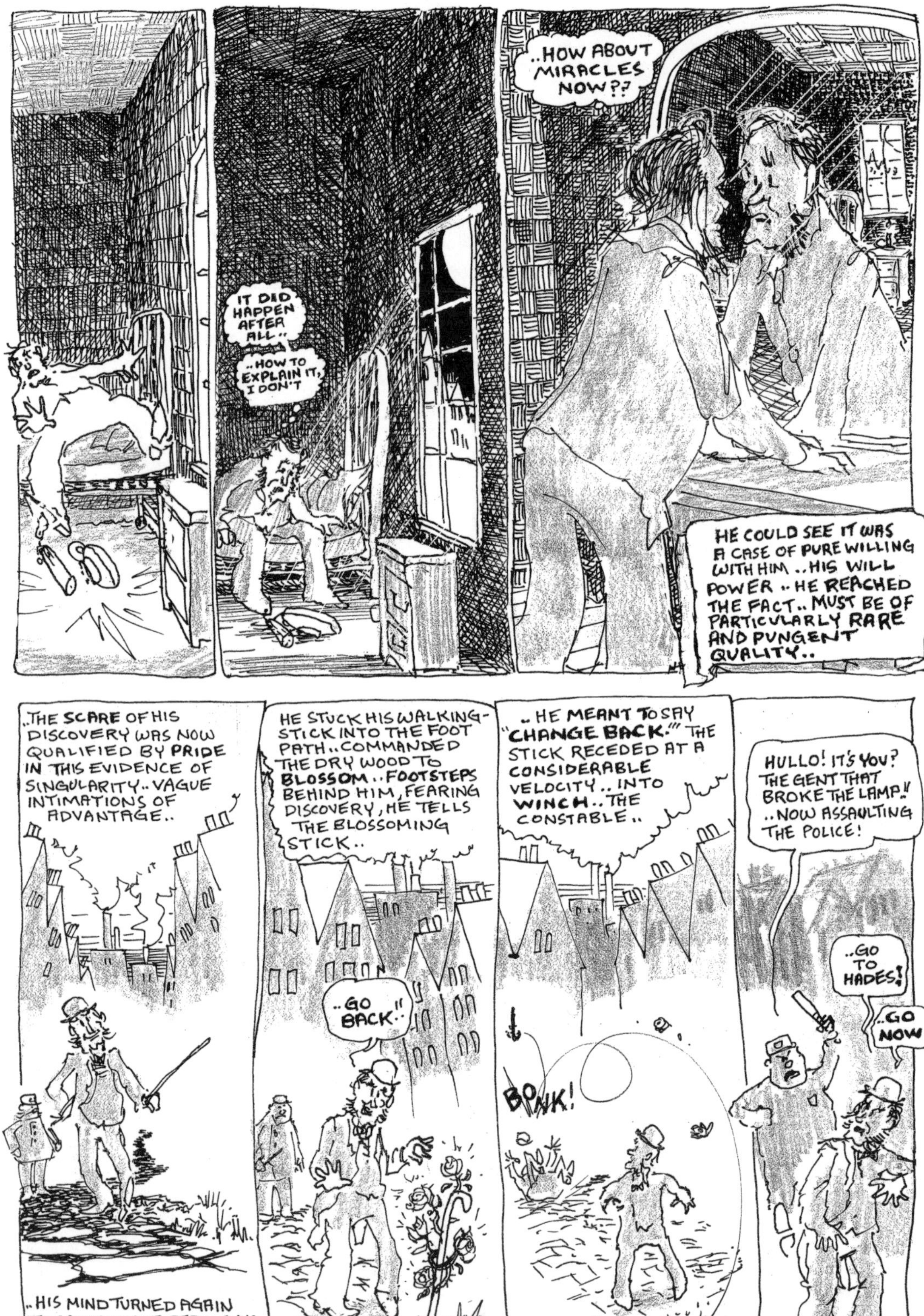
IT DID HAPPEN AFTER ALL..
..HOW TO EXPLAIN IT, I DON'T
..HOW ABOUT MIRACLES NOW??
HE COULD SEE IT WAS A CASE OF PURE WILLING WITH HIM ..HIS WILL POWER .. HE REACHED THE FACT.. MUST BE OF PARTICULARLY RARE AND PUNGENT QUALITY..
..THE SCARE OF HIS DISCOVERY WAS NOW QUALIFIED BY PRIDE IN THIS EVIDENCE OF SINGULARITY.. VAGUE INTIMATIONS OF ADVANTAGE..
..HIS MIND TURNED AGAIN TO CAUTIOUS EXPERIMENTS.. ..A WANT OF ORIGINALITY IN HIS ATTEMPTS..
HE STUCK HIS WALKING-STICK INTO THE FOOT PATH.. COMMANDED THE DRY WOOD TO BLOSSOM.. FOOTSTEPS BEHIND HIM, FEARING DISCOVERY, HE TELLS THE BLOSSOMING STICK..
..GO BACK.!!
.. HE MEANT TO SAY "CHANGE BACK."! THE STICK RECEDED AT A CONSIDERABLE VELOCITY.. INTO WINCH.. THE CONSTABLE..
BONK!
HULLO! IT'S YOU? THE GENT THAT BROKE THE LAMP!! ..NOW ASSAULTING THE POLICE!
..GO TO HADES!
..GO NOW!

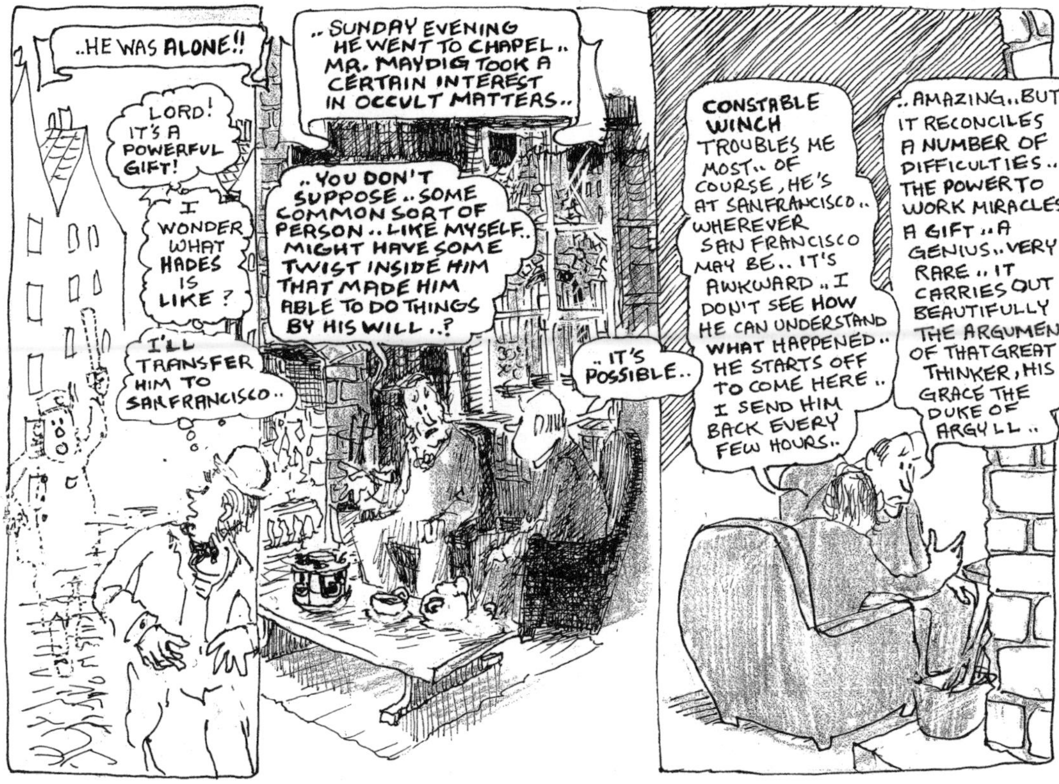
..HE WAS ALONE!!
LORD! IT'S A POWERFUL GIFT!
I WONDER WHAT HADES IS LIKE?
I'LL TRANSFER HIM TO SAN FRANCISCO..
..SUNDAY EVENING HE WENT TO CHAPEL.. MR. MAYDIG TOOK A CERTAIN INTEREST IN OCCULT MATTERS..
..YOU DON'T SUPPOSE.. SOME COMMON SORT OF PERSON.. LIKE MYSELF.. MIGHT HAVE SOME TWIST INSIDE HIM THAT MADE HIM ABLE TO DO THINGS BY HIS WILL..?
..IT'S POSSIBLE..
CONSTABLE WINCH TROUBLES ME MOST.. OF COURSE, HE'S AT SAN FRANCISCO.. WHEREVER SAN FRANCISCO MAY BE.. IT'S AWKWARD.. I DON'T SEE HOW HE CAN UNDERSTAND WHAT HAPPENED.. HE STARTS OFF TO COME HERE.. I SEND HIM BACK EVERY FEW HOURS..
..AMAZING..BUT IT RECONCILES A NUMBER OF DIFFICULTIES.. THE POWER TO WORK MIRACLES.. A GIFT.. A GENIUS.. VERY RARE.. IT CARRIES OUT BEAUTIFULLY THE ARGUMENTS OF THAT GREAT THINKER, HIS GRACE THE DUKE OF ARGYLL..

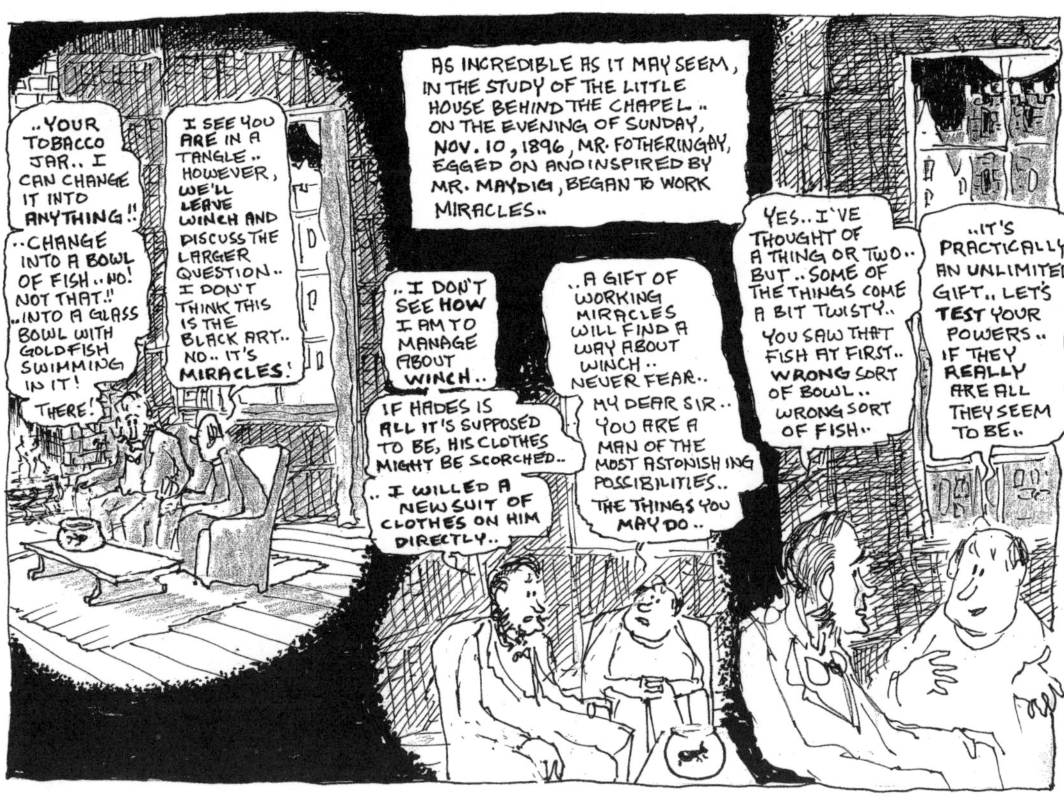
AS INCREDIBLE AS IT MAY SEEM, IN THE STUDY OF THE LITTLE HOUSE BEHIND THE CHAPEL.. ON THE EVENING OF SUNDAY, NOV. 10, 1896, MR. FOTHERINGAY, EGGED ON AND INSPIRED BY MR. MAYDIG, BEGAN TO WORK MIRACLES..
..YOUR TOBACCO JAR.. I CAN CHANGE IT INTO ANYTHING!!
..CHANGE INTO A BOWL OF FISH.. NO! NOT THAT.!" ..INTO A GLASS BOWL WITH GOLDFISH SWIMMING IN IT!
THERE!
I SEE YOU ARE IN A TANGLE.. HOWEVER, WE'LL LEAVE WINCH AND DISCUSS THE LARGER QUESTION.. I DON'T THINK THIS IS THE BLACK ART.. NO.. IT'S MIRACLES!
..I DON'T SEE HOW I AM TO MANAGE ABOUT WINCH..
IF HADES IS ALL IT'S SUPPOSED TO BE, HIS CLOTHES MIGHT BE SCORCHED..
..I WILLED A NEW SUIT OF CLOTHES ON HIM DIRECTLY..
..A GIFT OF WORKING MIRACLES WILL FIND A WAY ABOUT WINCH.. NEVER FEAR..
MY DEAR SIR.. YOU ARE A MAN OF THE MOST ASTONISHING POSSIBILITIES.. THE THINGS YOU MAY DO..
YES.. I'VE THOUGHT OF A THING OR TWO.. BUT.. SOME OF THE THINGS COME A BIT TWISTY.. YOU SAW THAT FISH AT FIRST.. WRONG SORT OF BOWL.. WRONG SORT OF FISH..
..IT'S PRACTICALLY AN UNLIMITED GIFT.. LET'S TEST YOUR POWERS.. IF THEY REALLY ARE ALL THEY SEEM TO BE..

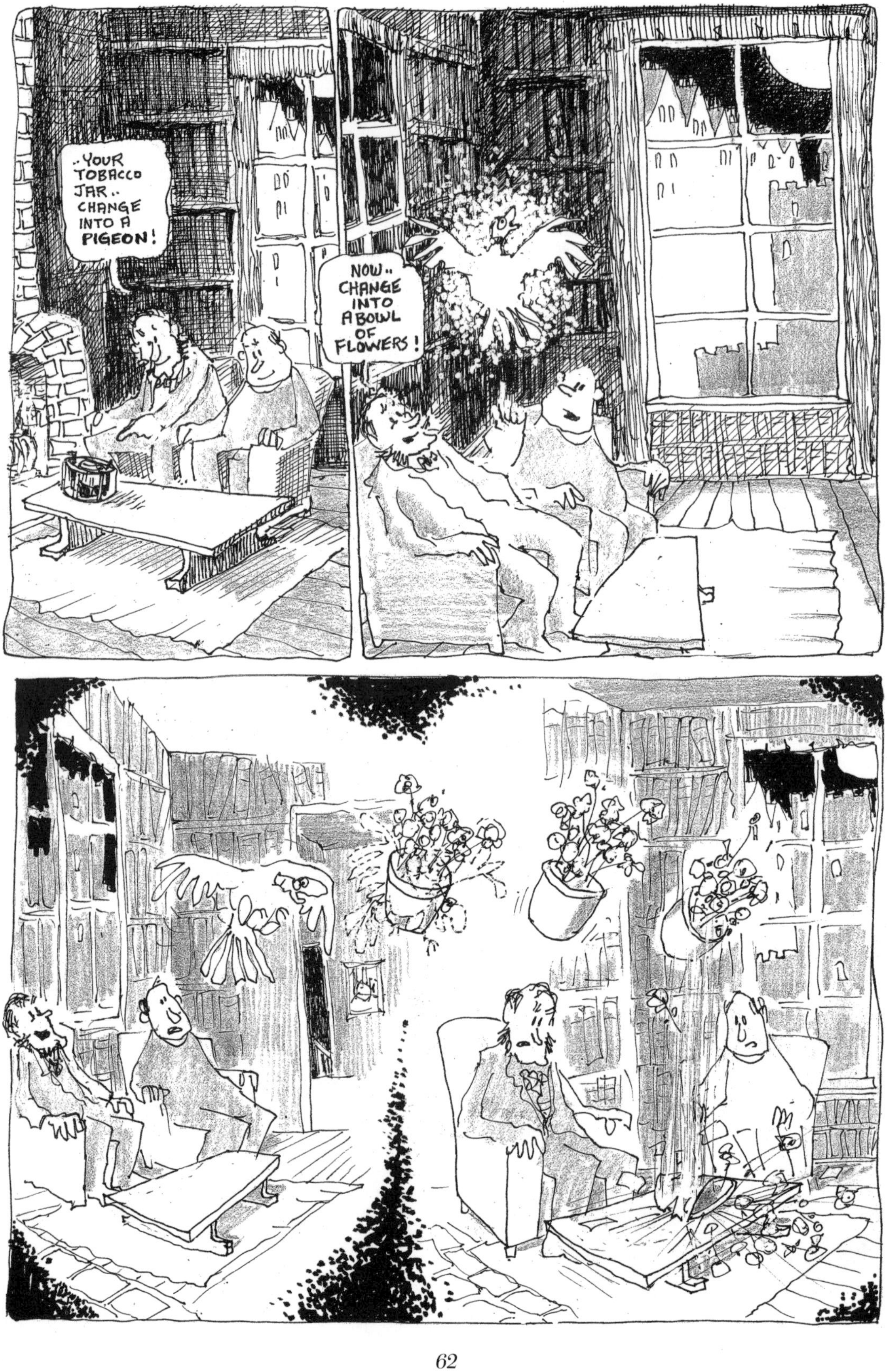
..YOUR TOBACCO JAR.. CHANGE INTO A PIGEON!
NOW.. CHANGE INTO A BOWL OF FLOWERS!

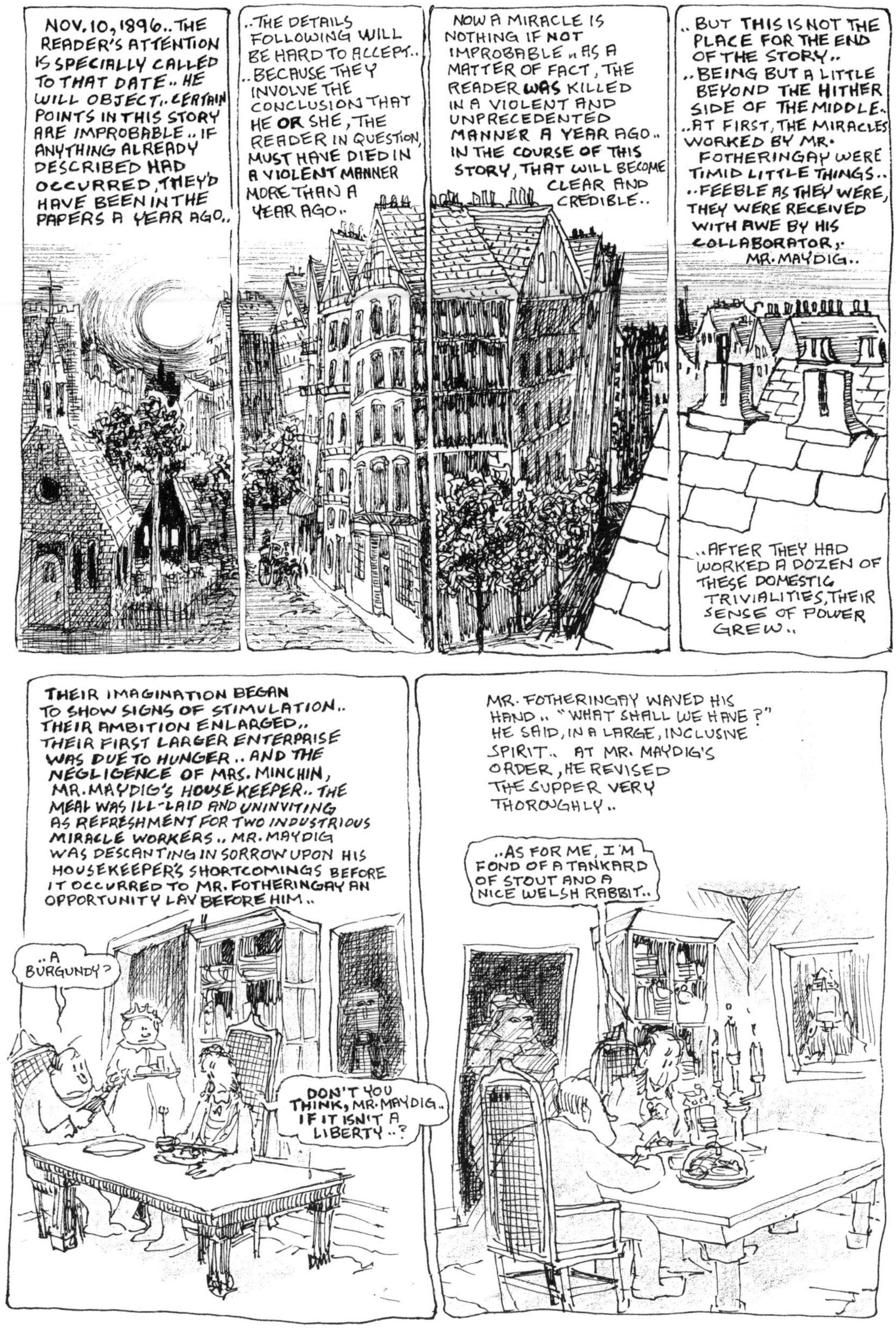
NOV. 10, 1896.. THE READER'S ATTENTION IS SPECIALLY CALLED TO THAT DATE.. HE WILL OBJECT.. CERTAIN POINTS IN THIS STORY ARE IMPROBABLE.. IF ANYTHING ALREADY DESCRIBED HAD OCCURRED, THEY'D HAVE BEEN IN THE PAPERS A YEAR AGO..
..THE DETAILS FOLLOWING WILL BE HARD TO ACCEPT.. ..BECAUSE THEY INVOLVE THE CONCLUSION THAT HE OR SHE, THE READER IN QUESTION, MUST HAVE DIED IN A VIOLENT MANNER MORE THAN A YEAR AGO..
NOW A MIRACLE IS NOTHING IF NOT IMPROBABLE.. AS A MATTER OF FACT, THE READER WAS KILLED IN A VIOLENT AND UNPRECEDENTED MANNER A YEAR AGO.. IN THE COURSE OF THIS STORY, THAT WILL BECOME CLEAR AND CREDIBLE..
.. BUT THIS IS NOT THE PLACE FOR THE END OF THE STORY.. ..BEING BUT A LITTLE BEYOND THE HITHER SIDE OF THE MIDDLE.. ..AT FIRST, THE MIRACLES WORKED BY MR. FOTHERINGAY WERE TIMID LITTLE THINGS.. ..FEEBLE AS THEY WERE, THEY WERE RECEIVED WITH AWE BY HIS COLLABORATOR, MR. MAYDIG..
..AFTER THEY HAD WORKED A DOZEN OF THESE DOMESTIC TRIVIALITIES, THEIR SENSE OF POWER GREW..
THEIR IMAGINATION BEGAN TO SHOW SIGNS OF STIMULATION.. THEIR AMBITION ENLARGED.. THEIR FIRST LARGER ENTERPRISE WAS DUE TO HUNGER.. AND THE NEGLIGENCE OF MRS. MINCHIN, MR. MAYDIG'S HOUSEKEEPER.. THE MEAL WAS ILL-LAID AND UNINVITING AS REFRESHMENT FOR TWO INDUSTRIOUS MIRACLE WORKERS.. MR. MAYDIG WAS DESCANTING IN SORROW UPON HIS HOUSEKEEPER'S SHORTCOMINGS BEFORE IT OCCURRED TO MR. FOTHERINGAY AN OPPORTUNITY LAY BEFORE HIM..
..A BURGUNDY?
DON'T YOU THINK, MR. MAYDIG.. IF IT ISN'T A LIBERTY..?
MR. FOTHERINGAY WAVED HIS HAND.. "WHAT SHALL WE HAVE?" HE SAID, IN A LARGE, INCLUSIVE SPIRIT.. AT MR. MAYDIG'S ORDER, HE REVISED THE SUPPER VERY THOROUGHLY..
..AS FOR ME, I'M FOND OF A TANKARD OF STOUT AND A NICE WELSH RABBIT..

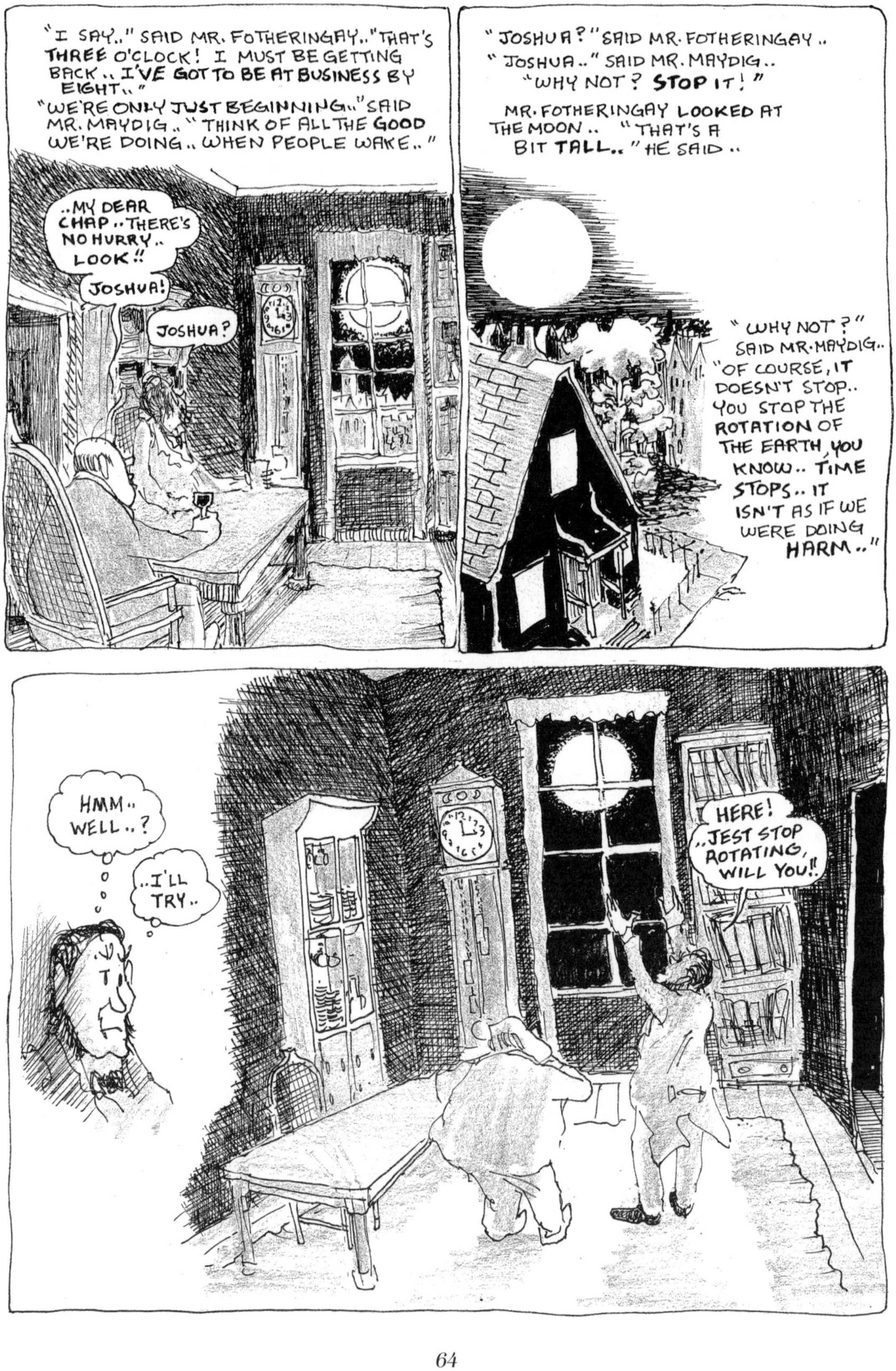
"I SAY.." SAID MR. FOTHERINGAY.."THAT'S THREE O'CLOCK! I MUST BE GETTING BACK.. I'VE GOT TO BE AT BUSINESS BY EIGHT.."
"WE'RE ONLY JUST BEGINNING.." SAID MR. MAYDIG.. "THINK OF ALL THE GOOD WE'RE DOING.. WHEN PEOPLE WAKE.."
..MY DEAR CHAP.. THERE'S NO HURRY.. LOOK!!
JOSHUA!
JOSHUA?
"JOSHUA?" SAID MR. FOTHERINGAY..
"JOSHUA.." SAID MR. MAYDIG..
"WHY NOT? STOP IT!"
MR. FOTHERINGAY LOOKED AT THE MOON.. "THAT'S A BIT TALL.." HE SAID..
"WHY NOT?" SAID MR. MAYDIG.. "OF COURSE, IT DOESN'T STOP.. YOU STOP THE ROTATION OF THE EARTH, YOU KNOW.. TIME STOPS.. IT ISN'T AS IF WE WERE DOING HARM.."
HMM.. WELL..?
..I'LL TRY..
HERE! ..JEST STOP ROTATING, WILL YOU!!

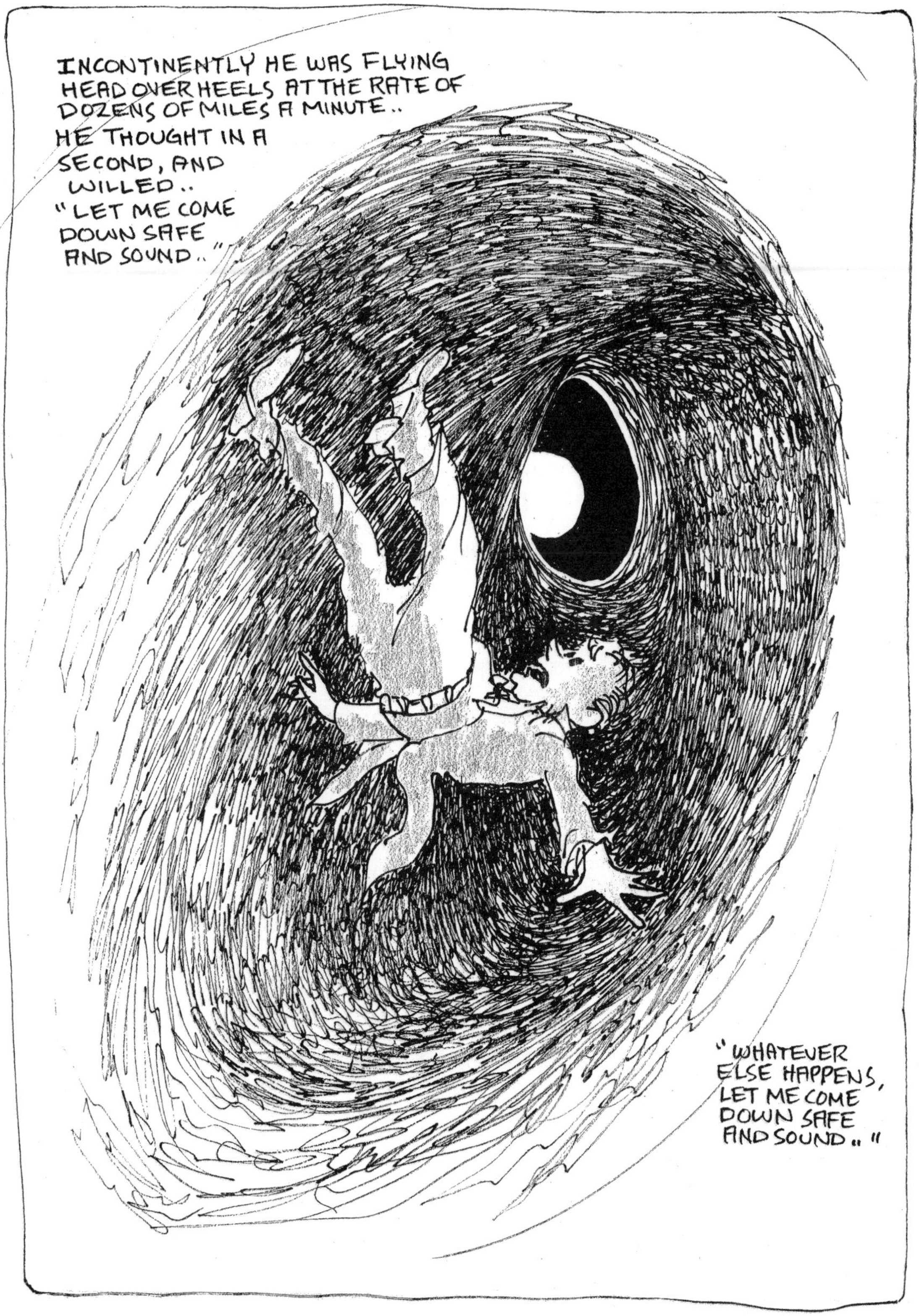
INCONTINENTLY HE WAS FLYING HEAD OVER HEELS AT THE RATE OF DOZENS OF MILES A MINUTE..
HE THOUGHT IN A SECOND, AND WILLED..
"LET ME COME DOWN SAFE AND SOUND.."
"WHATEVER ELSE HAPPENS, LET ME COME DOWN SAFE AND SOUND.."

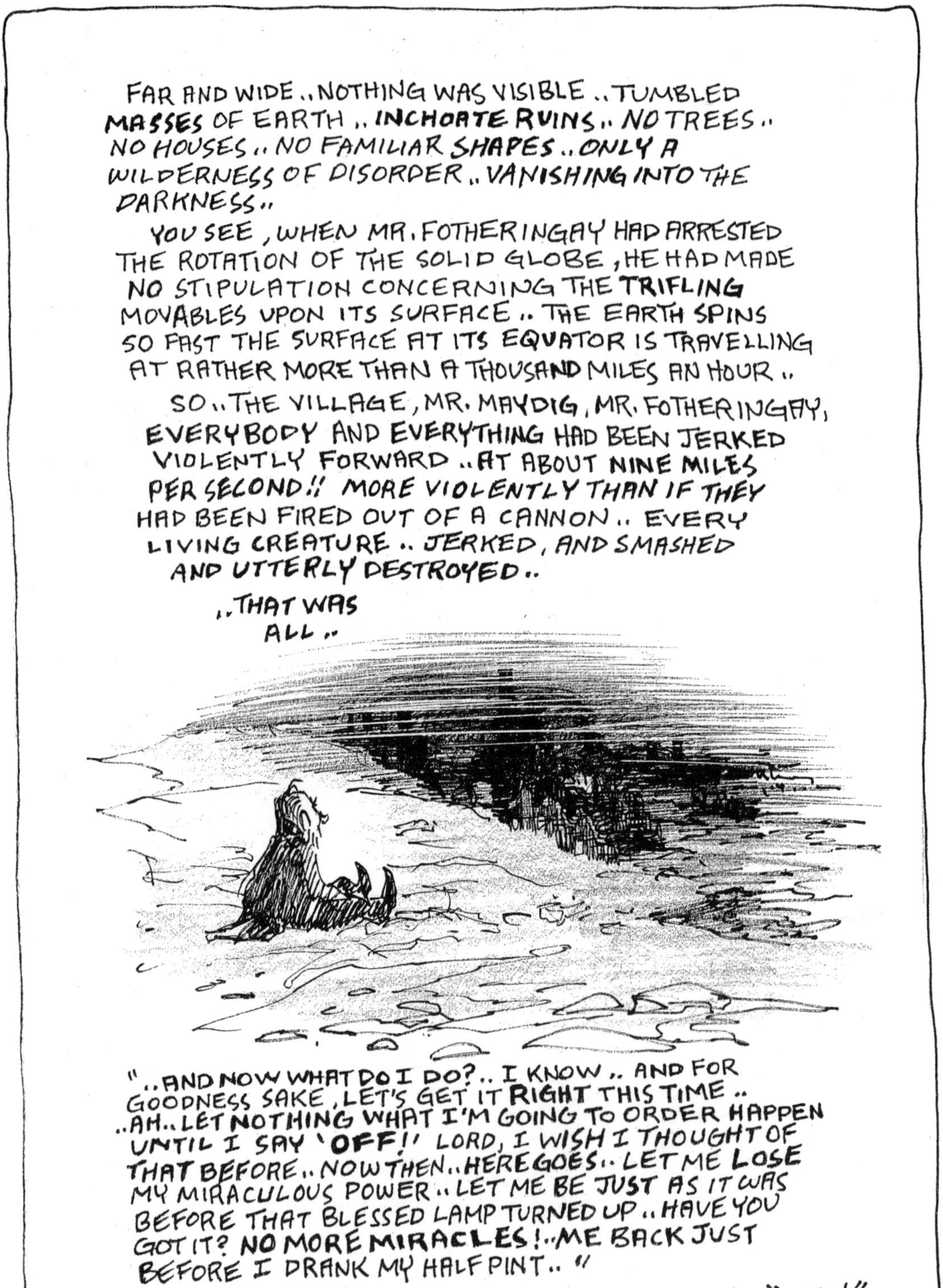
FAR AND WIDE .. NOTHING WAS VISIBLE .. TUMBLED MASSES OF EARTH .. INCHOATE RUINS .. NO TREES .. NO HOUSES .. NO FAMILIAR SHAPES .. ONLY A WILDERNESS OF DISORDER .. VANISHING INTO THE DARKNESS ..
YOU SEE, WHEN MR. FOTHERINGAY HAD ARRESTED THE ROTATION OF THE SOLID GLOBE, HE HAD MADE NO STIPULATION CONCERNING THE TRIFLING MOVABLES UPON ITS SURFACE .. THE EARTH SPINS SO FAST THE SURFACE AT ITS EQUATOR IS TRAVELLING AT RATHER MORE THAN A THOUSAND MILES AN HOUR ..
SO .. THE VILLAGE, MR. MAYDIG, MR. FOTHERINGAY, EVERYBODY AND EVERYTHING HAD BEEN JERKED VIOLENTLY FORWARD .. AT ABOUT NINE MILES PER SECOND!! MORE VIOLENTLY THAN IF THEY HAD BEEN FIRED OUT OF A CANNON .. EVERY LIVING CREATURE .. JERKED, AND SMASHED AND UTTERLY DESTROYED ..
.. THAT WAS ALL ..
".. AND NOW WHAT DO I DO? .. I KNOW .. AND FOR GOODNESS SAKE, LET'S GET IT RIGHT THIS TIME .. .. AH .. LET NOTHING WHAT I'M GOING TO ORDER HAPPEN UNTIL I SAY 'OFF!' LORD, I WISH I THOUGHT OF THAT BEFORE .. NOW THEN .. HERE GOES .. LET ME LOSE MY MIRACULOUS POWER .. LET ME BE JUST AS IT WAS BEFORE THAT BLESSED LAMP TURNED UP .. HAVE YOU GOT IT? NO MORE MIRACLES! .. ME BACK JUST BEFORE I DRANK MY HALF PINT .. "
.. HE CLOSED HIS EYES .. AND SAID .. "OFF!"

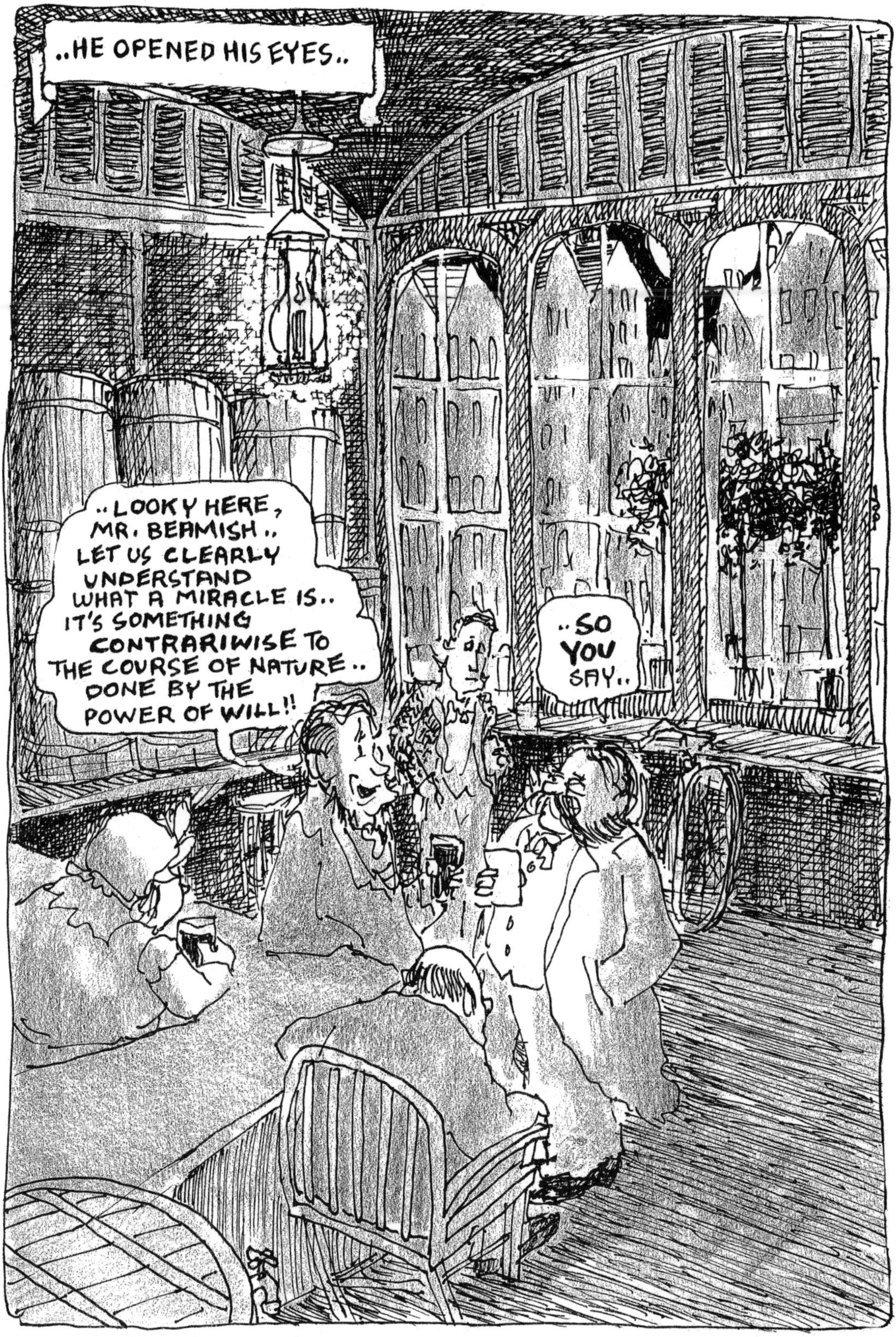
..HE OPENED HIS EYES..
..LOOKY HERE, MR. BEAMISH.. LET US CLEARLY UNDERSTAND WHAT A MIRACLE IS.. IT'S SOMETHING CONTRARIWISE TO THE COURSE OF NATURE.. DONE BY THE POWER OF WILL!!
..SO YOU SAY..

The Temptation of Harringay

A tale by **H. G. WELLS**

illustrated by **MILTON KNIGHT**

It is quite impossible to say whether this thing really happened. It depends entirely on the word of R. M. Harringay, who is an artist.

Following his version of the affair, the narrative deposes that Harringay went into his studio about ten o'clock to see what he could make of the head that he had been working at the day before. The head in question was that of an Italian organ-grinder, and Harringay thought — but was not quite sure — that the title would be the "Vigil." So far he is frank, and his narrative bears the stamp of truth. He had seen the man expectant for pennies, and with a promptness that suggested genius, had had him in at once.

"Kneel. Look up at that bracket," said Harringay. "As if you expected pennies.

"Don't *grin!*" said Harringay. "I don't want to paint your gums. Look as though you were unhappy."

Now, after a night's rest, the picture proved decidedly unsatisfactory. "It's good work," said Harringay. "That little bit in the neck... But."

He walked about the studio, and looked at the thing from this point and from that. Then he said a wicked word. In the original the word is given.

"Painting," he says he said. "Just a painting of an organ-grinder — a mere portrait. If it was a live organ-grinder

I wouldn't mind. But somehow I never make things alive. I wonder if my imagination is wrong."

This, too, has a truthful air. His imagination *is* wrong.

"That creative touch! To take canvas and pigment and make a man—as Adam was made of red ochre! But this thing! If you met it walking about the streets you would know it was only a studio production. The little boys would tell it to 'G'arn'ome and git frimed.' Some little touch... Well—it won't do as it is."

He went to the blinds and began to pull them down. They were made of blue holland with the rollers at the bottom of the window, so that you pull them down to get more light. He gathered his palette, brushes, and mahl stick from his table. Then he turned to the picture and put a speck of brown in the corner of the mouth; and shifted his attention thence to the pupil of the eye. Then he decided that the chin was a trifle too impassive for a vigil.

Presently he put down his impedimenta, and lighting a pipe surveyed the progress of his work. "I'm hanged if the thing isn't sneering at me," said Harringay, and he still believes it sneered.

The animation of the figure had certainly increased, but scarcely in the direction he wished. There was no mistake about the sneer. "Vigil of the Unbeliever," said Harringay. "Rather subtle and clever that! But the left eyebrow isn't cynical enough."

He went and dabbed at the eyebrow, and added a little to the lobe of the ear to suggest materialism. Further consideration ensued. "Vigil's off, I'm afraid," said Harringay. "Why not Mephistopheles? But that's a bit *too* common. 'A Friend of the Doge'—not so seedy. The armour won't do, though, too Camelot. How about a scarlet robe and call him 'One of the Sacred College'? Humor in that, and an appreciation of Middle Italian History.

"There's always Benvenuto Cellini," said Harringay; "with a clever suggestion of a gold cup in one corner. But that would scarcely suit the complexion."

He describes himself as babbling in this way in order to keep down an unaccountably unpleasant sensation of fear. The thing was certainly acquiring anything but a pleasing expression. Yet it was as certainly becoming far more of a living thing than it had been—if a sinister one—far more alive than anything he had ever painted before. "Call it 'Portrait of a Gentleman,'" said Harringay; "'A Certain Gentleman.'"

"Won't do," said Harringay, still keeping up his courage. "Kind of thing they call Bad Taste. That sneer will have to come out. That gone, and a little more fire in the eye—never noticed how warm his eye was before—and he might do for—? What price 'Passionate Pilgrim'? But that devilish face won't do—*this* side of the Channel.

"Some little inaccuracy does it," he said, "eyebrows probably too oblique"—therewith pulling the blind lower to get a better light, and resuming palette and brushes.

The face on the canvas seemed animated by a spirit of its own. Where the expression of diablerie came in he found impossible to discover. Experiment was necessary. The eyebrows—it could scarcely be the eyebrows? But he altered them. No, that was no better; in fact, if anything, a trifle more satanic. The corner of the mouth? Pah! more than ever a leer—and now, retouched, it was ominously grim. The eye, then? Catastrophe! He had filled his brush with vermilion instead of brown, and yet he had felt sure it was brown! The eye seemed now to have rolled in its socket, and was glaring at him an eye of fire. In a flash of passion, possibly with something of the courage of panic, he struck the brush full of bright red athwart the picture; and then a very curious thing, a very strange thing indeed, occurred—if it *did* occur.

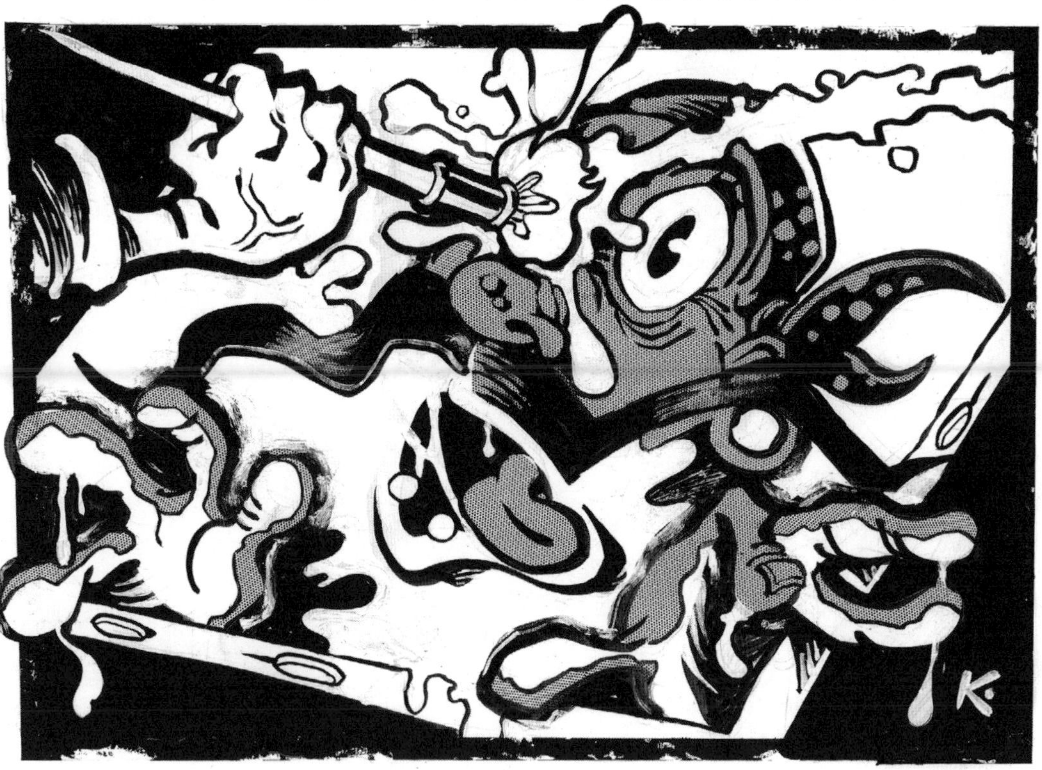
K.

The diabolified Italian before him shut both his eyes, pursed his mouth, and wiped the color off his face with his hand.

Then the red eye opened again, with a sound like the opening of lips, and the face smiled. "That was rather hasty of you," said the picture.

Harringay states that, now that the worst had happened, his self-possession returned. He had a saving persuasion that devils were reasonable creatures.

"Why do you keep moving about then," he said, "making faces and all that—sneering and squinting, while I am painting you?"

"I don't," said the picture.

"You *do*," said Harringay.

"It's yourself," said the picture.

"It's *not* myself," said Harringay.

"It *is* yourself," said the picture. "No! don't go hitting me with paint again, because it's true. You have been trying to fluke an expression on my face all the morning. Really, you haven't an idea what your picture ought to look like."

"I have," said Harringay.

"You have *not*," said the picture: "You *never* have with your pictures. You always start with the vaguest presentiment of what you are going to do; it is to be something beautiful—you are sure of that—and devout, perhaps, or tragic; but beyond that it is all experiment and chance. My dear fellow! You don't think you can paint a picture like that?"

Now it must be remembered that for what follows we have only Harringay's word.

"I shall paint a picture exactly as I like," said Harringay, calmly.

This seemed to disconcert the picture a little. "You can't paint a picture without an inspiration," it remarked.

"But I *had* an inspiration—for this."

"Inspiration!" sneered the sardonic figure, "a fancy that came from your seeing an organ-grinder looking up at a window! Vigil! Ha, ha! You just started painting on the chance of something coming—that's

what you did. And when I saw you at it I came. I want a talk with you!

"Art, with you," said the picture – "it's a poor business. You potter. I don't know how it is, but you don't seem able to throw your soul into it. You know too much. It hampers you. In the midst of your enthusiasms you ask yourself whether something like this has not been done before. And..."

"Look here," said Harringay, who had expected something better than criticism from the devil. "Are you going to talk studio to me?" He filled his number twelve hoghair with red paint.

"The true artist," said the picture, "is always an ignorant man. An artist who theorizes about his work is no longer artist but critic. Wagner... I say! – What's that red paint for?"

"I'm going to paint you out," said Harringay. "I don't want to hear all that Tommy Rot. If you think just because I'm an artist by trade I'm going to talk studio to you, you make a precious mistake."

"One minute," said the picture, evidently alarmed. "I want to make you an offer – a genuine offer. It's right what I'm saying. You lack inspirations. Well. No doubt you've heard of the Cathedral of Cologne, and the Devil's Bridge, and –"

"Rubbish," said Harringay. "Do you think I want to go to perdition simply for the pleasure of painting a good picture, and getting it slated. Take that."

His blood was up. His danger only nerved him to action, so he says. So he planted a dab of vermilion in his creature's mouth. The Italian spluttered and tried to wipe it off – evidently horribly surprised. And then – according to Harringay – there began a very remarkable struggle, Harringay splashing away with the red paint, and the picture wriggling about and wiping it off as fast as he put it on. "Two masterpieces," said the demon. "Two indubitable masterpieces for a Chelsea artist's soul. It's a bargain?" Harringay replied with the paint brush.

For a few minutes nothing could be heard but the brush going and the spluttering and ejaculations of the Italian. A lot of the strokes he caught on his arm and hand, though Harringay got over his guard often enough. Presently the paint on the palette gave out and the two antagonists stood breathless, regarding each other. The picture was so smeared with red that it looked as if it had been rolling about a slaughterhouse, and it was painfully out of breath and very uncomfortable with the wet paint trickling down its neck. Still, the first round was in its favour on the whole. "Think," it said, sticking pluckily to its point, "two supreme masterpieces – in different styles. Each equivalent to the Cathedral..."

"I know," said Harringay, and rushed out of the studio and along the passage towards his wife's boudoir.

In another minute he was back with a large tin of enamel – Hedge Sparrow's Egg Tint, it was, and a brush. At the sight of that the artistic devil with the red eye began to scream. "*Three* masterpieces – culminating masterpieces."

Harringay delivered cut two across the demon, and followed with a thrust in the eye. There was an indistinct rumbling. "*Four* masterpieces," and a spitting sound.

But Harringay had the upper hand now and meant to keep it. With rapid, bold strokes he continued to paint over the writhing canvas, until at last it was a uniform field of shining Hedge Sparrow tint. Once the mouth reappeared and got as far as "Five master –" before he filled it with enamel; and near the end the red eye opened and glared at him indignantly. But at last nothing remained save a gleaming panel of drying enamel. For a little while a faint stirring beneath the surface puckered it slightly here and there, but presently even that died away and the thing was perfectly still.

Then Harringay – according to Harringay's account – lit his pipe and sat down and stared at the enameled canvas, and tried to make out clearly what had happened. Then he walked round behind it, to see if the back of it was at all remarkable. Then it was he began to regret that he had not photographed the Devil before he painted him out.

This is Harringay's story – not mine. He supports it by a small canvas (24 by 20) enameled a pale green, and by violent asseverations. It is also true that he never has produced a masterpiece, and in the opinion of his intimate friends probably never will.

ILLUSTRATIONS ©2002 MILTON KNIGHT

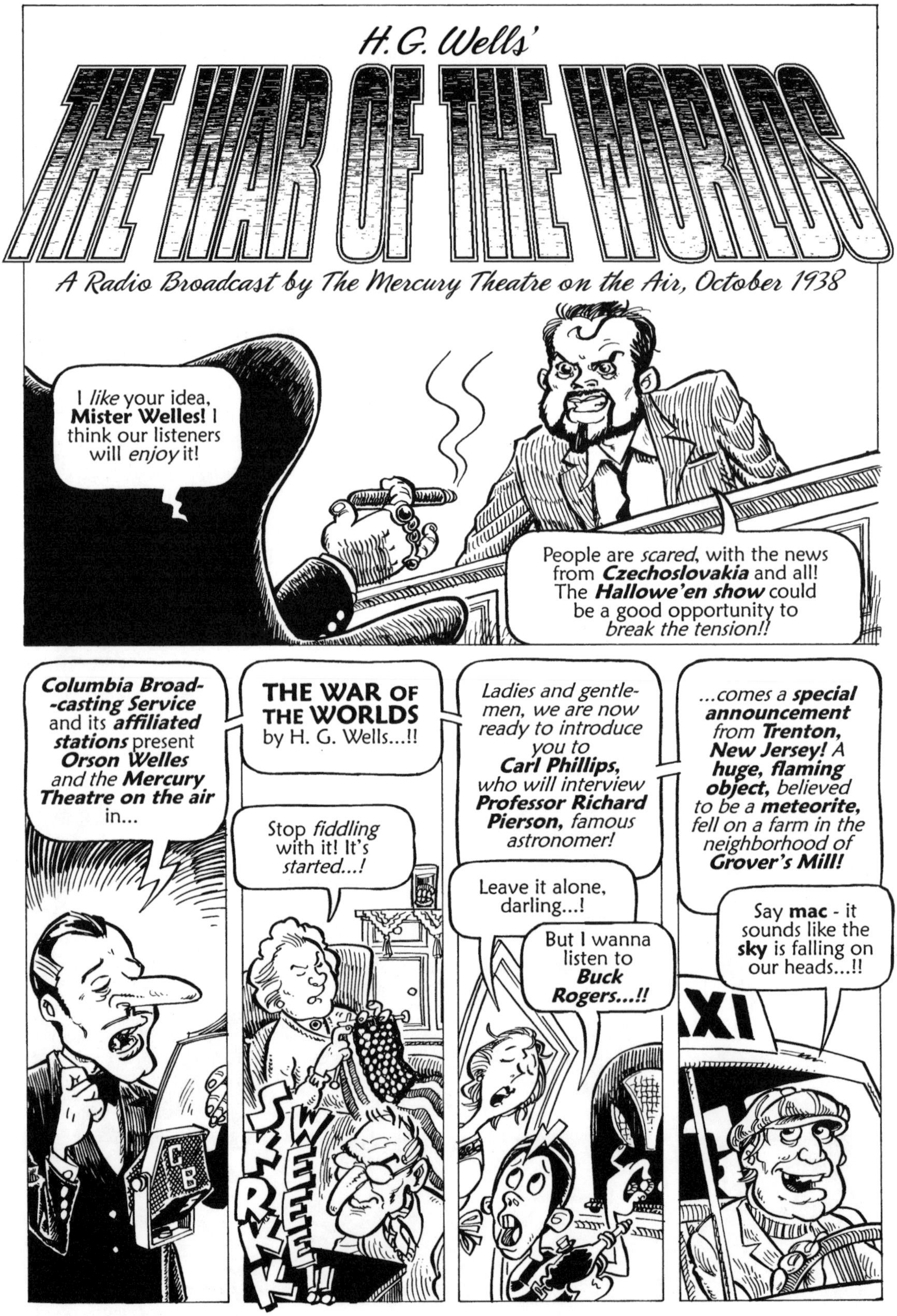
H. G. Wells'
THE WAR OF THE WORLDS
A Radio Broadcast by The Mercury Theatre on the Air, October 1938
I *like* your idea, **Mister Welles!** I think our listeners will *enjoy* it!
People are *scared*, with the news from ***Czechoslovakia*** and all! The ***Hallowe'en show*** could be a good opportunity to *break the tension!!*
Columbia Broad--casting Service *and its* ***affiliated stations*** *present* ***Orson Welles*** *and the* ***Mercury Theatre on the air*** *in...*
THE WAR OF THE WORLDS by H. G. Wells...!!
Stop *fiddling* with it! It's *started...!*
SKREEK
SWEEEEK!!
Ladies and gentle-men, we are now ready to introduce you to ***Carl Phillips,*** *who will interview* ***Professor Richard Pierson,*** *famous astronomer!*
Leave it alone, darling...!
But I wanna listen to ***Buck Rogers...!!***
...comes a ***special announcement*** *from* ***Trenton, New Jersey! A huge, flaming object,*** *believed to be a* ***meteorite,*** *fell on a farm in the neighborhood of* ***Grover's Mill!***
Say **mac** - it sounds like the **sky** is falling on our heads...!!
AXI

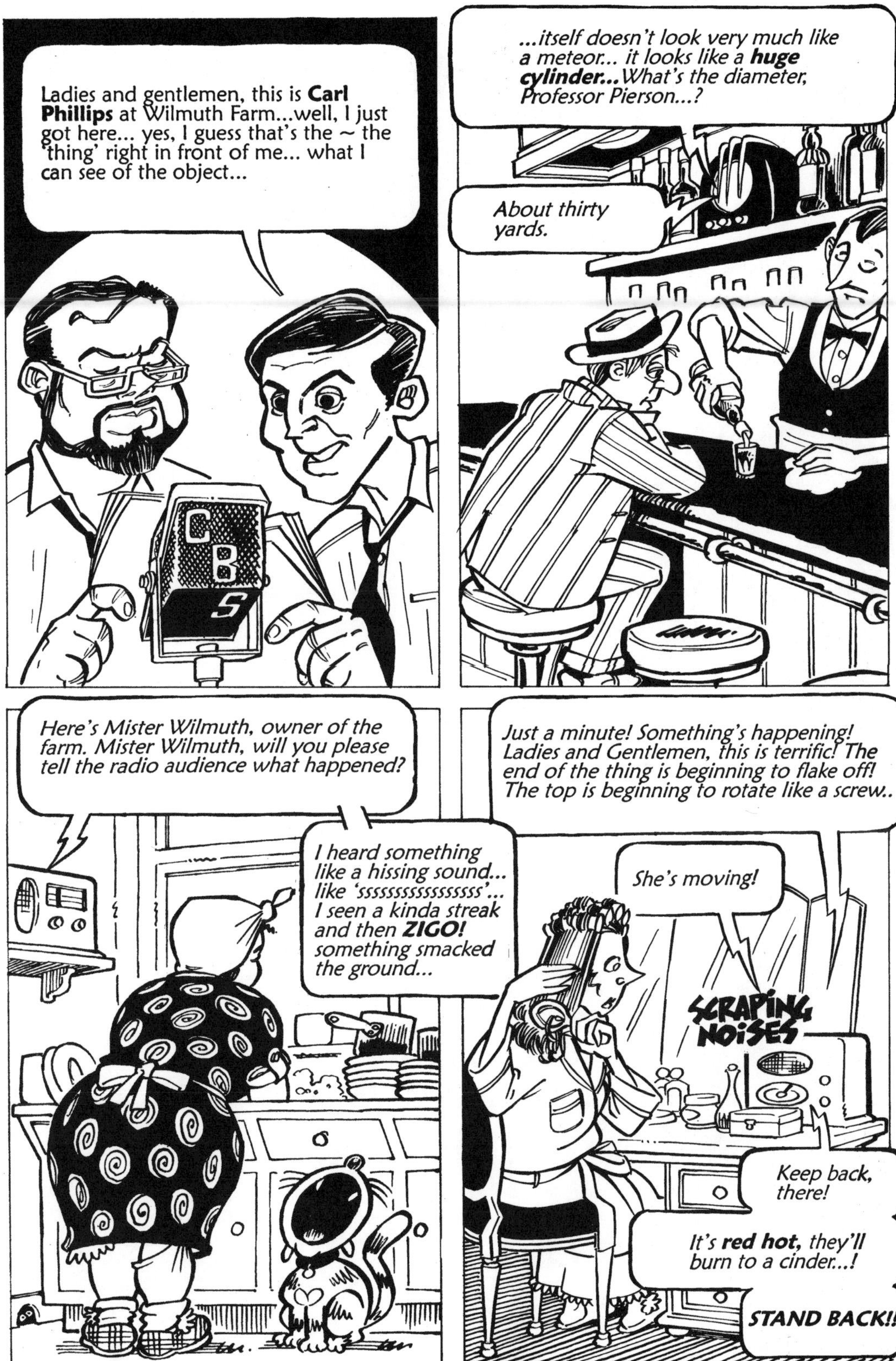
Ladies and gentlemen, this is **Carl Phillips** at Wilmuth Farm...well, I just got here... yes, I guess that's the ~ the 'thing' right in front of me... what I can see of the object...
CBS
*...itself doesn't look very much like a meteor... it looks like a **huge cylinder...** What's the diameter, Professor Pierson...?*
About thirty yards.
Here's Mister Wilmuth, owner of the farm. Mister Wilmuth, will you please tell the radio audience what happened?
*I heard something like a hissing sound... like 'ssssssssssssssss'... I seen a kinda streak and then **ZIGO!** something smacked the ground...*
Just a minute! Something's happening! Ladies and Gentlemen, this is terrific! The end of the thing is beginning to flake off! The top is beginning to rotate like a screw..
She's moving!
SCRAPING NOISES
Keep back, there!
*It's **red hot,** they'll burn to a cinder...!*
STAND BACK!!

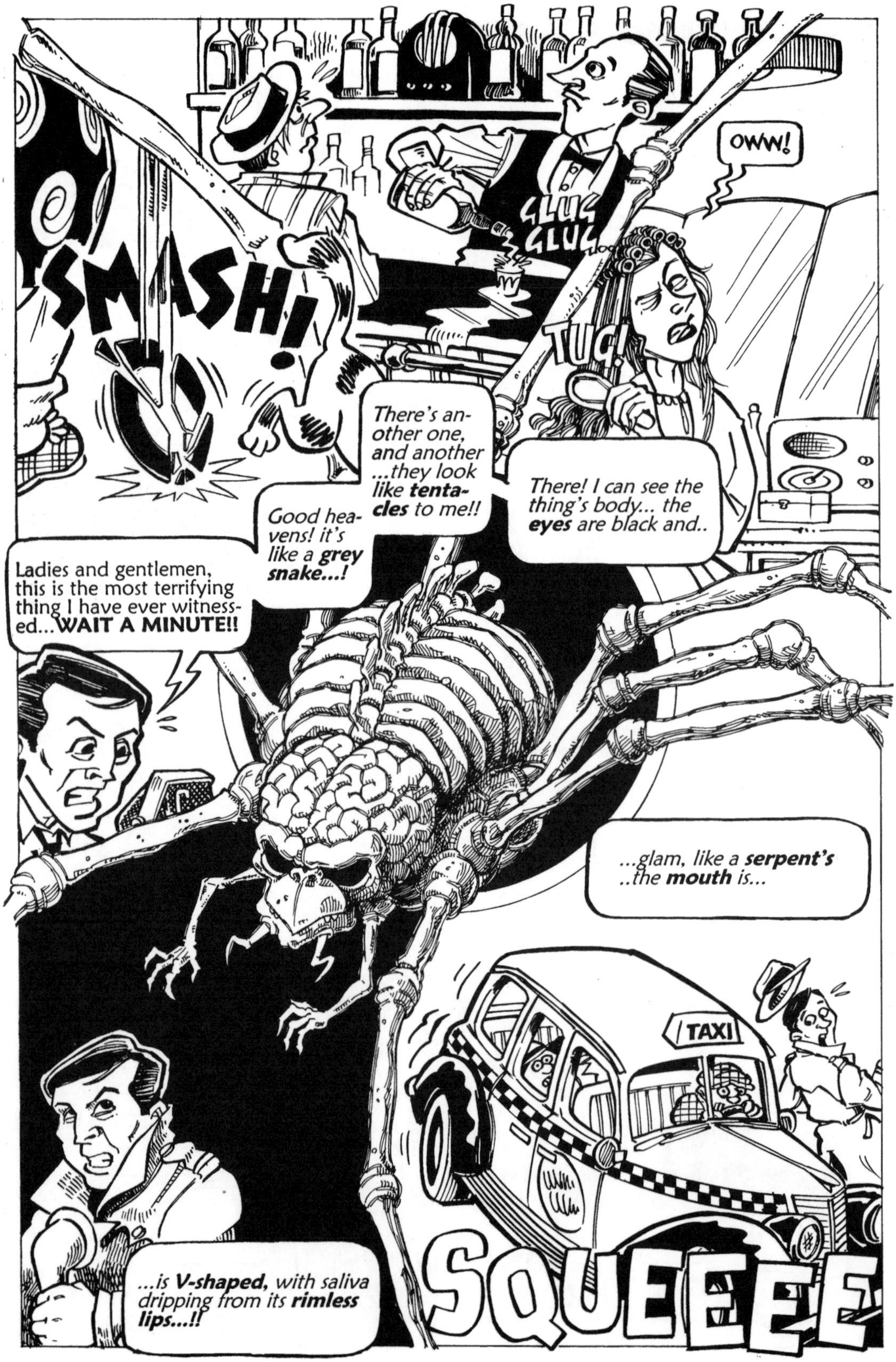
OWW!
GLUG GLUG
SMASH!
TUG!
There's another one, and another ...they look like **tentacles** to me!!
Good heavens! it's like a **grey snake...!**
There! I can see the thing's body... the **eyes** are black and..
Ladies and gentlemen, this is the most terrifying thing I have ever witnessed... **WAIT A MINUTE!!**
...glam, like a **serpent's** ..the **mouth** is...
TAXI
...is **V-shaped,** with saliva dripping from its **rimless lips...!!**
SQUEEEE

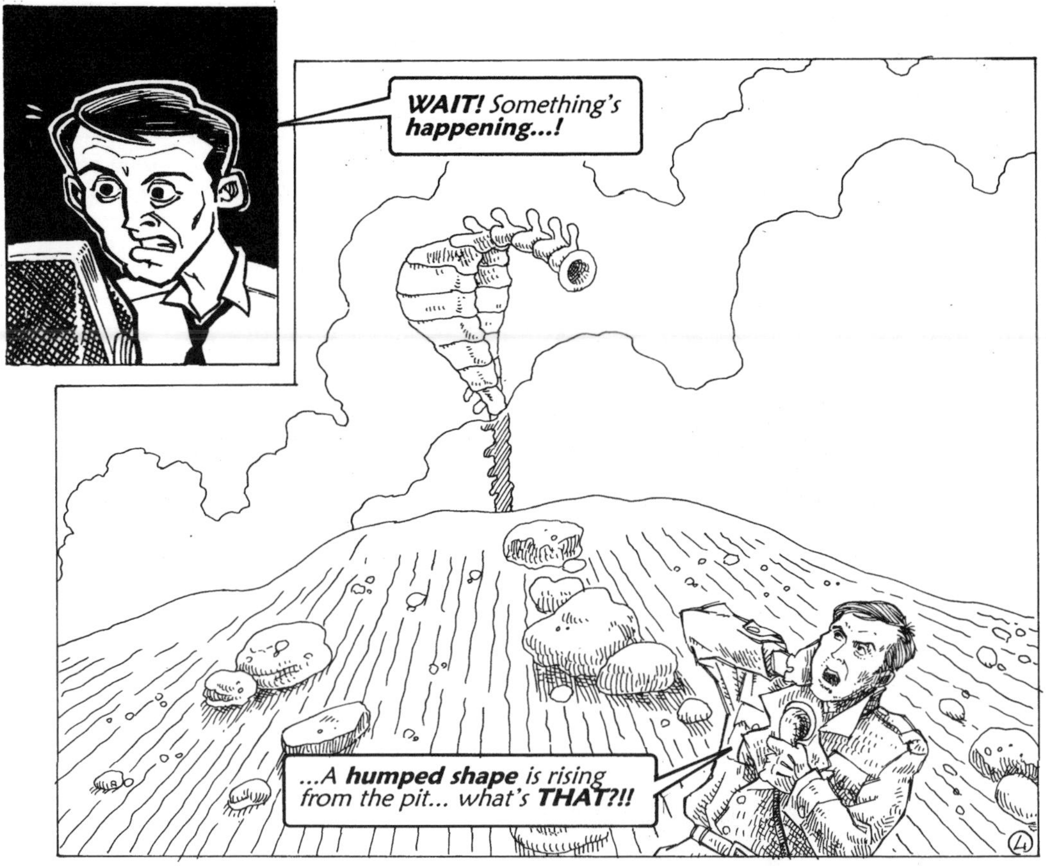
WAIT! Something's happening...!
...A humped shape is rising from the pit... what's THAT?!!

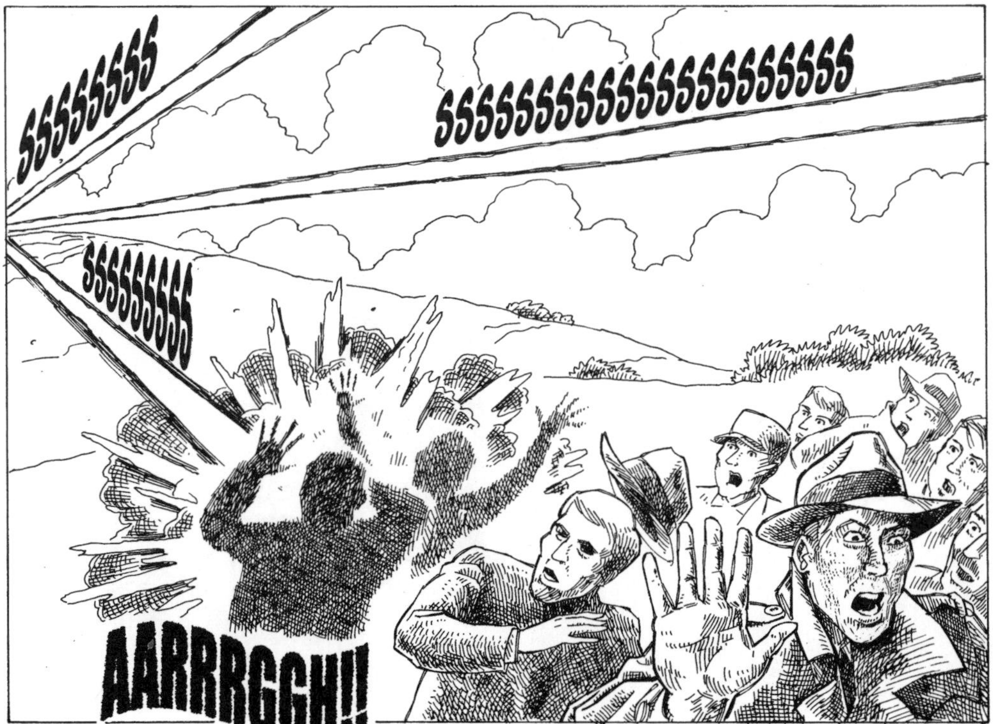
SSSSSSSS
SSSSSSSSSSSSSSSSSSSSSS
SSSSSSSSS
AARRRGGH!!

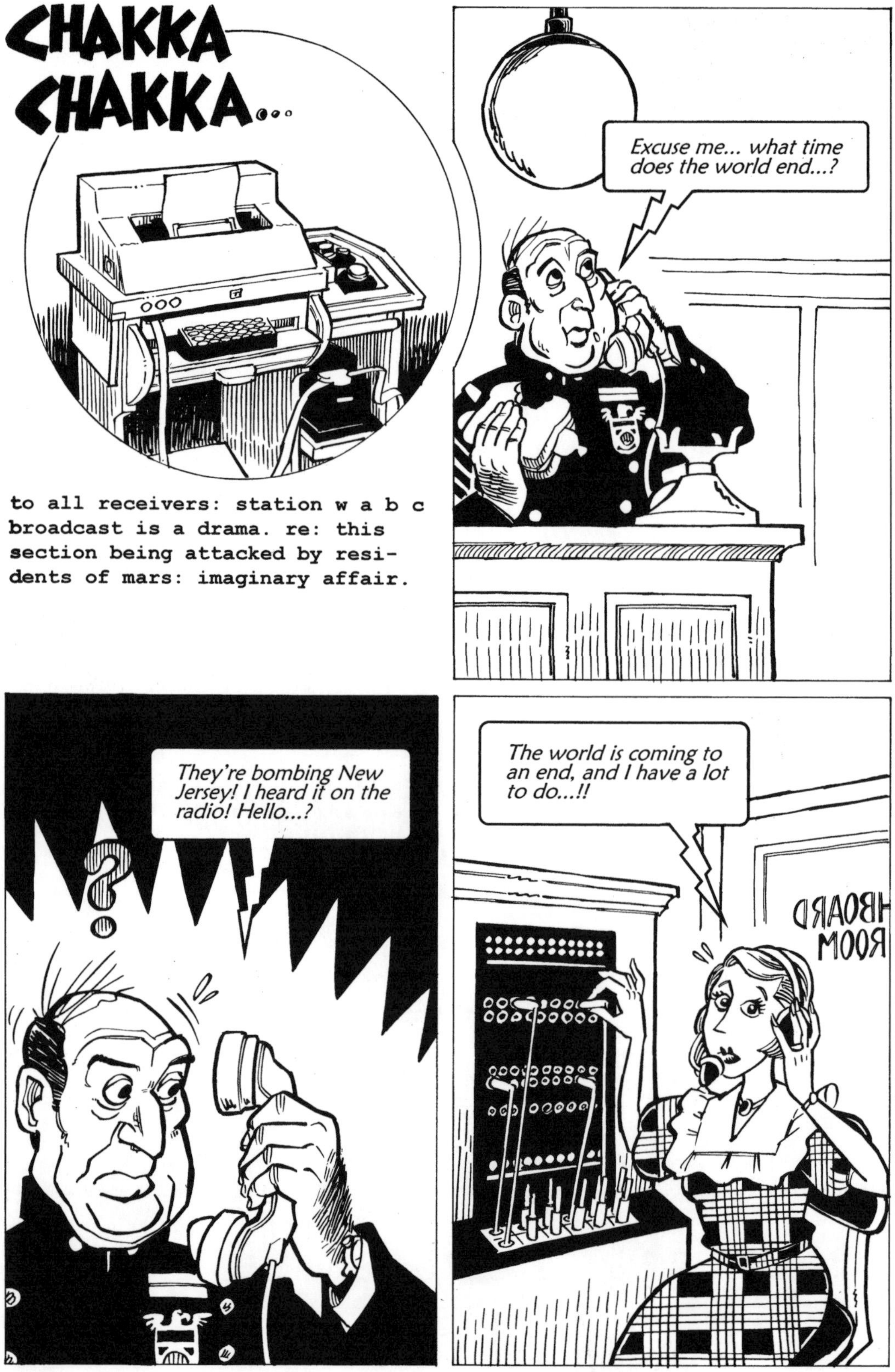
CHAKKA CHAKKA...
to all receivers: station w a b c broadcast is a drama. re: this section being attacked by residents of mars: imaginary affair.
Excuse me... what time does the world end...?
They're bombing New Jersey! I heard it on the radio! Hello...?
The world is coming to an end, and I have a lot to do...!!

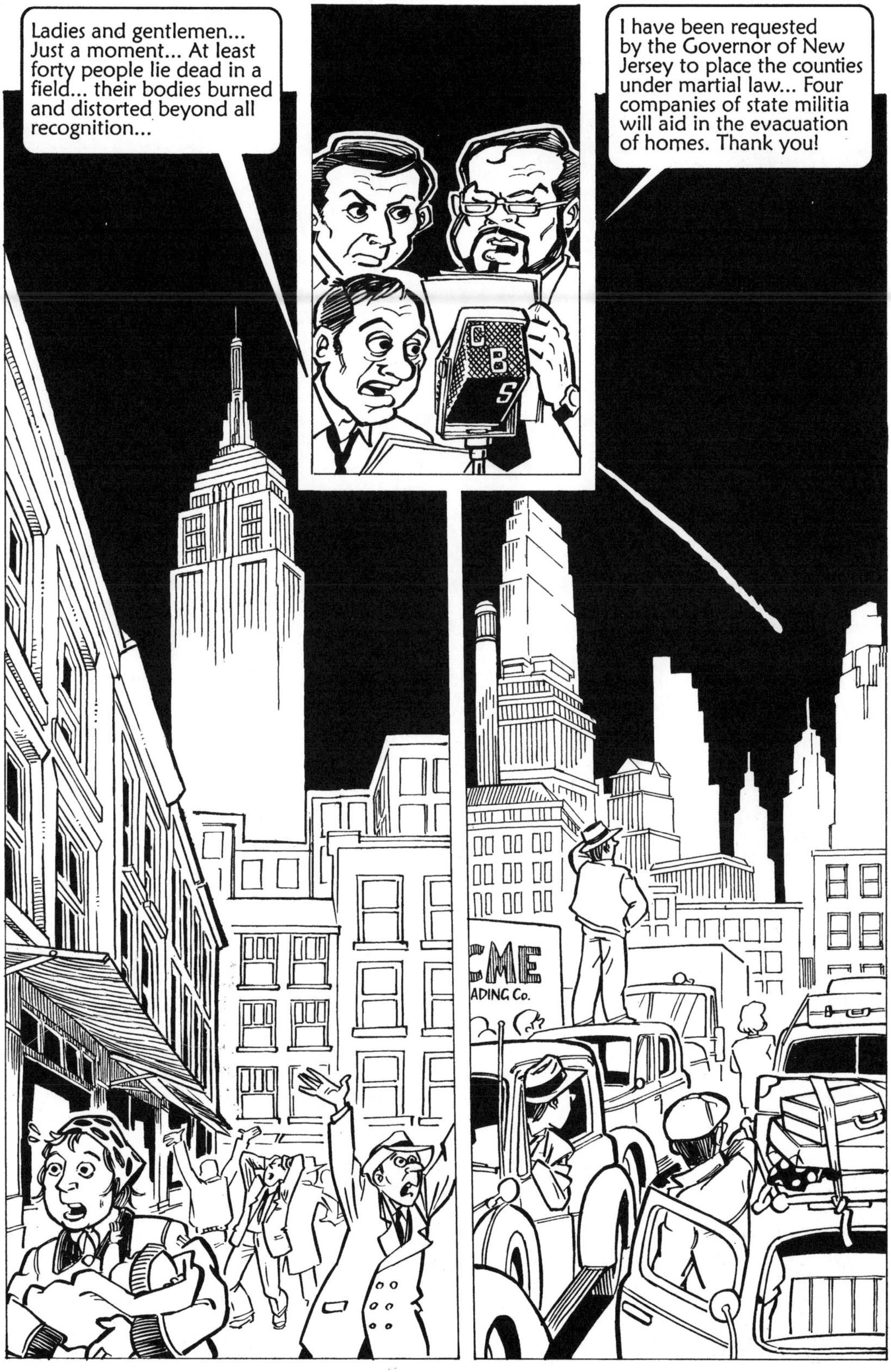
Ladies and gentlemen... Just a moment... At least forty people lie dead in a field... their bodies burned and distorted beyond all recognition...
CBS
I have been requested by the Governor of New Jersey to place the counties under martial law... Four companies of state militia will aid in the evacuation of homes. Thank you!
CME
ADING Co.

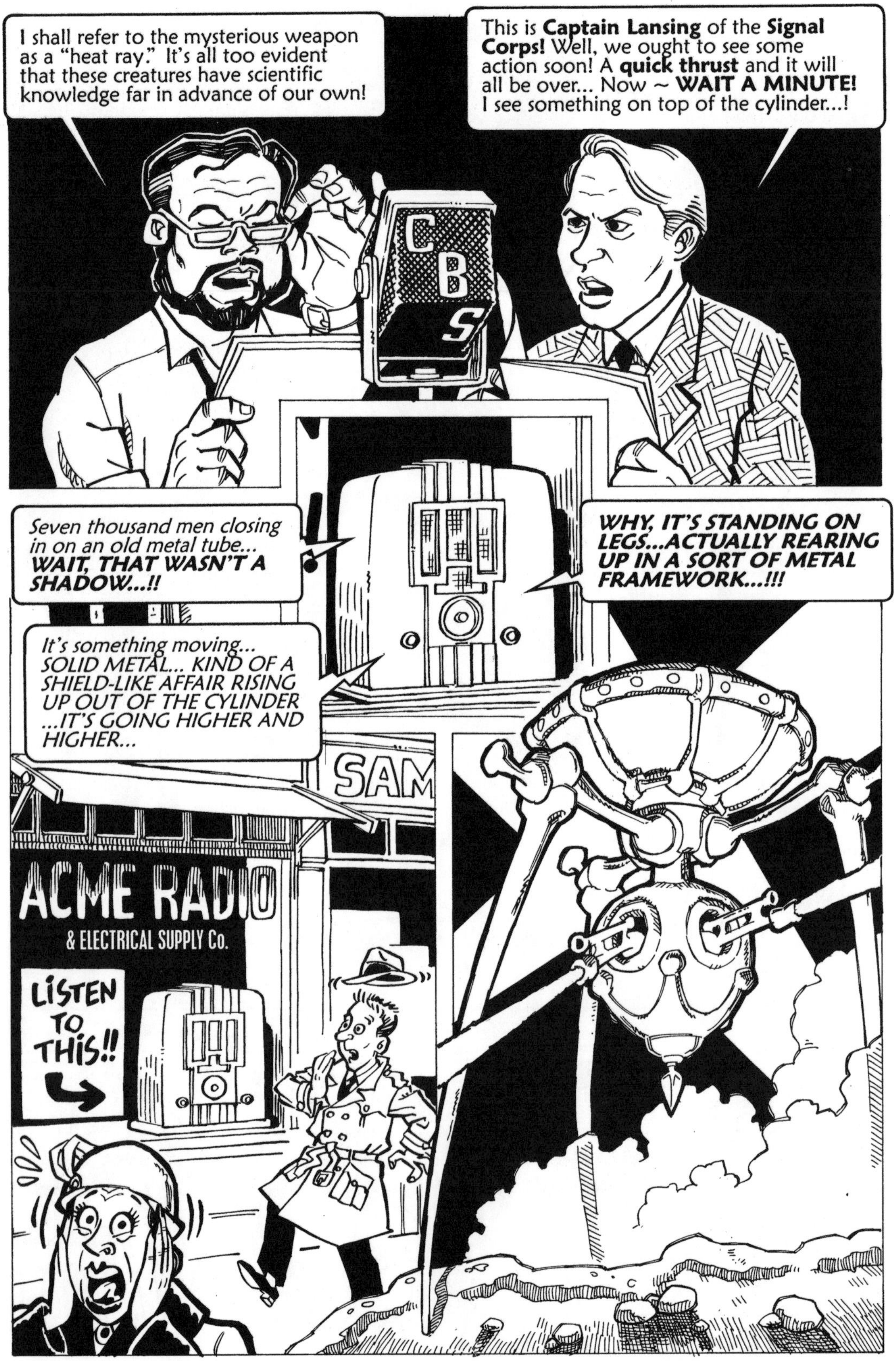

I shall refer to the mysterious weapon as a "heat ray." It's all too evident that these creatures have scientific knowledge far in advance of our own!
This is **Captain Lansing** of the **Signal Corps!** Well, we ought to see some action soon! A **quick thrust** and it will all be over... Now ~ **WAIT A MINUTE!** I see something on top of the cylinder...!
CBS
*Seven thousand men closing in on an old metal tube... **WAIT, THAT WASN'T A SHADOW...!!***
WHY, IT'S STANDING ON LEGS...ACTUALLY REARING UP IN A SORT OF METAL FRAMEWORK...!!!
It's something moving... SOLID METAL... KIND OF A SHIELD-LIKE AFFAIR RISING UP OUT OF THE CYLINDER ...IT'S GOING HIGHER AND HIGHER...
SAM
ACME RADIO
& ELECTRICAL SUPPLY Co.
LISTEN TO THIS!!

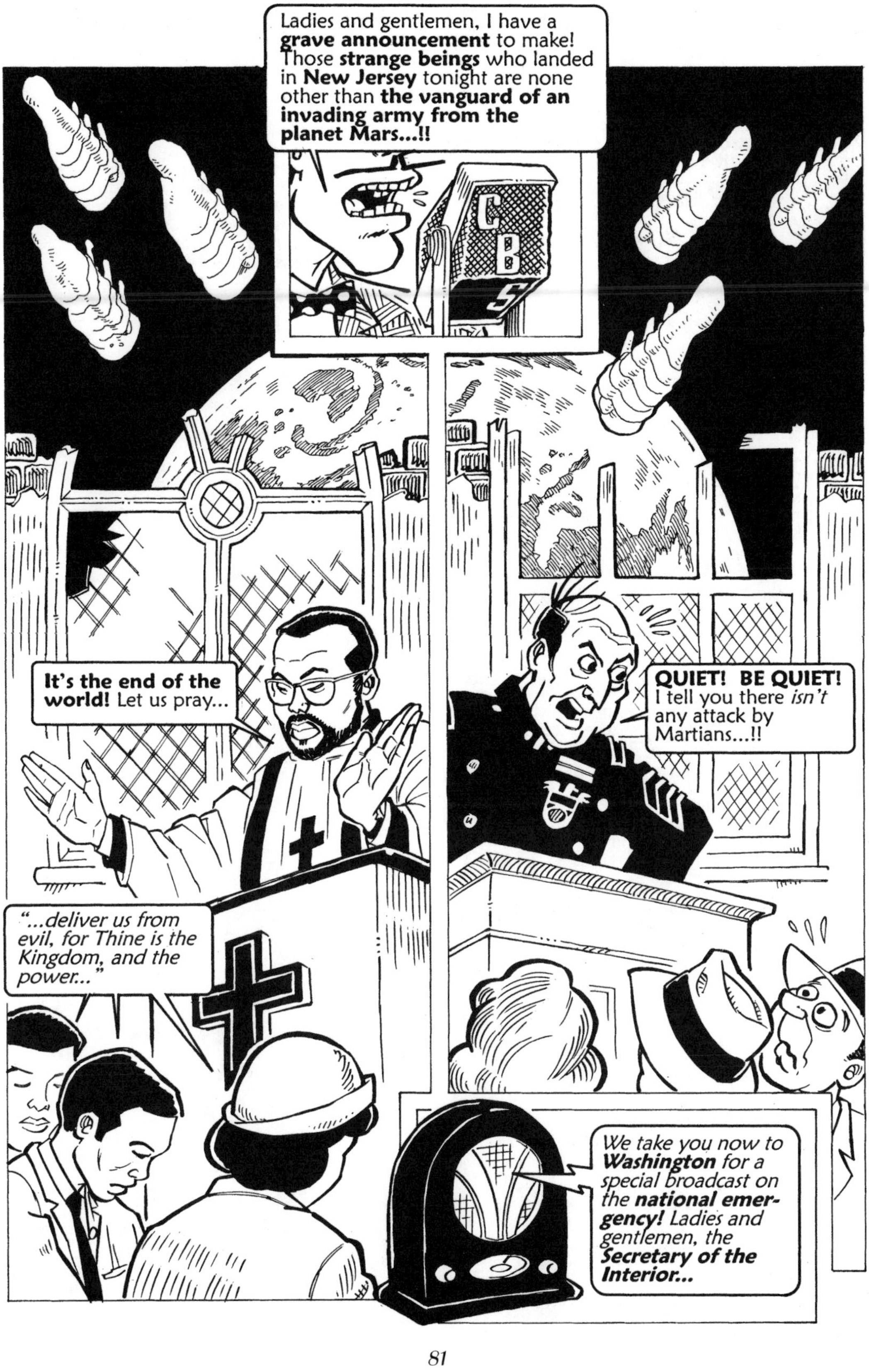
Ladies and gentlemen, I have a **grave announcement** to make! Those **strange beings** who landed in **New Jersey** tonight are none other than **the vanguard of an invading army from the planet Mars...!!**
C B S
It's the end of the world! Let us pray...
QUIET! BE QUIET! I tell you there *isn't* any attack by Martians...!!
"...deliver us from evil, for Thine is the Kingdom, and the power..."
*We take you now to **Washington** for a special broadcast on the **national emergency!** Ladies and gentlemen, the **Secretary of the Interior...***

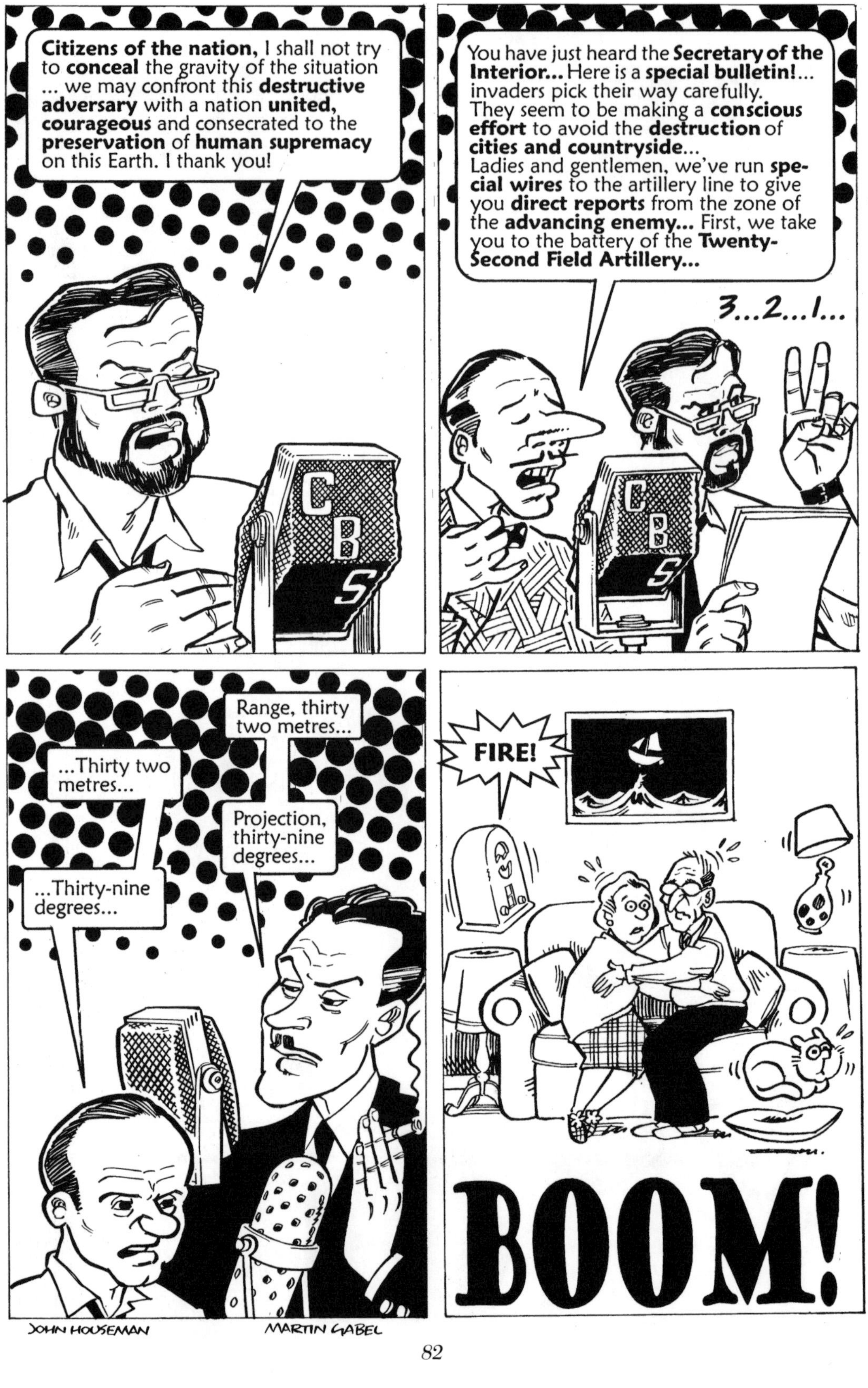
Citizens of the nation, I shall not try to conceal the gravity of the situation ... we may confront this destructive adversary with a nation united, courageous and consecrated to the preservation of human supremacy on this Earth. I thank you!
CBS
You have just heard the Secretary of the Interior... Here is a special bulletin!... invaders pick their way carefully. They seem to be making a conscious effort to avoid the destruction of cities and countryside... Ladies and gentlemen, we've run special wires to the artillery line to give you direct reports from the zone of the advancing enemy... First, we take you to the battery of the Twenty-Second Field Artillery...
3...2...1...
CBS
Range, thirty two metres...
...Thirty two metres...
Projection, thirty-nine degrees...
...Thirty-nine degrees...
JOHN HOUSEMAN
MARTIN GABEL
FIRE!
BOOM!

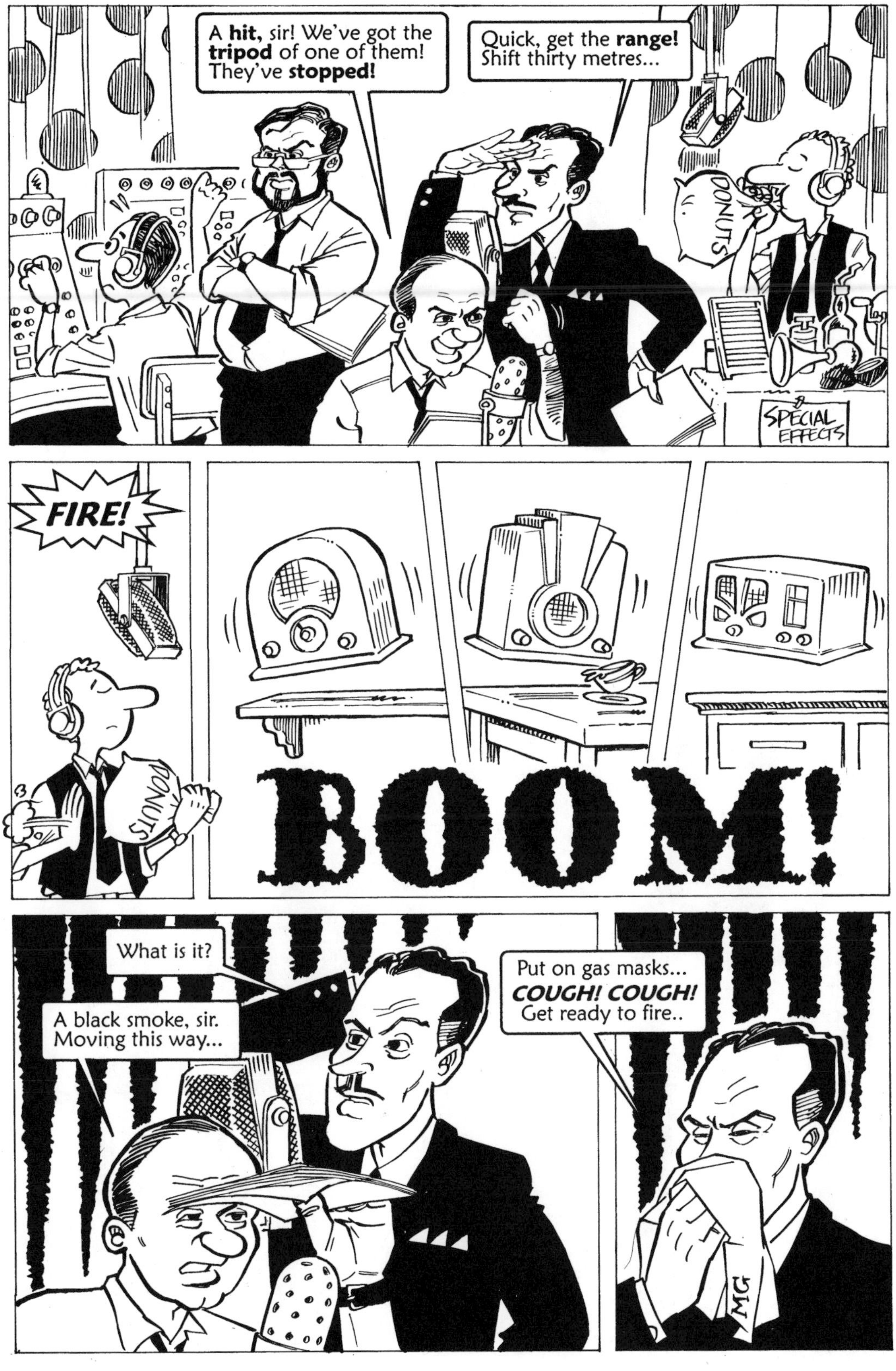
A hit, sir! We've got the tripod of one of them! They've stopped!
Quick, get the range! Shift thirty metres...
DONUTS
SPECIAL EFFECTS
FIRE!
DONUTS
BOOM!
What is it?
A black smoke, sir. Moving this way...
Put on gas masks... COUGH! COUGH! Get ready to fire..
MG

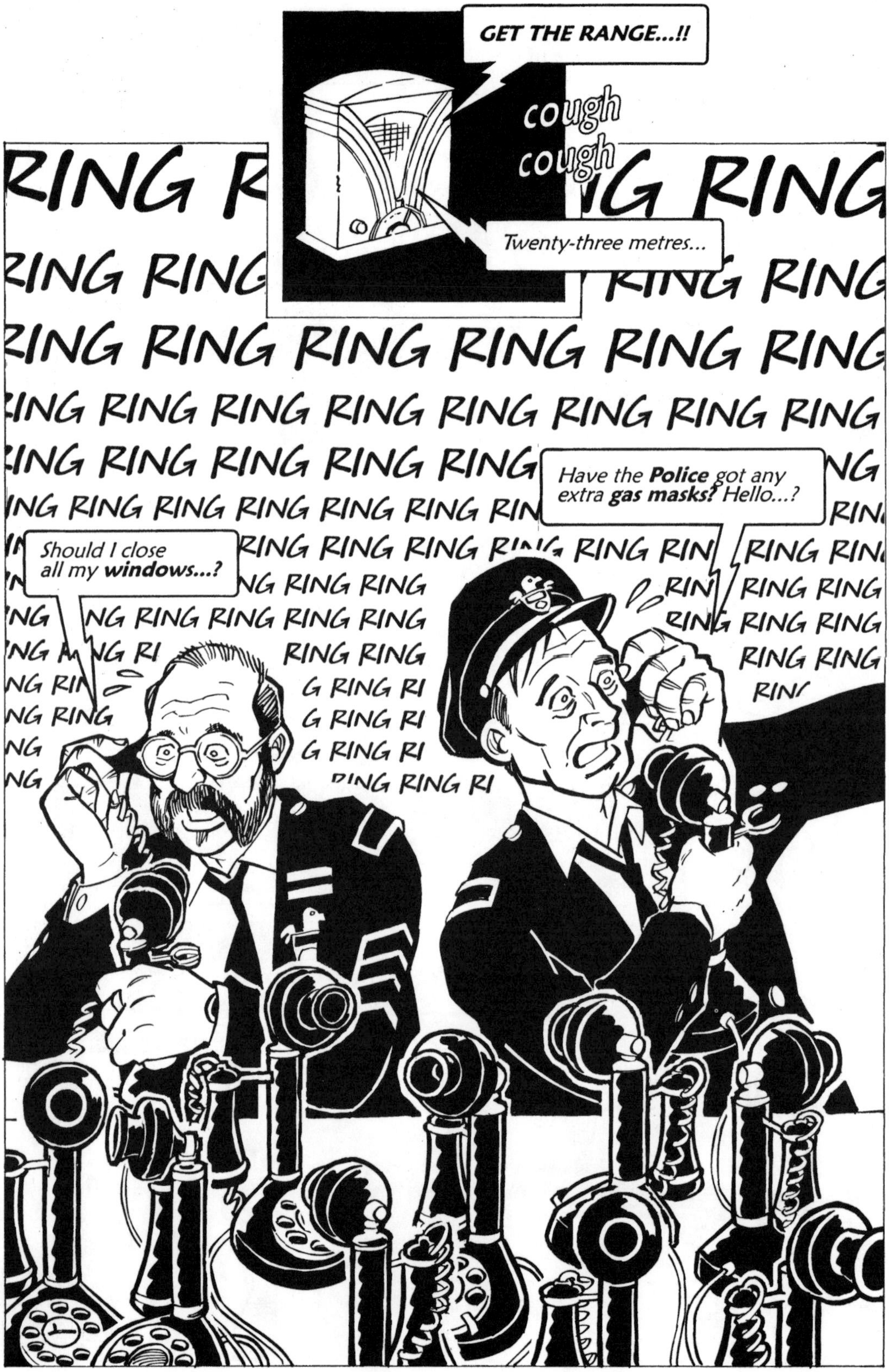
GET THE RANGE...!!
cough
cough
Twenty-three metres...
RING RING RING RING
Have the Police got any extra gas masks? Hello...?
Should I close all my windows...?

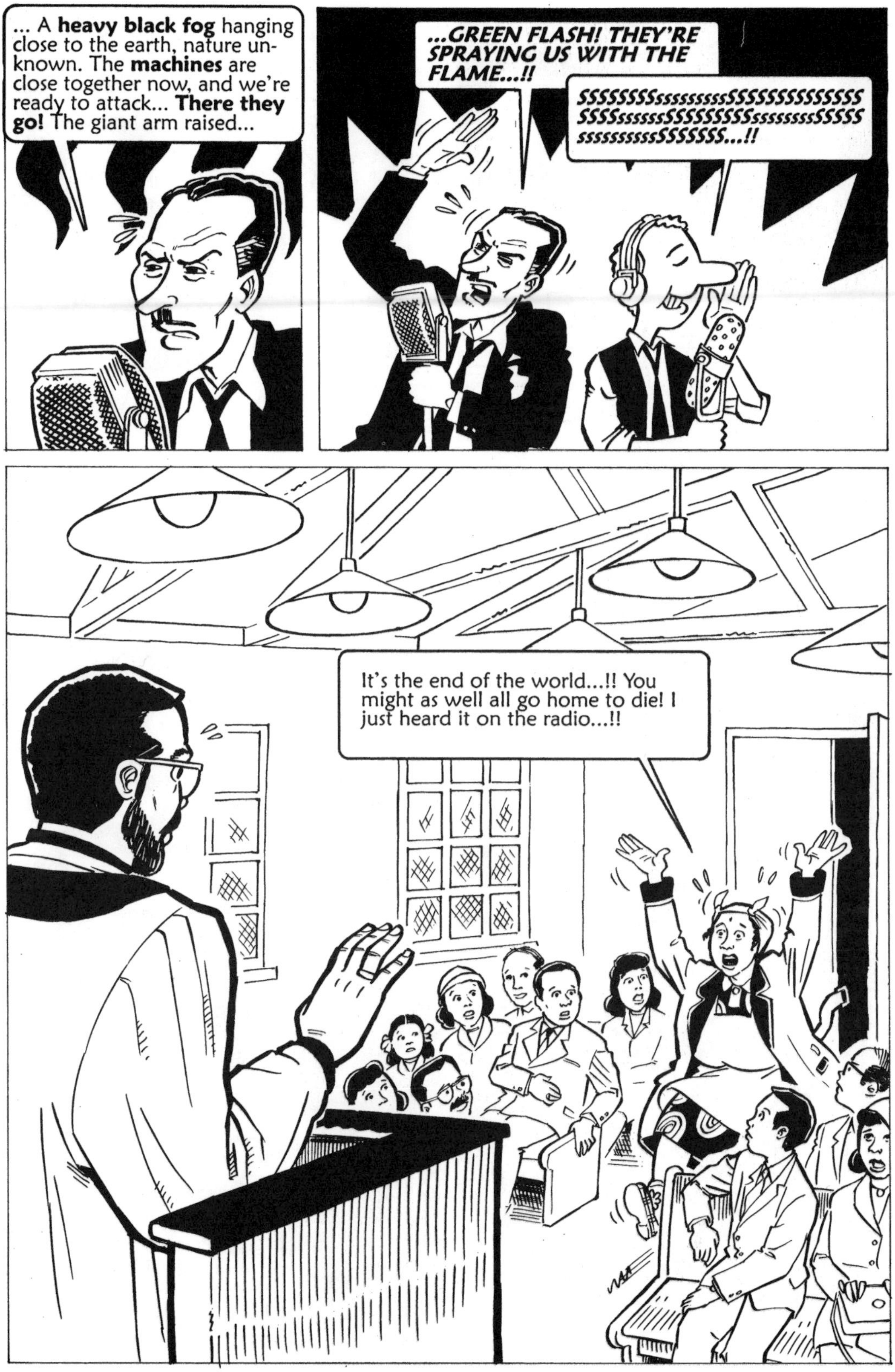
... A **heavy black fog** hanging close to the earth, nature unknown. The **machines** are close together now, and we're ready to attack... **There they go!** The giant arm raised...
...GREEN FLASH! THEY'RE SPRAYING US WITH THE FLAME...!!
SSSSSSSSsssssssssSSSSSSSSSSSSSS SSSSsssssssSSSSSSSSSssssssssssSSSSS ssssssssssSSSSSSS...!!
It's the end of the world...!! You might as well all go home to die! I just heard it on the radio...!!

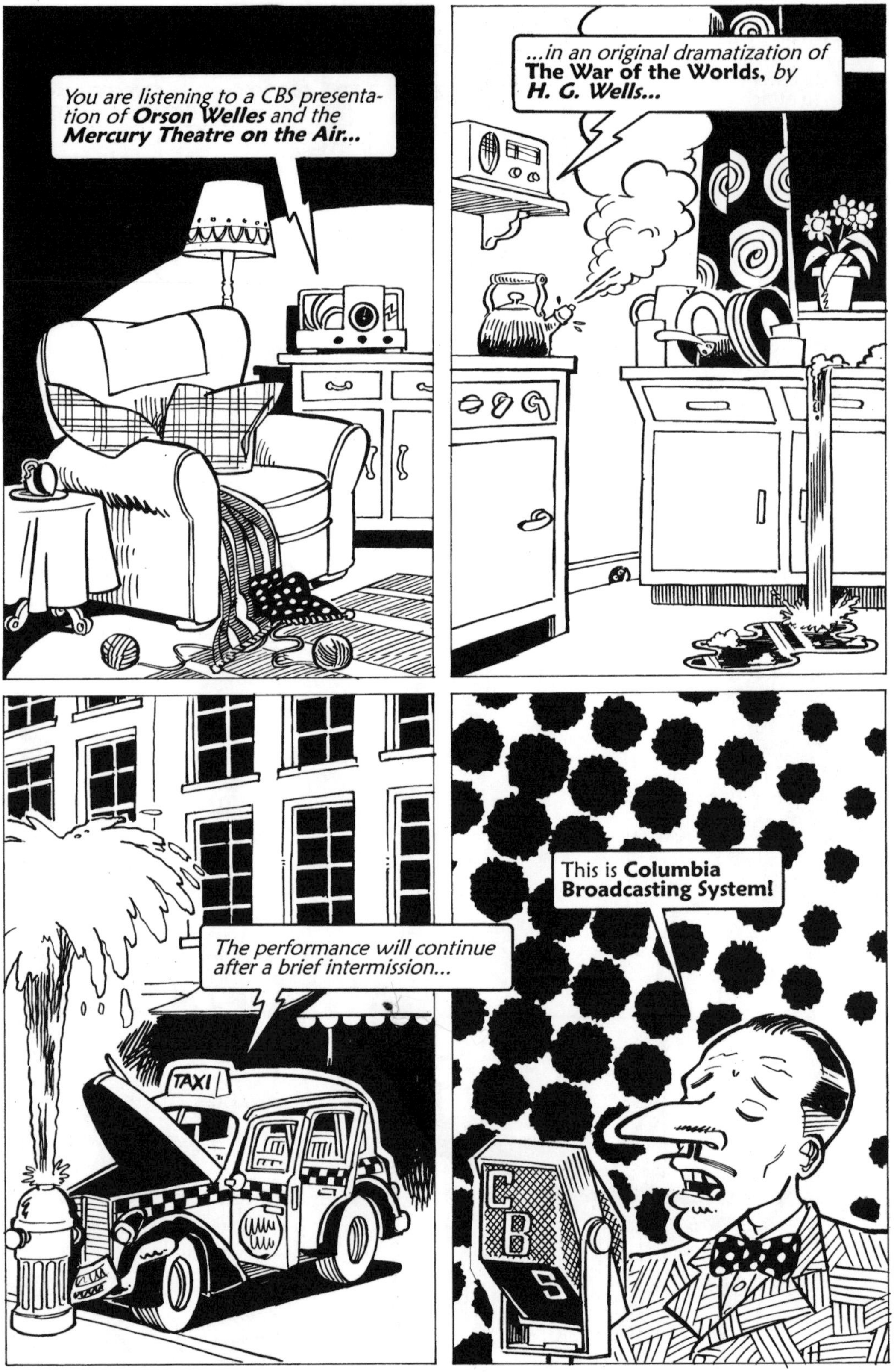
You are listening to a CBS presentation of **Orson Welles** and the **Mercury Theatre on the Air...**
...in an original dramatization of **The War of the Worlds,** by **H. G. Wells...**
TAXI
The performance will continue after a brief intermission...
This is **Columbia Broadcasting System!**
CBS

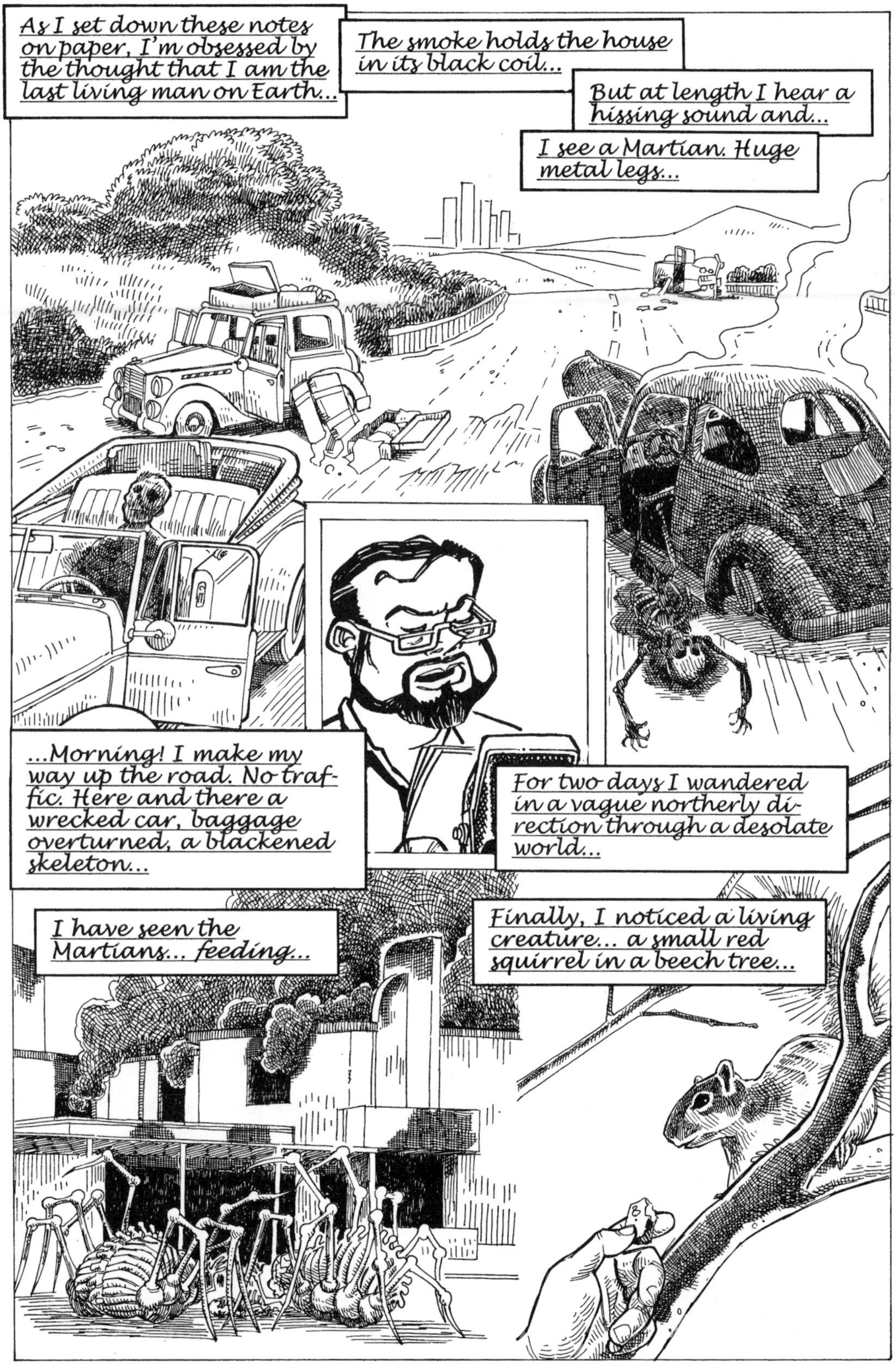
As I set down these notes on paper, I'm obsessed by the thought that I am the last living man on Earth...
The smoke holds the house in its black coil...
But at length I hear a hissing sound and...
I see a Martian. Huge metal legs...
...Morning! I make my way up the road. No traffic. Here and there a wrecked car, baggage overturned, a blackened skeleton...
For two days I wandered in a vague northerly direction through a desolate world...
I have seen the Martians... feeding...
Finally, I noticed a living creature... a small red squirrel in a beech tree...

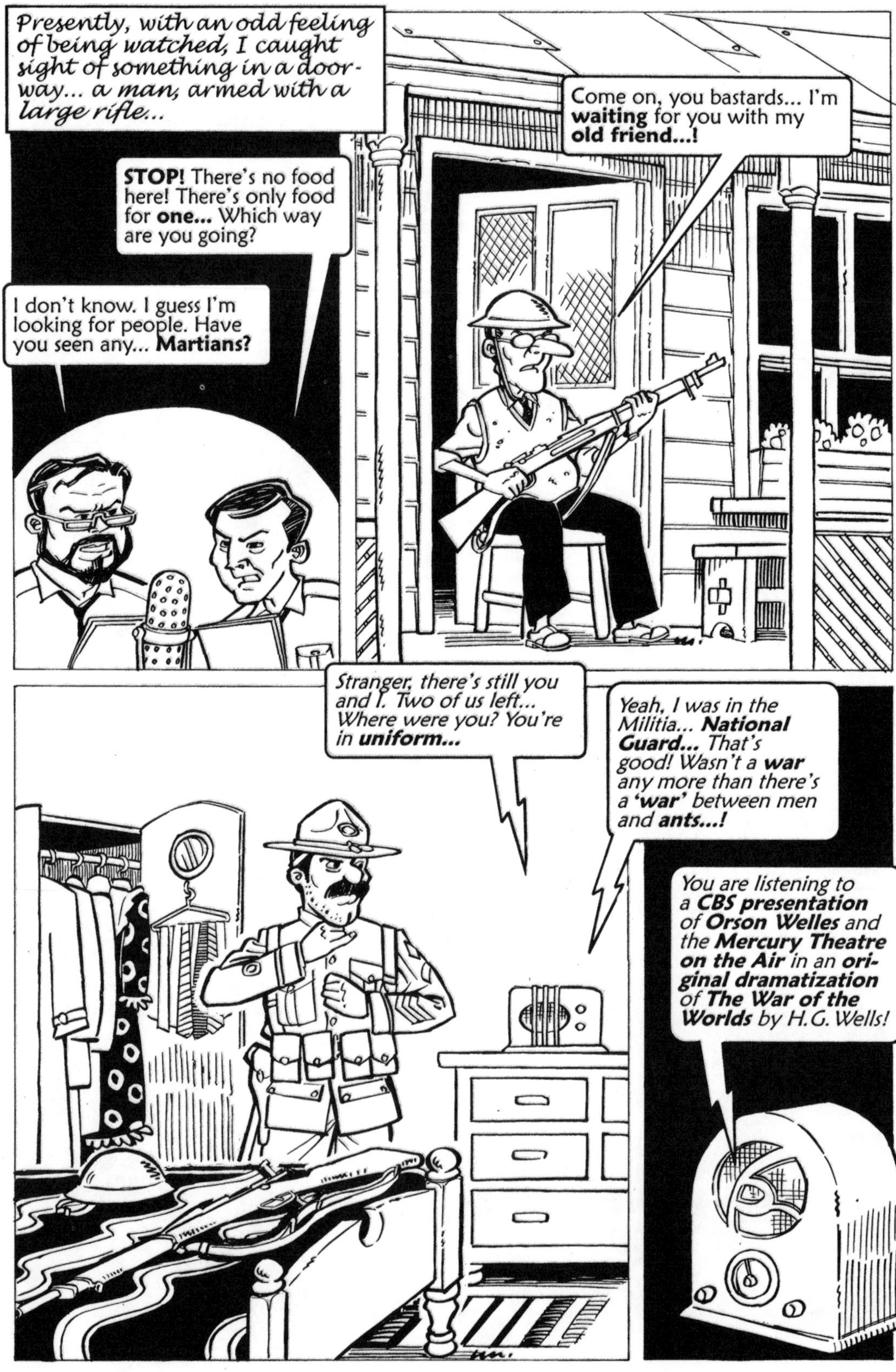
Presently, with an odd feeling of being watched, I caught sight of something in a doorway... a man, armed with a large rifle...
Come on, you bastards... I'm waiting for you with my old friend...!
STOP! There's no food here! There's only food for one... Which way are you going?
I don't know. I guess I'm looking for people. Have you seen any... Martians?
Stranger, there's still you and I. Two of us left... Where were you? You're in uniform...
Yeah, I was in the Militia... National Guard... That's good! Wasn't a war any more than there's a 'war' between men and ants...!
You are listening to a CBS presentation of Orson Welles and the Mercury Theatre on the Air in an original dramatization of The War of the Worlds by H.G. Wells!

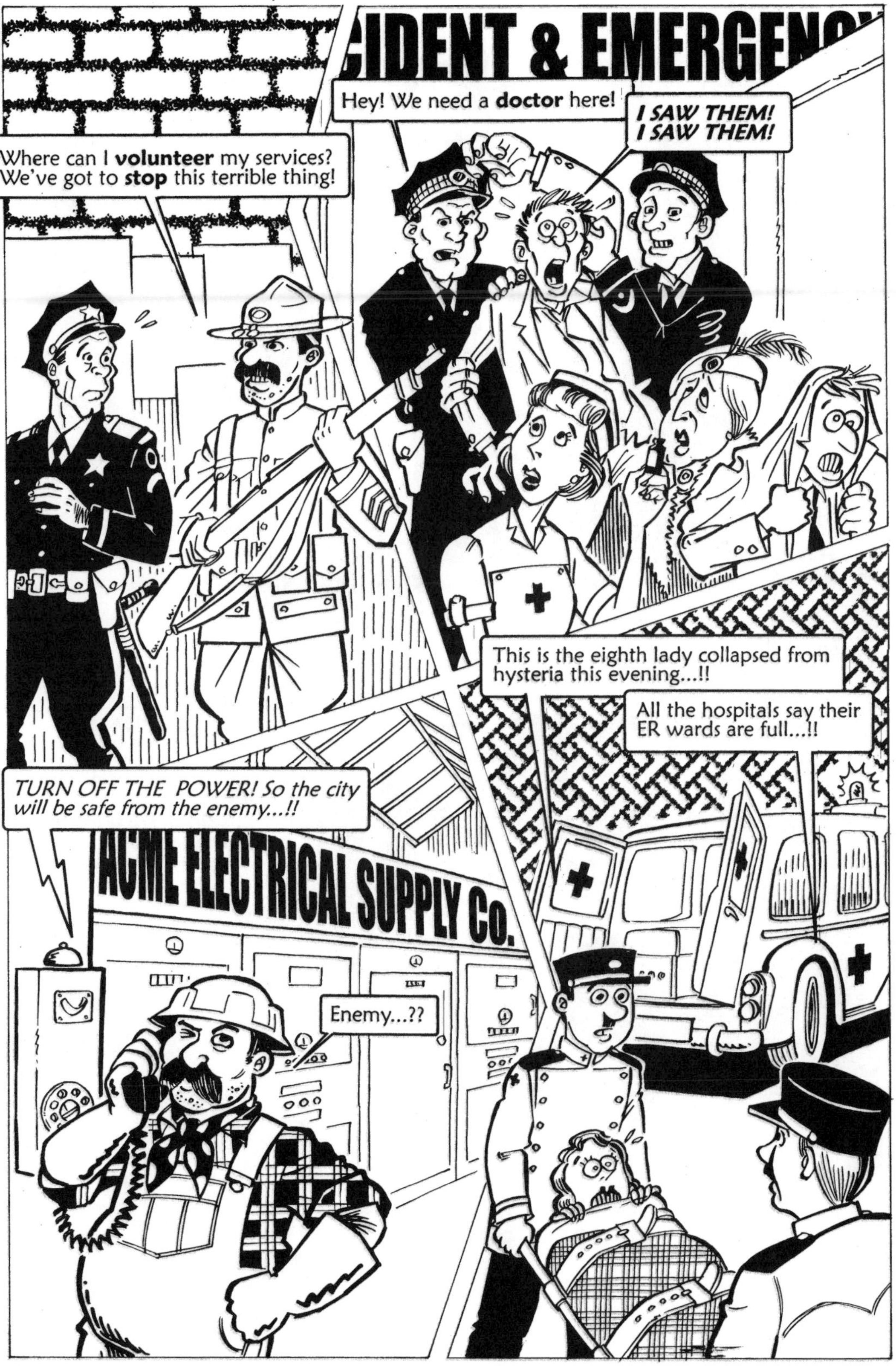

CIDENT & EMERGENC
Where can I **volunteer** my services? We've got to **stop** this terrible thing!
Hey! We need a **doctor** here!
I SAW THEM! I SAW THEM!
This is the eighth lady collapsed from hysteria this evening...!!
All the hospitals say their ER wards are full...!!
TURN OFF THE POWER! So the city will be safe from the enemy...!!
ACME ELECTRICAL SUPPLY Co.
Enemy...??

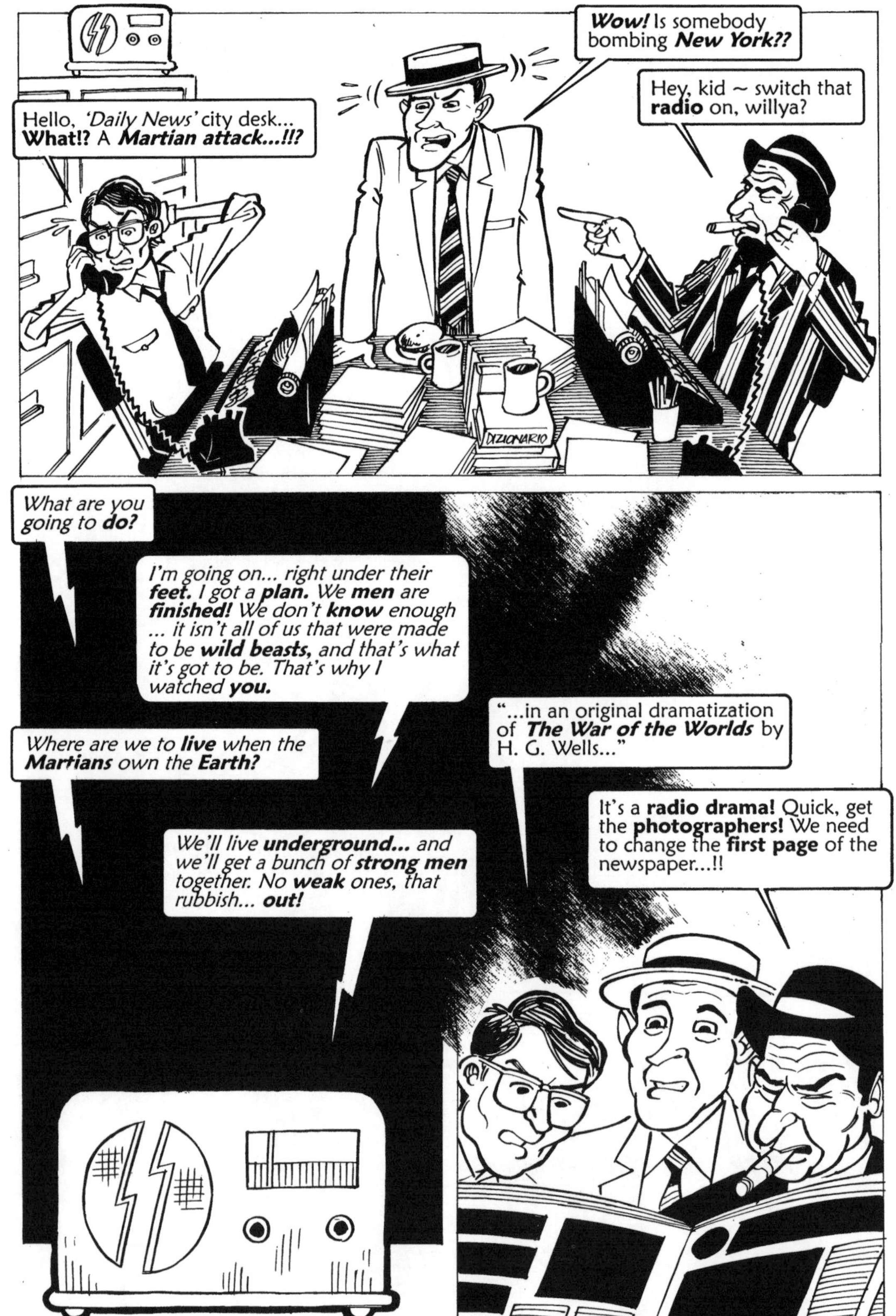
Hello, 'Daily News' city desk... What!? A Martian attack...!!?
Wow! Is somebody bombing New York??
Hey, kid ~ switch that radio on, willya?
DIZIONARIO
What are you going to do?
I'm going on... right under their feet. I got a plan. We men are finished! We don't know enough ... it isn't all of us that were made to be wild beasts, and that's what it's got to be. That's why I watched you.
Where are we to live when the Martians own the Earth?
We'll live underground... and we'll get a bunch of strong men together. No weak ones, that rubbish... out!
"...in an original dramatization of The War of the Worlds by H. G. Wells..."
It's a radio drama! Quick, get the photographers! We need to change the first page of the newspaper...!!

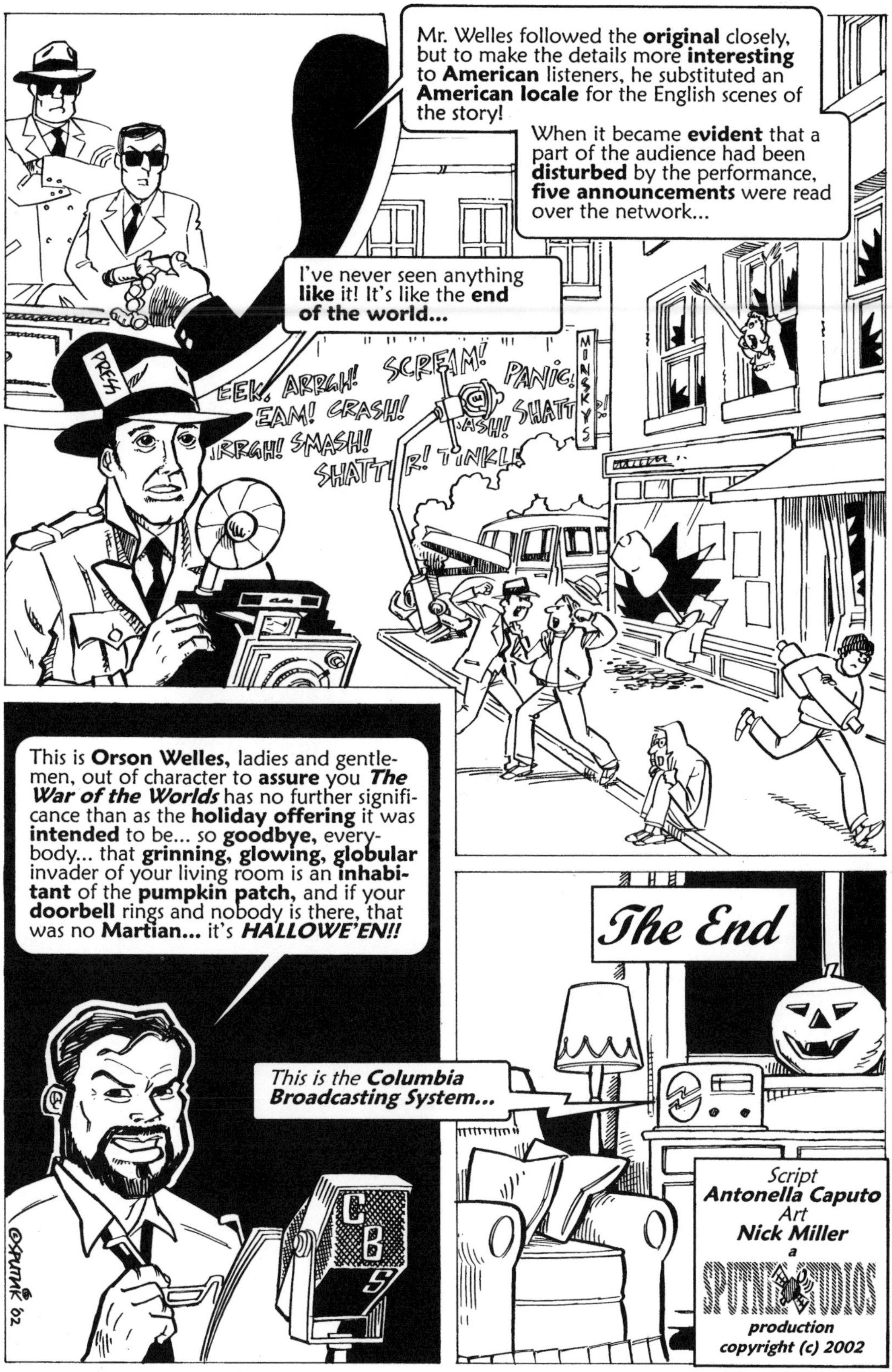
Mr. Welles followed the **original** closely, but to make the details more **interesting** to **American** listeners, he substituted an **American locale** for the English scenes of the story!
When it became **evident** that a part of the audience had been **disturbed** by the performance, **five announcements** were read over the network...
I've never seen anything **like** it! It's like the **end of the world...**
PRESS
EEK! ARRGH! SCREAM! PANIC!
CRASH! SMASH!
MINSKY'S
This is **Orson Welles**, ladies and gentlemen, out of character to **assure** you ***The War of the Worlds*** has no further significance than as the **holiday offering** it was **intended** to be... so **goodbye**, everybody... that **grinning, glowing, globular** invader of your living room is an **inhabitant** of the **pumpkin patch**, and if your **doorbell** rings and nobody is there, that was no **Martian...** it's ***HALLOWE'EN!!***
*This is the **Columbia Broadcasting System...***
CBS
©SPUTNIK '02
The End
Script
Antonella Caputo
Art
Nick Miller
a
SPUTNIK STUDIOS
production
copyright (c) 2002

ILLUSTRATION ©2005 LISA K. WEBER

Le Mari Terrible

from a story by **H.G. WELLS** / *illustrated by* **LISA K. WEBER**

You are always so sympathetic," she said; and added, reflectively, "and one can talk of one's troubles to you without any nonsense."

I wondered dimly if she meant that as a challenge. I helped myself to a biscuit thing that looked neither poisonous nor sandy. "You are one of the most puzzling human beings I ever met," I said,—a perfectly safe remark to any woman under any circumstances.

"Do you find me so hard to understand?" she said.

"You are dreadfully complex." I bit at the biscuit thing, and found it full of a kind of creamy bird-lime.

"How so?" she was saying, and smiling her most brilliant smile.

"Oh!" said I, and waved the cream biscuit thing. "You challenge me to dissect you."

"Well?"

"And that is precisely what I cannot do."

"I'm afraid you are very satirical," she said, with a touch of disappointment. She is always saying that when our conversation has become absolutely idiotic—as it invariably does.

She turned to pour hot water into the teapot, looking very prettily at me over her arm as she did so.

"Sympathy," she said, "is a very wonderful thing, and a very precious thing."

"You speak," said I (with a cough behind my hand), "as though you knew what it was to be lonely."

"There is solitude even in a crowd," she said, and looked round at the six other people — three discreet pairs—who were in the room.

"I, too..." I was beginning, when her husband (confound him!) came into the room.

He was a violent discord. He wore a short brown jacket and carpet slippers, and three of his waistcoat buttons were (as usual) undone. "Got any tea left, Millie?" he said, and came and sat down in the armchair beside the table.

"How do, Delalune?" he said to the man in the corner. "Damned hot, Bellows," he remarked to me, subsiding creakily.

She poured some more hot water into the teapot. (Why must charming married women always have these husbands?)

"It is very hot," I said.

There was a perceptible pause. He is one of those rather adipose people, who are not disconcerted by conversational gaps. "Are you, too, working at Argon?" I said. He is some kind of chemical investigator, I know.

He began at once to explain the most horribly complex things about elements to me. She gave him his tea, and rose and went and talked to the Giffens. "Yes," I said, not hearing what he was saying.

"'No' would be more appropriate," he said. "You are absent-minded, Bellows. Not in love, I hope—at your age?"

Really, I am not thirty, but a certain perceptible thinness in my hair may account for his invariably regarding me as a contemporary. But he should understand that nowadays the beginnings of baldness merely mark the virile epoch.

"I say, Millie," he said, out loud and across the room, "you haven't been collecting Bellows here—have you?"

She looked round startled, and I saw a pained look come into her eyes. "For the bazaar?" she said. "Not yet, dear." It seemed to me that she shot a glance of entreaty at him. Then she turned to the others again.

"My wife," he said, "has two distinctive traits. She is a born poetess and a born collector. I ought to warn you."

"I did not know," said I, "that she rhymed."

"I was speaking more of the imaginative quality, the temperament that finds a splendour in the grass, a glory in the flower, that clothes the whole world in a vestiture of interpretation."

"Indeed!" I said. I felt she was watching us anxiously. He could not, of course, suspect. But I was relieved to fancy he was simply talking nonsense.

I heard her dress rustle behind me.

"I want some more tea," he said to her. "But about the collecting, Bellows—"

"You *must* come to this bazaar," she interrupted.

"I shall be delighted," I said, boldly. "Where is it, and when?"

"About this collecting...," he began.

"It is in aid of that delightful orphanage at Wimblingham," she explained, and gave me an animated account of the charity. He emptied his second cup of tea.

"May I have a third cup?" he said.

The two girls signalled departure, and her attention was distracted. "She collects—and I will confess she does it with extraordinary skill—the surreptitious addresses—"

"John," she said over her shoulder, "I wish you would tell Miss Smithers all those interesting things about Argon." He gulped down his third cup, and rose with the easy obedience of the trained husband. Presently she returned to the tea-things. "Cannot I fill your cup?" she asked.

"I really hope John was not telling you his queer notions about me. He says the most remarkable things. Quite lately he has got it into his head that he has a formula for my character."

"I wish I had," I said, with a sigh.

"And he goes about explaining me to people, as though I was a mechanism. 'Scalp collector,' I think is the favorite phrase. Don't you think it perfectly horrid of him?"

"But he doesn't *understand* you," I said, not grasping his meaning quite at the minute.

She sighed.

"You have," I said, with infinite meaning, "my *sincere* sympathy—" I hesitated—"my *whole* sympathy."

"Thank you so much," she said, quite as meaningly. I rose forthwith, and we clasped hands, like souls who strike a compact.

Yet, thinking over what he said afterwards, I was troubled by a fancy that there was the faintest suggestion of a smile of triumph about her lips and mouth. I suppose he has poisoned my mind a little. Of course, I should not like to think of myself as one of a fortuitously selected multitude strung neatly together (if one may use the vulgarism) on a piece of string,—old gentlemen, nice boys, sympathetic and humorous men of thirty, kind fellows, gifted dreamers, and dashing blades, all trailing after her. It is confoundedly bad form of him, anyhow, to guy her visitors. She certainly took it like a saint. Of course, I shall see her again soon, and we shall talk to one another about one another.

Something or other cropped up and prevented my going there on her last Tuesday.

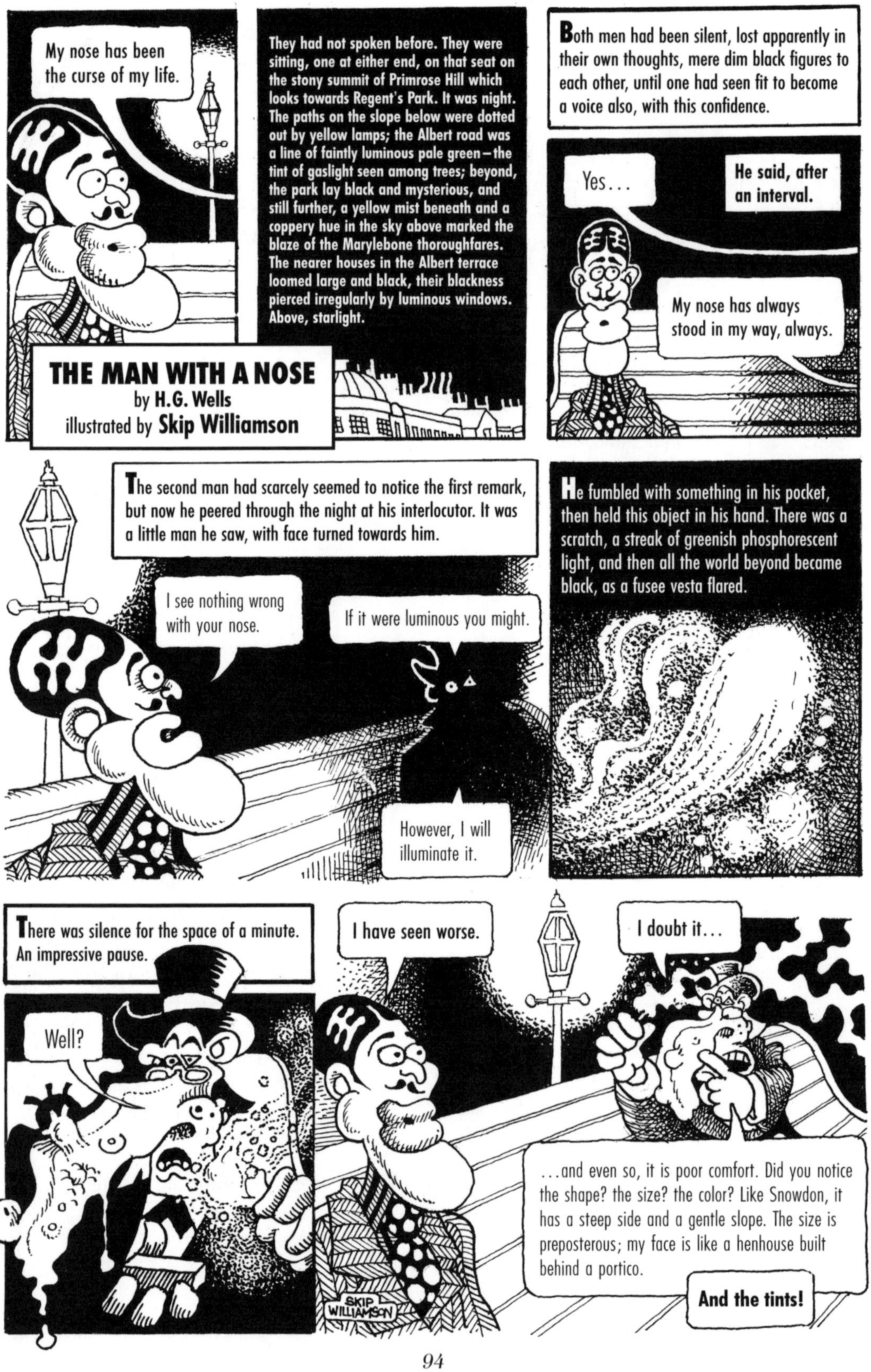
My nose has been the curse of my life.
They had not spoken before. They were sitting, one at either end, on that seat on the stony summit of Primrose Hill which looks towards Regent's Park. It was night. The paths on the slope below were dotted out by yellow lamps; the Albert road was a line of faintly luminous pale green—the tint of gaslight seen among trees; beyond, the park lay black and mysterious, and still further, a yellow mist beneath and a coppery hue in the sky above marked the blaze of the Marylebone thoroughfares. The nearer houses in the Albert terrace loomed large and black, their blackness pierced irregularly by luminous windows. Above, starlight.
THE MAN WITH A NOSE
by H.G. Wells
illustrated by Skip Williamson
Both men had been silent, lost apparently in their own thoughts, mere dim black figures to each other, until one had seen fit to become a voice also, with this confidence.
Yes...
He said, after an interval.
My nose has always stood in my way, always.
The second man had scarcely seemed to notice the first remark, but now he peered through the night at his interlocutor. It was a little man he saw, with face turned towards him.
I see nothing wrong with your nose.
If it were luminous you might.
However, I will illuminate it.
He fumbled with something in his pocket, then held this object in his hand. There was a scratch, a streak of greenish phosphorescent light, and then all the world beyond became black, as a fusee vesta flared.
There was silence for the space of a minute. An impressive pause.
Well?
I have seen worse.
I doubt it...
...and even so, it is poor comfort. Did you notice the shape? the size? the color? Like Snowdon, it has a steep side and a gentle slope. The size is preposterous; my face is like a henhouse built behind a portico.
And the tints!
SKIP WILLIAMSON

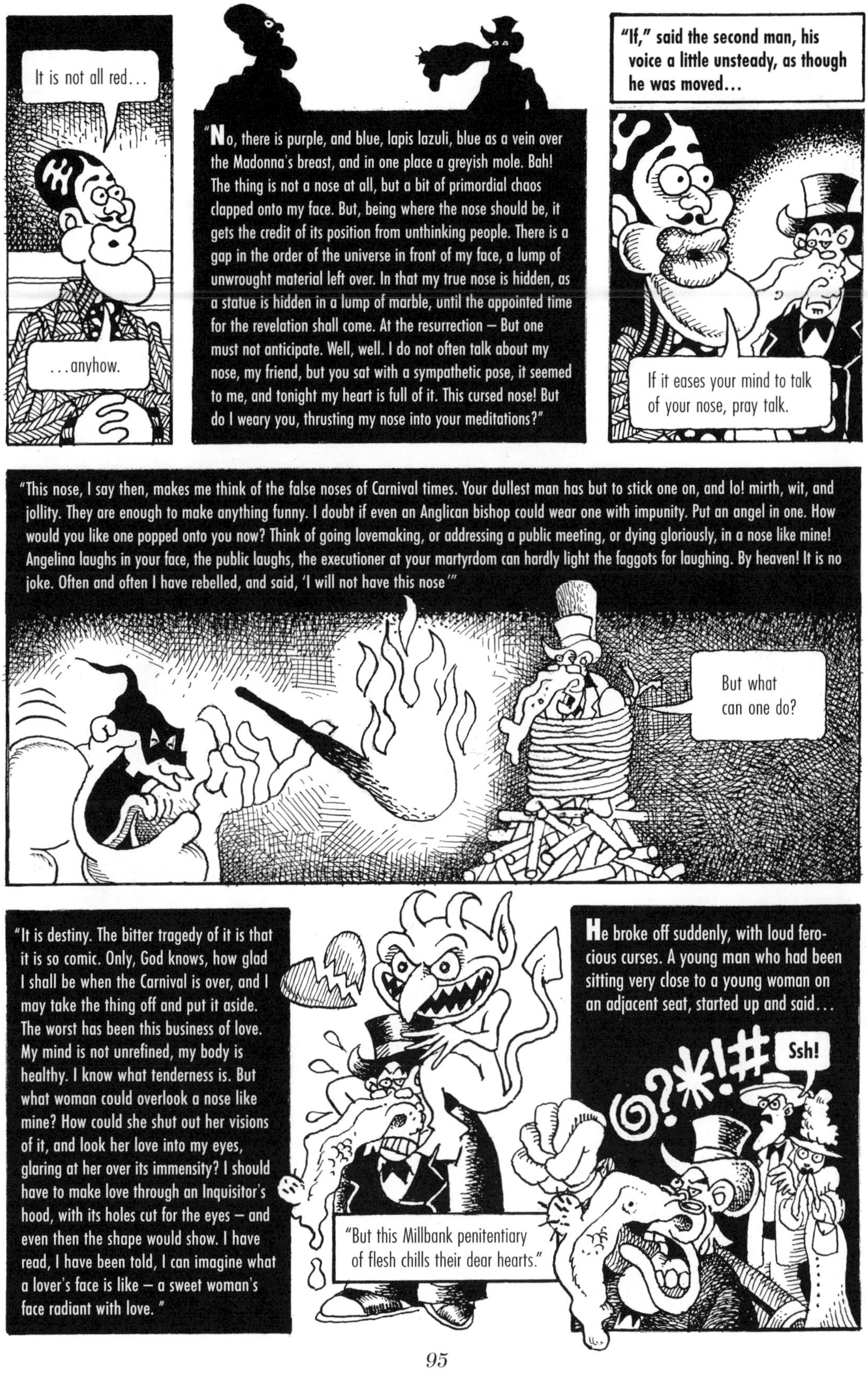
It is not all red…
…anyhow.
"No, there is purple, and blue, lapis lazuli, blue as a vein over the Madonna's breast, and in one place a greyish mole. Bah! The thing is not a nose at all, but a bit of primordial chaos clapped onto my face. But, being where the nose should be, it gets the credit of its position from unthinking people. There is a gap in the order of the universe in front of my face, a lump of unwrought material left over. In that my true nose is hidden, as a statue is hidden in a lump of marble, until the appointed time for the revelation shall come. At the resurrection – But one must not anticipate. Well, well. I do not often talk about my nose, my friend, but you sat with a sympathetic pose, it seemed to me, and tonight my heart is full of it. This cursed nose! But do I weary you, thrusting my nose into your meditations?"
"If," said the second man, his voice a little unsteady, as though he was moved…
If it eases your mind to talk of your nose, pray talk.
"This nose, I say then, makes me think of the false noses of Carnival times. Your dullest man has but to stick one on, and lo! mirth, wit, and jollity. They are enough to make anything funny. I doubt if even an Anglican bishop could wear one with impunity. Put an angel in one. How would you like one popped onto you now? Think of going lovemaking, or addressing a public meeting, or dying gloriously, in a nose like mine! Angelina laughs in your face, the public laughs, the executioner at your martyrdom can hardly light the faggots for laughing. By heaven! It is no joke. Often and often I have rebelled, and said, 'I will not have this nose'"
But what can one do?
"It is destiny. The bitter tragedy of it is that it is so comic. Only, God knows, how glad I shall be when the Carnival is over, and I may take the thing off and put it aside. The worst has been this business of love. My mind is not unrefined, my body is healthy. I know what tenderness is. But what woman could overlook a nose like mine? How could she shut out her visions of it, and look her love into my eyes, glaring at her over its immensity? I should have to make love through an Inquisitor's hood, with its holes cut for the eyes – and even then the shape would show. I have read, I have been told, I can imagine what a lover's face is like – a sweet woman's face radiant with love."
"But this Millbank penitentiary of flesh chills their dear hearts."
He broke off suddenly, with loud ferocious curses. A young man who had been sitting very close to a young woman on an adjacent seat, started up and said…
@?*!#
Ssh!

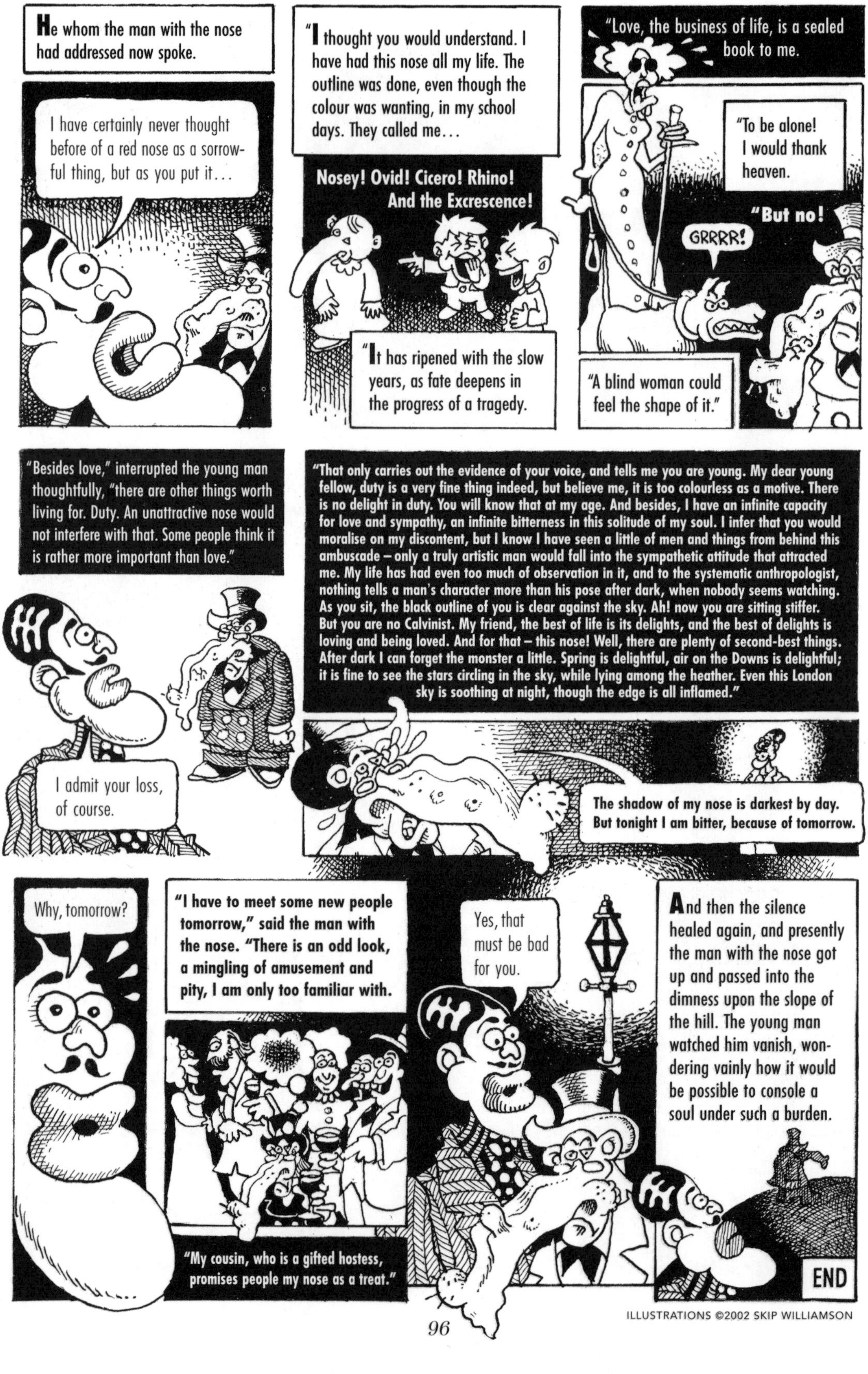
He whom the man with the nose had addressed now spoke.
I have certainly never thought before of a red nose as a sorrowful thing, but as you put it…
"I thought you would understand. I have had this nose all my life. The outline was done, even though the colour was wanting, in my school days. They called me…
Nosey! Ovid! Cicero! Rhino! And the Excrescence!
"It has ripened with the slow years, as fate deepens in the progress of a tragedy.
"Love, the business of life, is a sealed book to me.
"To be alone! I would thank heaven.
"But no!
GRRRR!
"A blind woman could feel the shape of it."
"Besides love," interrupted the young man thoughtfully, "there are other things worth living for. Duty. An unattractive nose would not interfere with that. Some people think it is rather more important than love."
"That only carries out the evidence of your voice, and tells me you are young. My dear young fellow, duty is a very fine thing indeed, but believe me, it is too colourless as a motive. There is no delight in duty. You will know that at my age. And besides, I have an infinite capacity for love and sympathy, an infinite bitterness in this solitude of my soul. I infer that you would moralise on my discontent, but I know I have seen a little of men and things from behind this ambuscade – only a truly artistic man would fall into the sympathetic attitude that attracted me. My life has had even too much of observation in it, and to the systematic anthropologist, nothing tells a man's character more than his pose after dark, when nobody seems watching. As you sit, the black outline of you is clear against the sky. Ah! now you are sitting stiffer. But you are no Calvinist. My friend, the best of life is its delights, and the best of delights is loving and being loved. And for that – this nose! Well, there are plenty of second-best things. After dark I can forget the monster a little. Spring is delightful, air on the Downs is delightful; it is fine to see the stars circling in the sky, while lying among the heather. Even this London sky is soothing at night, though the edge is all inflamed."
I admit your loss, of course.
The shadow of my nose is darkest by day. But tonight I am bitter, because of tomorrow.
Why, tomorrow?
"I have to meet some new people tomorrow," said the man with the nose. "There is an odd look, a mingling of amusement and pity, I am only too familiar with.
"My cousin, who is a gifted hostess, promises people my nose as a treat."
Yes, that must be bad for you.
And then the silence healed again, and presently the man with the nose got up and passed into the dimness upon the slope of the hill. The young man watched him vanish, wondering vainly how it would be possible to console a soul under such a burden.
END

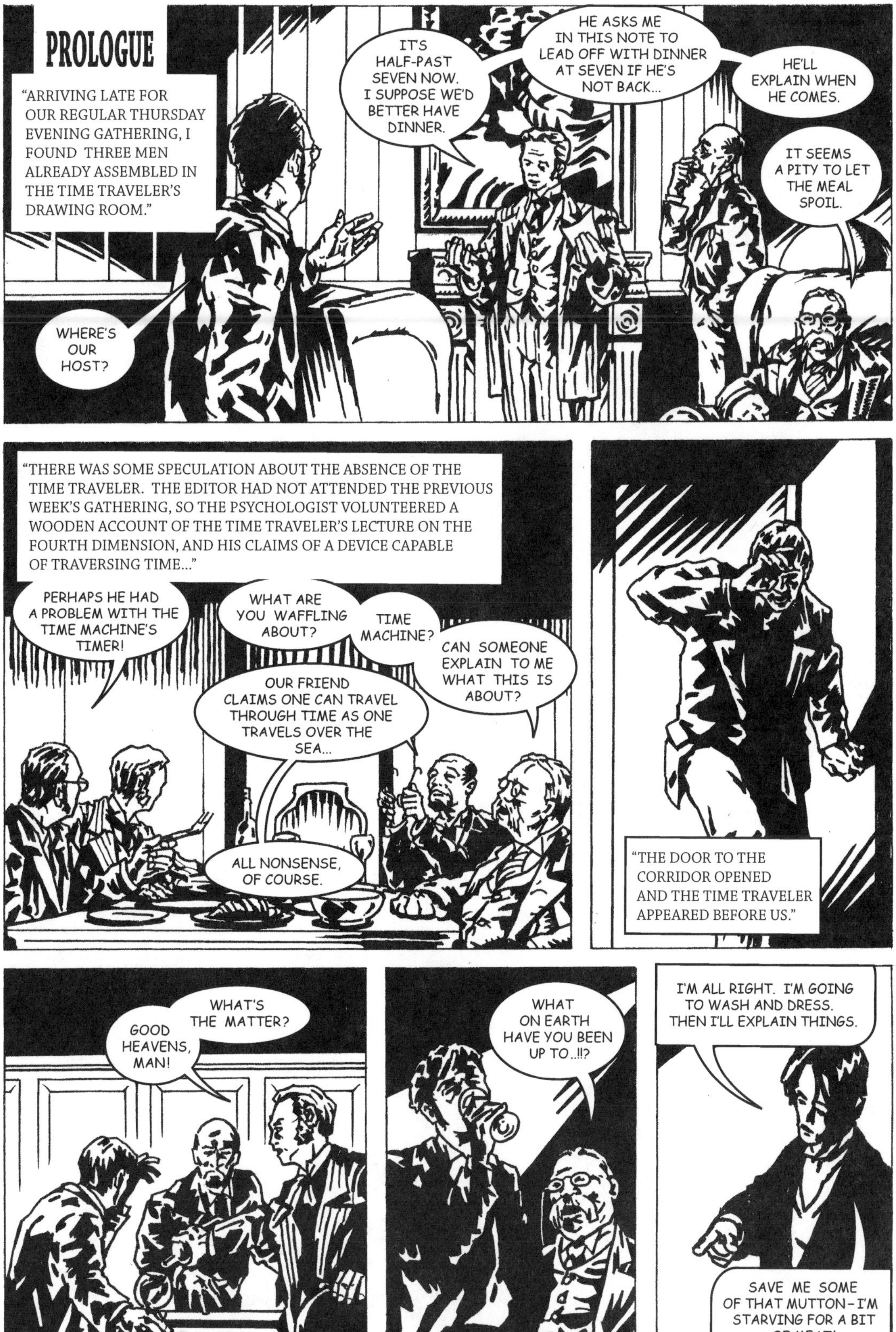
PROLOGUE
"ARRIVING LATE FOR OUR REGULAR THURSDAY EVENING GATHERING, I FOUND THREE MEN ALREADY ASSEMBLED IN THE TIME TRAVELER'S DRAWING ROOM."
WHERE'S OUR HOST?
IT'S HALF-PAST SEVEN NOW. I SUPPOSE WE'D BETTER HAVE DINNER.
HE ASKS ME IN THIS NOTE TO LEAD OFF WITH DINNER AT SEVEN IF HE'S NOT BACK...
HE'LL EXPLAIN WHEN HE COMES.
IT SEEMS A PITY TO LET THE MEAL SPOIL.
"THERE WAS SOME SPECULATION ABOUT THE ABSENCE OF THE TIME TRAVELER. THE EDITOR HAD NOT ATTENDED THE PREVIOUS WEEK'S GATHERING, SO THE PSYCHOLOGIST VOLUNTEERED A WOODEN ACCOUNT OF THE TIME TRAVELER'S LECTURE ON THE FOURTH DIMENSION, AND HIS CLAIMS OF A DEVICE CAPABLE OF TRAVERSING TIME..."
PERHAPS HE HAD A PROBLEM WITH THE TIME MACHINE'S TIMER!
WHAT ARE YOU WAFFLING ABOUT?
TIME MACHINE?
CAN SOMEONE EXPLAIN TO ME WHAT THIS IS ABOUT?
OUR FRIEND CLAIMS ONE CAN TRAVEL THROUGH TIME AS ONE TRAVELS OVER THE SEA...
ALL NONSENSE, OF COURSE.
"THE DOOR TO THE CORRIDOR OPENED AND THE TIME TRAVELER APPEARED BEFORE US."
GOOD HEAVENS, MAN!
WHAT'S THE MATTER?
WHAT ON EARTH HAVE YOU BEEN UP TO..!!?
I'M ALL RIGHT. I'M GOING TO WASH AND DRESS. THEN I'LL EXPLAIN THINGS.
SAVE ME SOME OF THAT MUTTON–I'M STARVING FOR A BIT OF MEAT!

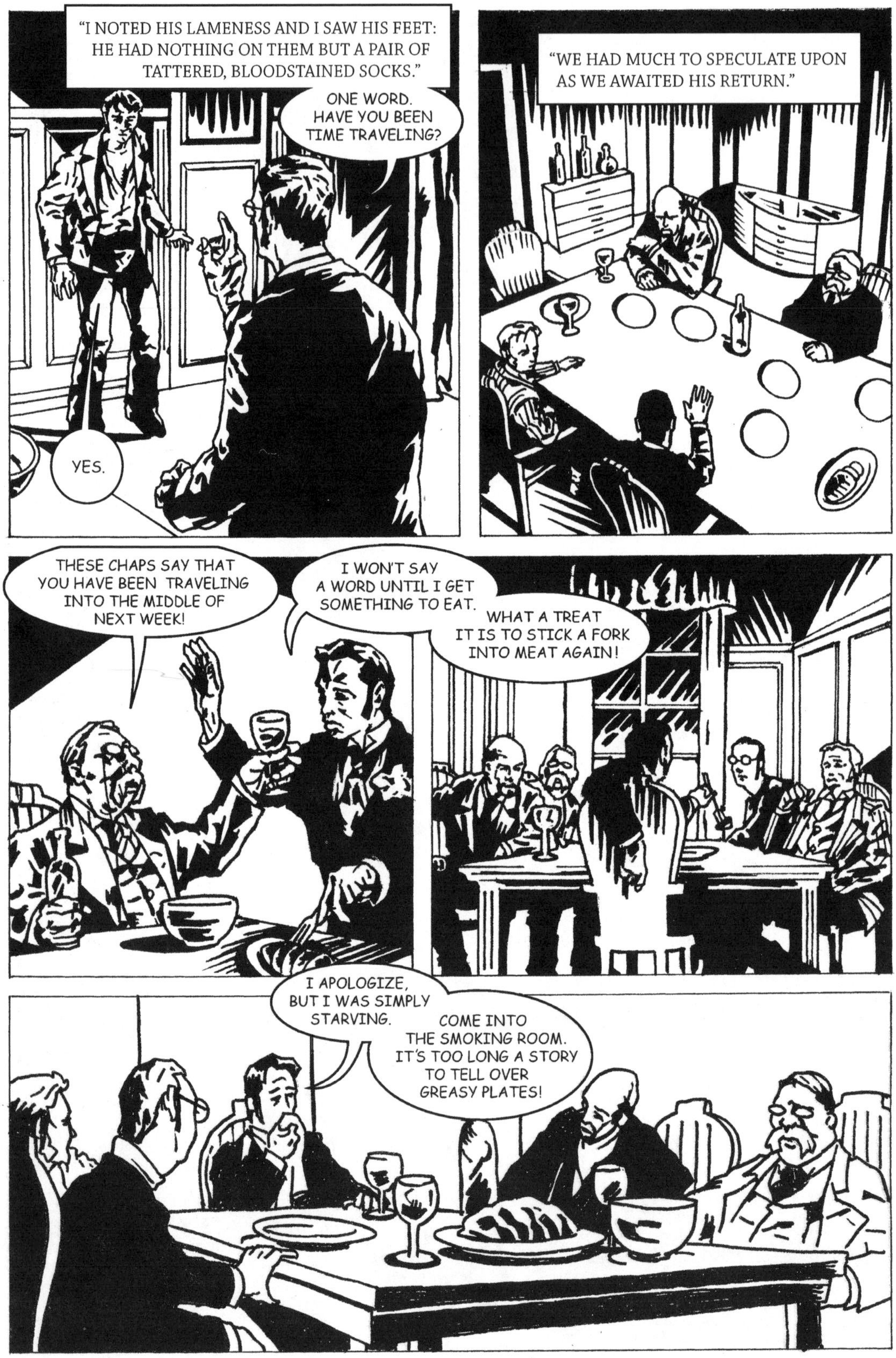
"I NOTED HIS LAMENESS AND I SAW HIS FEET: HE HAD NOTHING ON THEM BUT A PAIR OF TATTERED, BLOODSTAINED SOCKS."
ONE WORD. HAVE YOU BEEN TIME TRAVELING?
YES.
"WE HAD MUCH TO SPECULATE UPON AS WE AWAITED HIS RETURN."
THESE CHAPS SAY THAT YOU HAVE BEEN TRAVELING INTO THE MIDDLE OF NEXT WEEK!
I WON'T SAY A WORD UNTIL I GET SOMETHING TO EAT.
WHAT A TREAT IT IS TO STICK A FORK INTO MEAT AGAIN!
I APOLOGIZE, BUT I WAS SIMPLY STARVING.
COME INTO THE SMOKING ROOM. IT'S TOO LONG A STORY TO TELL OVER GREASY PLATES!

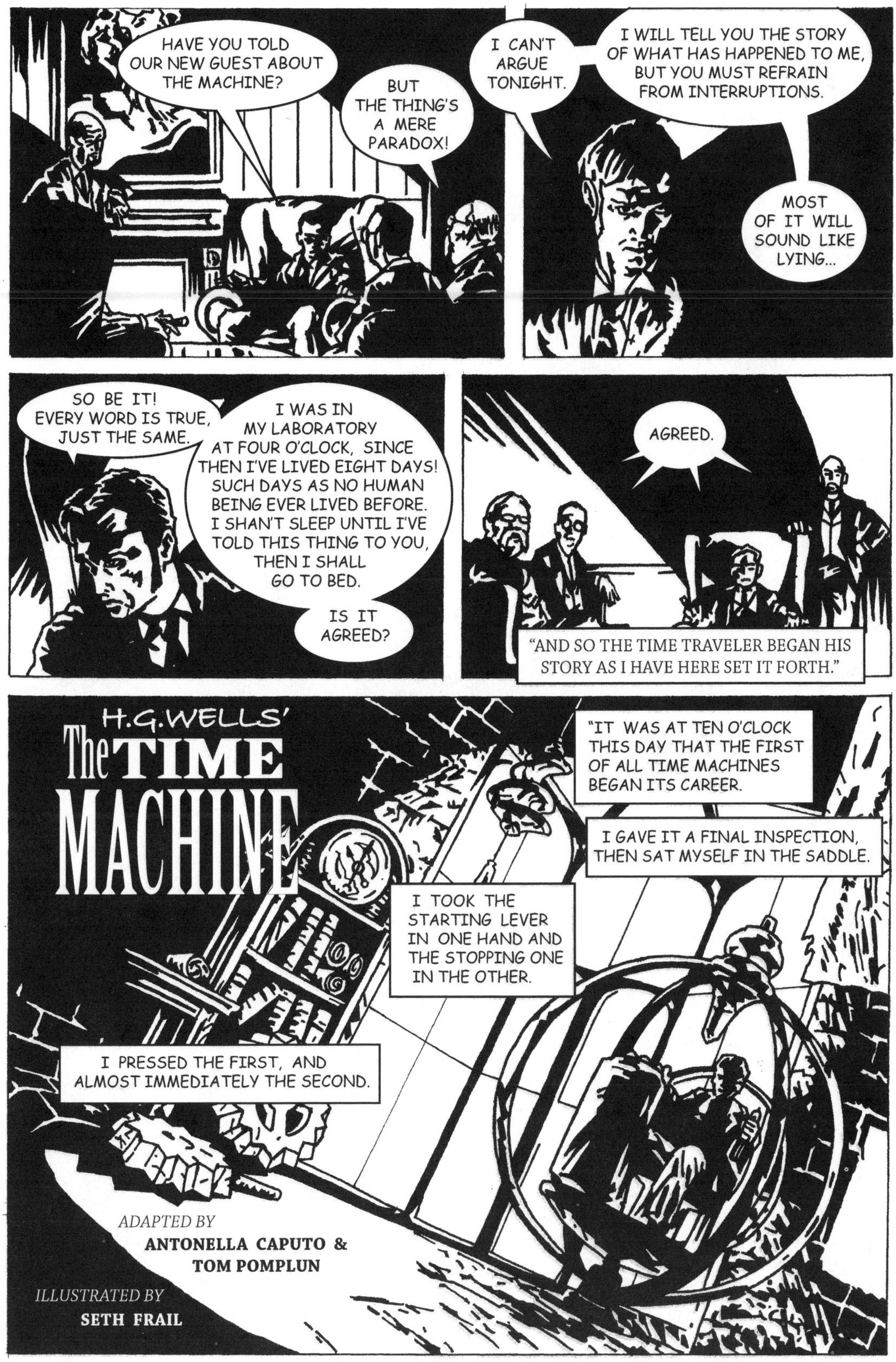
HAVE YOU TOLD OUR NEW GUEST ABOUT THE MACHINE?
BUT THE THING'S A MERE PARADOX!
I CAN'T ARGUE TONIGHT.
I WILL TELL YOU THE STORY OF WHAT HAS HAPPENED TO ME, BUT YOU MUST REFRAIN FROM INTERRUPTIONS.
MOST OF IT WILL SOUND LIKE LYING...
SO BE IT! EVERY WORD IS TRUE, JUST THE SAME.
I WAS IN MY LABORATORY AT FOUR O'CLOCK, SINCE THEN I'VE LIVED EIGHT DAYS! SUCH DAYS AS NO HUMAN BEING EVER LIVED BEFORE. I SHAN'T SLEEP UNTIL I'VE TOLD THIS THING TO YOU, THEN I SHALL GO TO BED.
IS IT AGREED?
AGREED.
"AND SO THE TIME TRAVELER BEGAN HIS STORY AS I HAVE HERE SET IT FORTH."
H.G.WELLS'
The TIME MACHINE
"IT WAS AT TEN O'CLOCK THIS DAY THAT THE FIRST OF ALL TIME MACHINES BEGAN ITS CAREER.
I GAVE IT A FINAL INSPECTION, THEN SAT MYSELF IN THE SADDLE.
I TOOK THE STARTING LEVER IN ONE HAND AND THE STOPPING ONE IN THE OTHER.
I PRESSED THE FIRST, AND ALMOST IMMEDIATELY THE SECOND.
ADAPTED BY
ANTONELLA CAPUTO &
TOM POMPLUN
ILLUSTRATED BY
SETH FRAIL

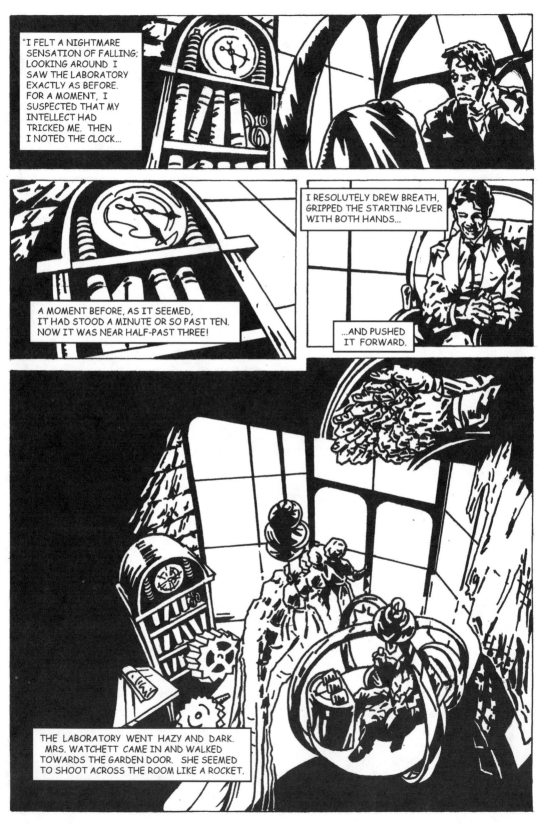

"I FELT A NIGHTMARE SENSATION OF FALLING; LOOKING AROUND I SAW THE LABORATORY EXACTLY AS BEFORE. FOR A MOMENT, I SUSPECTED THAT MY INTELLECT HAD TRICKED ME. THEN I NOTED THE CLOCK...

A MOMENT BEFORE, AS IT SEEMED, IT HAD STOOD A MINUTE OR SO PAST TEN. NOW IT WAS NEAR HALF-PAST THREE!

I RESOLUTELY DREW BREATH, GRIPPED THE STARTING LEVER WITH BOTH HANDS...

...AND PUSHED IT FORWARD.

THE LABORATORY WENT HAZY AND DARK. MRS. WATCHETT CAME IN AND WALKED TOWARDS THE GARDEN DOOR. SHE SEEMED TO SHOOT ACROSS THE ROOM LIKE A ROCKET.

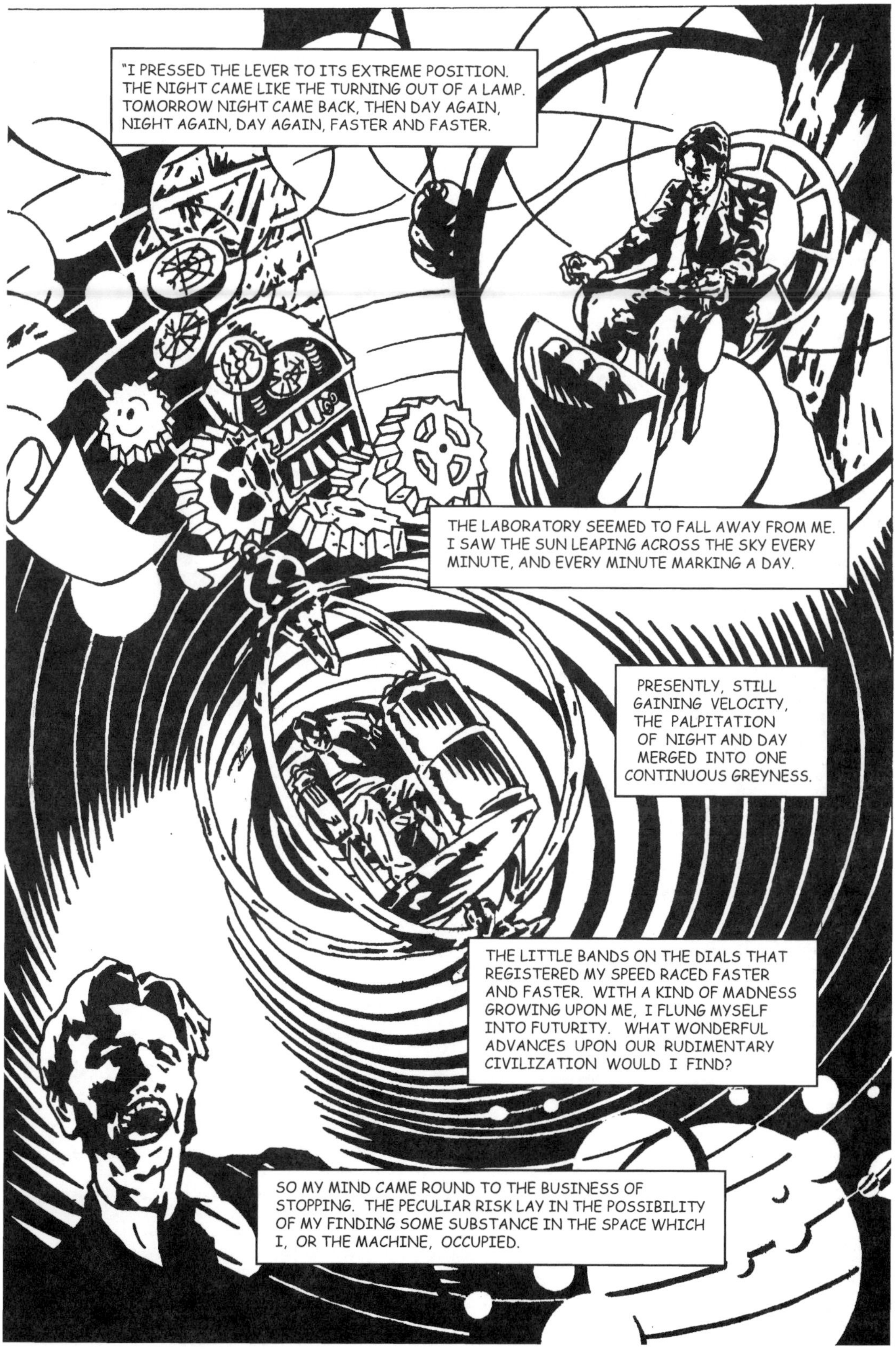
"I PRESSED THE LEVER TO ITS EXTREME POSITION. THE NIGHT CAME LIKE THE TURNING OUT OF A LAMP. TOMORROW NIGHT CAME BACK, THEN DAY AGAIN, NIGHT AGAIN, DAY AGAIN, FASTER AND FASTER.
THE LABORATORY SEEMED TO FALL AWAY FROM ME. I SAW THE SUN LEAPING ACROSS THE SKY EVERY MINUTE, AND EVERY MINUTE MARKING A DAY.
PRESENTLY, STILL GAINING VELOCITY, THE PALPITATION OF NIGHT AND DAY MERGED INTO ONE CONTINUOUS GREYNESS.
THE LITTLE BANDS ON THE DIALS THAT REGISTERED MY SPEED RACED FASTER AND FASTER. WITH A KIND OF MADNESS GROWING UPON ME, I FLUNG MYSELF INTO FUTURITY. WHAT WONDERFUL ADVANCES UPON OUR RUDIMENTARY CIVILIZATION WOULD I FIND?
SO MY MIND CAME ROUND TO THE BUSINESS OF STOPPING. THE PECULIAR RISK LAY IN THE POSSIBILITY OF MY FINDING SOME SUBSTANCE IN THE SPACE WHICH I, OR THE MACHINE, OCCUPIED.

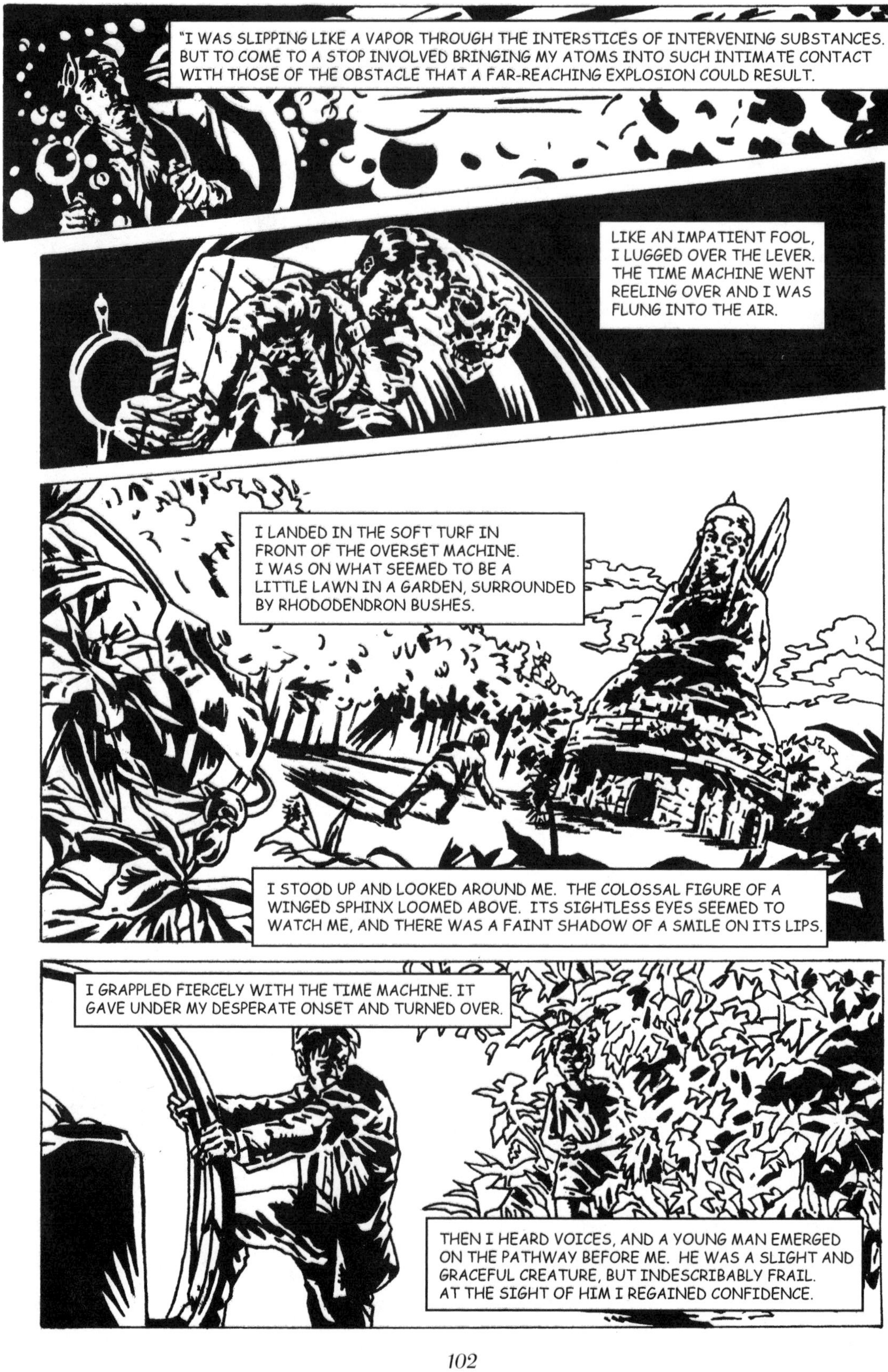
"I WAS SLIPPING LIKE A VAPOR THROUGH THE INTERSTICES OF INTERVENING SUBSTANCES. BUT TO COME TO A STOP INVOLVED BRINGING MY ATOMS INTO SUCH INTIMATE CONTACT WITH THOSE OF THE OBSTACLE THAT A FAR-REACHING EXPLOSION COULD RESULT.
LIKE AN IMPATIENT FOOL, I LUGGED OVER THE LEVER. THE TIME MACHINE WENT REELING OVER AND I WAS FLUNG INTO THE AIR.
I LANDED IN THE SOFT TURF IN FRONT OF THE OVERSET MACHINE. I WAS ON WHAT SEEMED TO BE A LITTLE LAWN IN A GARDEN, SURROUNDED BY RHODODENDRON BUSHES.
I STOOD UP AND LOOKED AROUND ME. THE COLOSSAL FIGURE OF A WINGED SPHINX LOOMED ABOVE. ITS SIGHTLESS EYES SEEMED TO WATCH ME, AND THERE WAS A FAINT SHADOW OF A SMILE ON ITS LIPS.
I GRAPPLED FIERCELY WITH THE TIME MACHINE. IT GAVE UNDER MY DESPERATE ONSET AND TURNED OVER.
THEN I HEARD VOICES, AND A YOUNG MAN EMERGED ON THE PATHWAY BEFORE ME. HE WAS A SLIGHT AND GRACEFUL CREATURE, BUT INDESCRIBABLY FRAIL. AT THE SIGHT OF HIM I REGAINED CONFIDENCE.

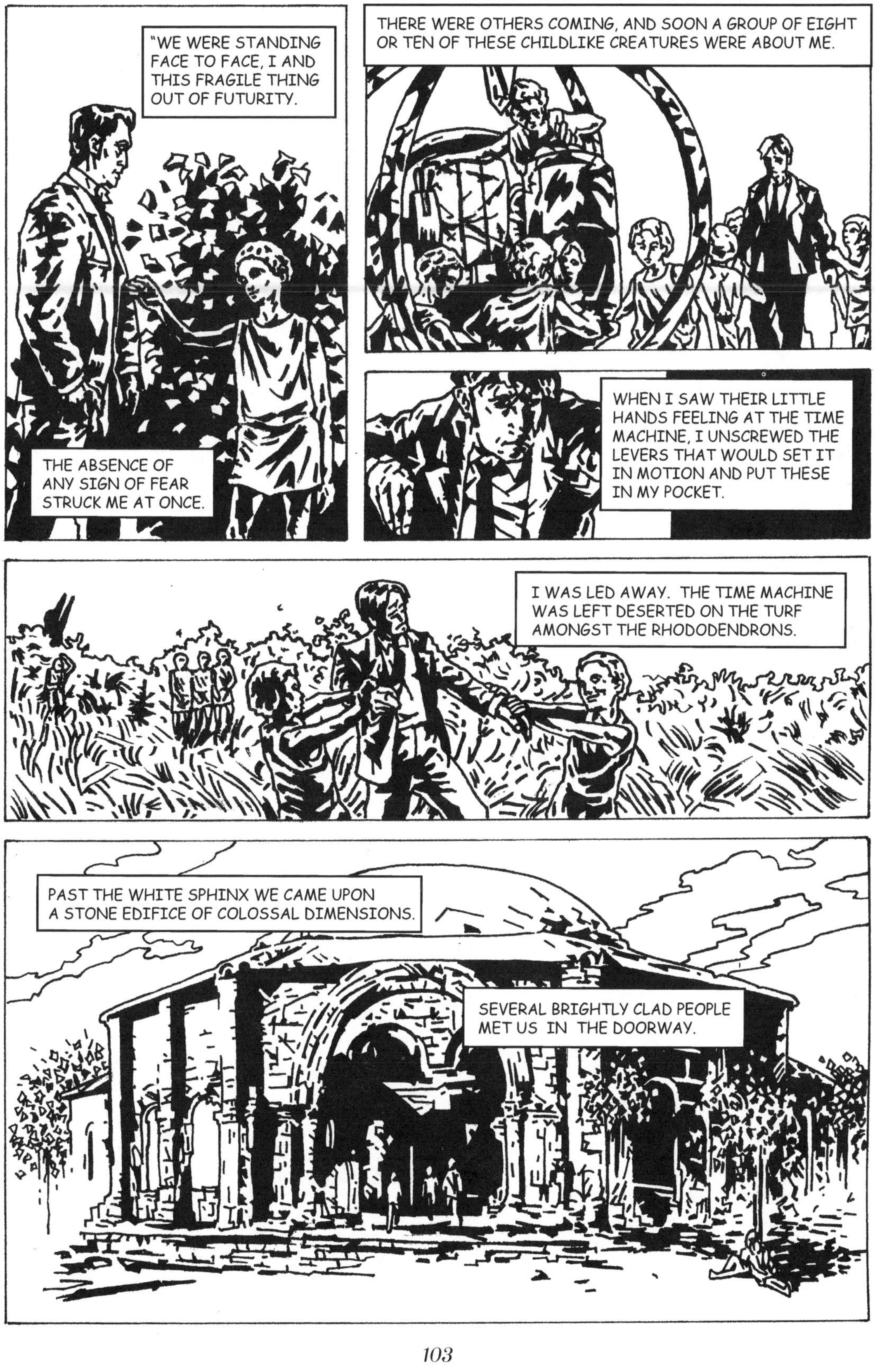
"WE WERE STANDING FACE TO FACE, I AND THIS FRAGILE THING OUT OF FUTURITY.
THE ABSENCE OF ANY SIGN OF FEAR STRUCK ME AT ONCE.
THERE WERE OTHERS COMING, AND SOON A GROUP OF EIGHT OR TEN OF THESE CHILDLIKE CREATURES WERE ABOUT ME.
WHEN I SAW THEIR LITTLE HANDS FEELING AT THE TIME MACHINE, I UNSCREWED THE LEVERS THAT WOULD SET IT IN MOTION AND PUT THESE IN MY POCKET.
I WAS LED AWAY. THE TIME MACHINE WAS LEFT DESERTED ON THE TURF AMONGST THE RHODODENDRONS.
PAST THE WHITE SPHINX WE CAME UPON A STONE EDIFICE OF COLOSSAL DIMENSIONS.
SEVERAL BRIGHTLY CLAD PEOPLE MET US IN THE DOORWAY.

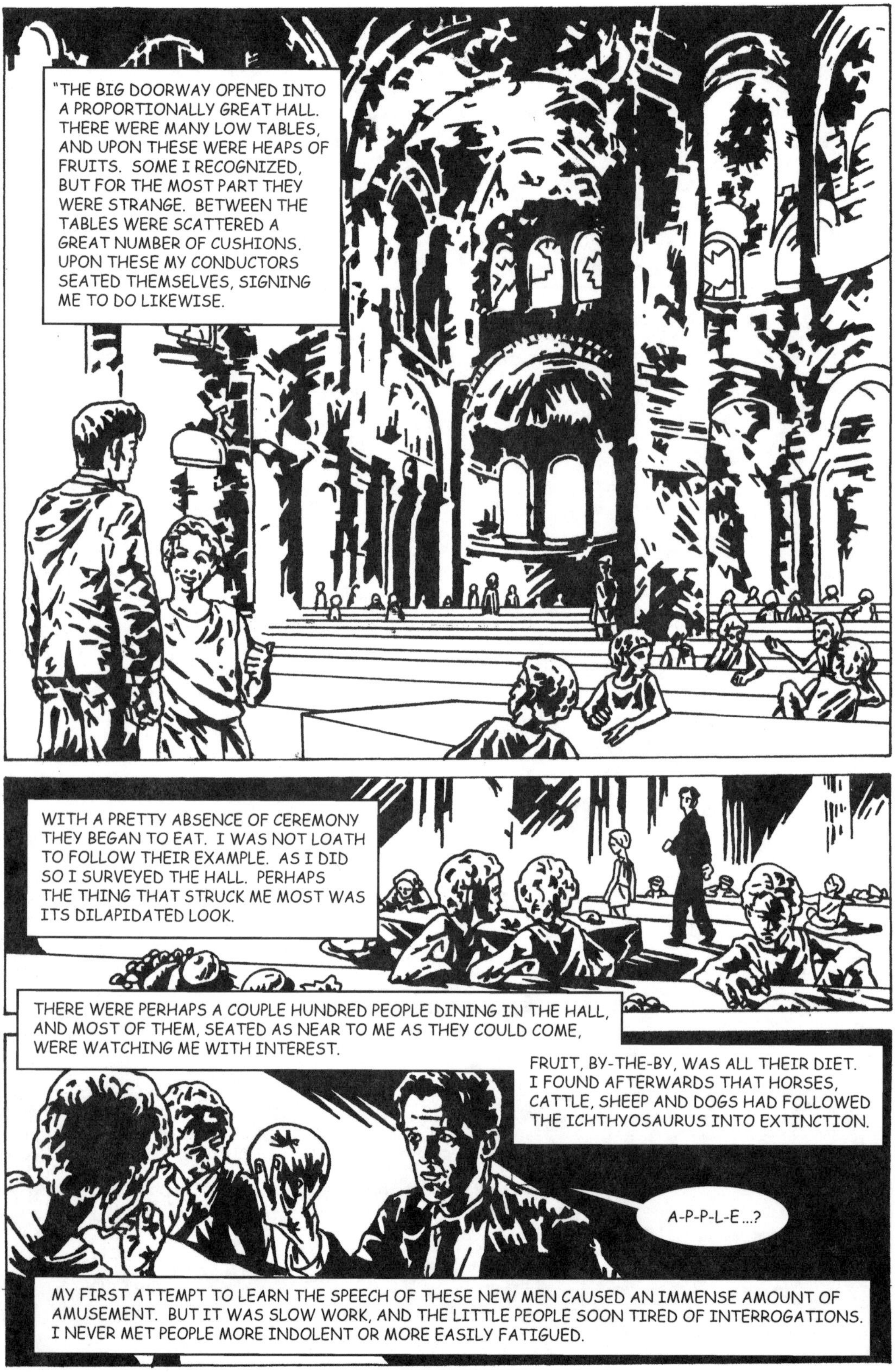
"THE BIG DOORWAY OPENED INTO A PROPORTIONALLY GREAT HALL. THERE WERE MANY LOW TABLES, AND UPON THESE WERE HEAPS OF FRUITS. SOME I RECOGNIZED, BUT FOR THE MOST PART THEY WERE STRANGE. BETWEEN THE TABLES WERE SCATTERED A GREAT NUMBER OF CUSHIONS. UPON THESE MY CONDUCTORS SEATED THEMSELVES, SIGNING ME TO DO LIKEWISE.
WITH A PRETTY ABSENCE OF CEREMONY THEY BEGAN TO EAT. I WAS NOT LOATH TO FOLLOW THEIR EXAMPLE. AS I DID SO I SURVEYED THE HALL. PERHAPS THE THING THAT STRUCK ME MOST WAS ITS DILAPIDATED LOOK.
THERE WERE PERHAPS A COUPLE HUNDRED PEOPLE DINING IN THE HALL, AND MOST OF THEM, SEATED AS NEAR TO ME AS THEY COULD COME, WERE WATCHING ME WITH INTEREST.
FRUIT, BY-THE-BY, WAS ALL THEIR DIET. I FOUND AFTERWARDS THAT HORSES, CATTLE, SHEEP AND DOGS HAD FOLLOWED THE ICHTHYOSAURUS INTO EXTINCTION.
A-P-P-L-E...?
MY FIRST ATTEMPT TO LEARN THE SPEECH OF THESE NEW MEN CAUSED AN IMMENSE AMOUNT OF AMUSEMENT. BUT IT WAS SLOW WORK, AND THE LITTLE PEOPLE SOON TIRED OF INTERROGATIONS. I NEVER MET PEOPLE MORE INDOLENT OR MORE EASILY FATIGUED.

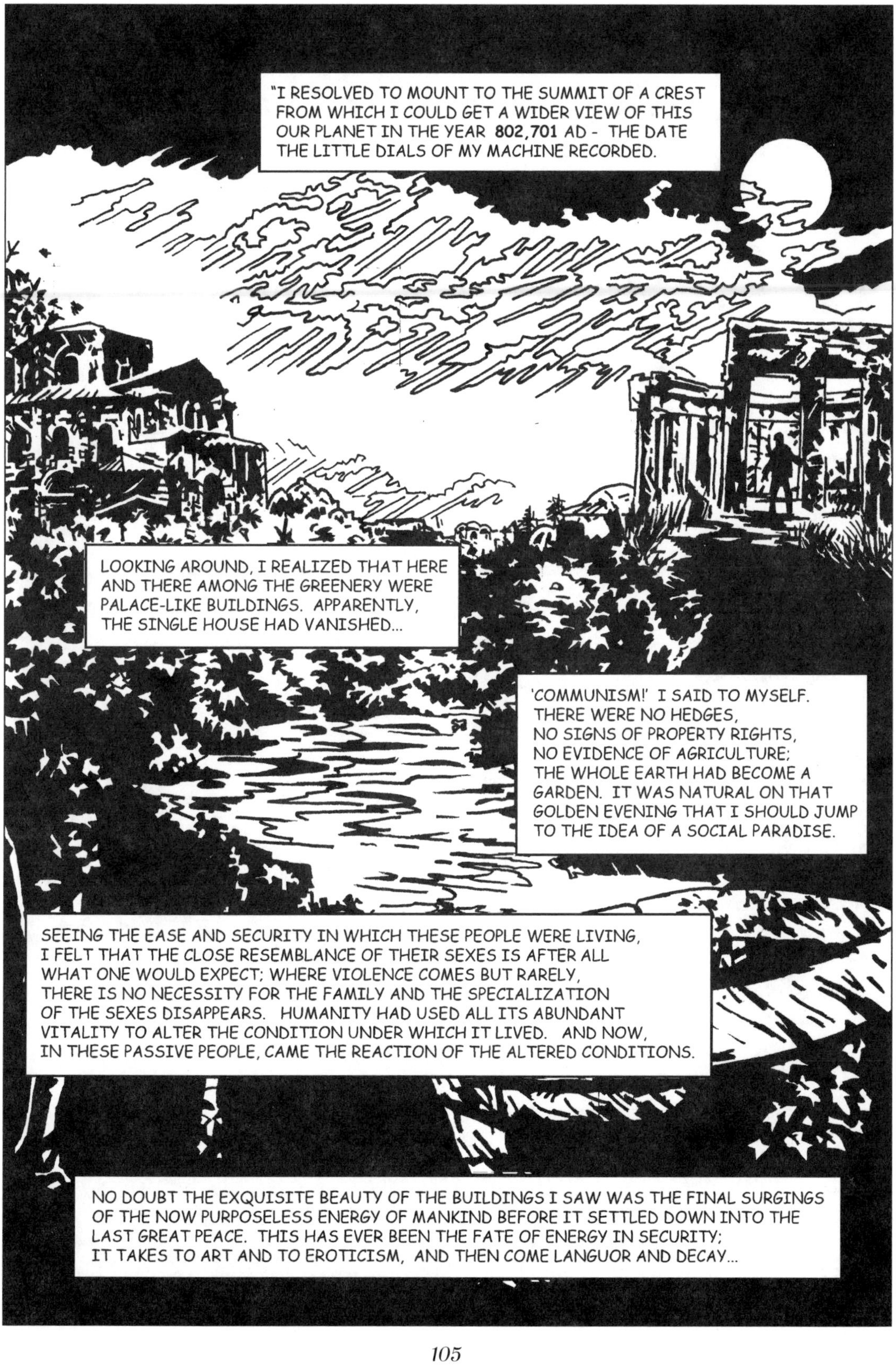
"I RESOLVED TO MOUNT TO THE SUMMIT OF A CREST FROM WHICH I COULD GET A WIDER VIEW OF THIS OUR PLANET IN THE YEAR **802,701** AD - THE DATE THE LITTLE DIALS OF MY MACHINE RECORDED.
LOOKING AROUND, I REALIZED THAT HERE AND THERE AMONG THE GREENERY WERE PALACE-LIKE BUILDINGS. APPARENTLY, THE SINGLE HOUSE HAD VANISHED...
'COMMUNISM!' I SAID TO MYSELF. THERE WERE NO HEDGES, NO SIGNS OF PROPERTY RIGHTS, NO EVIDENCE OF AGRICULTURE; THE WHOLE EARTH HAD BECOME A GARDEN. IT WAS NATURAL ON THAT GOLDEN EVENING THAT I SHOULD JUMP TO THE IDEA OF A SOCIAL PARADISE.
SEEING THE EASE AND SECURITY IN WHICH THESE PEOPLE WERE LIVING, I FELT THAT THE CLOSE RESEMBLANCE OF THEIR SEXES IS AFTER ALL WHAT ONE WOULD EXPECT; WHERE VIOLENCE COMES BUT RARELY, THERE IS NO NECESSITY FOR THE FAMILY AND THE SPECIALIZATION OF THE SEXES DISAPPEARS. HUMANITY HAD USED ALL ITS ABUNDANT VITALITY TO ALTER THE CONDITION UNDER WHICH IT LIVED. AND NOW, IN THESE PASSIVE PEOPLE, CAME THE REACTION OF THE ALTERED CONDITIONS.
NO DOUBT THE EXQUISITE BEAUTY OF THE BUILDINGS I SAW WAS THE FINAL SURGINGS OF THE NOW PURPOSELESS ENERGY OF MANKIND BEFORE IT SETTLED DOWN INTO THE LAST GREAT PEACE. THIS HAS EVER BEEN THE FATE OF ENERGY IN SECURITY; IT TAKES TO ART AND TO EROTICISM, AND THEN COME LANGUOR AND DECAY...

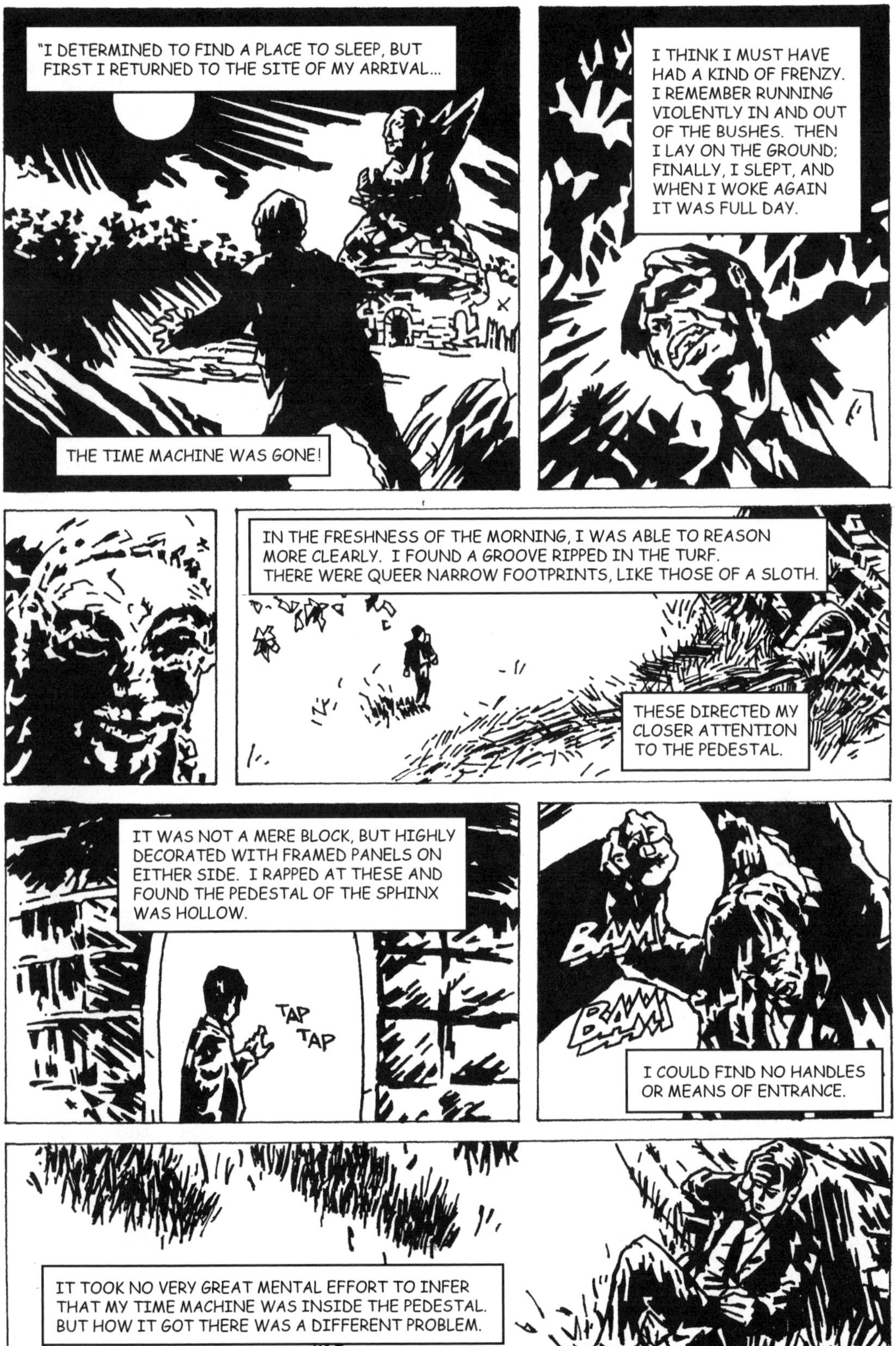
"I DETERMINED TO FIND A PLACE TO SLEEP, BUT FIRST I RETURNED TO THE SITE OF MY ARRIVAL...
THE TIME MACHINE WAS GONE!
I THINK I MUST HAVE HAD A KIND OF FRENZY. I REMEMBER RUNNING VIOLENTLY IN AND OUT OF THE BUSHES. THEN I LAY ON THE GROUND; FINALLY, I SLEPT, AND WHEN I WOKE AGAIN IT WAS FULL DAY.
IN THE FRESHNESS OF THE MORNING, I WAS ABLE TO REASON MORE CLEARLY. I FOUND A GROOVE RIPPED IN THE TURF. THERE WERE QUEER NARROW FOOTPRINTS, LIKE THOSE OF A SLOTH.
THESE DIRECTED MY CLOSER ATTENTION TO THE PEDESTAL.
IT WAS NOT A MERE BLOCK, BUT HIGHLY DECORATED WITH FRAMED PANELS ON EITHER SIDE. I RAPPED AT THESE AND FOUND THE PEDESTAL OF THE SPHINX WAS HOLLOW.
TAP
TAP
BAM
BAM
BAM
I COULD FIND NO HANDLES OR MEANS OF ENTRANCE.
IT TOOK NO VERY GREAT MENTAL EFFORT TO INFER THAT MY TIME MACHINE WAS INSIDE THE PEDESTAL. BUT HOW IT GOT THERE WAS A DIFFERENT PROBLEM.

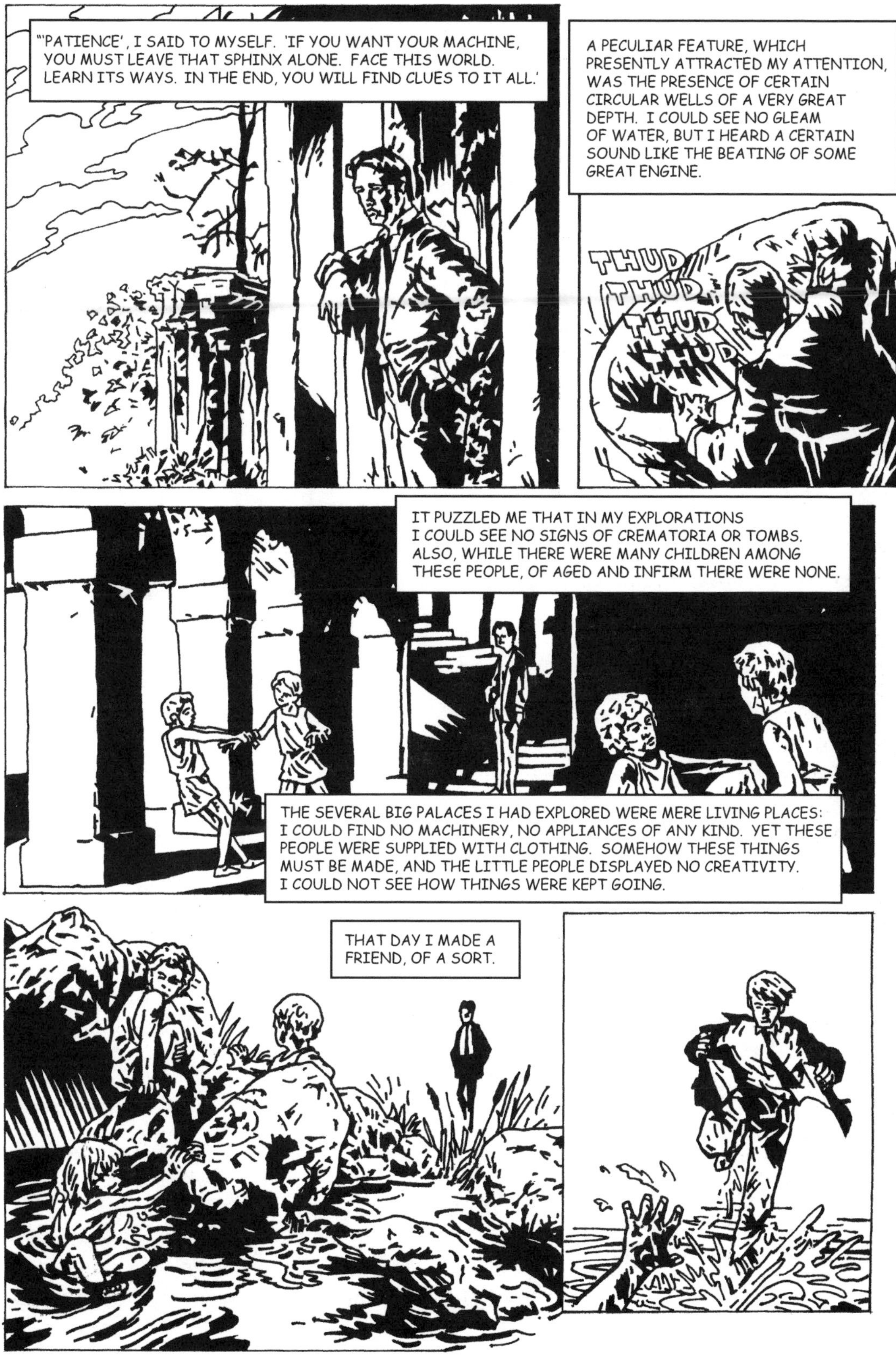
"'PATIENCE', I SAID TO MYSELF. 'IF YOU WANT YOUR MACHINE, YOU MUST LEAVE THAT SPHINX ALONE. FACE THIS WORLD. LEARN ITS WAYS. IN THE END, YOU WILL FIND CLUES TO IT ALL.'
A PECULIAR FEATURE, WHICH PRESENTLY ATTRACTED MY ATTENTION, WAS THE PRESENCE OF CERTAIN CIRCULAR WELLS OF A VERY GREAT DEPTH. I COULD SEE NO GLEAM OF WATER, BUT I HEARD A CERTAIN SOUND LIKE THE BEATING OF SOME GREAT ENGINE.
THUD
THUD
THUD
THUD
IT PUZZLED ME THAT IN MY EXPLORATIONS I COULD SEE NO SIGNS OF CREMATORIA OR TOMBS. ALSO, WHILE THERE WERE MANY CHILDREN AMONG THESE PEOPLE, OF AGED AND INFIRM THERE WERE NONE.
THE SEVERAL BIG PALACES I HAD EXPLORED WERE MERE LIVING PLACES: I COULD FIND NO MACHINERY, NO APPLIANCES OF ANY KIND. YET THESE PEOPLE WERE SUPPLIED WITH CLOTHING. SOMEHOW THESE THINGS MUST BE MADE, AND THE LITTLE PEOPLE DISPLAYED NO CREATIVITY. I COULD NOT SEE HOW THINGS WERE KEPT GOING.
THAT DAY I MADE A FRIEND, OF A SORT.

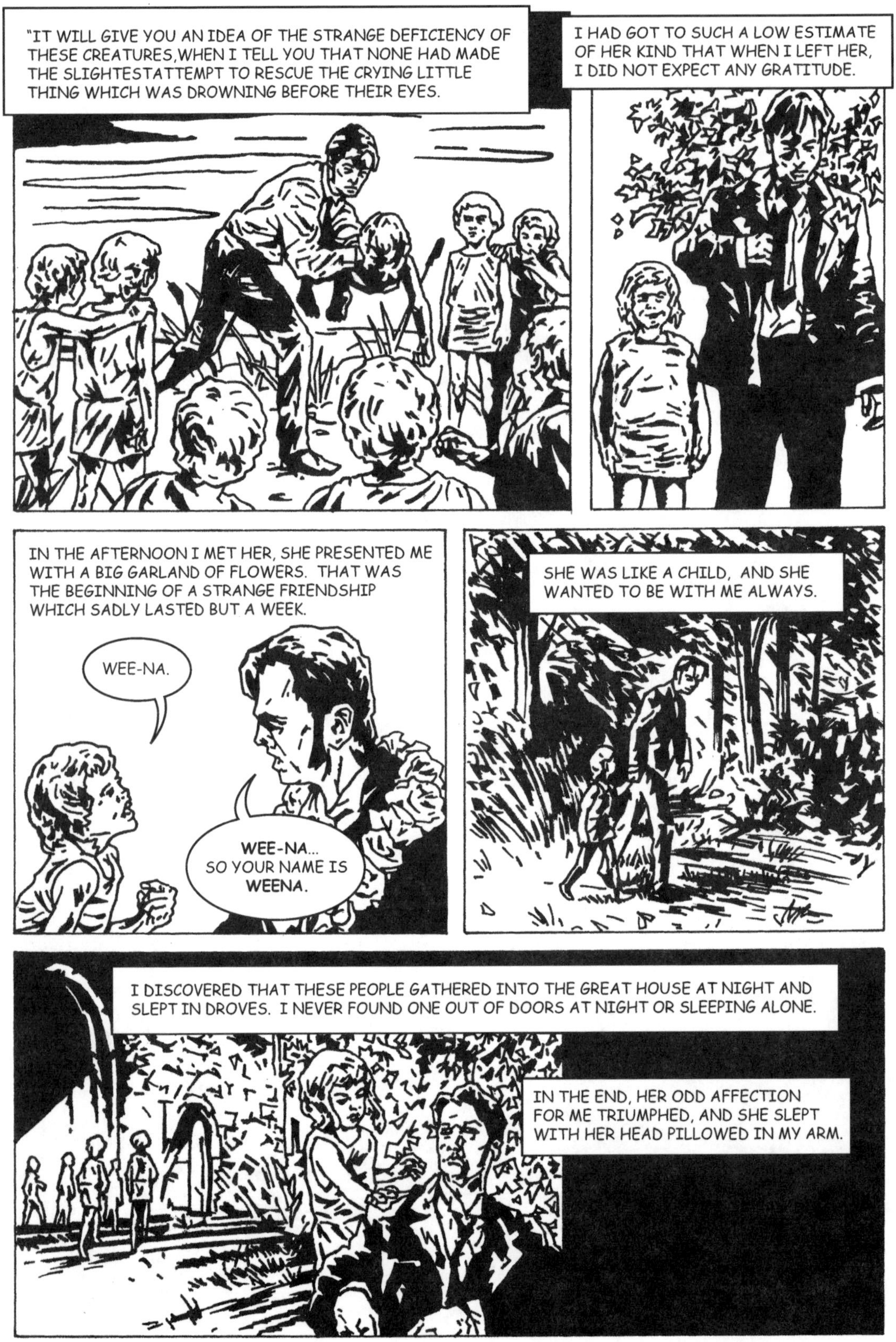
"IT WILL GIVE YOU AN IDEA OF THE STRANGE DEFICIENCY OF THESE CREATURES, WHEN I TELL YOU THAT NONE HAD MADE THE SLIGHTESTATTEMPT TO RESCUE THE CRYING LITTLE THING WHICH WAS DROWNING BEFORE THEIR EYES.
I HAD GOT TO SUCH A LOW ESTIMATE OF HER KIND THAT WHEN I LEFT HER, I DID NOT EXPECT ANY GRATITUDE.
IN THE AFTERNOON I MET HER, SHE PRESENTED ME WITH A BIG GARLAND OF FLOWERS. THAT WAS THE BEGINNING OF A STRANGE FRIENDSHIP WHICH SADLY LASTED BUT A WEEK.
WEE-NA.
WEE-NA... SO YOUR NAME IS WEENA.
SHE WAS LIKE A CHILD, AND SHE WANTED TO BE WITH ME ALWAYS.
I DISCOVERED THAT THESE PEOPLE GATHERED INTO THE GREAT HOUSE AT NIGHT AND SLEPT IN DROVES. I NEVER FOUND ONE OUT OF DOORS AT NIGHT OR SLEEPING ALONE.
IN THE END, HER ODD AFFECTION FOR ME TRIUMPHED, AND SHE SLEPT WITH HER HEAD PILLOWED IN MY ARM.

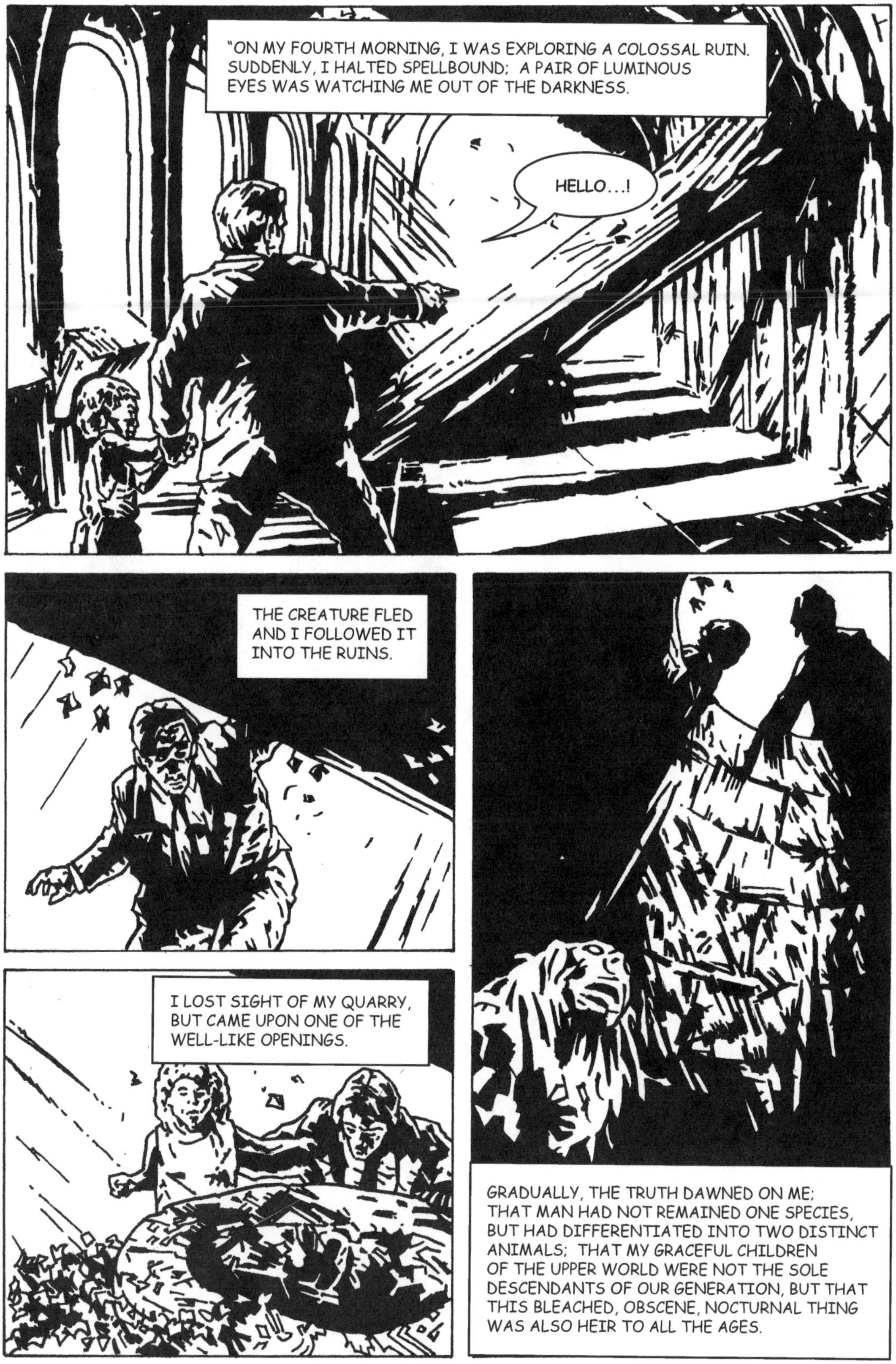
"ON MY FOURTH MORNING, I WAS EXPLORING A COLOSSAL RUIN. SUDDENLY, I HALTED SPELLBOUND; A PAIR OF LUMINOUS EYES WAS WATCHING ME OUT OF THE DARKNESS.
HELLO...!
THE CREATURE FLED AND I FOLLOWED IT INTO THE RUINS.
I LOST SIGHT OF MY QUARRY, BUT CAME UPON ONE OF THE WELL-LIKE OPENINGS.
GRADUALLY, THE TRUTH DAWNED ON ME; THAT MAN HAD NOT REMAINED ONE SPECIES, BUT HAD DIFFERENTIATED INTO TWO DISTINCT ANIMALS; THAT MY GRACEFUL CHILDREN OF THE UPPER WORLD WERE NOT THE SOLE DESCENDANTS OF OUR GENERATION, BUT THAT THIS BLEACHED, OBSCENE, NOCTURNAL THING WAS ALSO HEIR TO ALL THE AGES.

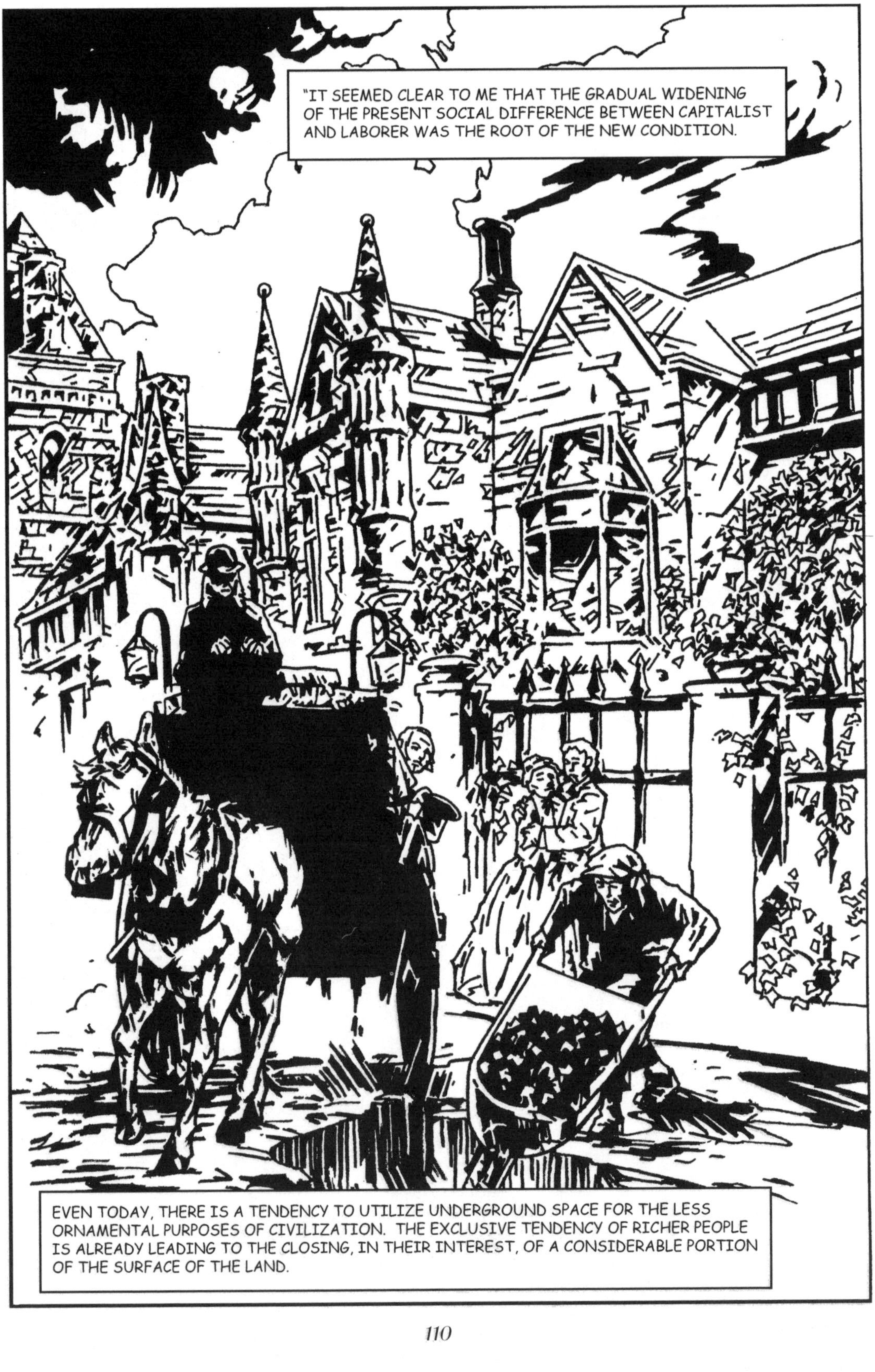
"IT SEEMED CLEAR TO ME THAT THE GRADUAL WIDENING OF THE PRESENT SOCIAL DIFFERENCE BETWEEN CAPITALIST AND LABORER WAS THE ROOT OF THE NEW CONDITION.
EVEN TODAY, THERE IS A TENDENCY TO UTILIZE UNDERGROUND SPACE FOR THE LESS ORNAMENTAL PURPOSES OF CIVILIZATION. THE EXCLUSIVE TENDENCY OF RICHER PEOPLE IS ALREADY LEADING TO THE CLOSING, IN THEIR INTEREST, OF A CONSIDERABLE PORTION OF THE SURFACE OF THE LAND.

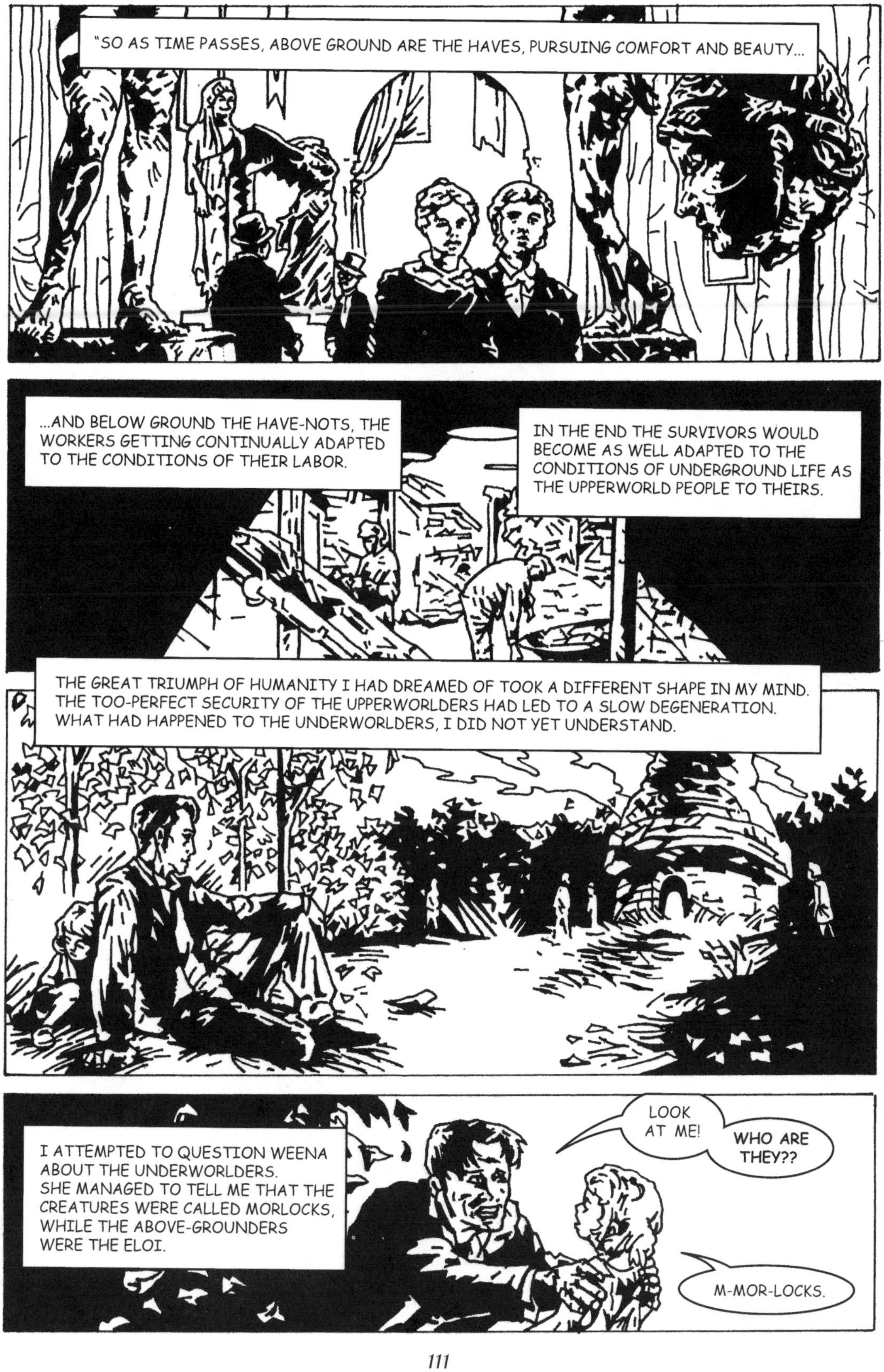
"SO AS TIME PASSES, ABOVE GROUND ARE THE HAVES, PURSUING COMFORT AND BEAUTY...
...AND BELOW GROUND THE HAVE-NOTS, THE WORKERS GETTING CONTINUALLY ADAPTED TO THE CONDITIONS OF THEIR LABOR.
IN THE END THE SURVIVORS WOULD BECOME AS WELL ADAPTED TO THE CONDITIONS OF UNDERGROUND LIFE AS THE UPPERWORLD PEOPLE TO THEIRS.
THE GREAT TRIUMPH OF HUMANITY I HAD DREAMED OF TOOK A DIFFERENT SHAPE IN MY MIND. THE TOO-PERFECT SECURITY OF THE UPPERWORLDERS HAD LED TO A SLOW DEGENERATION. WHAT HAD HAPPENED TO THE UNDERWORLDERS, I DID NOT YET UNDERSTAND.
I ATTEMPTED TO QUESTION WEENA ABOUT THE UNDERWORLDERS. SHE MANAGED TO TELL ME THAT THE CREATURES WERE CALLED MORLOCKS, WHILE THE ABOVE-GROUNDERS WERE THE ELOI.
LOOK AT ME!
WHO ARE THEY??
M-MOR-LOCKS.

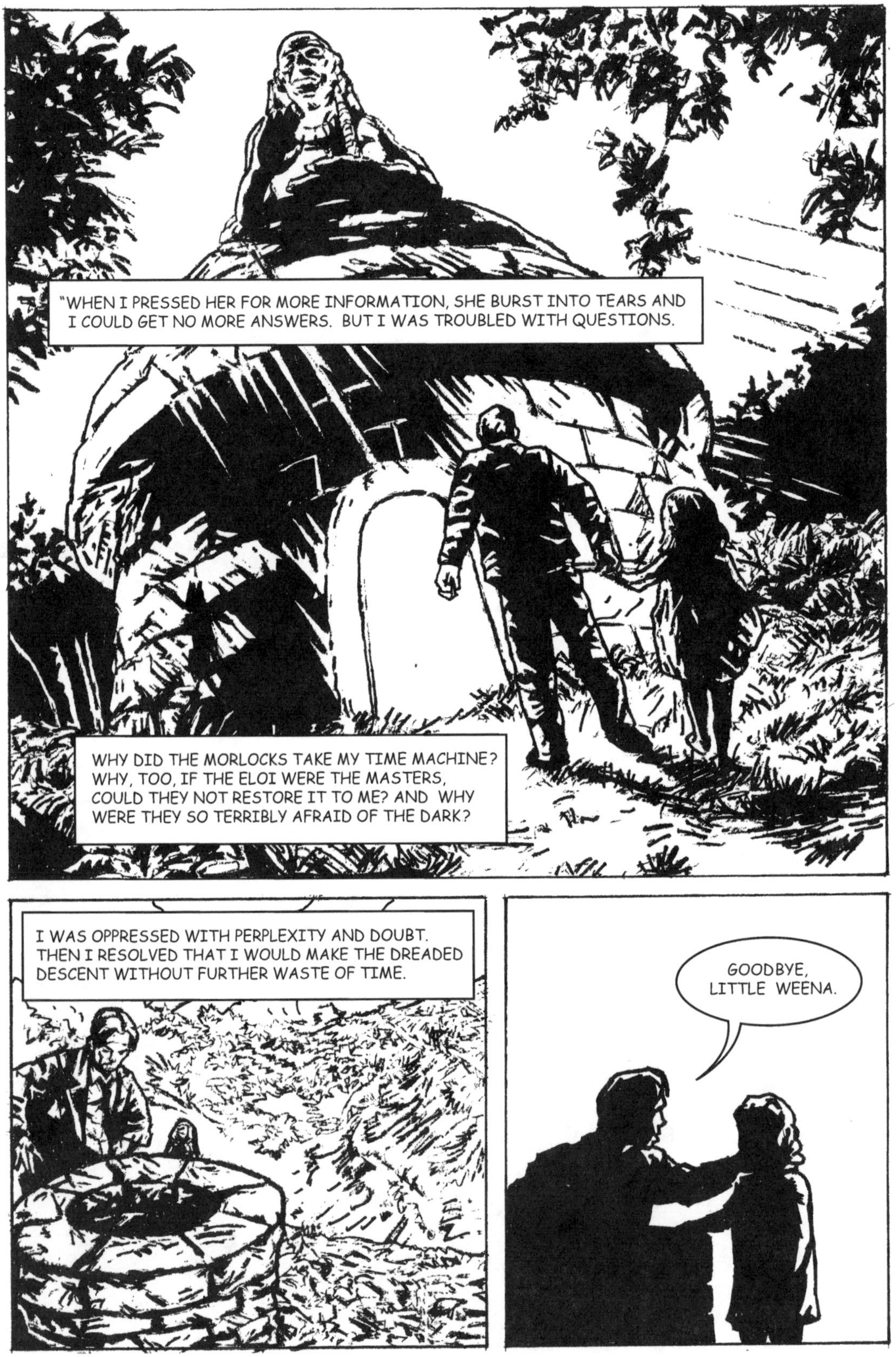
"WHEN I PRESSED HER FOR MORE INFORMATION, SHE BURST INTO TEARS AND I COULD GET NO MORE ANSWERS. BUT I WAS TROUBLED WITH QUESTIONS.
WHY DID THE MORLOCKS TAKE MY TIME MACHINE? WHY, TOO, IF THE ELOI WERE THE MASTERS, COULD THEY NOT RESTORE IT TO ME? AND WHY WERE THEY SO TERRIBLY AFRAID OF THE DARK?
I WAS OPPRESSED WITH PERPLEXITY AND DOUBT. THEN I RESOLVED THAT I WOULD MAKE THE DREADED DESCENT WITHOUT FURTHER WASTE OF TIME.
GOODBYE, LITTLE WEENA.

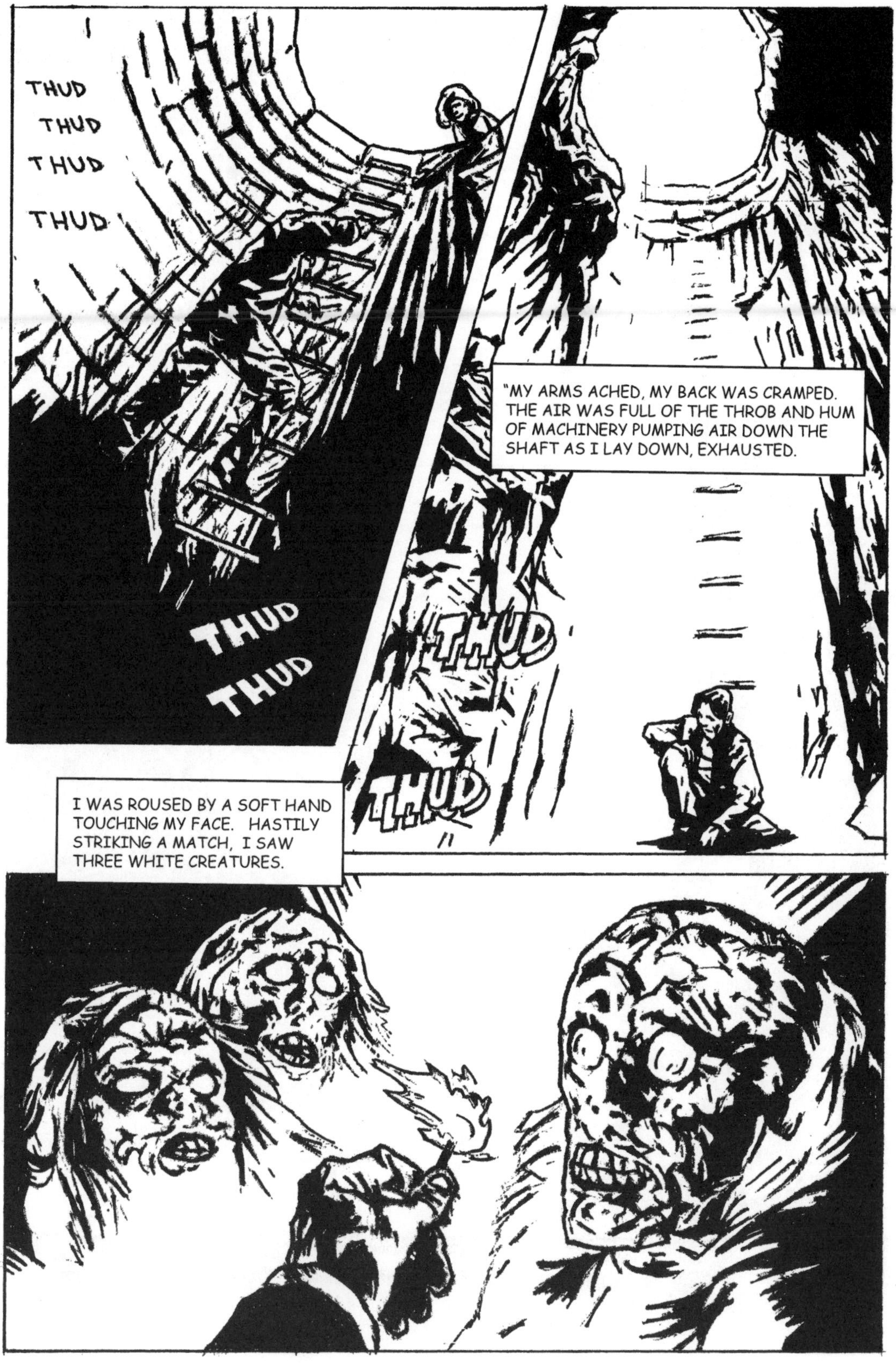
THUD
THUD
THUD
THUD
THUD
THUD
"MY ARMS ACHED, MY BACK WAS CRAMPED. THE AIR WAS FULL OF THE THROB AND HUM OF MACHINERY PUMPING AIR DOWN THE SHAFT AS I LAY DOWN, EXHAUSTED.
THUD
THUD
I WAS ROUSED BY A SOFT HAND TOUCHING MY FACE. HASTILY STRIKING A MATCH, I SAW THREE WHITE CREATURES.

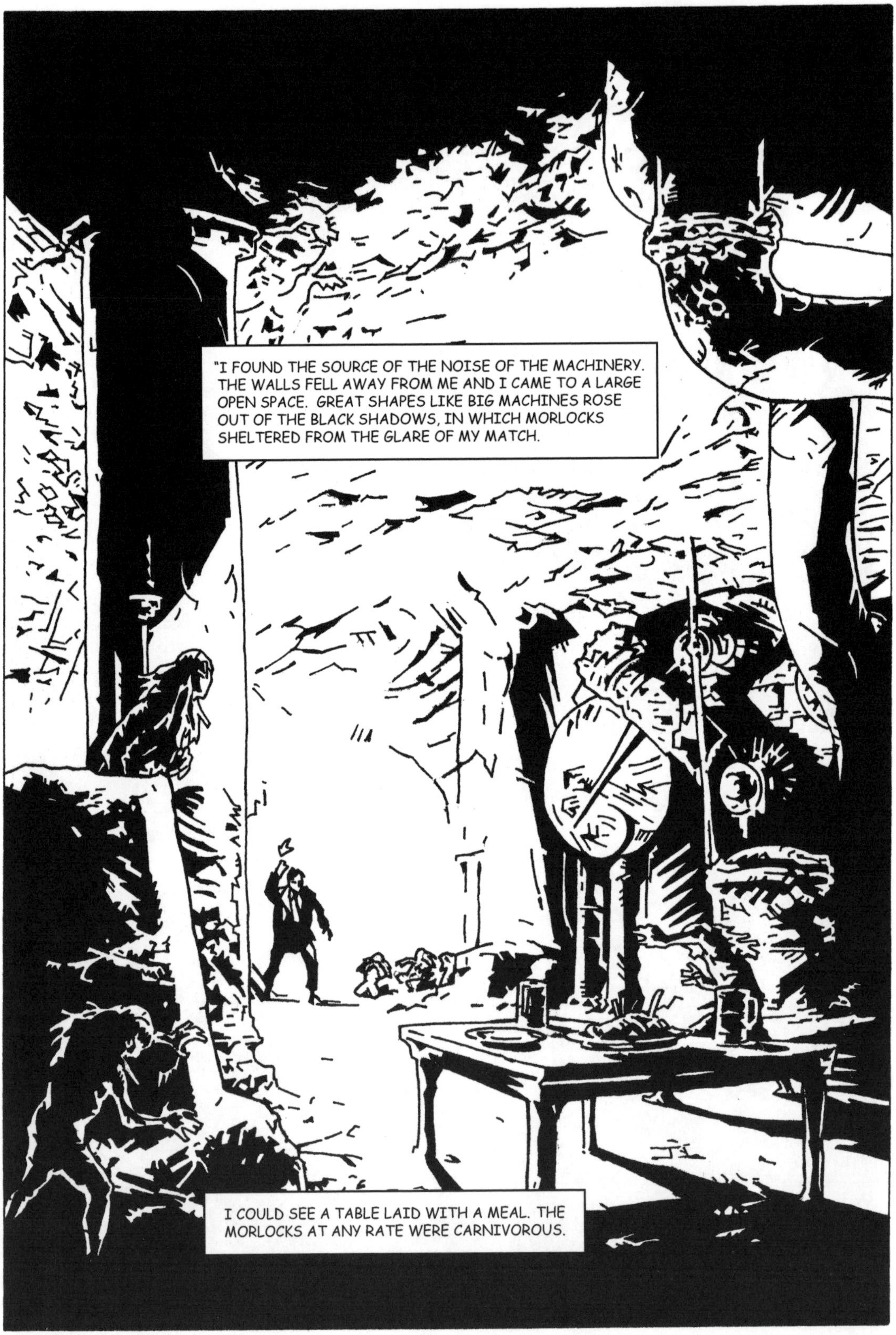
"I FOUND THE SOURCE OF THE NOISE OF THE MACHINERY. THE WALLS FELL AWAY FROM ME AND I CAME TO A LARGE OPEN SPACE. GREAT SHAPES LIKE BIG MACHINES ROSE OUT OF THE BLACK SHADOWS, IN WHICH MORLOCKS SHELTERED FROM THE GLARE OF MY MATCH.
I COULD SEE A TABLE LAID WITH A MEAL. THE MORLOCKS AT ANY RATE WERE CARNIVOROUS.

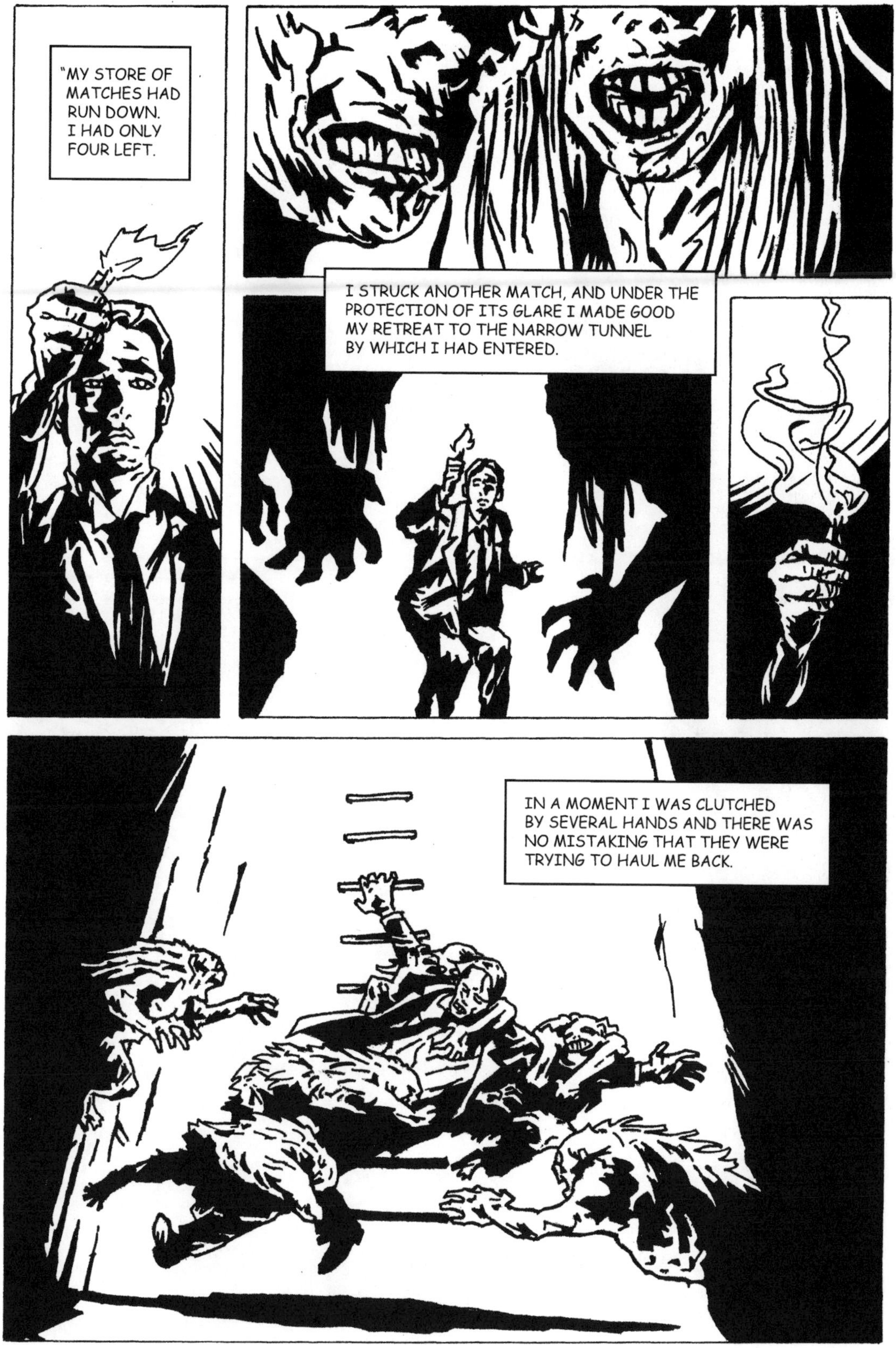
"MY STORE OF MATCHES HAD RUN DOWN. I HAD ONLY FOUR LEFT.
I STRUCK ANOTHER MATCH, AND UNDER THE PROTECTION OF ITS GLARE I MADE GOOD MY RETREAT TO THE NARROW TUNNEL BY WHICH I HAD ENTERED.
IN A MOMENT I WAS CLUTCHED BY SEVERAL HANDS AND THERE WAS NO MISTAKING THAT THEY WERE TRYING TO HAUL ME BACK.

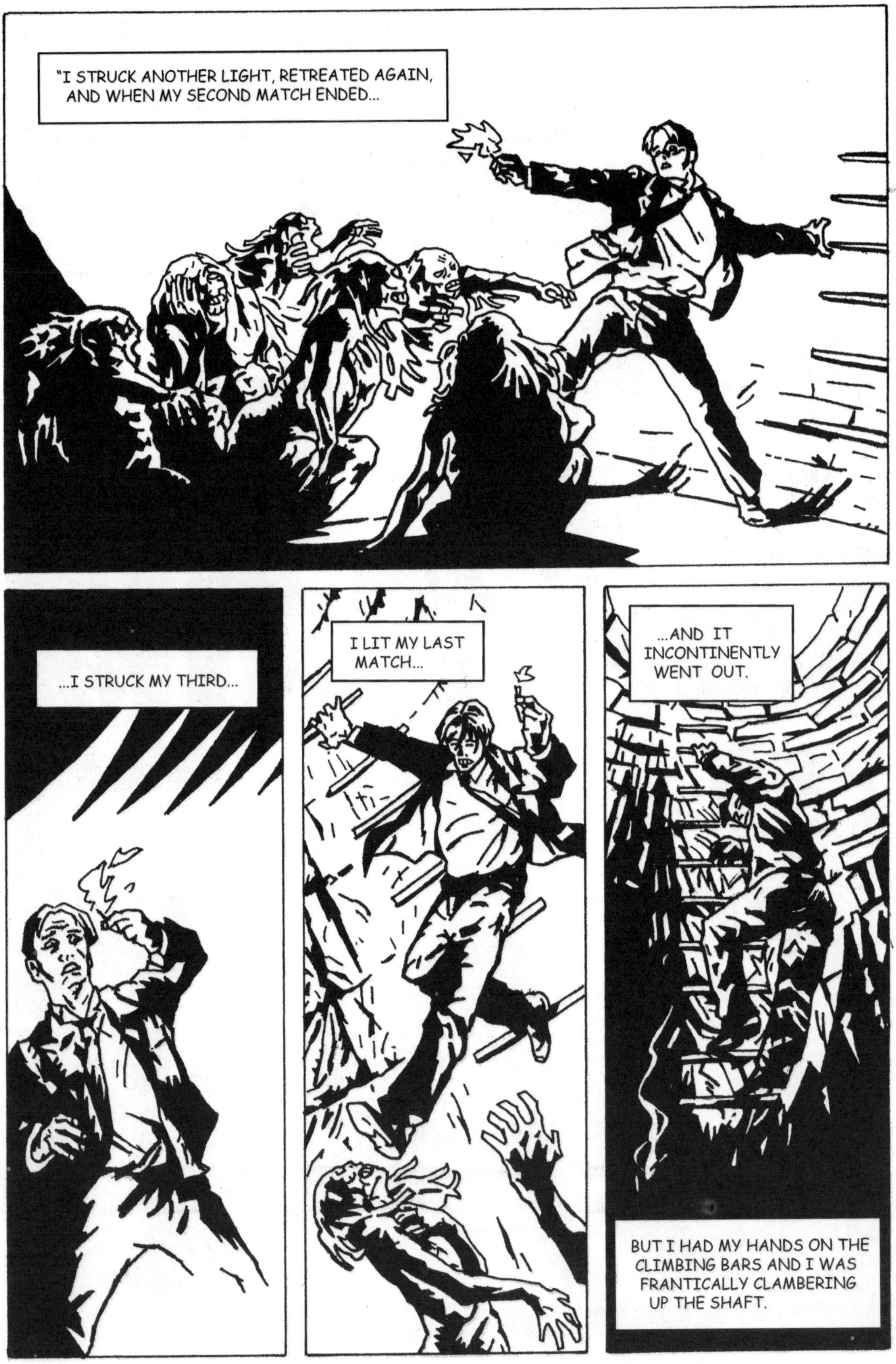
"I STRUCK ANOTHER LIGHT, RETREATED AGAIN, AND WHEN MY SECOND MATCH ENDED...
...I STRUCK MY THIRD...
I LIT MY LAST MATCH...
...AND IT INCONTINENTLY WENT OUT.
BUT I HAD MY HANDS ON THE CLIMBING BARS AND I WAS FRANTICALLY CLAMBERING UP THE SHAFT.

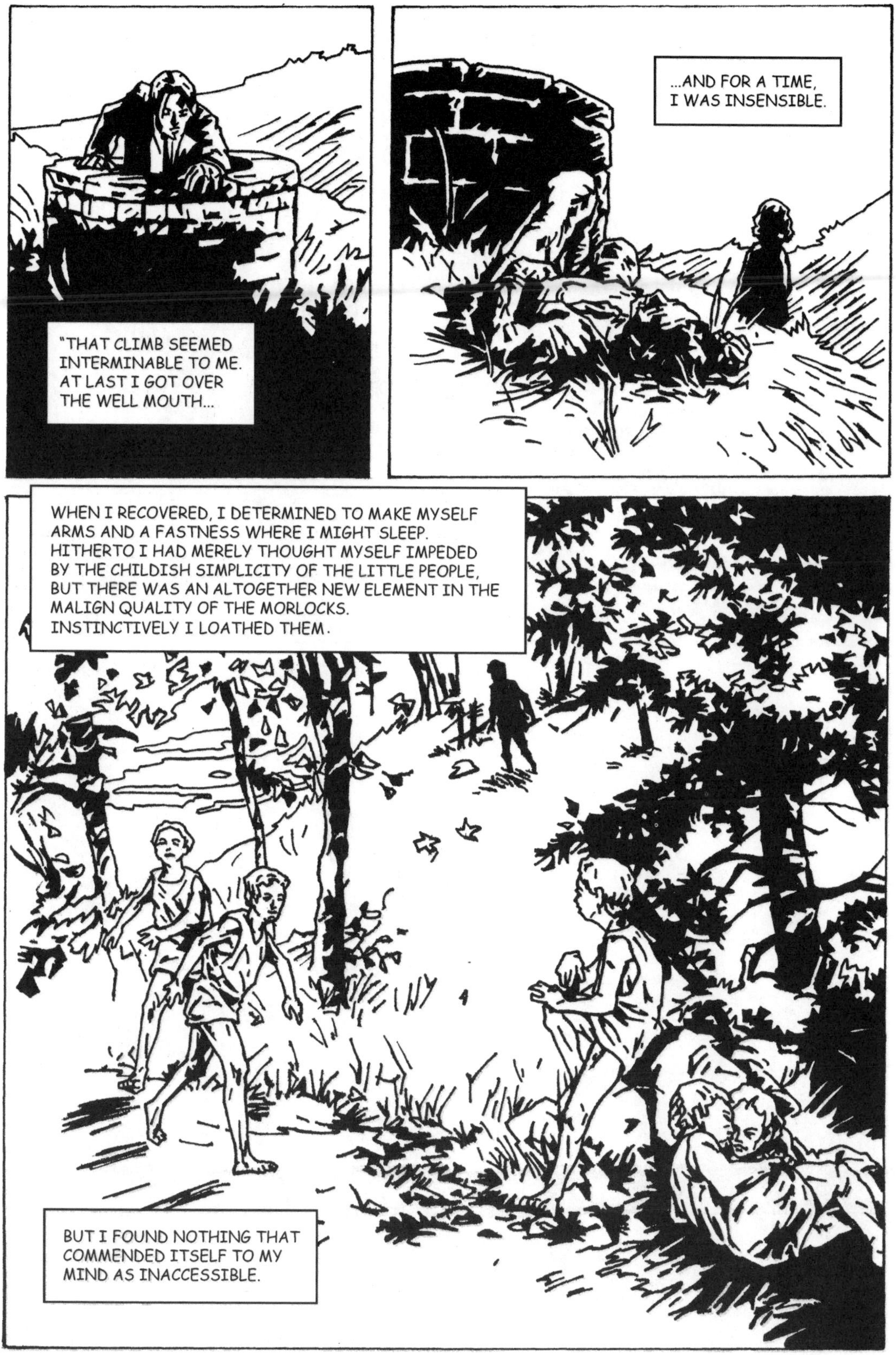
"THAT CLIMB SEEMED INTERMINABLE TO ME. AT LAST I GOT OVER THE WELL MOUTH...
...AND FOR A TIME, I WAS INSENSIBLE.
WHEN I RECOVERED, I DETERMINED TO MAKE MYSELF ARMS AND A FASTNESS WHERE I MIGHT SLEEP. HITHERTO I HAD MERELY THOUGHT MYSELF IMPEDED BY THE CHILDISH SIMPLICITY OF THE LITTLE PEOPLE, BUT THERE WAS AN ALTOGETHER NEW ELEMENT IN THE MALIGN QUALITY OF THE MORLOCKS. INSTINCTIVELY I LOATHED THEM.
BUT I FOUND NOTHING THAT COMMENDED ITSELF TO MY MIND AS INACCESSIBLE.

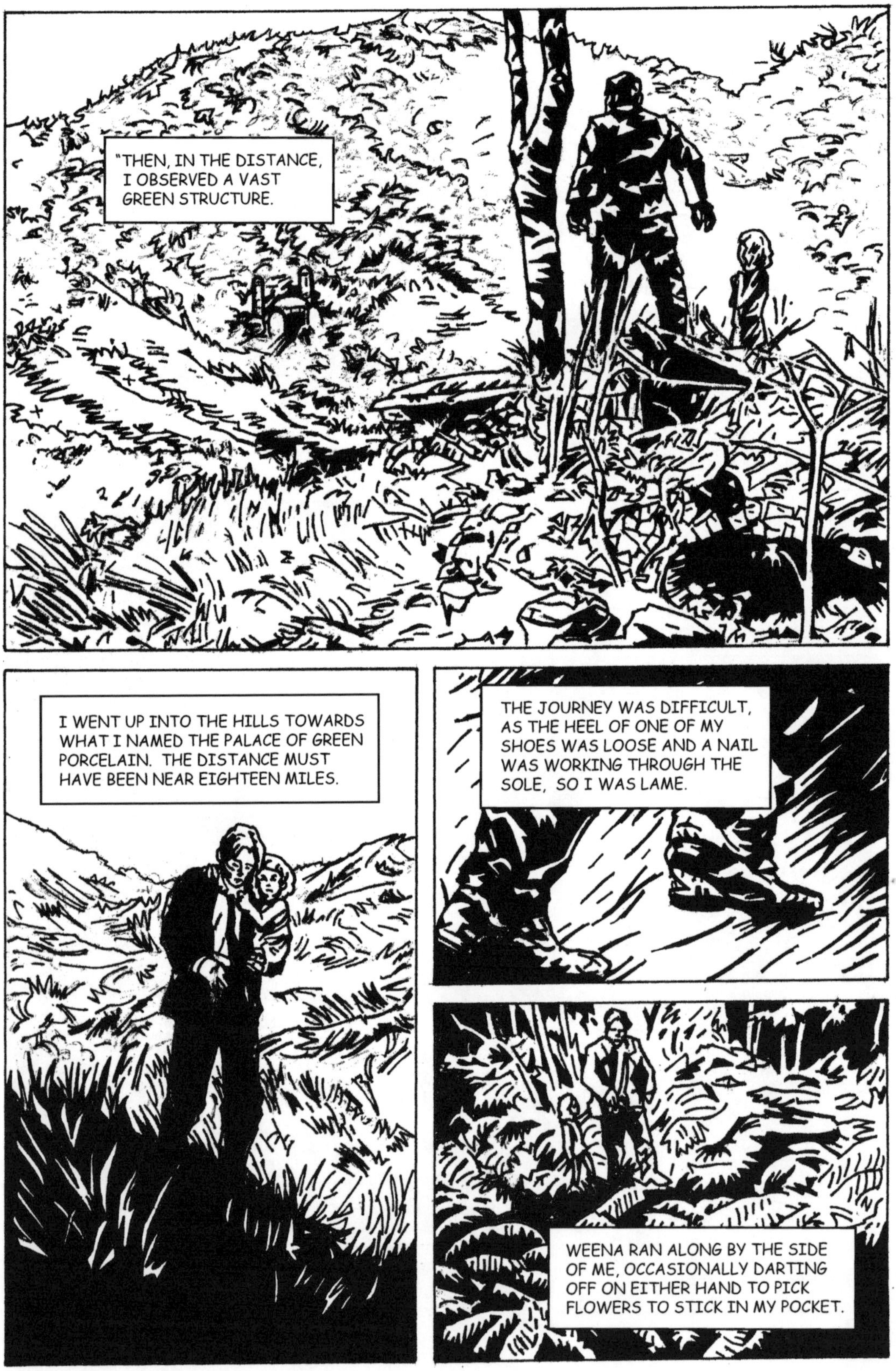
"THEN, IN THE DISTANCE, I OBSERVED A VAST GREEN STRUCTURE.
I WENT UP INTO THE HILLS TOWARDS WHAT I NAMED THE PALACE OF GREEN PORCELAIN. THE DISTANCE MUST HAVE BEEN NEAR EIGHTEEN MILES.
THE JOURNEY WAS DIFFICULT, AS THE HEEL OF ONE OF MY SHOES WAS LOOSE AND A NAIL WAS WORKING THROUGH THE SOLE, SO I WAS LAME.
WEENA RAN ALONG BY THE SIDE OF ME, OCCASIONALLY DARTING OFF ON EITHER HAND TO PICK FLOWERS TO STICK IN MY POCKET.

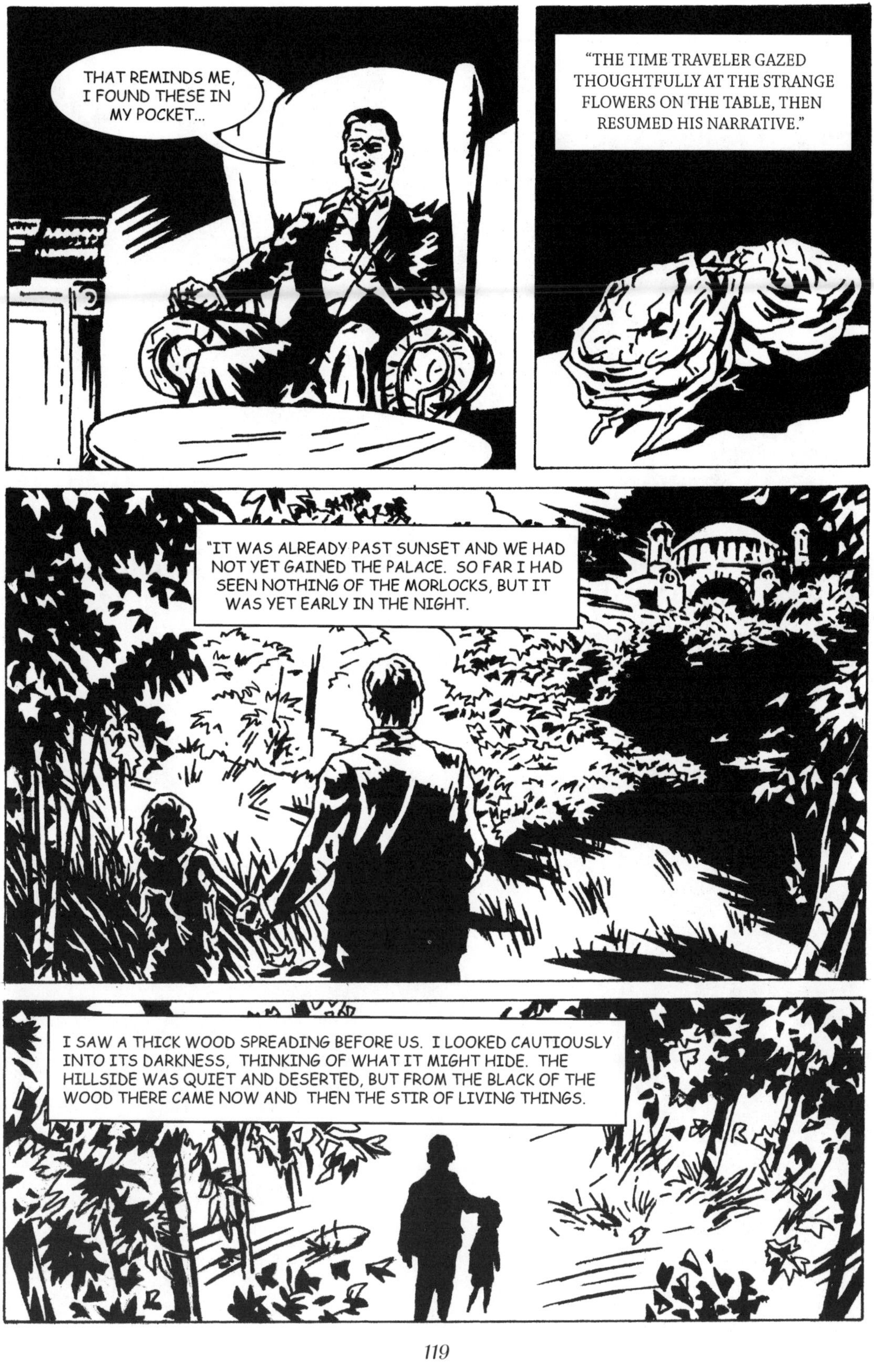
THAT REMINDS ME, I FOUND THESE IN MY POCKET...
"THE TIME TRAVELER GAZED THOUGHTFULLY AT THE STRANGE FLOWERS ON THE TABLE, THEN RESUMED HIS NARRATIVE."
"IT WAS ALREADY PAST SUNSET AND WE HAD NOT YET GAINED THE PALACE. SO FAR I HAD SEEN NOTHING OF THE MORLOCKS, BUT IT WAS YET EARLY IN THE NIGHT.
I SAW A THICK WOOD SPREADING BEFORE US. I LOOKED CAUTIOUSLY INTO ITS DARKNESS, THINKING OF WHAT IT MIGHT HIDE. THE HILLSIDE WAS QUIET AND DESERTED, BUT FROM THE BLACK OF THE WOOD THERE CAME NOW AND THEN THE STIR OF LIVING THINGS.

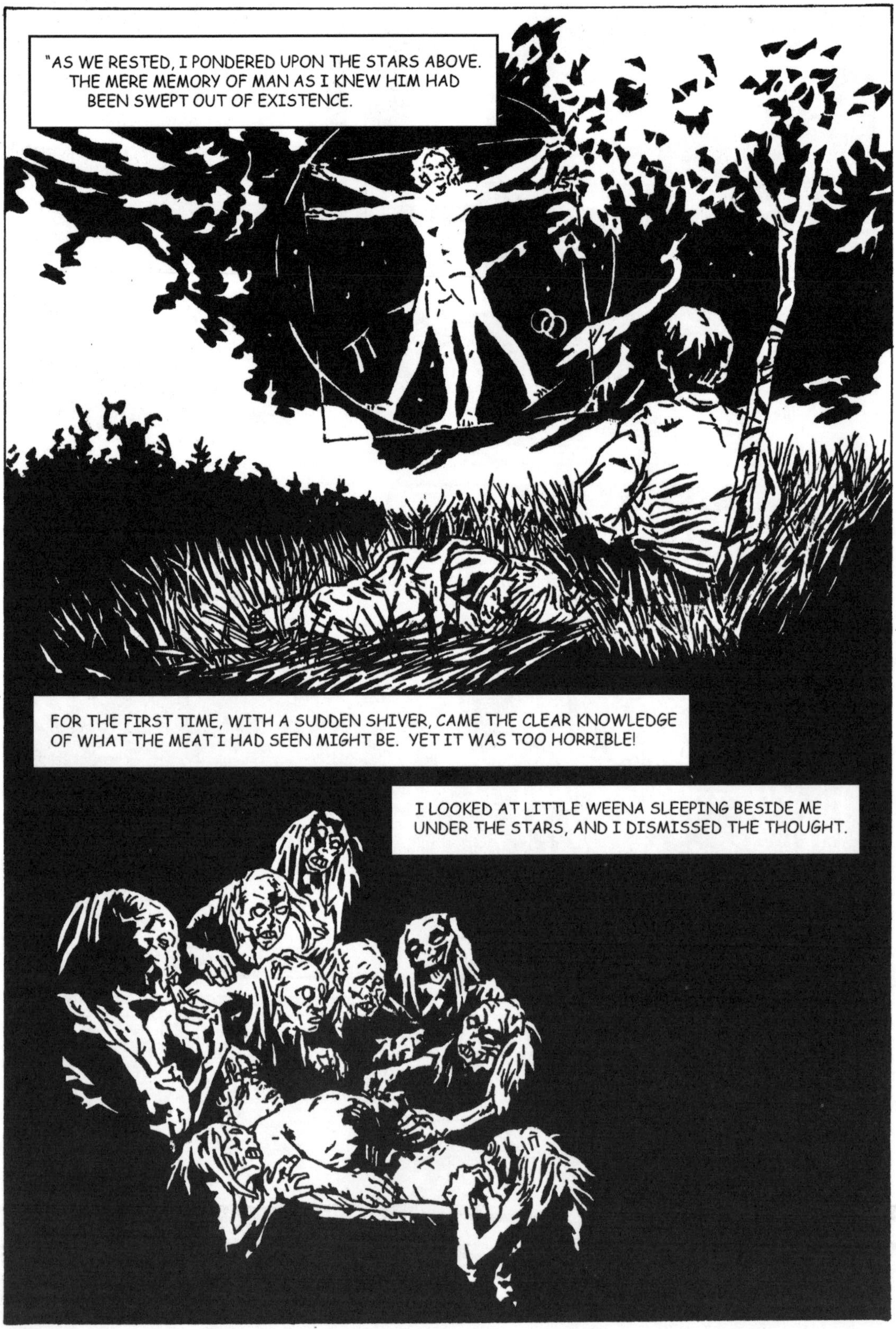
"AS WE RESTED, I PONDERED UPON THE STARS ABOVE. THE MERE MEMORY OF MAN AS I KNEW HIM HAD BEEN SWEPT OUT OF EXISTENCE.
FOR THE FIRST TIME, WITH A SUDDEN SHIVER, CAME THE CLEAR KNOWLEDGE OF WHAT THE MEAT I HAD SEEN MIGHT BE. YET IT WAS TOO HORRIBLE!
I LOOKED AT LITTLE WEENA SLEEPING BESIDE ME UNDER THE STARS, AND I DISMISSED THE THOUGHT.

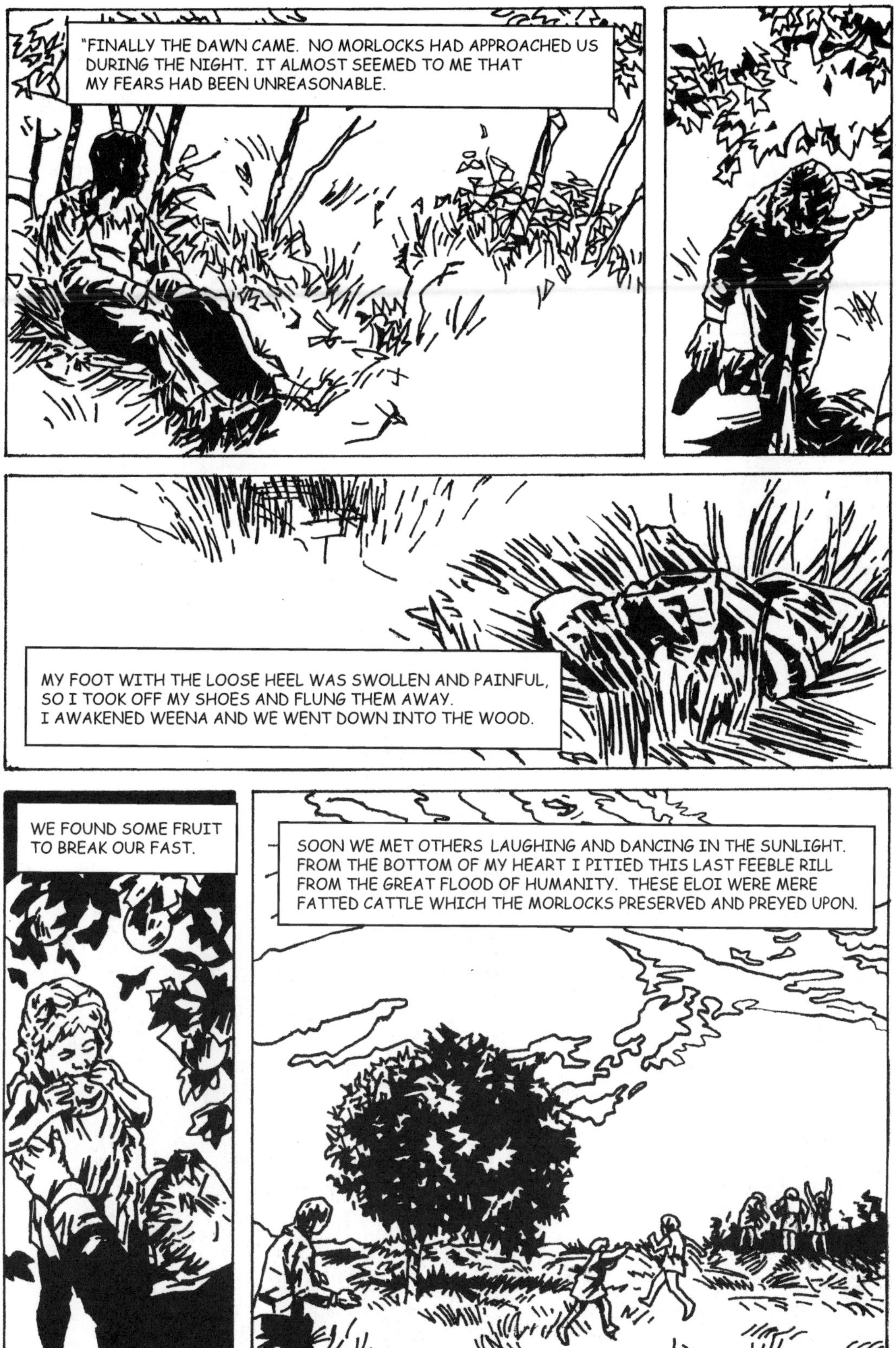
"FINALLY THE DAWN CAME. NO MORLOCKS HAD APPROACHED US DURING THE NIGHT. IT ALMOST SEEMED TO ME THAT MY FEARS HAD BEEN UNREASONABLE.
MY FOOT WITH THE LOOSE HEEL WAS SWOLLEN AND PAINFUL, SO I TOOK OFF MY SHOES AND FLUNG THEM AWAY. I AWAKENED WEENA AND WE WENT DOWN INTO THE WOOD.
WE FOUND SOME FRUIT TO BREAK OUR FAST.
SOON WE MET OTHERS LAUGHING AND DANCING IN THE SUNLIGHT. FROM THE BOTTOM OF MY HEART I PITIED THIS LAST FEEBLE RILL FROM THE GREAT FLOOD OF HUMANITY. THESE ELOI WERE MERE FATTED CATTLE WHICH THE MORLOCKS PRESERVED AND PREYED UPON.

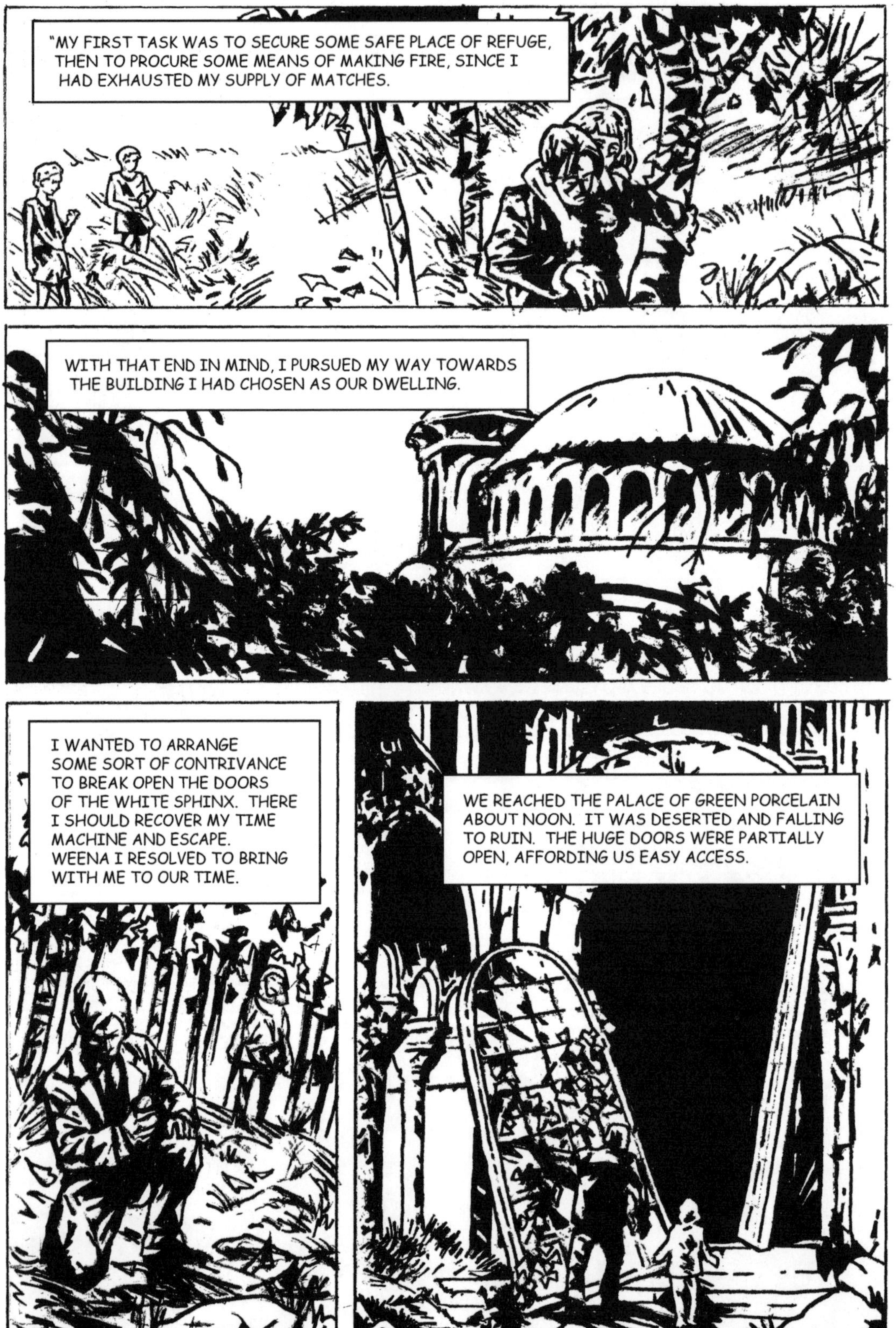
"MY FIRST TASK WAS TO SECURE SOME SAFE PLACE OF REFUGE, THEN TO PROCURE SOME MEANS OF MAKING FIRE, SINCE I HAD EXHAUSTED MY SUPPLY OF MATCHES.
WITH THAT END IN MIND, I PURSUED MY WAY TOWARDS THE BUILDING I HAD CHOSEN AS OUR DWELLING.
I WANTED TO ARRANGE SOME SORT OF CONTRIVANCE TO BREAK OPEN THE DOORS OF THE WHITE SPHINX. THERE I SHOULD RECOVER MY TIME MACHINE AND ESCAPE. WEENA I RESOLVED TO BRING WITH ME TO OUR TIME.
WE REACHED THE PALACE OF GREEN PORCELAIN ABOUT NOON. IT WAS DESERTED AND FALLING TO RUIN. THE HUGE DOORS WERE PARTIALLY OPEN, AFFORDING US EASY ACCESS.

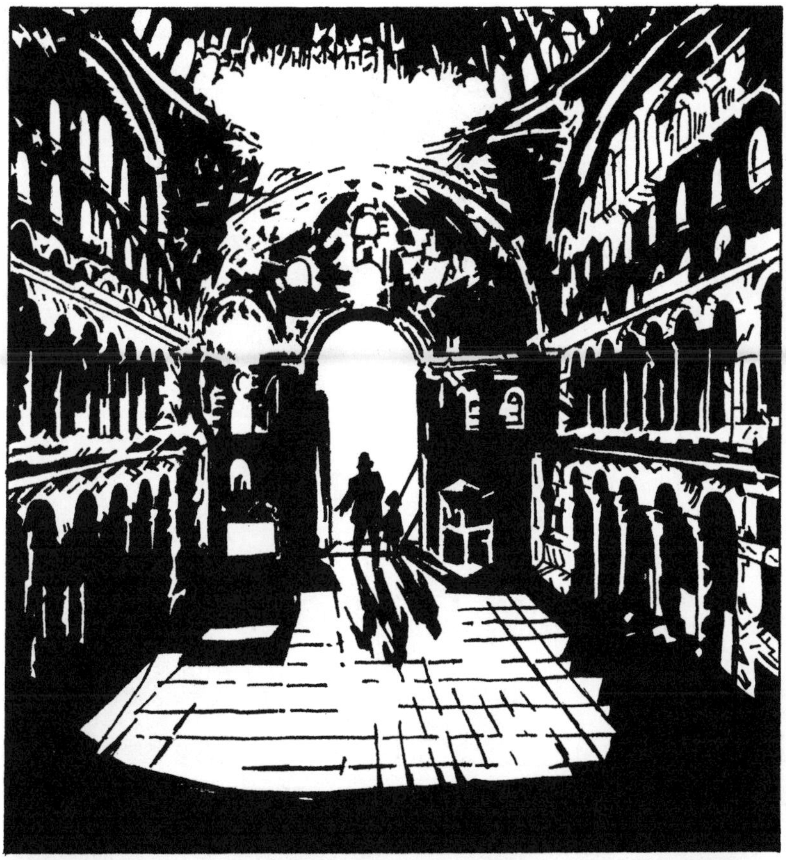

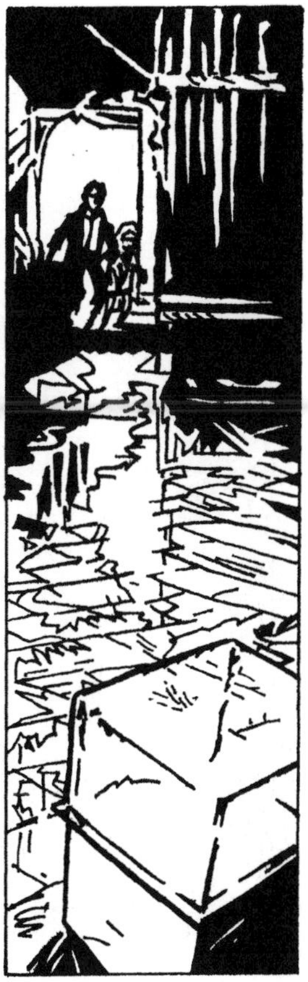

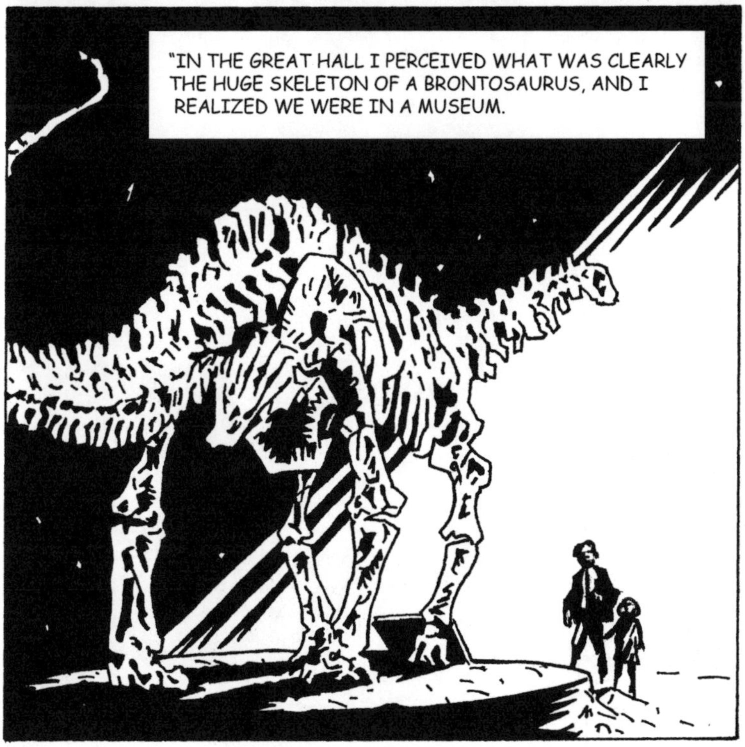
"IN THE GREAT HALL I PERCEIVED WHAT WAS CLEARLY THE HUGE SKELETON OF A BRONTOSAURUS, AND I REALIZED WE WERE IN A MUSEUM.

HERE, APPARENTLY, WAS THE PALEONTOLOGICAL SECTION, THOUGH TO JUDGE FROM THE SIZE OF THE PLACE, THIS PALACE HAD A GREAT DEAL MORE IN IT. PERHAPS HISTORICAL GALLERIES; IT MIGHT BE, EVEN A LIBRARY!

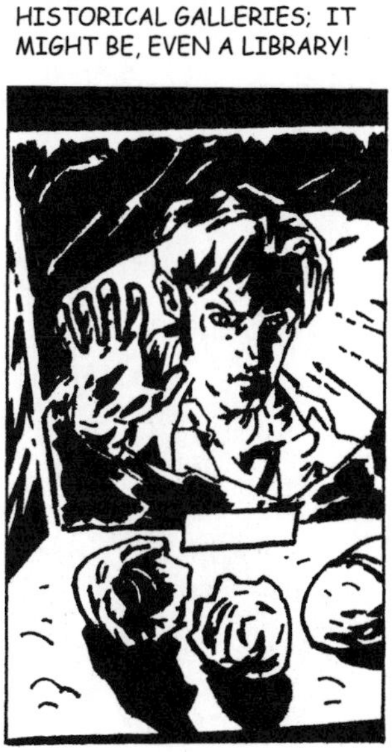

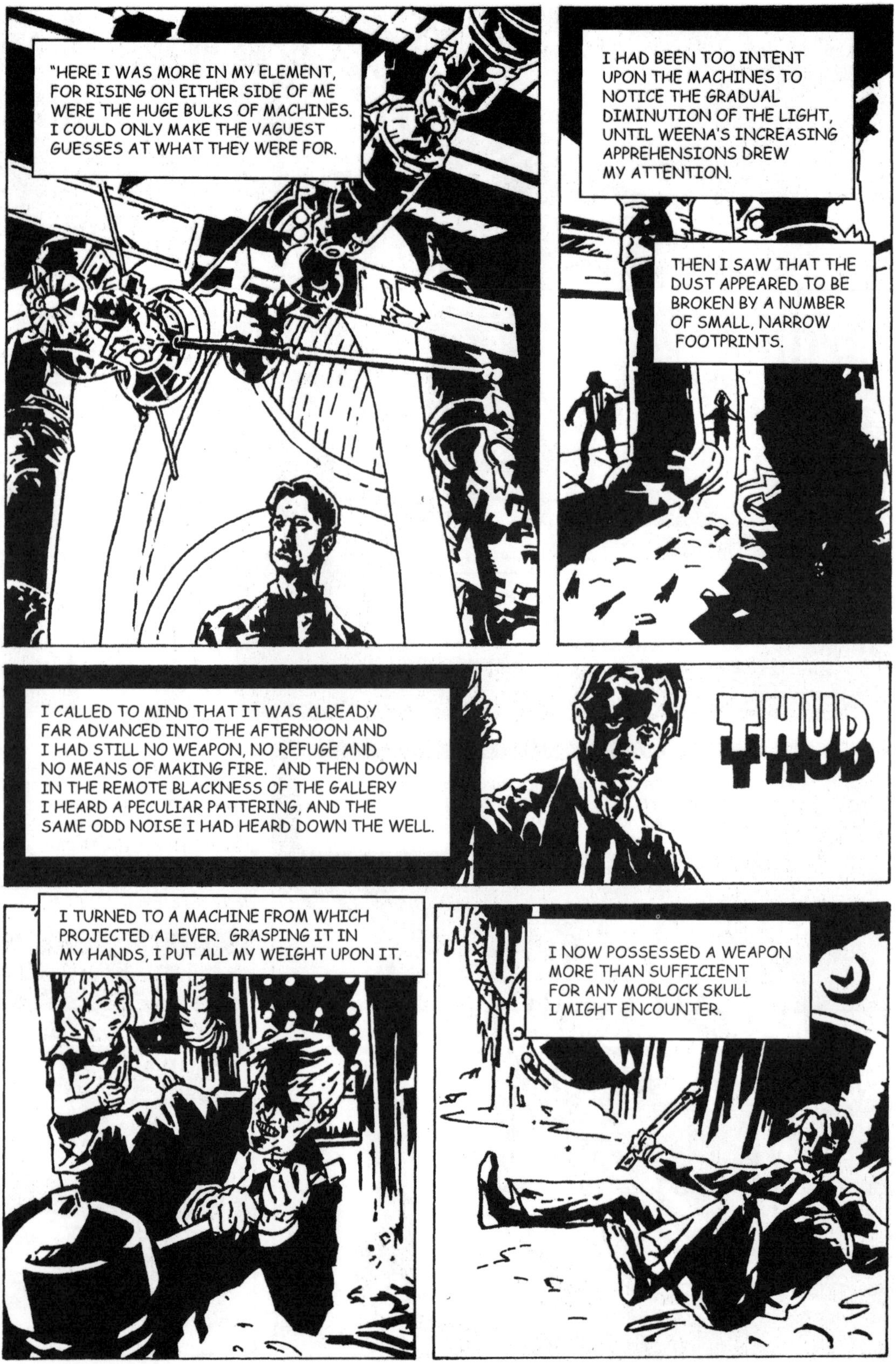
"HERE I WAS MORE IN MY ELEMENT, FOR RISING ON EITHER SIDE OF ME WERE THE HUGE BULKS OF MACHINES. I COULD ONLY MAKE THE VAGUEST GUESSES AT WHAT THEY WERE FOR.
I HAD BEEN TOO INTENT UPON THE MACHINES TO NOTICE THE GRADUAL DIMINUTION OF THE LIGHT, UNTIL WEENA'S INCREASING APPREHENSIONS DREW MY ATTENTION.
THEN I SAW THAT THE DUST APPEARED TO BE BROKEN BY A NUMBER OF SMALL, NARROW FOOTPRINTS.
I CALLED TO MIND THAT IT WAS ALREADY FAR ADVANCED INTO THE AFTERNOON AND I HAD STILL NO WEAPON, NO REFUGE AND NO MEANS OF MAKING FIRE. AND THEN DOWN IN THE REMOTE BLACKNESS OF THE GALLERY I HEARD A PECULIAR PATTERING, AND THE SAME ODD NOISE I HAD HEARD DOWN THE WELL.
THUD
I TURNED TO A MACHINE FROM WHICH PROJECTED A LEVER. GRASPING IT IN MY HANDS, I PUT ALL MY WEIGHT UPON IT.
I NOW POSSESSED A WEAPON MORE THAN SUFFICIENT FOR ANY MORLOCK SKULL I MIGHT ENCOUNTER.

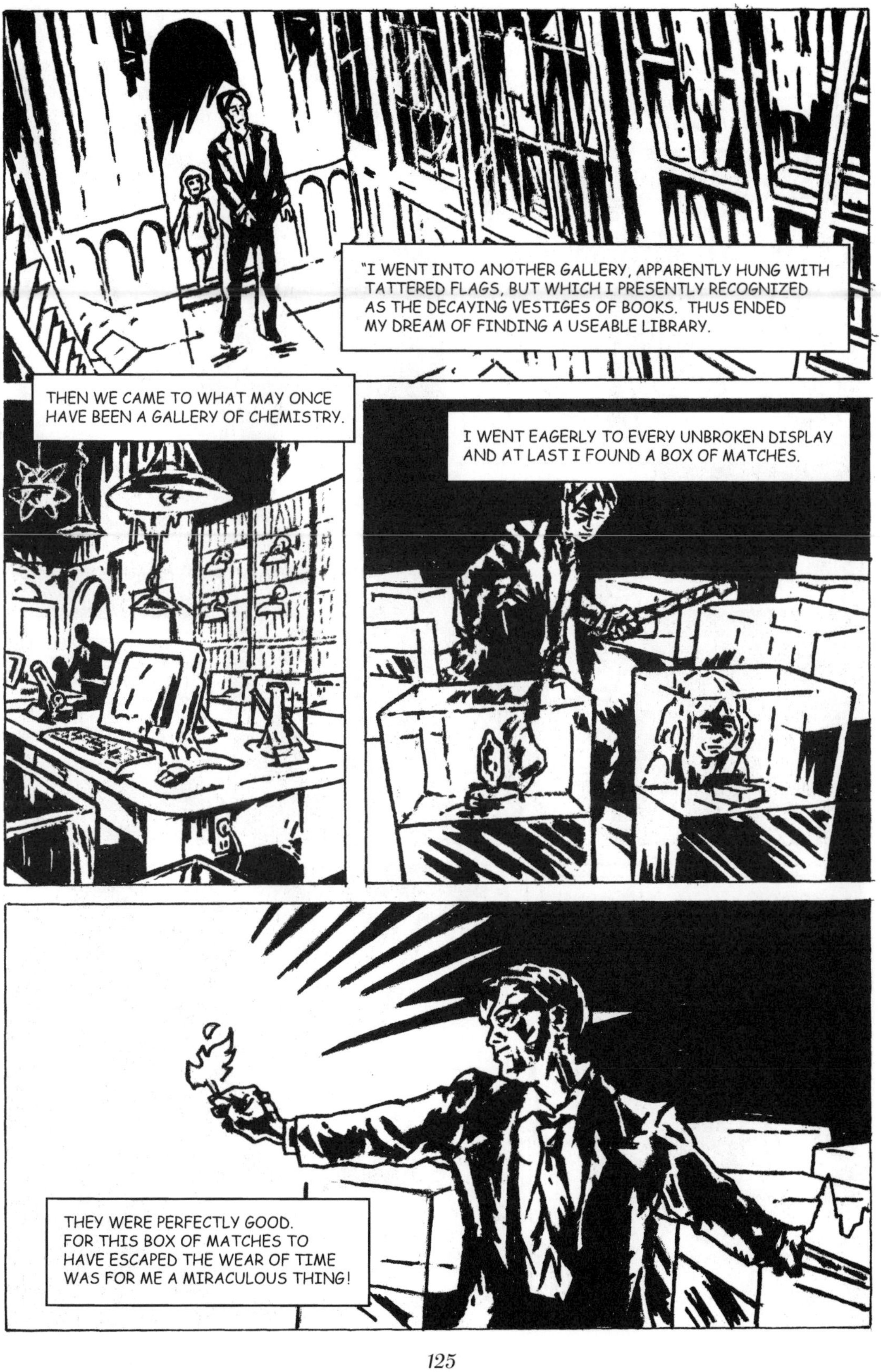
"I WENT INTO ANOTHER GALLERY, APPARENTLY HUNG WITH TATTERED FLAGS, BUT WHICH I PRESENTLY RECOGNIZED AS THE DECAYING VESTIGES OF BOOKS. THUS ENDED MY DREAM OF FINDING A USEABLE LIBRARY.
THEN WE CAME TO WHAT MAY ONCE HAVE BEEN A GALLERY OF CHEMISTRY.
I WENT EAGERLY TO EVERY UNBROKEN DISPLAY AND AT LAST I FOUND A BOX OF MATCHES.
THEY WERE PERFECTLY GOOD. FOR THIS BOX OF MATCHES TO HAVE ESCAPED THE WEAR OF TIME WAS FOR ME A MIRACULOUS THING!

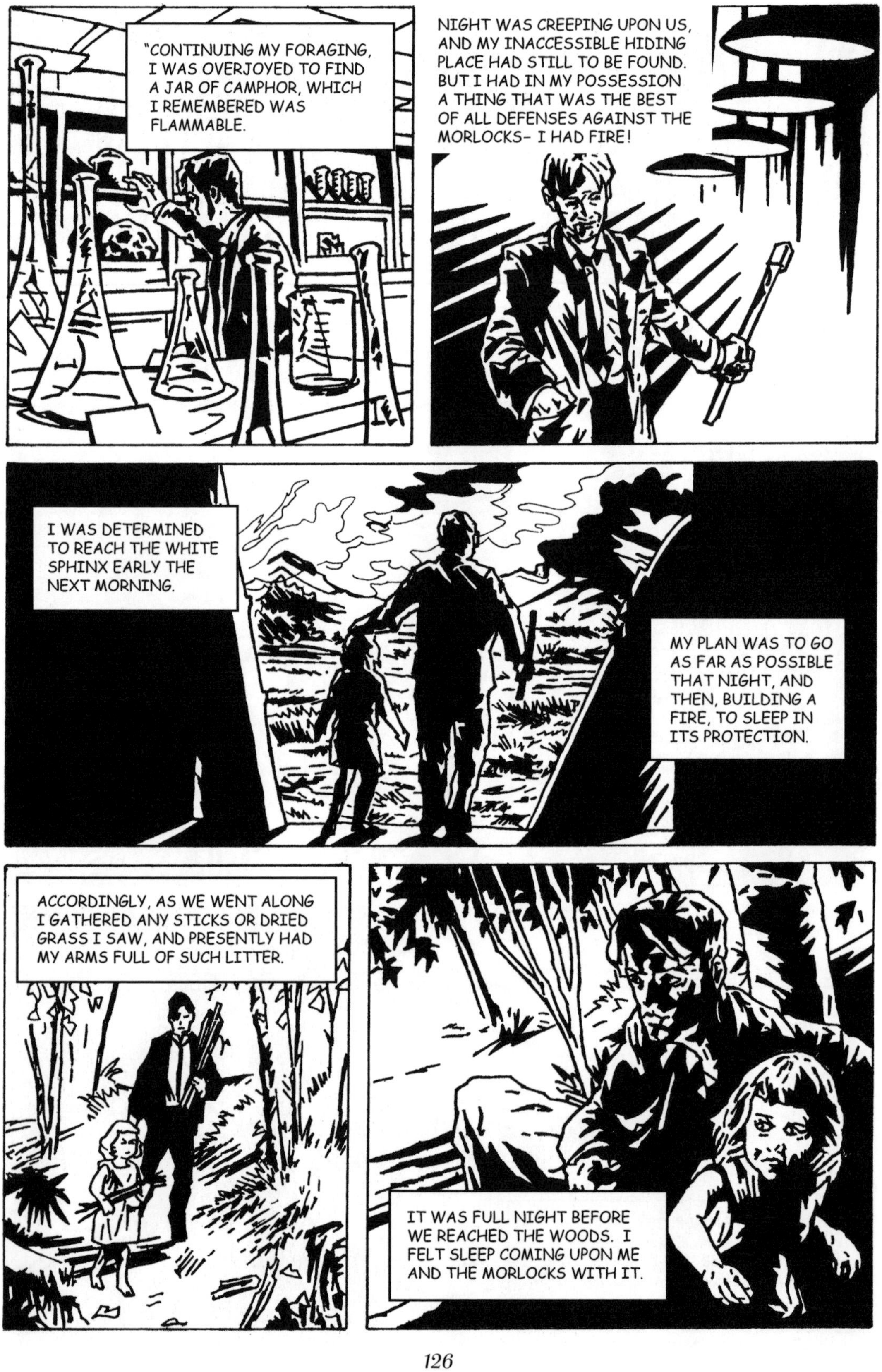
"CONTINUING MY FORAGING, I WAS OVERJOYED TO FIND A JAR OF CAMPHOR, WHICH I REMEMBERED WAS FLAMMABLE.
NIGHT WAS CREEPING UPON US, AND MY INACCESSIBLE HIDING PLACE HAD STILL TO BE FOUND. BUT I HAD IN MY POSSESSION A THING THAT WAS THE BEST OF ALL DEFENSES AGAINST THE MORLOCKS– I HAD FIRE!
I WAS DETERMINED TO REACH THE WHITE SPHINX EARLY THE NEXT MORNING.
MY PLAN WAS TO GO AS FAR AS POSSIBLE THAT NIGHT, AND THEN, BUILDING A FIRE, TO SLEEP IN ITS PROTECTION.
ACCORDINGLY, AS WE WENT ALONG I GATHERED ANY STICKS OR DRIED GRASS I SAW, AND PRESENTLY HAD MY ARMS FULL OF SUCH LITTER.
IT WAS FULL NIGHT BEFORE WE REACHED THE WOODS. I FELT SLEEP COMING UPON ME AND THE MORLOCKS WITH IT.

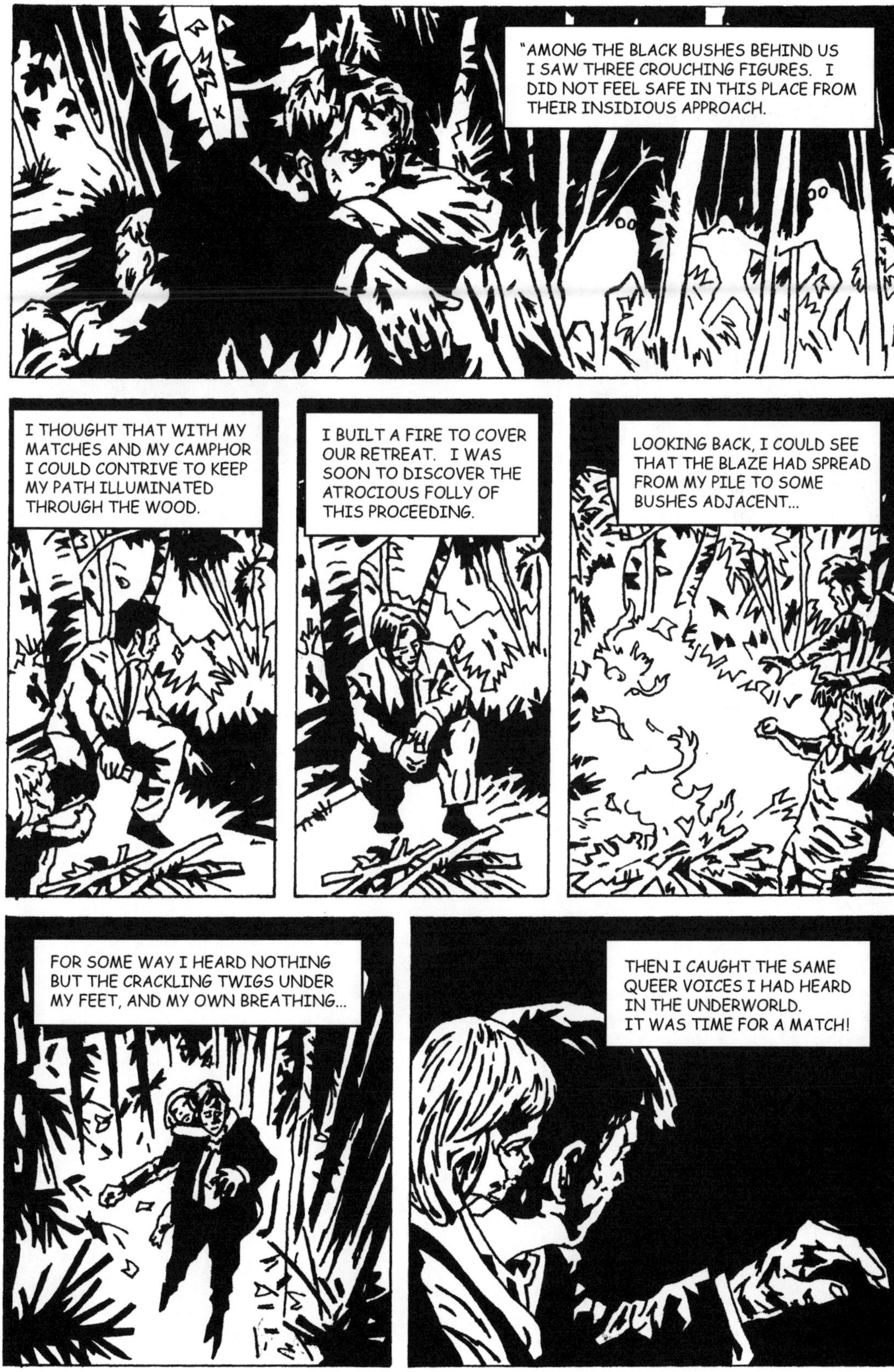
"AMONG THE BLACK BUSHES BEHIND US I SAW THREE CROUCHING FIGURES. I DID NOT FEEL SAFE IN THIS PLACE FROM THEIR INSIDIOUS APPROACH.
I THOUGHT THAT WITH MY MATCHES AND MY CAMPHOR I COULD CONTRIVE TO KEEP MY PATH ILLUMINATED THROUGH THE WOOD.
I BUILT A FIRE TO COVER OUR RETREAT. I WAS SOON TO DISCOVER THE ATROCIOUS FOLLY OF THIS PROCEEDING.
LOOKING BACK, I COULD SEE THAT THE BLAZE HAD SPREAD FROM MY PILE TO SOME BUSHES ADJACENT...
FOR SOME WAY I HEARD NOTHING BUT THE CRACKLING TWIGS UNDER MY FEET, AND MY OWN BREATHING...
THEN I CAUGHT THE SAME QUEER VOICES I HAD HEARD IN THE UNDERWORLD.
IT WAS TIME FOR A MATCH!

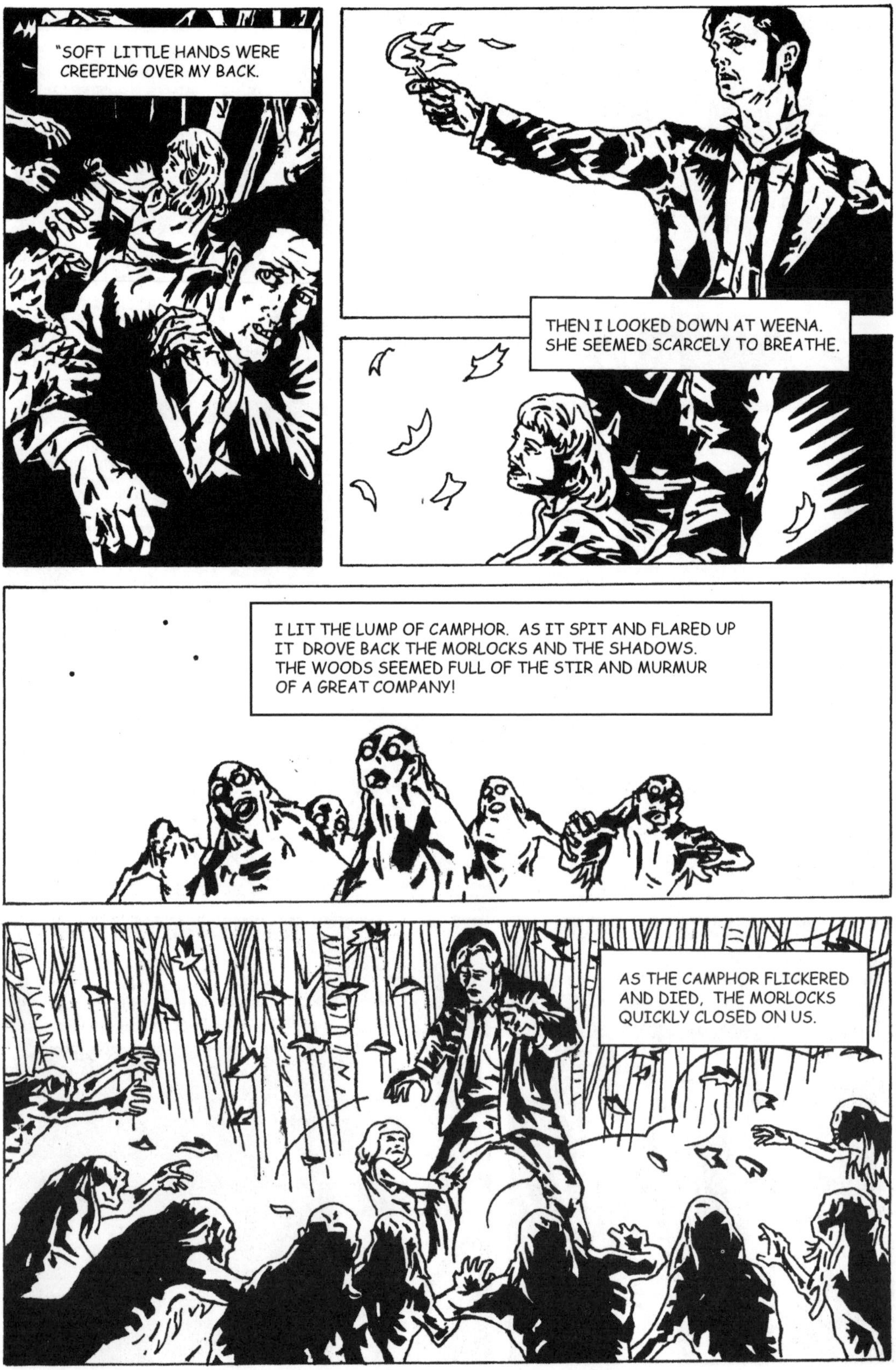
"SOFT LITTLE HANDS WERE CREEPING OVER MY BACK.
THEN I LOOKED DOWN AT WEENA. SHE SEEMED SCARCELY TO BREATHE.
I LIT THE LUMP OF CAMPHOR. AS IT SPIT AND FLARED UP IT DROVE BACK THE MORLOCKS AND THE SHADOWS. THE WOODS SEEMED FULL OF THE STIR AND MURMUR OF A GREAT COMPANY!
AS THE CAMPHOR FLICKERED AND DIED, THE MORLOCKS QUICKLY CLOSED ON US.

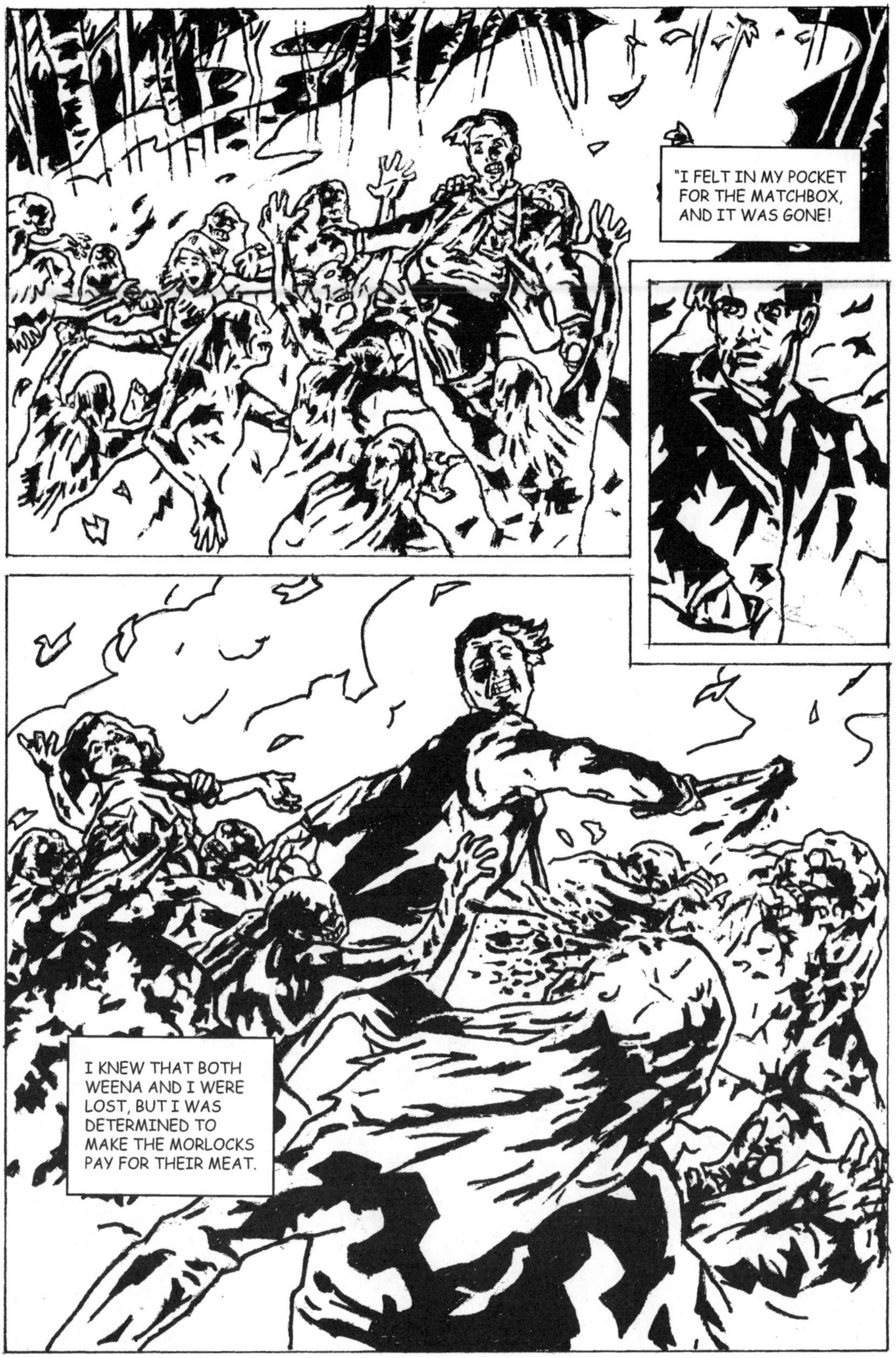
"I FELT IN MY POCKET FOR THE MATCHBOX, AND IT WAS GONE!
I KNEW THAT BOTH WEENA AND I WERE LOST, BUT I WAS DETERMINED TO MAKE THE MORLOCKS PAY FOR THEIR MEAT.

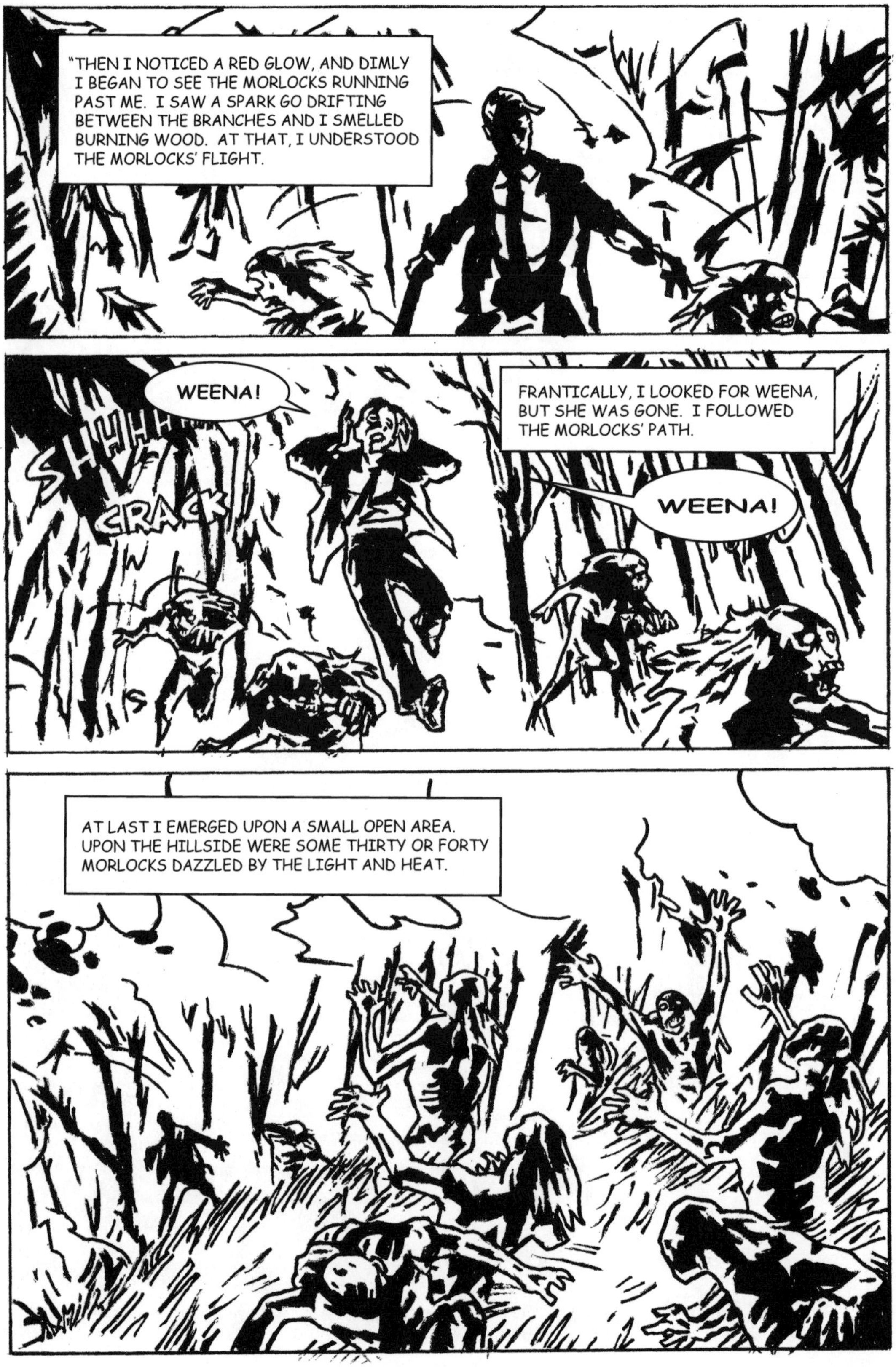
"THEN I NOTICED A RED GLOW, AND DIMLY I BEGAN TO SEE THE MORLOCKS RUNNING PAST ME. I SAW A SPARK GO DRIFTING BETWEEN THE BRANCHES AND I SMELLED BURNING WOOD. AT THAT, I UNDERSTOOD THE MORLOCKS' FLIGHT.
WEENA!
CRACK
FRANTICALLY, I LOOKED FOR WEENA, BUT SHE WAS GONE. I FOLLOWED THE MORLOCKS' PATH.
WEENA!
AT LAST I EMERGED UPON A SMALL OPEN AREA. UPON THE HILLSIDE WERE SOME THIRTY OR FORTY MORLOCKS DAZZLED BY THE LIGHT AND HEAT.

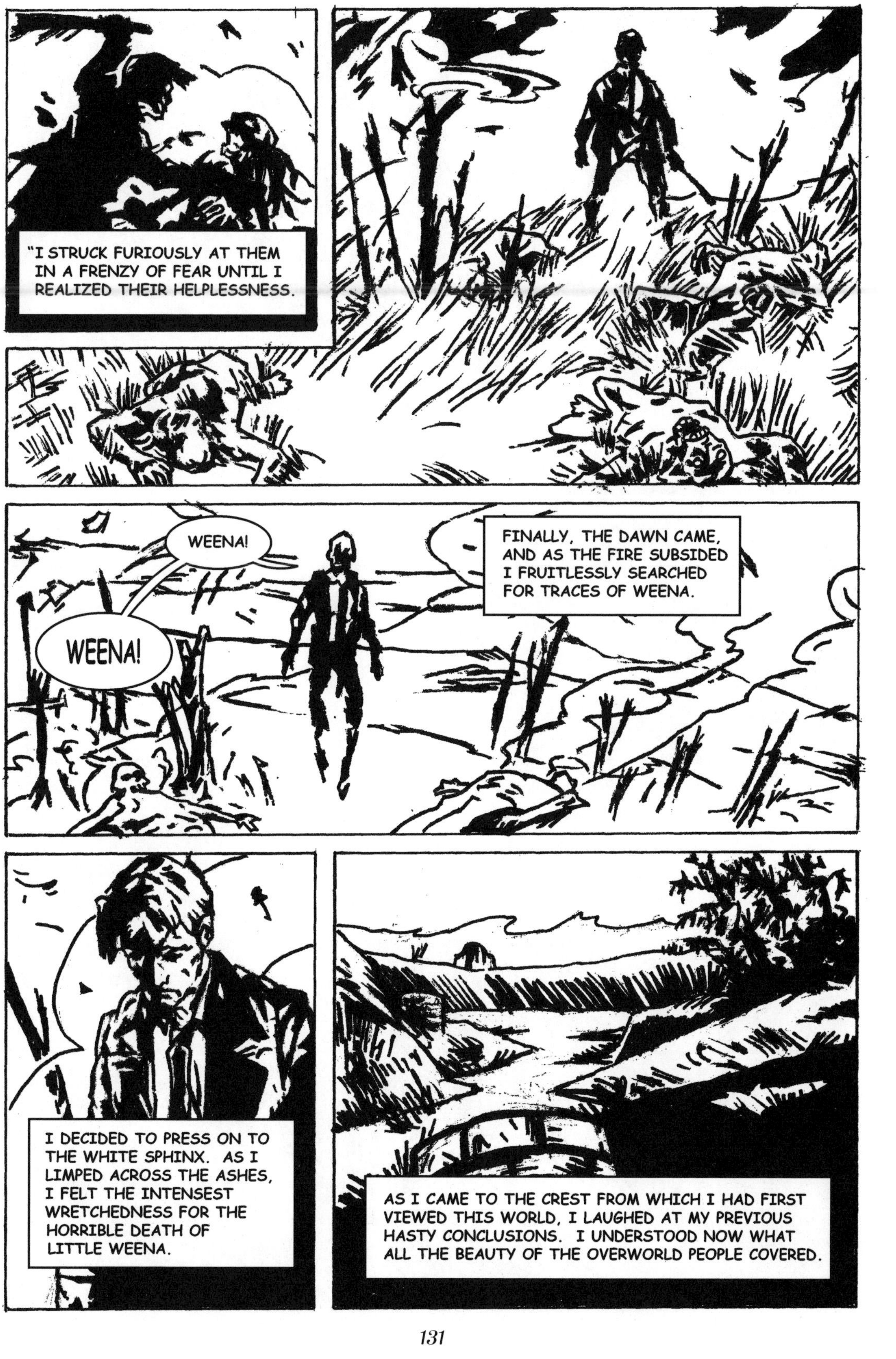
"I STRUCK FURIOUSLY AT THEM IN A FRENZY OF FEAR UNTIL I REALIZED THEIR HELPLESSNESS.
WEENA!
WEENA!
FINALLY, THE DAWN CAME, AND AS THE FIRE SUBSIDED I FRUITLESSLY SEARCHED FOR TRACES OF WEENA.
I DECIDED TO PRESS ON TO THE WHITE SPHINX. AS I LIMPED ACROSS THE ASHES, I FELT THE INTENSEST WRETCHEDNESS FOR THE HORRIBLE DEATH OF LITTLE WEENA.
AS I CAME TO THE CREST FROM WHICH I HAD FIRST VIEWED THIS WORLD, I LAUGHED AT MY PREVIOUS HASTY CONCLUSIONS. I UNDERSTOOD NOW WHAT ALL THE BEAUTY OF THE OVERWORLD PEOPLE COVERED.

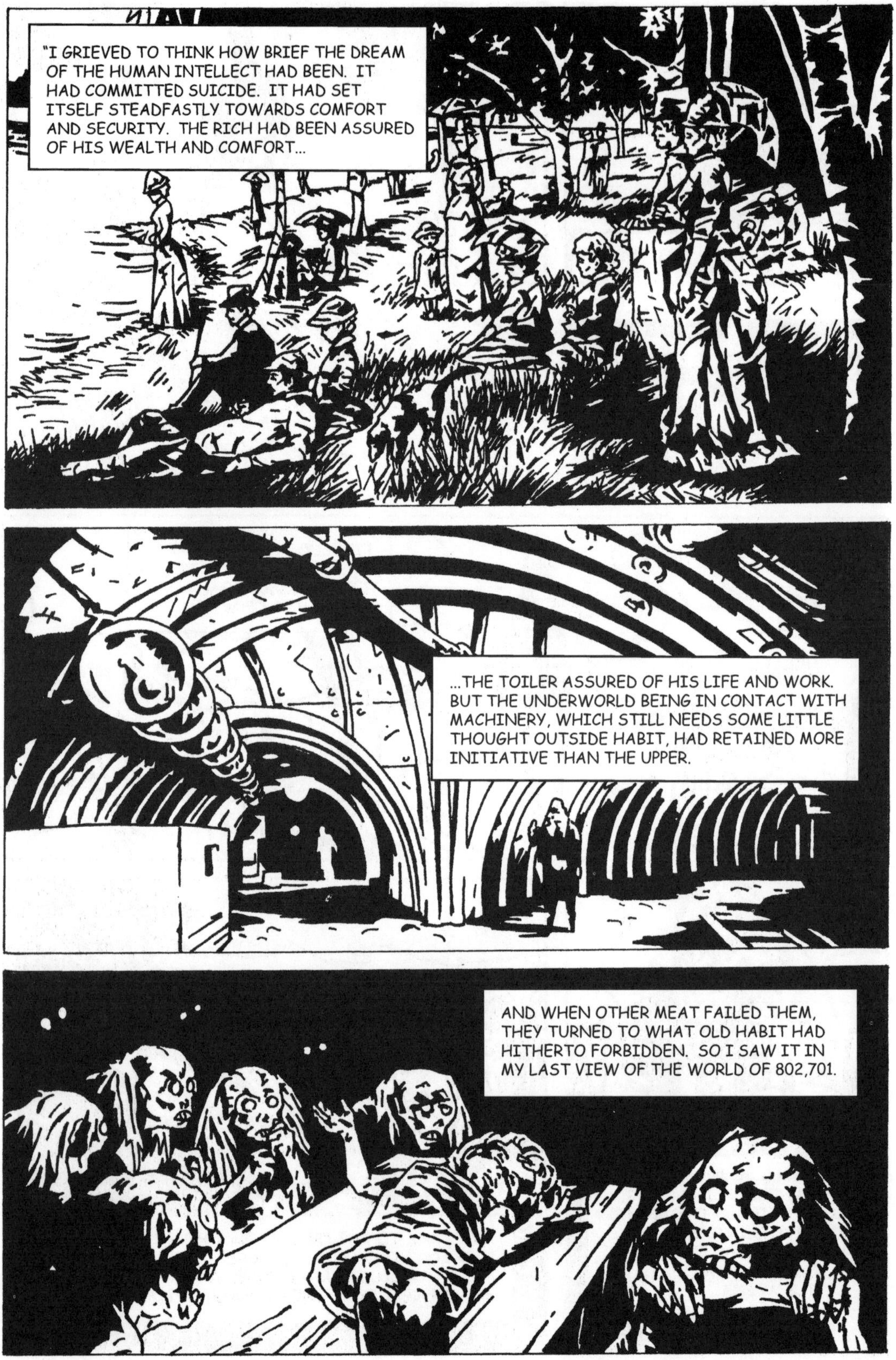
"I GRIEVED TO THINK HOW BRIEF THE DREAM OF THE HUMAN INTELLECT HAD BEEN. IT HAD COMMITTED SUICIDE. IT HAD SET ITSELF STEADFASTLY TOWARDS COMFORT AND SECURITY. THE RICH HAD BEEN ASSURED OF HIS WEALTH AND COMFORT...
...THE TOILER ASSURED OF HIS LIFE AND WORK. BUT THE UNDERWORLD BEING IN CONTACT WITH MACHINERY, WHICH STILL NEEDS SOME LITTLE THOUGHT OUTSIDE HABIT, HAD RETAINED MORE INITIATIVE THAN THE UPPER.
AND WHEN OTHER MEAT FAILED THEM, THEY TURNED TO WHAT OLD HABIT HAD HITHERTO FORBIDDEN. SO I SAW IT IN MY LAST VIEW OF THE WORLD OF 802,701.

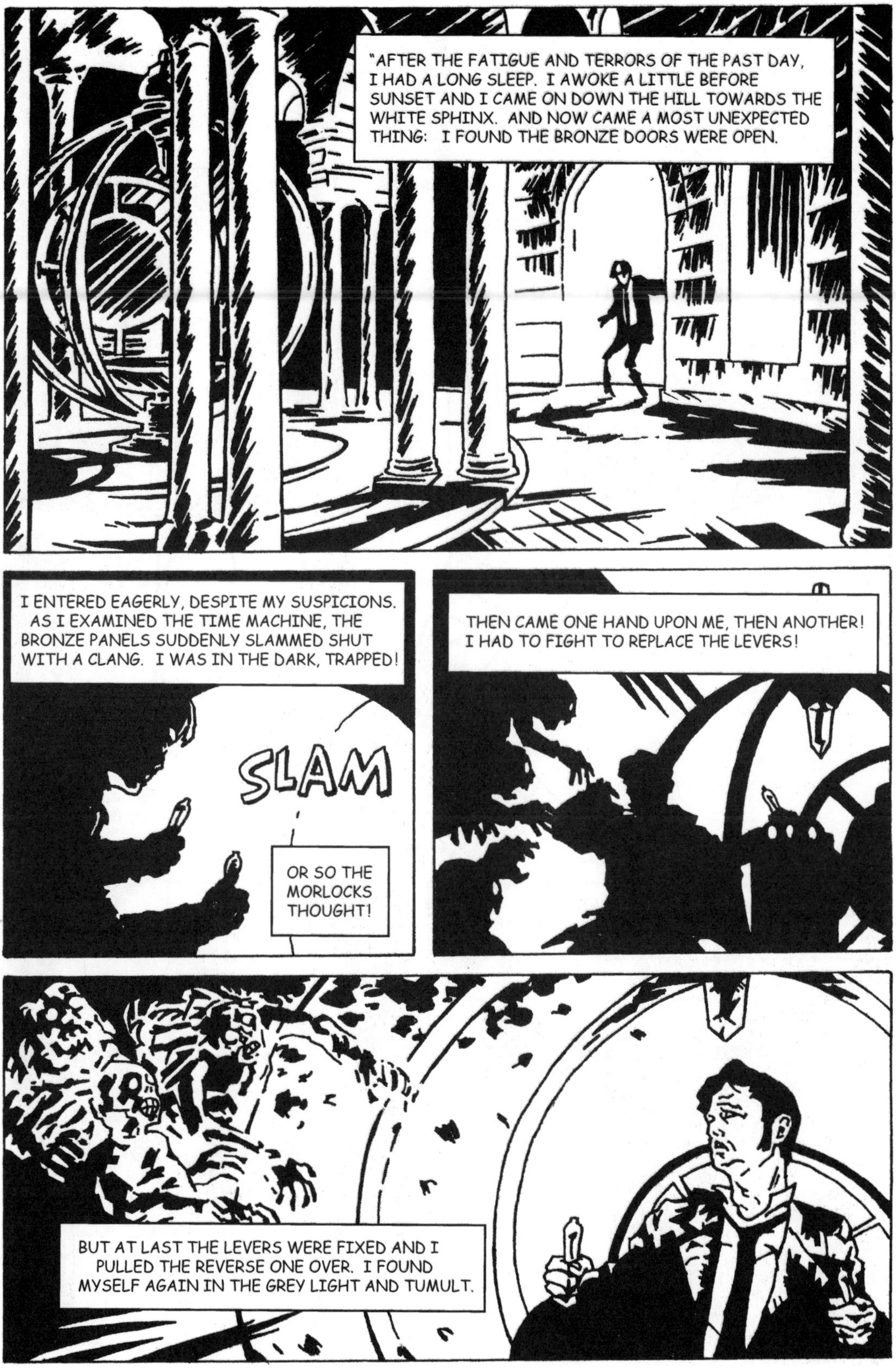
"AFTER THE FATIGUE AND TERRORS OF THE PAST DAY, I HAD A LONG SLEEP. I AWOKE A LITTLE BEFORE SUNSET AND I CAME ON DOWN THE HILL TOWARDS THE WHITE SPHINX. AND NOW CAME A MOST UNEXPECTED THING: I FOUND THE BRONZE DOORS WERE OPEN.
I ENTERED EAGERLY, DESPITE MY SUSPICIONS. AS I EXAMINED THE TIME MACHINE, THE BRONZE PANELS SUDDENLY SLAMMED SHUT WITH A CLANG. I WAS IN THE DARK, TRAPPED!
SLAM
OR SO THE MORLOCKS THOUGHT!
THEN CAME ONE HAND UPON ME, THEN ANOTHER! I HAD TO FIGHT TO REPLACE THE LEVERS!
BUT AT LAST THE LEVERS WERE FIXED AND I PULLED THE REVERSE ONE OVER. I FOUND MYSELF AGAIN IN THE GREY LIGHT AND TUMULT.

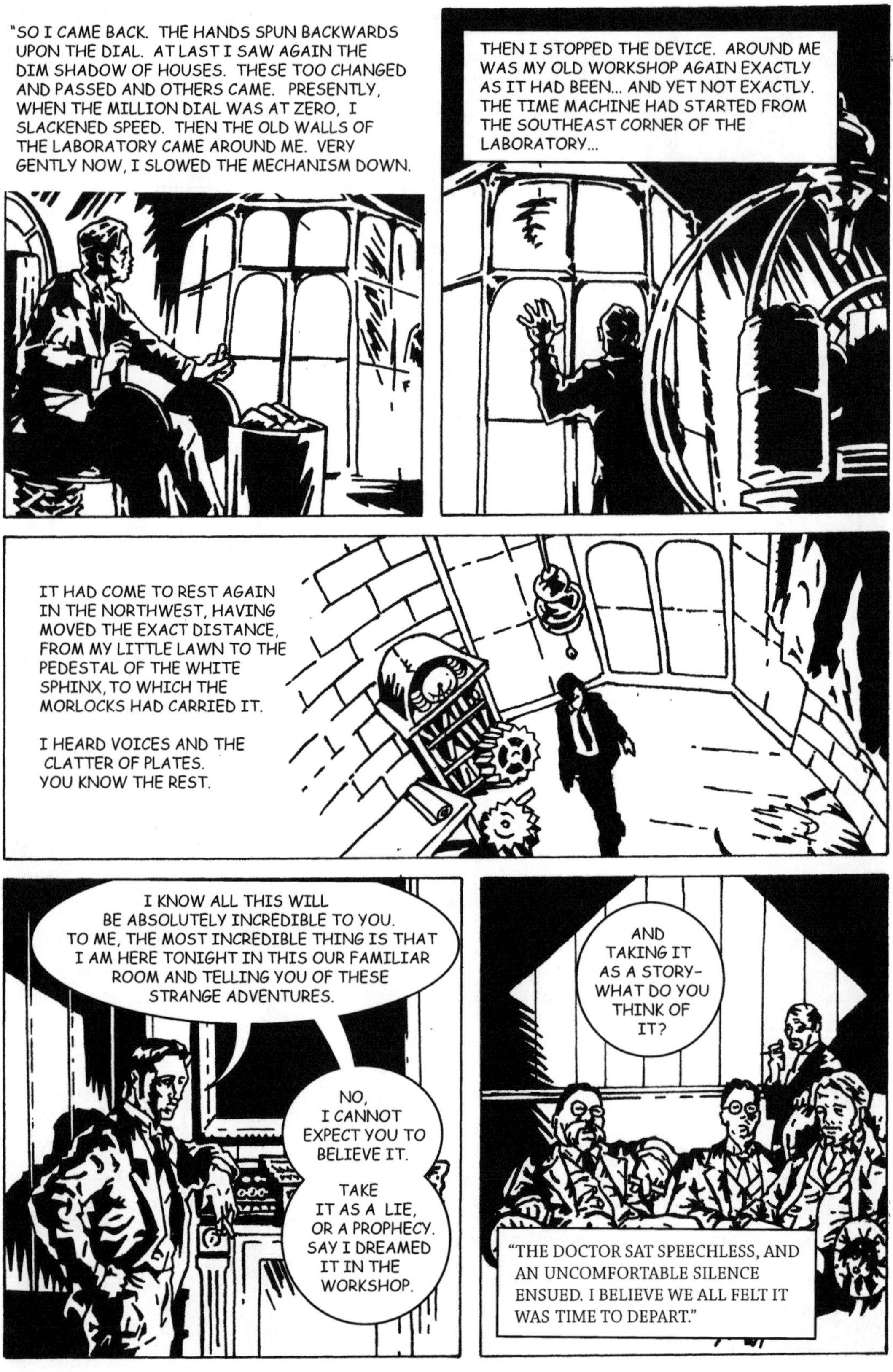
"SO I CAME BACK. THE HANDS SPUN BACKWARDS UPON THE DIAL. AT LAST I SAW AGAIN THE DIM SHADOW OF HOUSES. THESE TOO CHANGED AND PASSED AND OTHERS CAME. PRESENTLY, WHEN THE MILLION DIAL WAS AT ZERO, I SLACKENED SPEED. THEN THE OLD WALLS OF THE LABORATORY CAME AROUND ME. VERY GENTLY NOW, I SLOWED THE MECHANISM DOWN.
THEN I STOPPED THE DEVICE. AROUND ME WAS MY OLD WORKSHOP AGAIN EXACTLY AS IT HAD BEEN... AND YET NOT EXACTLY. THE TIME MACHINE HAD STARTED FROM THE SOUTHEAST CORNER OF THE LABORATORY...
IT HAD COME TO REST AGAIN IN THE NORTHWEST, HAVING MOVED THE EXACT DISTANCE, FROM MY LITTLE LAWN TO THE PEDESTAL OF THE WHITE SPHINX, TO WHICH THE MORLOCKS HAD CARRIED IT.
I HEARD VOICES AND THE CLATTER OF PLATES. YOU KNOW THE REST.
I KNOW ALL THIS WILL BE ABSOLUTELY INCREDIBLE TO YOU. TO ME, THE MOST INCREDIBLE THING IS THAT I AM HERE TONIGHT IN THIS OUR FAMILIAR ROOM AND TELLING YOU OF THESE STRANGE ADVENTURES.
NO, I CANNOT EXPECT YOU TO BELIEVE IT.
TAKE IT AS A LIE, OR A PROPHECY. SAY I DREAMED IT IN THE WORKSHOP.
AND TAKING IT AS A STORY- WHAT DO YOU THINK OF IT?
"THE DOCTOR SAT SPEECHLESS, AND AN UNCOMFORTABLE SILENCE ENSUED. I BELIEVE WE ALL FELT IT WAS TIME TO DEPART."

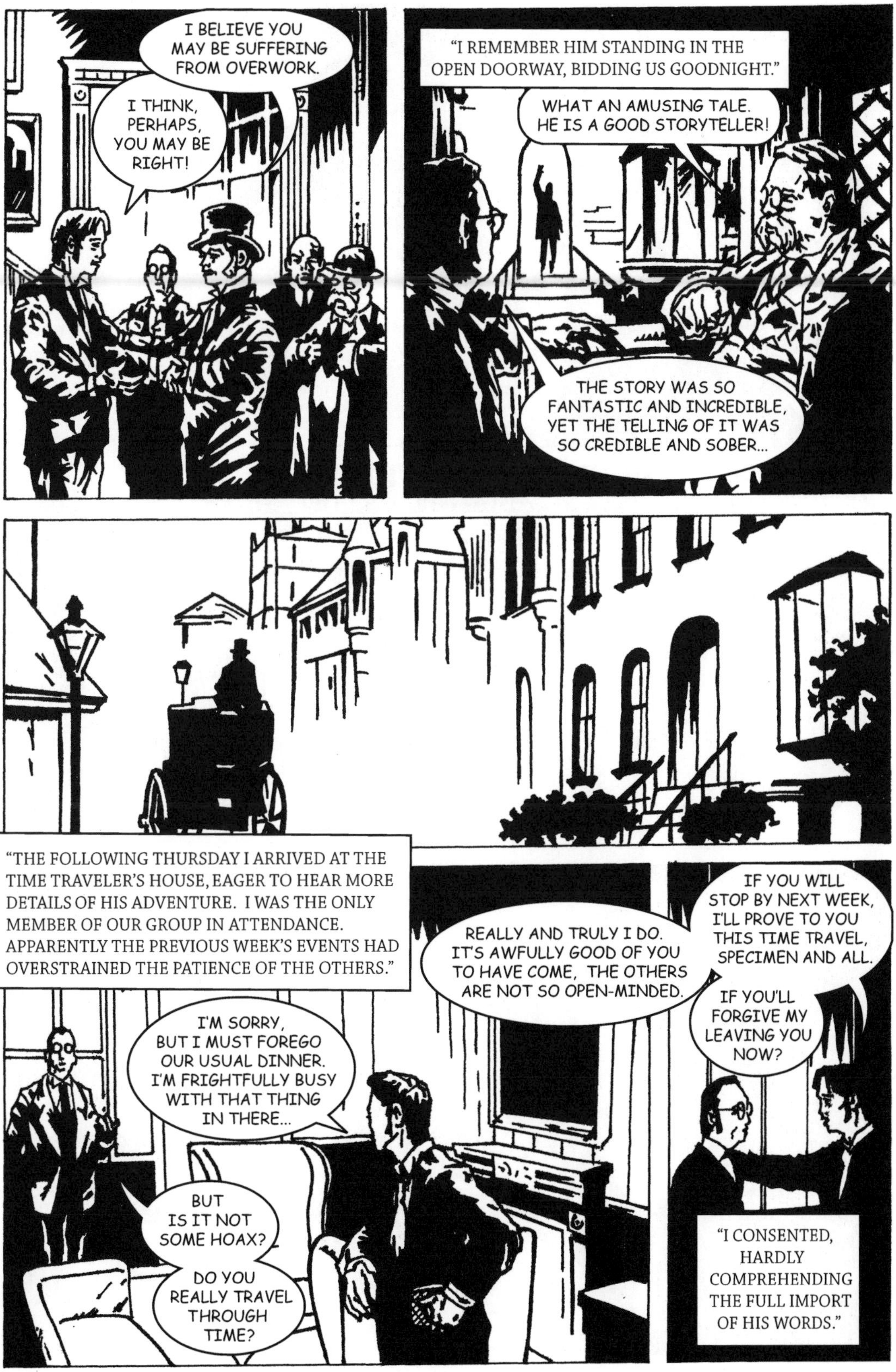
I BELIEVE YOU MAY BE SUFFERING FROM OVERWORK.
I THINK, PERHAPS, YOU MAY BE RIGHT!
"I REMEMBER HIM STANDING IN THE OPEN DOORWAY, BIDDING US GOODNIGHT."
WHAT AN AMUSING TALE. HE IS A GOOD STORYTELLER!
THE STORY WAS SO FANTASTIC AND INCREDIBLE, YET THE TELLING OF IT WAS SO CREDIBLE AND SOBER...
"THE FOLLOWING THURSDAY I ARRIVED AT THE TIME TRAVELER'S HOUSE, EAGER TO HEAR MORE DETAILS OF HIS ADVENTURE. I WAS THE ONLY MEMBER OF OUR GROUP IN ATTENDANCE. APPARENTLY THE PREVIOUS WEEK'S EVENTS HAD OVERSTRAINED THE PATIENCE OF THE OTHERS."
I'M SORRY, BUT I MUST FOREGO OUR USUAL DINNER. I'M FRIGHTFULLY BUSY WITH THAT THING IN THERE...
BUT IS IT NOT SOME HOAX?
DO YOU REALLY TRAVEL THROUGH TIME?
REALLY AND TRULY I DO. IT'S AWFULLY GOOD OF YOU TO HAVE COME, THE OTHERS ARE NOT SO OPEN-MINDED.
IF YOU WILL STOP BY NEXT WEEK, I'LL PROVE TO YOU THIS TIME TRAVEL, SPECIMEN AND ALL.
IF YOU'LL FORGIVE MY LEAVING YOU NOW?
"I CONSENTED, HARDLY COMPREHENDING THE FULL IMPORT OF HIS WORDS."

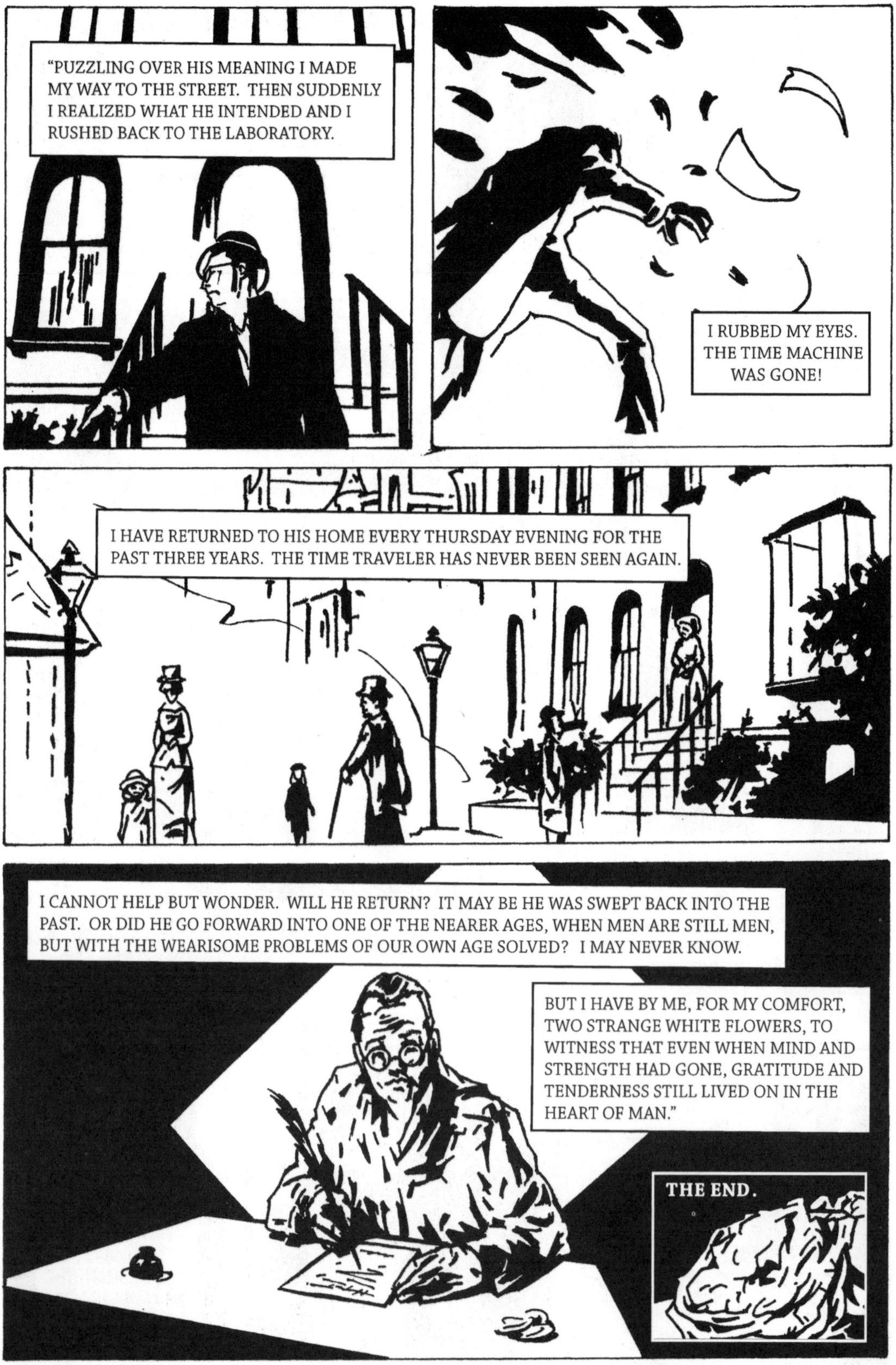
"PUZZLING OVER HIS MEANING I MADE MY WAY TO THE STREET. THEN SUDDENLY I REALIZED WHAT HE INTENDED AND I RUSHED BACK TO THE LABORATORY.
I RUBBED MY EYES. THE TIME MACHINE WAS GONE!
I HAVE RETURNED TO HIS HOME EVERY THURSDAY EVENING FOR THE PAST THREE YEARS. THE TIME TRAVELER HAS NEVER BEEN SEEN AGAIN.
I CANNOT HELP BUT WONDER. WILL HE RETURN? IT MAY BE HE WAS SWEPT BACK INTO THE PAST. OR DID HE GO FORWARD INTO ONE OF THE NEARER AGES, WHEN MEN ARE STILL MEN, BUT WITH THE WEARISOME PROBLEMS OF OUR OWN AGE SOLVED? I MAY NEVER KNOW.
BUT I HAVE BY ME, FOR MY COMFORT, TWO STRANGE WHITE FLOWERS, TO WITNESS THAT EVEN WHEN MIND AND STRENGTH HAD GONE, GRATITUDE AND TENDERNESS STILL LIVED ON IN THE HEART OF MAN."
THE END.

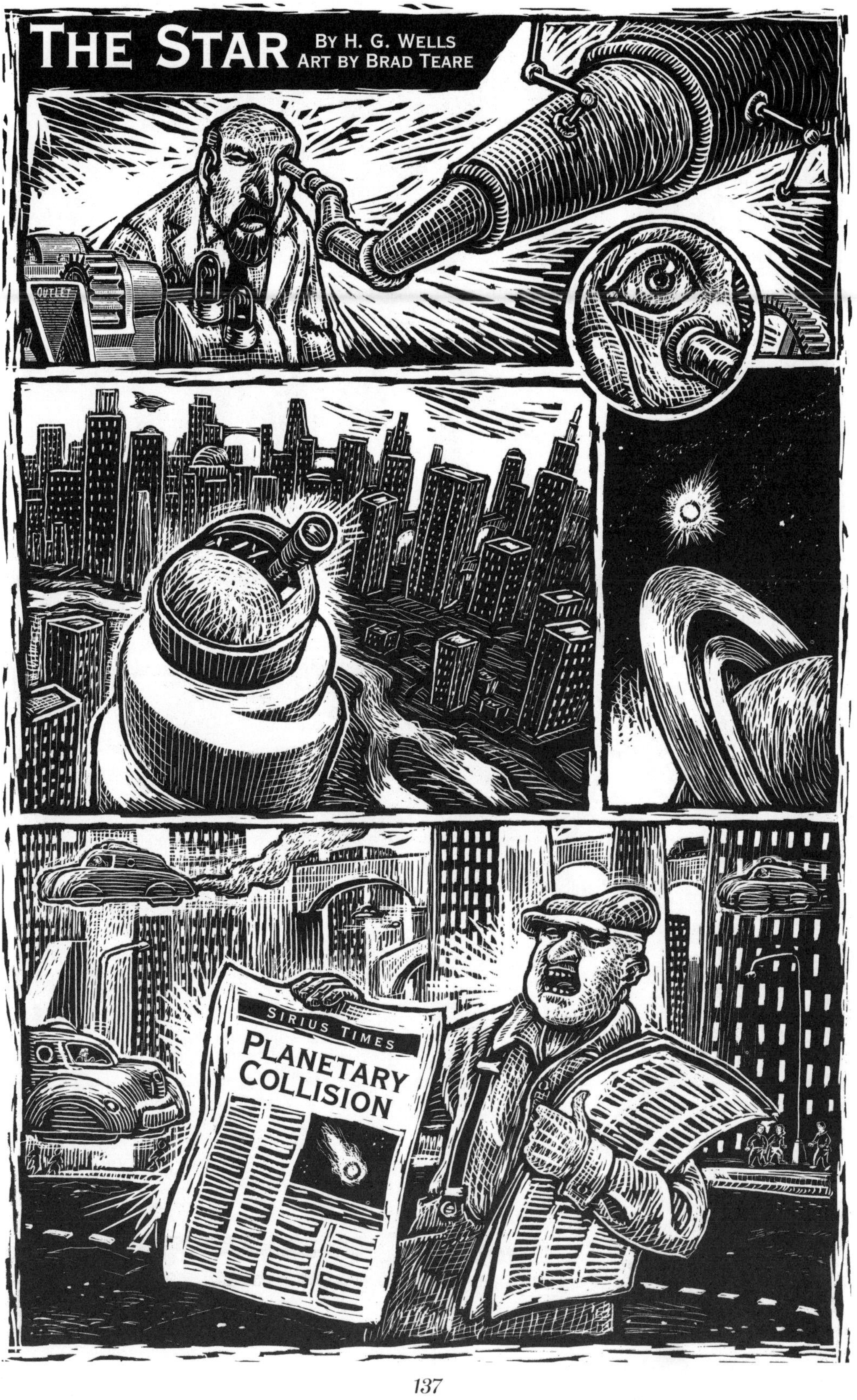
THE STAR
BY H. G. WELLS
ART BY BRAD TEARE
OUTLET
SIRIUS TIMES
PLANETARY COLLISION

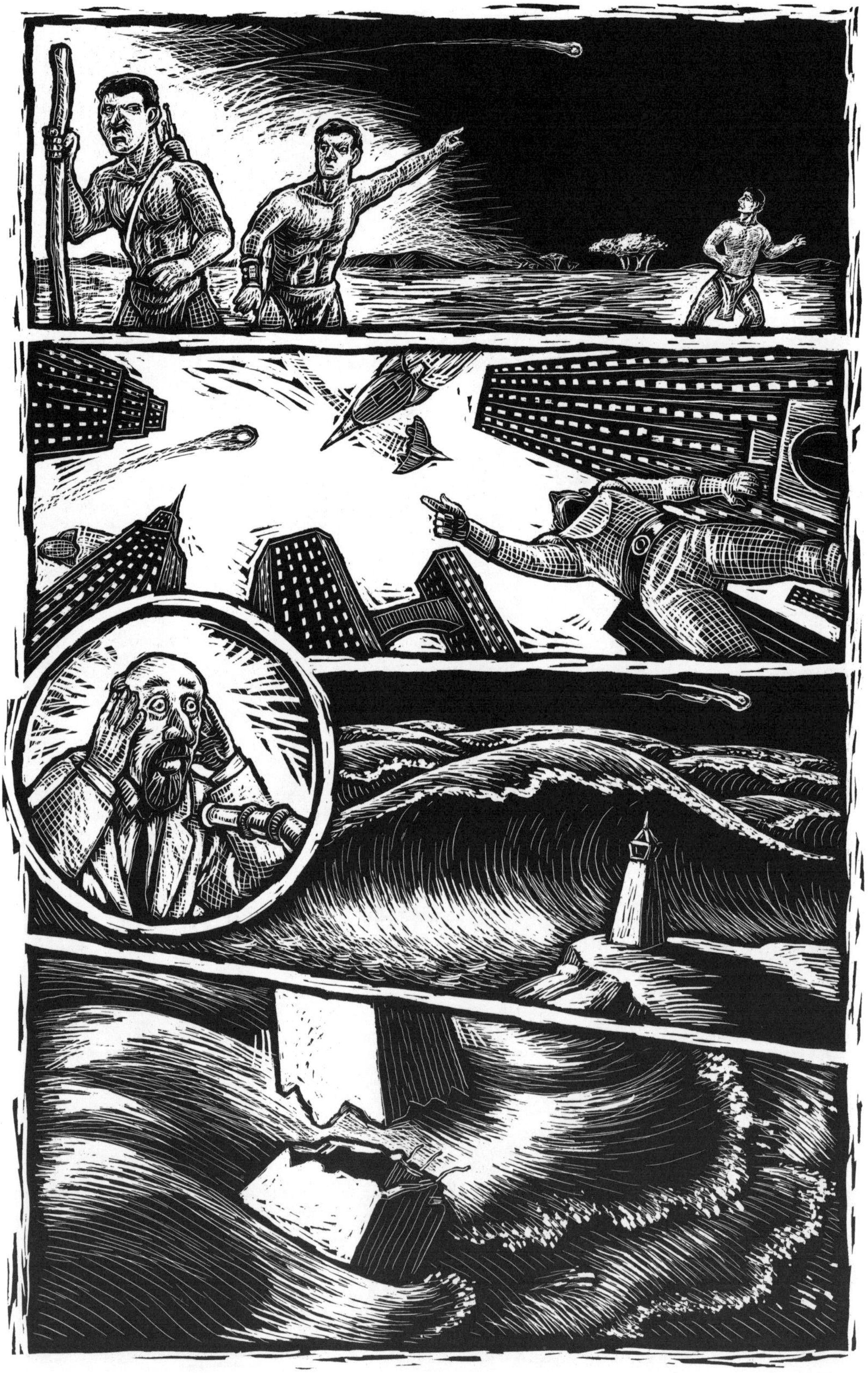

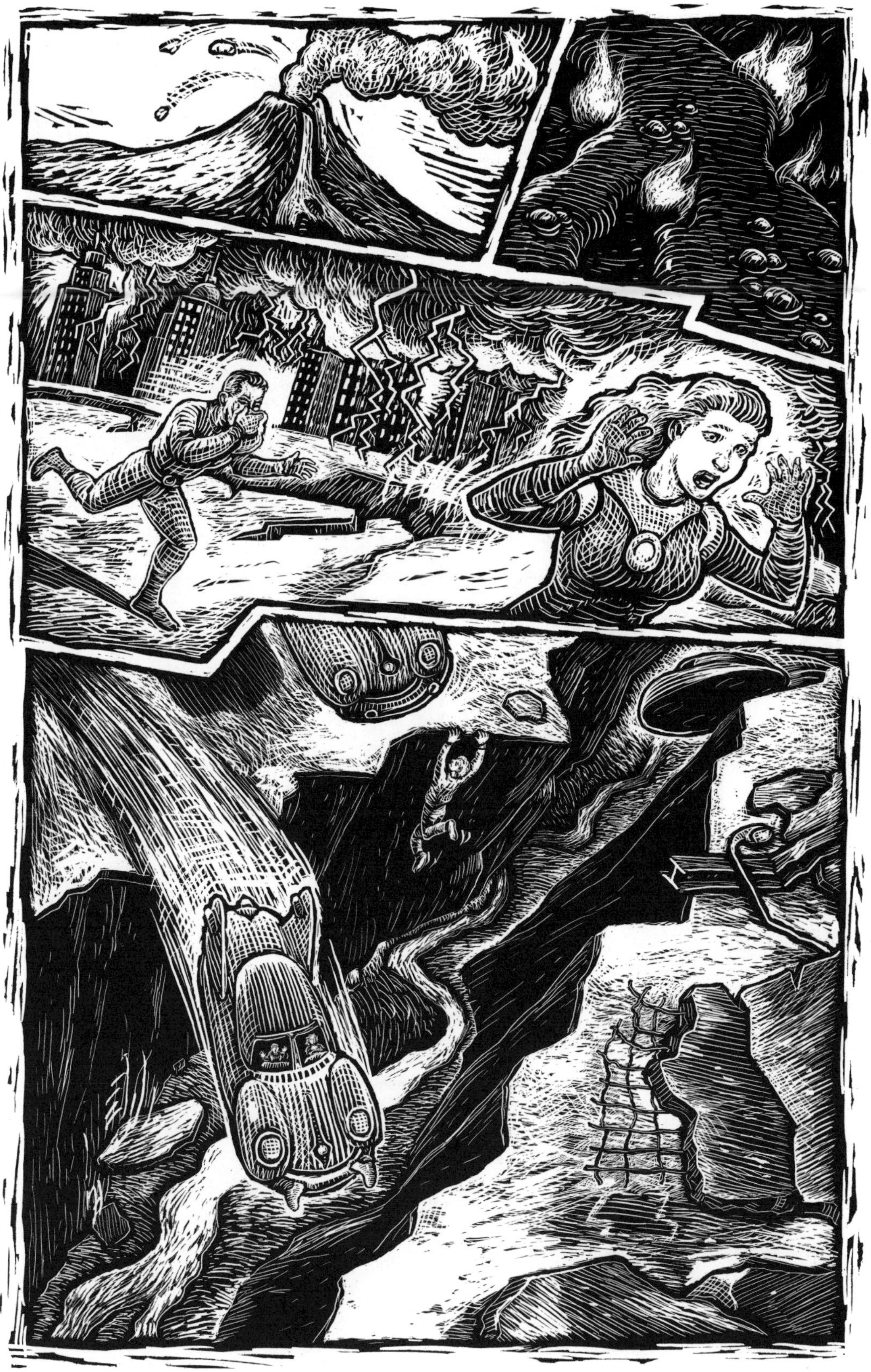

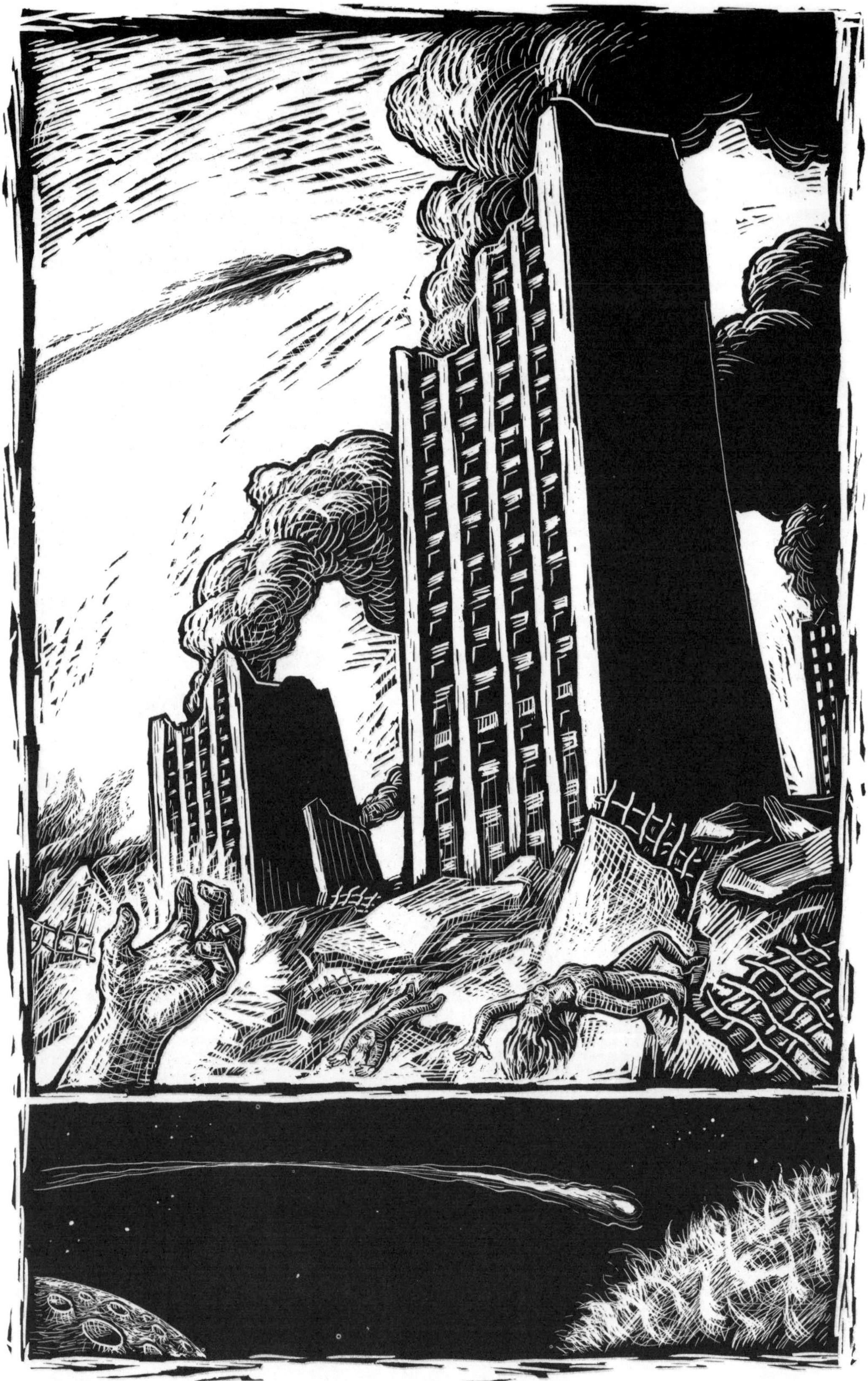

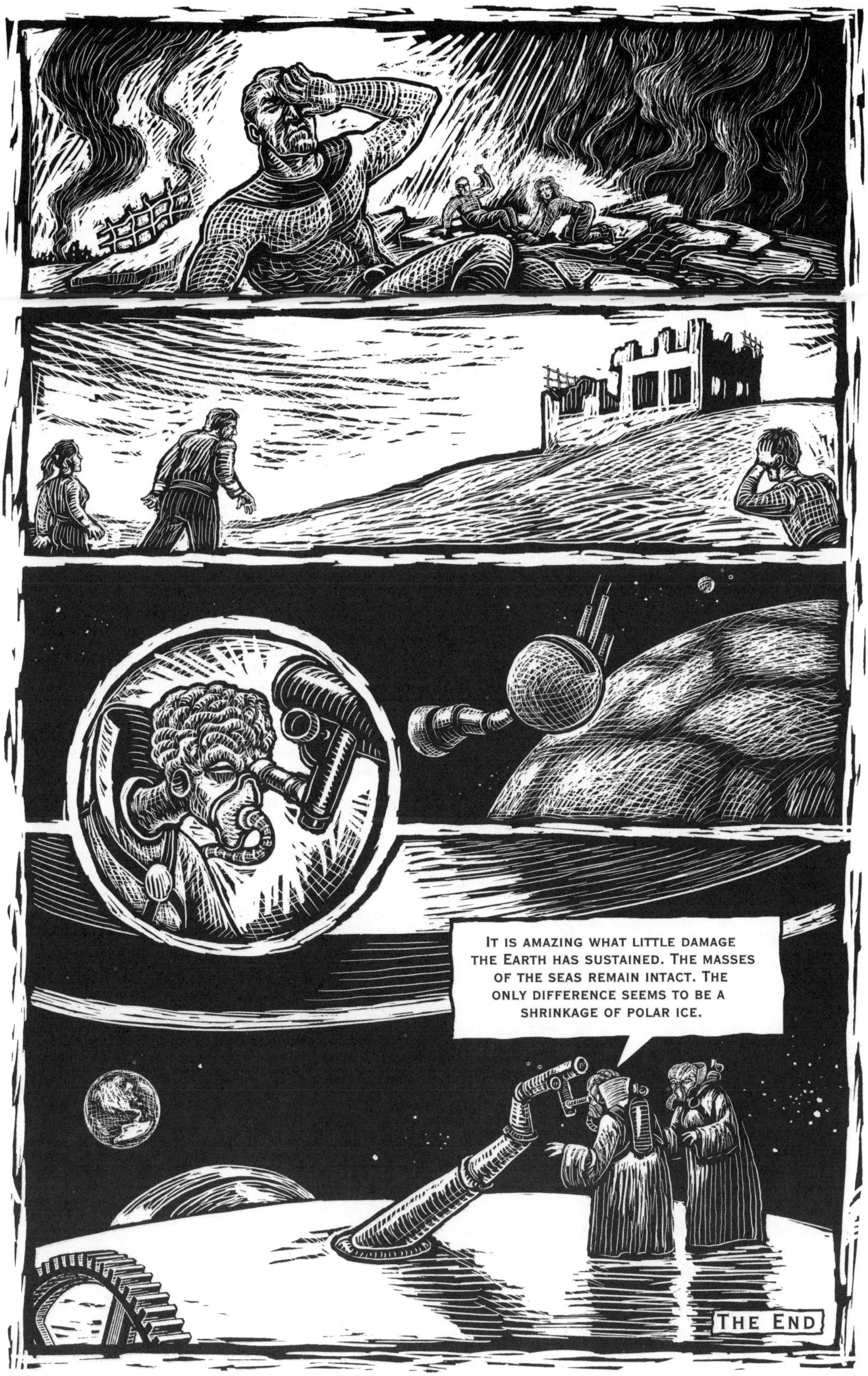
IT IS AMAZING WHAT LITTLE DAMAGE THE EARTH HAS SUSTAINED. THE MASSES OF THE SEAS REMAIN INTACT. THE ONLY DIFFERENCE SEEMS TO BE A SHRINKAGE OF POLAR ICE.
THE END

H.G. WELLS

Herbert George Wells was born to English working-class parents in 1866. At age eighteen he earned a scholarship to Imperial College, where he came under the tutelage of Darwinian scholar T. H. Huxley. Evolutionary theory strongly influenced Wells' early "scientific romances." The first of these, *The Chronic Argonauts*, was serialized in his college newspaper in 1888. Seven years later he rewrote it as *The Time Machine: An Invention*, which became the first published in a series of popular novels including *The Island of Dr. Moreau*, *The Invisible Man* and *The War of the Worlds*. These "romances" became the foundation of modern science fiction. Their seminal influence in the field is challenged only by that of the French fantasist Jules Verne, who Wells claimed "can't write himself out of a paper sack." Wells briefly joined England's socialist movement and in later novels promoted socialism, feminism, and free love, which he put into personal practice. He was a leading proponent of the League of Nations and chaired the original proposal. Wells wrote numerous short stories and essays and more than one hundred fifty books, including the nonfiction *Outline of History*, which sold over two million copies. But it is his early science fiction that remains his most enduring legacy. Before his death in 1946 Wells provided his own epitaph to an interviewer: "God damn you all, I told you so."

SETH FRAIL (front cover, page 97)

Starting with drawing bulletin covers for his father's church at the age of seven, Seth Frail has been working in freelance illustration for many years, doing everything from logo design to gallery exhibits. While staying at home with his two kids for the last four years, he finally decided to focus on his first love: comics. "*Graphic Classics: H.G. Wells* marks my most widely distributed work to date," Seth says, "unless you count the fact that my family and I have moved all over the country for the last five years. I now live and work in St. Louis, Missouri... but that really isn't particularly interesting." Fortunately, Seth's work is, and he plans to do much more of it. He can be reached through his website, www.abnormalcomics.com.

KENT STEINE (page 1)

Kent Steine began his career producing advertising and editorial illustration and has done cover art for over fifty periodicals. For the past twenty years he has been painting pretty girls for a living. His first major exposure as a glamour artist came in 1992 with the creation of his *Hollywood Glamour* limited edition prints. These contemporary images helped reestablish an interest in classic pinup and glamour art. Kent's pinup illustrations have appeared in numerous magazines, and have been published in the form of prints, lithographs, posters, trading cards and calendars. Steine has authored *The J.C. Leyendecker Collection* and *Billy DeVorss Pinup*, and he has been a contributing writer to *Step-By-Step Graphics* and *Illustration* magazine. More of Kent's art can be seen at www.kentsteine.com.

CHRIS MOORE (page 2)

English artist Chris Moore is one of the premier illustrators of science fiction working today. In 1974 he did his first SF covers, for books by Alfred Bester and Philip K. Dick. He has specialized in the field ever since, and the roster of his covers reads like a *Who's Who* of the SF elite, including Isaac Asimov, Larry Niven, Frederick Pohl, Anne McCaffrey, Clifford D. Simak, Kurt Vonnegut, J.G. Ballard, Arthur C. Clarke and Samuel R. Delany. His painting of *The War of the Worlds* was done for the cover of a 1998 Orion volume that combined *The War of the Worlds* and *The Time Machine* in one book. "I very much wanted the atmosphere to be both British and Wellsian," states Chris. "I thought it would be nice to have Big Ben standing as a timepiece along with the Martian tripod, giving a presence to both themes in the same image." Chris Moore's art is featured in *Fantasy Art Masters* (1999, Watson-Guptill), in *Rosebud 23*, and on the cover of the upcoming *Graphic Classics* anthology *Adventure Classics*. *Journeyman*, a collection of his work, was published in 2000 by Paper Tiger. His website is at www.illust.demon.co.uk.

RICK GEARY (page 3)

Rick is best known for his thirteen years as a contributor to *The National Lampoon*. His work has also appeared in Marvel, DC, and Dark Horse comics, *Rolling Stone*, *Mad*, *Heavy Metal*, *Disney Adventures*, *The Los Angeles Times*, and *The New York Times Book Review*. He is a regular cartoonist in *Rosebud*. Rick has written and illustrated five children's books and published a collection of his comics, *Housebound with Rick Geary*. The fifth volume in his continuing book series *A Treasury of Victorian Murder* is *The Beast of Chicago* (NBM Publishing, 2003). More of Rick's work has appeared in the *Graphic Classics* anthologies *Edgar Allan Poe*, *Arthur Conan Doyle*, *H.P. Lovecraft*, *Jack London*, *Ambrose Bierce*, *Mark Twain* and *O. Henry*. You can also view his art at www.rickgeary.com.

ROD LOTT (page 4)

Based in Oklahoma City, Rod Lott is a freelance writer and graphic designer in the worlds of journalism, advertising and beyond. For the past ten years, he has served as editor and publisher of the more-or-less quarterly magazine *Hitch: The Journal of Pop Culture Absurdity*. Rod's humorous essays have been published in anthologies including *More Mirth of a Nation*, *101 Damnations* and *May Contain Nuts*. Rod's work appeared in *Graphic Classics: O. Henry*. He also adapted stories by Edgar Allan Poe and Clark Ashton Smith in *Horror Classics*, and is now working on scripts for the upcoming anthology *Adventure Classics: Graphic Classics Volume Twelve*. You can learn more about his work online at www.rodlott.com and www.hitchmagazine.com.

SIMON GANE (page 4)

British artist Simon Gane lives and works in Bath as a magazine and children's book illustrator and graphic designer. His first published strips appeared in the self-produced punk fanzine *Arnie*, and others followed in self-contained mini comics and eventually the collection *Punk Strips*. He recently completed *All Flee*, a comic about a "finishing school for monsters" and is working on a four-issue series set in the Paris and New York of the 1950s for Slave Labor Graphics. "I especially enjoyed drawing *The Policeman and the Citizen* in *Graphic Classics: Ambrose Bierce*," says Simon, "because it encompasses many of my favorite themes: alcohol, police aggression, a past-times setting and a sense that whilst largely forgotten now, comics remain a peerless medium for satire." For *Is He Living or Is He Dead?*, in *Graphic Classics: Mark Twain*, Simon spent time sketching in Menton, the setting of the story, which contributes to the rich backgrounds and detail that are also evident in his interpretation of *Dr. Jekyll and Mr. Hyde* for *Graphic Classics: Robert Louis Stevenson* and *The Invisible Man* in this volume.

RICH TOMMASO (page 44)

Atlanta resident Rich Tomasso grew up in what he calls "one of the dullest parts of the New Jersey suburban-lands." He became a student at The Joe Kubert Art School, but quit after his first year, never being interested in a career drawing superheroes, and instead spent many years making pizza while trying to find more personal things to write and draw about. He says he has been "struggling to do a decent comic for over ten years, and after eight years at it, my recent works, *Perverso* and *8½ Ghosts*, make me *sometimes* think I just may accomplish this feat some day." His work (much more "decent" than Rich admits) has appeared in collections from Fantagraphics, Dark Horse, Top Shelf and Alternative Comics.

DAN O'NEILL (page 58)

In 1963 Dan O'Neill dropped out of college and started his comic *Odd Bodkins* for the *San Francisco Chronicle*. The strip was soon syndicated to over 350 papers, with a combined readership of 50 million. For seven years O'Neill proceeded to entertain readers and offend editors by satirizing religion and politics, targeting characters from Superman to Abraham Lincoln to Jesus Christ. He managed to lose 90% of the feature's syndication before finally being fired by the *Chronicle*. These strips are collected in two books, *Hear the Sound of My Feet Walking Drown the Sound of My Voice Talking* and *The Collective Unconscience of Odd Bodkins*. In 1970, at the height of the underground comix movement, O'Neill met four cartoonists who would form the core of his infamous comics collective, The Air Pirates: Ted Richards, Gary Hallgren, Bobby London and Shary Flenniken. They produced three issues of *Dan O'Neill's Comics and Stories*, which consisted largely of satires of Disney cartoon characters, two issues of *Air Pirates Funnies* and several books by individual members of the collective. O'Neill's intent was to provoke a reaction from the Disney empire and in 1971 he succeeded. The highly-publicized court case dragged out for nine years, eventually resulting in an injunction against the Pirates and a financial judgement that was never collected by Disney. Dan returned to newspaper comics with his *Dan O'Neill* strip that continues today in the *San Francisco Bay Guardian* and other papers. His work also appears in *Graphic Classics: Ambrose Bierce* and *Graphic Classics: Mark Twain*.

MILTON KNIGHT (page 68)

Milton Knight claims he started drawing, painting and creating his own attempts at comic books and animation at age two. "I've never formed a barrier between fine art and cartooning," says Milt. "Growing up, I treasured Chinese watercolors, Breughel, Charlie

THE TIME MACHINE ©2002 JIM NELSON

Brown and Terrytoons equally." His work has appeared in magazines including *Heavy Metal*, *High Times*, *National Lampoon* and *Nickelodeon Magazine*, and he has illustrated record covers, posters, candy packaging and T-shirts, and occasionally exhibited his paintings. Labor on *Ninja Turtles* comics allowed him to get up a grubstake to move to the West Coast in 1991, where he became an animator and director on *Felix the Cat* cartoons. Milt's comics titles include *Midnite the Rebel Skunk*, *Hinkley*, and *Slug and Ginger* and *Hugo*. He has contributed to the *Graphic Classics* volumes *Edgar Allan Poe*, *Jack London*,

Ambrose Bierce, Mark Twain and *Horror Classics.* Check the latest news at www.miltonknight.net.

ANTONELLA CAPUTO (pages 74, 97)

Antonella Caputo was born and educated in Rome, Italy, and is now living in England. She has been an architect, archaeologist, art restorer, photographer, calligrapher, interior designer, theater designer, actress and theater director. Antonella's first published work was *Casa Montesi*, a weekly comic strip that appeared in *Il Journalino.* She has since written comedies for children and scripts for comics in Europe and the U.S., before joining Nick Miller as a partner in Sputnik Studios. Antonella has collaborated with Nick, as well as with artists Francesca Ghermandi and Rick Geary in *Graphic Classics: Jack London, Graphic Classics: Ambrose Bierce, Graphic Classics: Mark Twain, Graphic Classics: O. Henry* and *Horror Classics.*

NICK MILLER (page 74, back cover)

The son of two artists, Nick Miller learned to draw at an early age. After leaving college, he worked as a graphic designer before switching to cartooning full-time. Since then, his work has appeared in numerous adult and children's magazines as well as comics anthologies in Britain, Europe and the U.S. His weekly newspaper comics run in *The Planet on Sunday.* He shares his Lancaster, England house with two cats, a lodger and Antonella Caputo. His stories have appeared in *Graphic Classics: Jack London, Graphic Classics: Ambrose Bierce, Graphic Classics: Mark Twain* and *Horror Classics.* See more of Nick's work at http://www.cat-box.net/sputnik.

LISA K. WEBER (page 92)

Lisa is a graduate of Parsons School of Design in New York City, where she is currently employed in the fashion industry, designing prints and characters for teenage girls' jammies, while freelancing work on children's books and character design for animation. Other projects include her "creaturized" opera posters and playing cards. Lisa has provided illustrations for *Graphic Classics: Edgar Allan Poe, Graphic Classics: H.P. Lovecraft, Graphic Classics: Ambrose Bierce, Graphic Classics: Bram Stoker, Graphic Classics: Mark Twain, Graphic Classics: Robert Louis Stevenson* and *Graphic Classics: O. Henry.* Illustrations from her in-progress book *The Shakespearean ABCs* were printed in *Rosebud 25.* More of Lisa's art can be seen online at www.creatureco.com.

SKIP WILLIAMSON (page 94)

A Chicago native, Skip Williamson began his cartooning in the alternative newspapers *The Chicago Mirror* and *The Chicago Seed.* In 1968 he produced *Bijou Funnies*, one of the earliest and longest-running underground comix titles, with Robert Crumb and Jay Lynch. During the 1970s and 1980s Williamson was an art director for what he calls "the carnal fleshpool of Hugh Hefner's *Playboy* magazine." In addition to numerous comics including *Smoot, Naked Hostility, Gag Reflex*, and *Class War Comix*, he has published two anthologies of his work, *Halsted Street* and *The Scum Also Rises.* Skip is now editing and assembling a 300-page anthology entitled *My Bitter Agenda.* Williamson now lives in the Atlanta area, where he is concentrating on painting large-scale canvases. His paintings have shown in numerous art galleries and were featured in *Rosebud 24.* His comics appear in *Graphic Classics: Mark Twain* and *Graphic Classics: Ambrose Bierce.* You can see more of Skip's bitter agenda at www.skipwilliamson.com.

BRAD TEARE (page 137)

Utah artist Brad Teare maintains a career as both illustrator and fine arts painter. Clients include *The New York Times, Fortune* and Random House, where he has created book covers for authors such as James Michener, Ann Tyler, and Rafael Yglesias. Teare's comics creations have appeared in *Heavy Metal* and the *Big Book* series from Paradox Press. He is currently Senior Designer at *The Friend* magazine. Brad is now turning his graphic novel *Cypher* (excerpted in *Rosebud 20*) into a screenplay. You can check out his work at www.st45.com/cypher.

JIM NELSON *(page 143)*

Jim Nelson's work has appeared in fantasy role-playing games, books and magazines. He has been represented in *Spectrum: The Best in Contemporary Fantastic Art* as both an artist and art director. Jim lives in Chicago, where he is currently working on Wizards of the Coast's popular *Magic: The Gathering* card game and is also involved in projects for White Wolf, *Weekly Reader* and *Riotminds.* More of his art can be seen in *Graphic Classics: H.P. Lovecraft* and at http://www.theispot.com/artist/jnelson.

TOM POMPLUN

The designer, editor and publisher of the *Graphic Classics* series, Tom previously designed and produced *Rosebud*, a journal of poetry, fiction and illustration, from 1993 to 2003. He is now working on *Adventure Classics,* the second multi-author volume in the *Graphic Classics* series. The book will present new adaptations of stories by Sax Rohmer, Arthur Conan Doyle, Zane Grey, Rudyard Kipling, Damon Runyon, Johnston McCulley, Rafael Sabatini, O. Henry and more. *Adventure Classics* is scheduled for release in July 2005. You can see previews, sample art, and much more at www.graphicclassics.com.

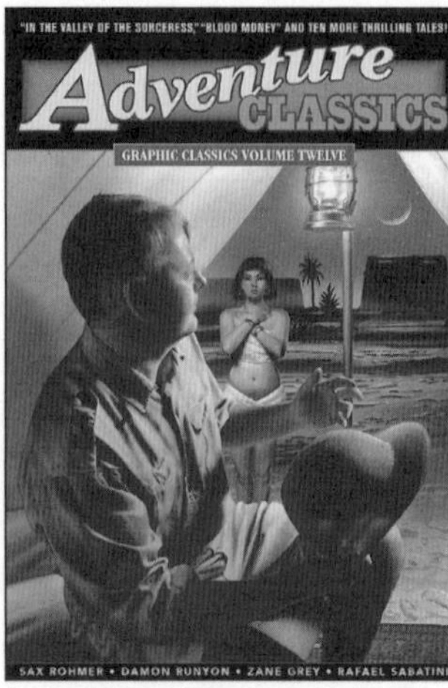
"IN THE VALLEY OF THE SORCERESS," "BLOOD MONEY" AND TEN MORE THRILLING TALES!
Adventure CLASSICS
GRAPHIC CLASSICS VOLUME TWELVE
SAX ROHMER • DAMON RUNYON • ZANE GREY • RAFAEL SABATINI